State of California
GOVERNOR'S OFFICE
SACRAMENTO 95814

Of the many pageants staged in California over the years, few have attained the fame and prestige enjoyed by the Tournament of Roses. As an outstanding showcase for the originality, artistry and community pride identified with California and Californians, the Tournament continues to draw spectators from all over the world every New Year's Day.

Each year the entries manage to surpass those which were considered to be the ultimate the previous year. All California is proud to be a part of this colorful pageant and takes pleasure in extolling its beauty and excellence to those from outside our state.

The Tournament of Roses is truly one of the living wonders of the West.

Sincerely,

RONALD REAGAN
Governor

The

Tournament

of

Roses

A Pictorial History

BY

Joe Hendrickson

IN COLLABORATION WITH

Maxwell Stiles

Brooke House, Publishers

Los Angeles, California

This work is dedicated to the spirit and philosophy of the late John Cabot and the fourteen hundred volunteer members of the Tournament of Roses who each year unselfishly offer their time and effort to stage the Granddaddy of the New Year's festivals. After twenty-six years of Tournament activity, Cabot passed away on January 21, 1971, at the Tournament headquarters, less than an hour after being inducted as president.

Contents

Foreword by Max Colwell   xiii

Preface   xv

1   Life Is a Rose   1

2   The Mediterranean of the West   4

3   Football? We Want Chariots   10

4   King Football Returns to Stay   24

5   A Wonder of Our Times — The Living Float   30

6   Granddaddy Is Born   42

7   The Four Horsemen   48

8   The Age of Dixie   58

9   "Roses Are in Bloom"   62

10   The Run that Stunned the Nation   66

11   The Tournament Band Is Born   70

12   Queens, Horses, and Bands   75

13   Year of the Olympics   90

14   "America's Sweetheart"   92

15   The Great Flood   96

16   Yippee! Texas Invades   102

17   The Second Leishman   109

18   Confessions of a Queen   115

19   The Age of Negotiation   117

20   "T" Is Served in the Bowl   121

21   Hardy Days   128

22   Marriage with the Big Ten   133

23   The Golden West   140

24   Survival Against Opposition   148

25   Max Colwell   158

26   Richard Nixon Comes to Pasadena   163

27   It Rains — Money and Water   171

28 Big Ten Dominance Continues   179

29 First of the Pamelas — and a Fellow Named Jim   188

30 Minnesota Gets Repaid   196

31 The Space Age   201

32 Mr. Eisenhower Finally Comes to Pasadena   205

33 Mickey Mouse Makes Good   213

34 Rose Bowl Put on U.S.C. Schedule   218

35 O.J.   225

36 Moon Men Land in Pasadena   238

37 Lewis the Second   250

38 Tragedy   259

39 Trends and Fashions   265

40 By Way of a Summary   272

    Appendixes:

       I — Rose Bowl Scores   279

      II — Individual Records   280

     III — Tournament Royalty — Presidents, Grand
            Marshals, Queens   281

      IV — Band Participation   283

    Index   291

List of Illustrations

C. F. Holder, 1
Lewis Shingler, 2
Dr. Francis F. Rowland, 4
Dr. Rowland in first parade, 5
Carriages in early parades, 6
Tournament games, 1890, 7
An 1890 attraction, 7
B. Marshall Wotkyns, 8
Frank C. Bolt, 8
Charles D. Daggett, 8
Mr. and Mrs. Thaddeus S. C. Lowe, 1895, 9
Chariot racing, 10
Maj. Gen. Shafter, Mayor Patten, Brig. Gen.
   Harrison Gray Otis, 1900, 11
Horseless carriage, 1901, 11
Herman Hertel, 11
F. B. Weatherby, 11
James B. Wagner, 12
Michigan team, 1902, 13
Stanford team, 1902, 13
Neil Snow, 14
Hallie Woods, 16
Ed Off, 16
Elsie Armitage and her court, 17
Joan Woodbury, 18
A chariot race, 18
May Sutton, 19
Mayor Early and the city council, 1908, 19
Ruth Palmer, 20
Alhambra's float, 1908, 20
Harrison Drummond and Jean French, 21
Anita Baldwin's peacock float, 22
M. S. Pashgian, 1915, 23
George Halas, 1919, 24
Lewis Turner, 25
Fritz Pollard, 25
Japan's float, 1917, 26
Paddy Driscoll, 29
Isabella Coleman, 1971, 30
Mrs. Coleman and Swan Lake float, 33
Isabella, 1919, 34
Chrysler's float, 1965, 36
Farmers Insurance float, 1965, 38
Farmers Insurance float, 1971, 41
Knott's Berry Farm float, 1971, 41
W. L. Leishman, 42
The Birth of the Rose Bowl, 43
Eddie Casey, 44

Action, Harvard vs. Oregon, 1920, 45
Brick Muller, 46
Knute Rockne, 48
May McAvoy, 49
Ericson of W and J runs against California, 1922, 50
Hugo Bezdek, 50
Gus Henderson, 50
Glendale's float, 1923, 51
Crowley of Notre Dame runs away, 52
Ernie Nevers, 53
The Four Horsemen, 53
Pop Warner, 54
1925 parade scene, Pasadena, 57
Johnny Mack Brown, 58
Fay Lanphier, 59
Harry Ticknor, 59
Wallace Wade, 60
Wade advises his players, 60
George Wilson, 61
Alabama vs. Washington, 1926, 61
One-Eye Connolly, 62
Dick Hyland runs for Stanford, 1927, 63
Freddie Pickard, 63
One-Eye Connolly crashes Rose Bowl, 64
Harriet B. Sterling, 65
Roy Riegels, 66
Riegels runs wrong way, 68
"What have I done?" 69
Albert Einstein, 70
C. Hal Reynolds, 71
James Rolph, 71
Holly Halstead, 71
Russ Saunders, 72
Ernie Pinckert, 1971, 72
Gen. C. S. Farnsworth, 73
Mary Lou Waddell, 73
Babe Hollingberry, 74
Rose Bowl, 1931, 74
Queen tryouts, 75
Queen judging, 77
San Marino float, 1932, 90
Howard Jones, 91
Bernie Bierman, 91
Ernie Pinckert runs for U.S.C., 1932, 91
Mary Pickford, 92
Miss Pickford acknowledges crowd's greetings, 93
D. E. McDaneld and Dorothy Edwards, 93
William May Garland, 93

Cotton Warburton, 95
Lou Little, 96
Long Beach's float, 1934, 97
Adm. Sims and Treva Scott, 97
Al Barabas of Columbia scores, 1934, 98
Harold Lloyd, Muriel Cowan, and C. Elmer
    Anderson, 99
Don Hutson, Phyllis Brooks, and Dixie Howell, 100
Frank Thomas, 101
Leo Carrillo, 102
Barbara Nichols, 103
Nancy Bumpus, 103
Cheryl Walker, 103
South Pasadena float, 1936, 103
Stanford's Vow Boys, 104
Matty Bell, 104
Bob Reynolds, 104
Bobby La Rue eludes Washington tackler, 104
Marshall Goldberg runs for Pitt, 105
Don Hensley of Pitt intercepts, 105
Walter Merrill of Alabama, 105
J. V. Allred, 106
Eugene Biscailuz, 106
Cyril Bennett, 106
First big float, Santa Barbara's, 1936, 107
Will Rogers float, 1936, 107
George S. Campbell, 108
Lathrop Leishman, 109
Lathrop Leishman and Shirley Temple, 110
Barbara Dougall, 110
Burbank float, 1939, 111
The Last Supper, Laguna Beach float, 1939, 111
Doyle Nave, 112
Al Krueger, 113
Krueger catches Nave's winning pass, 1939, 114
Margaret Huntley, 115
Charlie McCarthy and Edgar Bergen, 117
Mr. and Mrs. Harlan Loud, 118
Charlie McCarthy, Margaret Huntley,
    and Edgar Bergen, 118
El Monte's African float, 119
Bob Neyland, 120
Ambrose Schindler, 120
Clark Shaughnessy, 121
Biff Jones, 122
Frankie Albert, 122
J. W. McCall, Sally Stanton, and E. O. Nay, 122
Stanford's "T" Boys, 123
Vike Francis, 123
Duke Stadium, 1942, 124
Lon Stiner, 124
Robert H. McCurdy, 125
Kay Kyser, 125
Dolores Brubach, 125
Mildred Miller, 126
James K. Ingham, 127
Frankie Sinkwich, 127
Alonzo A. Stagg, 128
Frank Brooks, 129
Naomi Riordan, 129

Mary Rutte, 129
Don Burnside, 130
Blake Headley of U.S.C. in action, 130
Max Turner, Herbert Hoover,
    and William Dunkerley, 131
Stella Morrill, 131
Ted Tannehill, 132
Adm. William F. Halsey, 132
Patricia Auman, 132
Bob Hope, 133
Tug Wilson, 134
Bill Reed, 135
Red Mackey, 135
William Welsh, Norma Christopher,
    and Bob Hope, 137
Paul Patterson scores for Illinois, 138
Ray Eliot, 138
Al Hoisch, U.S.C., returns kickoff 102 yards, 139
Burt LaBrucherie, 139
Gen. Omar Bradley, 140
Louis Vincenti, 141
Virginia Goodhue, 141
Bob Chappuis, 142
Jack Weisenburger, 142
Perry Brown, 143
Harold Schaffer and Virginia Bower, 144
Pappy Waldorf and Jackie Jensen, 145
Did Murakowski score? 146
Drummond McCunn, 148
Marion Brown, 149
Paul G. Hoffman, 149
Wesley Fesler, 150
Robert S. Gray, 152
Mr. and Mrs. Clifford Kenworthy, 153
Eleanor Payne, 154
Ben Oosterbaan, 156
Max Colwell, 158
Nancy Thorne, 161
Seven Medal of Honor winners as grand marshals, 161
Richard Nixon, 1953, 163
William Nicholas and Leah Feland, 164
Jess Hill, 165
Biggie Munn, 167
Red Sanders, 167
Harry W. Hurry and Gen. William F. Dean, 169
Barbara Schmidt, 169
Earl Warren, 171
Elmer Wilson and Earl Warren, 172
Roy Rogers, Dale Evans, Elmer Wilson, and
    Earl Warren, 173
Dinah Shore, 174
Carlota Busch Giersch with St. Louis float, 1955, 175
Marilyn Smuin and Elmer Wilson, 176
Woody Hayes, 176
Duffy Daugherty, 179
Joan Culver, 180
David Llewellyn, 180
Alfred L. Gerrie and Charles E. Wilson, 181
Forest Evashevski, 182
Ann Mossberg, 183

Eddie Rickenbacker and John S. Davidson, 183
Robert Gordon Sproul and John H. Biggar, 184
Gertrude Wood, 184
Don Clark and Frank Kremblas of O.S.U., 186
Len Casanova, 187
Pamela Prather, 188
E. L. Bartlett dances with Pamela Prather, 189
Wrigley Mansion, the Tournament House, 191
Ray Dorn and Richard Nixon, 1960, 193
Ray Dorn and Margarethe Bertelson, 193
Margarethe Bertelson and her court, 194
Bob Schloredt, 194
Tom Hamilton, 194
Hobbs, Wisconsin, and Wooten, Washington,
    scramble for ball, 195
Jim Owens, 195
William F. Quinn, 196
Arthur W. Althouse, 197
Carole Washburn, 197
Albert D. Rosellini, 198
Martha Sissell, 199
Murray Warmath, 199
H. Burton Noble, 200
Bill Barnes, 200
Ron VanderKelen, 201
Stanley L. Hahn, 202
William H. Pickering, 202
Pete Beathard, 203
Milt Bruhn, 203
Nancy Davis, 204
Dwight D. Eisenhower, 205
Hilles Bedell, 206
Pete Elliott, 207
Dwight Eisenhower and the 1964 court, 208
Fritz Crisler and Dawn Baker, 209
Mr. and Mrs. Arnold Palmer, 209
Walter R. Hoefflin, 210
Bump Elliott and Bob Timberlake, 211
Mel Anthony's 84-yard run, 212
Tommy Prothro, 213
Walt Disney and Mickey Mouse, 214
J. Randolph Richards and Carole Cota, 215
Bob Stiles, 216
Henry Kearns and Thanat Khoman, 220
Barbara Hewitt and her court, 221
Catch by Rod Sherman, U.S.C., 222
George Catavolos, Purdue, intercepts, 222
John McKay, 223
O. J. Simpson, 225
H. W. Bragg and Everett Dirksen, 226
Dirksen dances with Queen Linda Strother, 226
The official Tournament family, 1968, 226
Indiana cheer leaders, 227
Johnny Pont, 228
Bob Hope and Gleeson L. Payne, 230

Pamela Anicich, 231
O. J. Simpson at full speed, 233
O. J. Simpson scores, 234
Rex Kern passes, 235
Leo Hayden passes some U.S.C. tacklers, 235

Michigan tumbles, 238
Bo Schembechler leaves hospital, 239
Curt Gowdy and Lathrop Leishman, 239
Alex Gaal, C. Lewis Edwards, and
    Pamela Dee Tedesco, 240
Lathrop Leishman, Stanley Hahn, Ray Dorn,
    William Nicholas, 241
Linda Lanphear, Charles Manos, and pet dog
    Rosey, 243
The Wild Bunch, 244
Bob Chandler catches Jimmy Jones' pass, 245
Stanley Hahn, Lathrop Leishman, Bill Nicholas,
    C. Lewis Edwards, and President Nixon, 248
Billy Graham, 250
Kathy Howie and Kathy Parker, 253
Jim Plunkett, Jack Schultz, and Kyle Rote, 254
Steve Horowitz kicks a 48-yard field goal, 255
Randy Vataha catches a touchdown pass, 256
Bob Moore catch sets up touchdown, 256
Stanford pompon dance, 257
Victory ride for John Ralston, 257
Geordie Lawry's bicycle "strip ride," 257
Rex Kern runs behind interference, 258
John Cabot, 259
Otis Blasingham, 260
Edward Wilson, 260
William Lawson, 261
Terry Chambers, 263
H. Lewis Shingler puts president's pin on
    John Cabot, 264
Mary Lou Waddell, 1931, 265
May McAvoy, 1923, 266
The daring look, 1925, 266
The crowning of Muriel Cowan, 1935, 267
Cheryl Walker and court, 267
Court of Margaret Huntley, 1940, 267
Dolores Brubach's court, 1942, 268
Court of Mildred Miller, 1943, 268
Patricia Auman, 1946, 269
Court of Virginia Goodhue, 1948, 269
William Holden with Eleanor Payne's court, 270
Harry W. Hurry crowns Barbara Schmidt, 270
Nancy Kneeland's court, 1964, 270
Pamela Anicich and princesses, 1969, 271
Pamela Dee Tedesco's court, 1970, 271
Jet Propulsion Laboratory, 272
Pasadena City Hall, 273
Huntington Library, 273
Entrance, Beckman Auditorium, California
    Institute of Technology, 274

Color Pictures

(section following page 46)

The Rose Bowl, 1970
Richard M. Nixon, Ronald Reagan, with their ladies and their
    escort, at the Rose Bowl, 1969
The Tournament parade, Colorado Boulevard
Pasadena City College Lancer Band
Long Beach Mounted Police Posse, 1971
St. Louis float, 1970
Bekins Moving and Storage float, 1970
Florists Transworld Delivery Association float, 1971
Barbara Trisler
George Putnam
Equestrian unit, Marshal Bill Crook

(section following page 110)

The Queen's Court, 1969
The Queen's Court, 1970
Chief Eagle Friend
Georgia's float, 1970
Republic of Mexico's float, 1970
Bank of America's floats, 1970 and 1971
City of Los Angeles' float, 1970
Union Oil's float, 1970
Jay Jackson
Belle Starr
O. J. Simpson
Joe Hendrickson and O. J. Simpson
Gunn, U.S.C., tackles Mandich, Michigan
Jones, U.S.C., hands off

(section following page 174)

Cordelia and Walter Knott ride the Knott's Berry Farm float, 1970
Universal Studios' float, 1970
Charles L. Conrad, Jr., Richard F. Gordon, Jr., and Alan L. Bean,
    spacemen, 1970
Billy Graham
Lawrence Welk
Hillary Shockley, Stanford, tackled by Beecroft, Ohio State
Jankowski, Ohio State, eludes Barnes, Stanford, as Sampson comes in
Knott's Berry Farm's float, 1971
Farmers Insurance Group's float, 1971
John Cabot
Virgil White
Granada Hills Marching Band, 1971
The 1971 Court

Floats in the 1971 Rose Parade

(section following page 238)

Georgia
Bakery and Confectionery Workers Union
Eastman Kodak
Chrysler Corporation
National Exchange Club
Dr. Pepper Company
Salvation Army
Hi-C Drinks
Union Oil Company of California
Al Malaikah Shrine Temple
Portland Rose Festival Association
Continental Airlines
Occidental Life of California
Soroptimists International
Bekins Moving and Storage
St. Louis, Missouri

Foreword

Since the early morning hours of January 1, 1890, when Pasadena families drove through the streets in buggies and tallyhos all decorated with roses plucked from their own gardens, the Tournament of Roses has developed into the world's greatest floral spectacle.

Likewise, the Rose Bowl football game, which came into being through the same Pasadena families who comprise the Tournament of Roses Association, has developed into one of the world's greatest and most respected sporting events.

Both the Rose Parade and the Rose Bowl game have been copied by other communities, but never matched. There is no parade anywhere in the same class, and the Rose Bowl remains the Granddaddy of all bowl games.

Both have become institutions on the American scene. They did not reach this pinnacle without some effort. It took the time and talents of hundreds of volunteers. There were trying moments as well as triumphs.

The Tournament of Roses and the Rose Bowl have a great story to tell. Only a person who could catch the spirit that has inoculated Tournament workers could do justice to the story. Such a man is Joe Hendrickson, the talented editor and writer. Joe writes with feeling and with authority. He has the true story and, as you will note as you read, he relates the story of the Tournament of Roses in a most entertaining and heartwarming fashion.

MAX COLWELL
General Manager

Preface

This is the first attempt by any writer to record the complete Tournament of Roses story from its beginning to the present in total makeup — not solely an account of the tremendous Rose Bowl games but also a compilation of many of the happenings in the Tournament of Roses since the inception of this festival in 1890.

The story of the Tournament parade, the crowning of the Tournament queen, and the festive events leading up to the climactic Rose Bowl game represent a unique example of community cooperation and world-wide response.

The late Maxwell Stiles, sports editor of the Hollywood *Citizen News* at the time of his passing in 1969, left this writer much exciting history of those Rose Bowl games that dominated the New Year's Day scene up to the time the Pacific Eight-Big Ten series began in 1947. These reports have been augmented to complete the first full story of this Rose Bowl New Year's football domination that has been maintained through 57 years of exciting gridiron action.

While the beauty of a queen such as Nancy Davis or the wholesome smile of a grand marshal like Shirley Temple cannot exactly be likened to the symmetry of a winning forward pass from a Doyle Nave to an "Antelope Al" Krueger, there is a common tie in all that has made the festival great. Since 1890, this has been an operation of expanding cooperation, spirit, hard work, and good will — and that is the story this writer has put on paper.

Sports observer Stiles, a most competent newspaperman for nearly fifty years and my fine friend, has contributed a great deal of information to this story of the Tournament of Roses that has merited permanent recording. I trust that this book will be a tribute to the career in sports and human relations that Maxwell loved and upheld.

Of considerable satisfaction to me are the words of my editor at the Pasadena *Star-News*, Arnold Huss, who thus appraised *The Tournament of Roses Story*: "You have captured the spirit of Pasadena's big day. You have put into the book warmth with touches of humor and an amazing amount of detail, not generally known to followers of the pageant."

To me, the opportunity to live and work in Pasadena through one of the eight decades in Tournament of Roses history has provided much personal satisfaction and appreciation for my good fortune. Life really has become a rose, with some thorns up the stem but with a beautiful flower atop.

JOE HENDRICKSON
Sports Editor
Pasadena *Star-News*

The author wishes to thank many people who have been helpful in making possible this picture and story compilation of the Tournament of Roses. Especially in the collection of photographic material were Sam Akers, Public Relations Director of the Tournament of Roses, and his assistant, Walter Hoefflin, most cooperative. Bill Schroeder and his Helms Hall staff lent valuable service as did "Mr. D" and Doris Wilson, Tournament photographers, and Clem Inskeep, photographer and reproduction specialist. The assistance of editorial consultant Sandra Whelan Hittson and fashion authority Phyllis Touchie-Specht was most vital to the completion of this work. Charles Cherniss, Jerome Fried, and Bernice and Lou Eaton were helpful consultants.

The
Tournament
of
Roses

A Pictorial History

1

Life Is a Rose

C. F. HOLDER

MAX COLWELL insists life is a rose.

When the Tournament of Roses celebrated its 75th anniversary at the 1964 festival, general manager Colwell received a letter from one Mary Martenson of Alta Vista, Kansas.

"I am 75 years old and my birthday is January 1. I would like to celebrate by seeing the Tournament of Roses in person," wrote the Kansan, who was especially proud that a native of her state, former President Dwight D. Eisenhower, was to be grand marshal of the Rose Parade.

"Congratulations," replied Colwell in his usual considerate pattern of answering all mail. "If ever you are here on New Year's Day, we will be happy to help you enjoy your visit."

About ten days before New Year's, Colwell received a phone call from the agent at the Pasadena bus depot.

"Mr. Colwell, your distinguished guest is here," said the agent.

Surprised and bewildered, Colwell asked questions until he learned that Mary Martenson of Kansas was in Pasadena, without any reservations or spending money.

Colwell and Tournament of Roses officials acted quickly. J. Randolph Richards, destined to ascend to the presidency of the association in two years, who also was owner of the Pasadena Athletic Club, said he would put up the visitor at the club. Other members passed the hat and soon there was money to provide living expenses. Even General Eisenhower, when he arrived, contributed some cash. Mary Martenson became the visiting "little old lady of Pasadena," and she enjoyed every minute of her stay — truly as a guest carrying unique if not exactly distinguished standing. Three days after the parade, she was provided transportation back to Kansas. The case was forgotten by Colwell and his associates, but not by Mary Martenson.

Five years later, in early December, Colwell received another letter from "Queen Mary."

"My 80th birthday on January 1 coincides with your 80th Tournament of Roses," she wrote. "I will be very happy to come to Pasadena

1

as your honored guest. I hope I can ride in the first or second car of the parade. I will have my hair combed and I will wear my white shoes. Should I come to Pasadena by train or will you send an airplane for me this time?"

Colwell, a former newspaperman with writing tact, replied: "It is not our custom to invite distinguished guests twice. If we ever change our policy and invite General Eisenhower to return, we will include you."

Lewis Shingler, president of the 1971 Tournament of Roses, agrees that life is a rose. A twenty-three-year veteran Tournament of Roses member who has been chairman of fifteen committees, including the equestrian committee, he tells an equally amusing story of the persistence that has made the Tournament of Roses so fascinating.

"In the chilly pre-dawn hours of New Year's Day 1950, an uninvited seventy-three-year-old self-styled cowboy with long beard, silverless saddle, long barreled rifle, and shaggy horse appeared in the equestrian unloading area near Orange Grove Avenue where the parade was formed," recalls Shingler.

LEWIS SHINGLER

"In no uncertain terms, the equestrian chairman advised the stranger, 'You have not been invited — neither you, your horse, saddle, nor costume qualify for this parade, so load your horse and leave.'

"Standing erect to his six feet two inch height, the stranger declared so all around could hear: 'I'm seventy-seven years old; I own this horse, saddle, and rifle; and I pay taxes on these streets; and I'm going to ride in this parade.'

"An equestrian committeeman was secretly instructed to keep the man out of the parade, regardless of the effort required. The chairman felt so good when no outlaw rider filed into the Orange Grove and Palmetto parade line-up at 9 a.m., he bragged of his success until the official film of the parade, which arrived a few days later, showed the modern Bill Cody prancing his shaggy nag down the center of Colorado Street at Orange Grove Avenue before the official reviewing stand."

Terry Chambers, assistant manager of the Tournament, a man who left a successful contracting business in Pasadena to join the festival staff because he found the work so fascinating, further substantiates that life is a rose.

An expert on parades (he directed Richard Nixon's 1969 inaugural parade in Washington, D.C., a few days after the Pasadena event was history), Chambers insists Pasadena staged the "first topless parade" — almost.

"We had a float entry from Reno," relates Chambers. "It was decorated with show girls who were garbed in feathers made of flowers and pampas grass. One of the girls apparently was allergic to the pampas grass which formed her brassiere, and she repeatedly kept on inserting her hand under her bra as she smiled to the crowd. The distraction became so noticeable, we decided we had to do something. All that was needed was a bottle of glue. Her bra was glued down, and the float continued on its way without any further distractions."

A resident of Pasadena on a world tour found himself in Africa distressingly short of cash, so he headed to the nearest bank to try to cash a check. He produced a driver's license, a gasoline credit card, and all manner of identification, none of which seemed to make an impression on the African banker. Ultimately, the Pasadenan's Tournament of Roses membership card came into view. This hit the jackpot. The banker smiled for the first time, cashed the check, and then insisted that his caller come to the Rotary Club luncheon to tell about the New Year's Day activities in Pasadena.

It never has been substantiated that zoologist Charles Frederick Holder had such events as these in mind in 1889 when he addressed his fellow members of the socially elite Valley Hunt Club of Pasadena with these words: "What our city needs is an expression of our inspiration."

Holder amplified: "There can be no more spontaneous illustration of pure inspiration than the natural beauties of Pasadena and its vicinity — inspiration from the petals of thousands of roses in bloom while our former eastern homes are buried in snow." Thus was the idea for the Tournament of Roses born.

"Holder was a great Pasadenan and hardly has received the recognition he deserves. He was an outstanding community leader," states Paul Bryan, who among many contributions made during thirty years of service as a committeeman for the Tournament has researched the festival's historic moments.

Holder had business sense in addition to his understanding of inspiration and the artistry of mountain and valley. One of his friends was Walter Raymond, a Pasadena pioneer who owned the then-famed Hotel Raymond.

"We need visitors from the east to fill up our hotels," said Raymond to his friend.

"I think I know how to help you," replied Holder.

Little did Holder realize that the help he was to launch would one day bring more than two million visitors to Pasadena each New Year's. Nor did he suspect that his festival dream would provide the setting for the first date of a future President of the United States with the girl who was to become his First Lady. For it was at the annual Rose festival that Richard M. Nixon first dated Pat Ryan.

2

The Mediterranean of the West

DR. FRANCIS F. ROWLAND

THE VALLEY HUNT CLUB, where gentlemen convened with more grace than any other place in Pasadena, was a proper setting for the birth of the Tournament of Roses.

Professor Holder, with newspaper clippings in his hand telling of the great blizzard of 1888 in New York, addressed the membership of the Valley Hunt Club.

"Gentlemen," he said, "I came from the east to this beautiful area for my health. I found it here. I also discovered happiness and beauty. In New York, people are buried in snow. Here our flowers are blooming and our oranges are about to bear. Let's have a festival and tell the world about our paradise."

A willing listener was Dr. Francis F. Rowland.

"I agree with your idea," said Dr. Rowland. "My wife has just returned from a festival of roses in Nice, France. Let's call our festival 'The Battle of Roses.' "

Some of the listeners chimed in: "We will be the Mediterranean of the West."

Thus was the Tournament of Roses born. The members of the Valley Hunt Club voted to stage, on January 1, 1890, a parade of decorated carriages and an afternoon of public games on the "town lot" east of Los Robles between Colorado and Santa Fe.

The young men of Pasadena's 4,882 population competed in a variety of foot races, tugs of war, jousts, and a tourney of rings, an old Spanish game in which mounted horsemen, each carrying a twelve-foot lance, try to spear three rings hung about thirty feet apart while riding at top speed. The tourney of rings, coupled with the display of roses, prompted Professor Holder to say, "Now we have the name we want— the Tournament of Roses."

The Pasadena *Evening Star* gave the event a smash review. "The greatest festival of similar nature ever held in the country," said the *Evening Star,* pointing out that one thousand people were fed and three thousand attended.

Newspaper announcements invited citizens to watch the promenade and games as they enjoyed a picnic lunch under the giant oak trees.

4

DR. ROWLAND LEADS THE FIRST PARADE, 1890

A wagon load of ripe oranges was distributed. Youngsters scattered rose petals along the dirt road that was Pasadena's main street.

"I do not recall the prize winners of the entries in the parade, but I remember that, due to a mistake in time, Mr. C. D. Daggett reached the grounds after the decision of the judges, in a carriage so beautifully decorated he would have won first place," said Holder.

Daggett later was to distinguish himself—as Tournament of Roses president, grand marshal, and originator of the idea to stage chariot races as a major attraction.

Now, in 1971, it impresses Max Colwell that the message given to the Pasadenans who participated in the original Tournament of Roses was "Go home and pick your natural flowers and turn them into displays." This the natives did in the first year of the Tournament. The policy set in the beginning is the policy that has survived and expanded to its present magnificent splendor.

"That," said Colwell, "is one of the wonders of our festival. The founders knew what would succeed. The same idea has always prevailed."

Eva Townsend, who celebrated her 100th birthday on July 26, 1969, in Pasadena, recalled the first Tournament of Roses. "It was a nice event," she reminisced with a smile. "My suitor, Harry Townsend, wanted to show me what he could do. He rented a buggy and a team of bay horses and decorated it. We got our rig in the line of march. Then we went to the picnic on North Los Robles."

Dr. Rowland and Professor Holder led the first parade riding on their favorite mounts. The carriages were decorated with flowers. Valley Hunt Club hounds were led on leashes by their proud masters. The theme of the affair was "A Time to Remember" (a theme repeated on the 80th Anniversary in 1969).

C. V. Howard won the first Tournament of Roses sports event, a 100-yard foot race. For his 11¼ second effort, Howard received the Pickwick Cup, donated by Pickwick House. Howard was versatile: he also won the one-mile foot race in 5:40. Most novel of the 1890 races was an orange race. Each contestant picked up a line of fifty oranges

CARRIAGES DECORATED WITH FLOWERS AP-
PEARED IN THE EARLY PARADES: FIRST PRIZE
IN 1890 (LEFT) AND A STUNNER IN 1891
(RIGHT)

placed two feet apart and put them into a basket. Bob Collingwood
won the event but received a whip for a prize. In the quarter-mile pony
race, Clayton Raymond aboard Dr. Rowland's Elsie nosed out Capt.
A. B. Anderson aboard Fairy. Raymond received a silver watch. Anderson's second prize was a complete set of Dickens' literary works.

The first Tournament of Roses showed a cash profit of $229.30. In
staging the 1891 festival, Valley Hunt Club members urged the residents
of the city to join the parade along with club members. A prize was
offered for the best decorated carriage.

"Who will say that Life, Liberty and the Pursuit of Happiness is
not more desirable in southern California than elsewhere on earth!" the
official announcement of the Tournament exclaimed. B. Marshall Wotkyns was president of this second festival.

To impress upon easterners the stunning beauty of Pasadena on
January 1, the Valley Hunt Clubbers called their 1891 festival "Dead of
Winter." It was held at Devil's Gate Park to accommodate picnickers.
A major feature was the appearance of the Monrovia Town Band, the
first musical organization ever to participate in the Tournament of
Roses.

"I think we have something started," said Dr. Rowland, who was
to serve as parade grand marshal seven times, more than anyone else in
the event's history. Since 1930, when it was decided to invite a distinguished personality from outside Pasadena to be the grand marshal,
only three people have had the honor of serving in that capacity twice
—Richard Nixon, Earl Warren, and Bob Hope. Equally enthusiastic in
their response were other members of the Valley Hunt Club, who were
dedicated to "the hunting of the jackrabbit, fox, and other wild game
with horses and hounds."

The 1891 line of march started on South Orange Grove Avenue,
virtually the same site used today, and led to Devil's Gate, a wooded

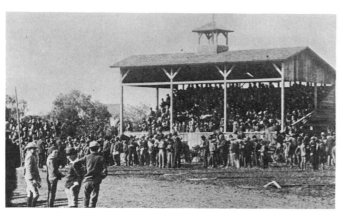

SCENE AT THE TOURNAMENT GAMES IN 1890 (LEFT). DANDY DRIVEN BY VIRA BARKER AND

JENNIE GRAHAM IS AN 1890 ATTRACTION (RIGHT)

amphitheater in the northern part of Pasadena where the games were held.

The 1892 parade produced an edict from the Valley Hunt Club in paid newspaper advertisements that "every man, woman, and child plus horse and carriage should be decorated with flowers." This celebration was returned to the east-central part of the city.

The name of the festival almost became the Orange Tournament in 1892 when a severe winter caused a shortage of roses. The *Daily Star* campaigned to call the Pasadena fete the Orange Tournament whenever there is a shortage of roses, "so there will be no misnomer attached to our great celebration." However, when warm weather brought out plenty of blossoms before the 1893 event, the idea of changing the name was dropped. The president for the two years was Frank C. Bolt.

Reviewing stands were built for the first time along the parade route in 1894. Perhaps a step-up in public interest was precipitated by the 1893 decision to permit female equestrians in the parade to wear "bifurcated skirts" (divided skirts which permitted a woman to ride astride a horse).

The "bifurcated skirts" ruling also precipitated the Tournament's first public debate on accepted style and fashion. In the first three parades, the women rode sidesaddle. Opponents of the new way argued it wasn't a "natural, graceful, and becoming act."

The 1894 parade represented a growth from the few teams decorated with flowers and greens to a parade of many classes with six-in-hand and four-in-hand turnouts, double and single teams, and equestrians. Floats also were entered by organizations. The Columbia Hill Tennis Club, the Valley Hunt Club, and Hotel Raymond had the first float entries.

Then came a historic decision by members of the Valley Hunt Club.

"We have grown to the extent the staging of this festival is more

B. MARSHALL WOTKYNS

FRANK C. BOLT

CHARLES D. DAGGETT

than we, as a club, can handle," said President Daggett in 1895. He was right. The parade had become so big that the incline-railway man, Thaddeus S. C. Lowe, had seven entries alone. Included were a single rig, four pairs, a four-in-hand, and a six-in-hand!

The Valley Hunt Club also was finding that staging the festival was costly. It rained steadily a week before the 1895 event. Club members decided there was less risk in sticking to their hunting. Many ladies refused to ride in the parade. Wettest of all were the young high school girls, their colors dripping in stains over their dainty white gowns, their heads protected by marguerite petals. But one float seemed right at home. The San Pedro Chamber of Commerce had created a full-rigged brig with spectacular masts and rigging on a sea of flowers which read, "San Pedro to Pasadena." One jokester remarked, "It took a day like this to get a full-rigged brig this far up the San Gabriel."

Although 1895 marked the Valley Hunt Club's last parade, their present home still remains in the parade's formation area, a tribute to southern California's oldest social club.

A public subscription campaign raised $595 to underwrite expenses of the 1896 festival. At a public meeting, the Tournament of Roses Association was formed. Edwin Stearns was its first president. Nature gave the world a hint the Tournament of Roses Association would cause a stir in years to come. Clouds of dust harassed the 1896 proceedings.

Little did the citizens realize, as they petitioned for better sprinkling of the streets to prevent such disturbances in the future, that the second great rain in the history of the Tournament was to strike Pasadena in 1899. It had been Pasadena's good fate that rain has troubled the festivities only nine times in its eighty-one-year history—1895, 1899, 1906, 1910, 1916, 1922, 1934, 1937, and 1955. (This will be discussed at greater length in Chapter 15.)

Communities from outside Pasadena joined in the Pasadena parade in 1896 when South Pasadena had an official entry. The Los Angeles Chamber of Commerce entered a float in 1897.

Chamber officers gave a yell during the parade, "Pasadena, Pasadena. What's the matter with Pasadena? She's all right."

"We have started to achieve the goal of our founders and the cities around us are beginning to join in making our festival one of national interest," said President Martin H. Weight when, in 1898, he welcomed reporters from large eastern newspapers who came west for the first time to bring the story to their readers. Of significance that year was the vote of confidence Pasadena received from United States President William McKinley, who told the festival to continue even though the country was at war with Spain. The 12,000 citizens of Pasadena, just 10 per cent of what the population is today, cheered McKinley's blessing, but the high school band of Whittier wasn't so happy. It couldn't make the twenty-mile trip to Pasadena to appear in the parade because every rig had been rented by the stables of southern California and there were none left for so long a trip.

G. A. W. Haas, who rode a bicycle from New York to Pasadena, appeared in the parade with his cross-country costume and bike.

When the rainstorm struck in 1899, Tournament officials displayed their first example of collective cool by waiting until 3:45 in the afternoon for the skies to clear. Although the downpour had made Colorado Avenue a sea of mud, the parade finally started — and finished. The sports events, however, were called off.

Horse races and bicycle races shared the sports spotlight with track events in the 1890s. A winner of a one-mile college bike race was a young student from Occidental, Dean Cromwell, who later became the nation's No. 1 track coach at U.S.C. Track records were far from what the world today considers noteworthy. In 1899, E. B. Helpinstein of San Diego won the 12-pound shot-put with an effort of 36 feet 10 inches and the high jump at 5 feet 5 inches.

A BROUGHAM, THE PRIDE OF MR. AND MRS.
THADDEUS S. C. LOWE IN THE 1895 PARADE

3

Football? We Want Chariots

CHARIOT RACING

WHEN PRESIDENT Herman Hertel made a deal with the Vitascope Company granting that firm exclusive rights to make movies of the 1900 parade, the Tournament of Roses was brought "live" to audiences throughout the United States. Even though shown days, weeks, and months later, the parade scenes became a motion-picture feature in many cities. Newspaper coverage increased also, and so did the number of visitors to Pasadena.

The 1900 festival also was famous for having the Tournament's first visiting parade guests of distinction — General William Rufus Shafter, commander of the American forces in Santiago de Cuba during the Spanish-American War, and Brig. General Harrison Gray Otis, newspaper publisher and veteran of two wars.

"The end of the century" parade attracted 50,000 visitors, who came with Fourth of July feeling. Every five minutes a trolley car from Los Angeles rolled in with men and boys clinging to its sides and riding on the roof.

Although unnoticed at the time, one of the Tournament standard bearers accompanying herald Paul Heydenreich was sixteen-year-old George Patton, Jr., later to become the famed, colorful general of World War II.

Hertel's term as Tournament president also was significant because he proposed that money be raised to obtain a permanent site for sports activities. After $2,043 was earned from selling post cards with parade pictures, Patton Field was leased and renamed Tournament Park.

When the Indians sold Manhattan to some Dutch settlers for $24, the bargain was not a great deal more profitable than the purchase of Tournament Park by Tournament of Roses officers in 1901. Fourteen "country acres" at Wilson Avenue and California Street were purchased for $6,300; the amount that was needed beyond the post-card profits was borrowed at 5 per cent interest. The land, deeded to the city of Pasadena with the proviso that it would be available each January as a disbanding area for the sporting events, eventually was sold by the city to California Institute of Technology for $650,000.

HERMAN HERTEL

F. B. WEATHERBY

1901

"The automobile is here to stay. Let's let automobiles appear in our parade," said President F. B. Weatherby as the 1901 festival approached. "But they must appear in the rear of the parade so they don't scare the horses," he added.

Five chugging automobiles, decorated with flowers, entered the competition.

Autos were not accepted with total enthusiasm. One Tournament official said, in comparing autos with horse-drawn vehicles: "The pesky things stand there puffing like a frosty force pump and the flowers seem to have caught on by accident."

An annual parade feature in these years was competition for the best float between Throop Polytechnic Institute, a private school, and Pasadena High School. Throop had the best of it for several years until Leroy Ely, who was to become principal of Pasadena High, took over the designing and decorating of high school floats and soon developed the Tournament's first pretentious and elaborately conceived entry, drawn by six horses.

To inspire the entry of ladies, the Tournament advised: "Ladies who wish to ride in the parade will be welcome and they will be furnished escorts by contacting F. E. Burnham and Ed Braly."

1902

In 1902 under the Tournament administration of James B. Wagner, the idea of staging a football game as the major sports attraction came to the fore. Up until that year, the sports events had not been of a scope to attract visitors. People came to Pasadena to see the parade and remained for the sports events only as a side show during their afternoon picnic. One Don Arturo Bandini had won some fame as an expert in

LEFT: MAJOR GENERAL WILLIAM RUFUS SHAFTER, MAYOR G. D. PATTEN, BRIGADIER GENERAL HARRISON GRAY OTIS (1900)

HORSELESS CARRIAGE DRIVEN BY ROBERT GAYLORD (1901)

JAMES B. WAGNER

the tourney of rings. A tug-of-war team from Duarte had defeated a strong-armed group from Pasadena. There had been bicycle and running races, picnic style. Riverside defeated Santa Barbara 4-1 in polo. But none of this received much attention in the Chicago *Tribune* or the New York *Times*.

"We are national in everything but a sports attraction that will get people in the icy north and east talking," said President Wagner when he took over the duties of heading the Tournament.

Fielding H. Yost's Michigan football team had won ten straight games and had outscored its opposition 501-0. "Let's match our best against them. Stanford will test them," agreed other Tournament members. The invitations to the two teams were extended, both accepted, and the game was scheduled to be played at Tournament Park after the parade on January 1, 1902.

A crisis was averted after the Tournament offered the Michigan team $2 a day as meal money. Charles Baird, graduate manager of the Wolverines, replied, "We won't come unless we can go comfortably and in reasonable style. We want $3 a day meal money." The raise was granted.

It was a hot, dusty day. After the parade, people started to head for Tournament Park, which was located on part of what now is the athletic field of California Institute of Technology, then known as Throop Polytechnic Institute. The city was decorated in blue and gold, the official colors adopted by the Tournament. Blue and gold pennants were everywhere. The colors so closely resembled the maize and blue of Michigan that Stanford followers became miffed. Stanford fans began to tear down the pennants and streamers, some shouting, "Those colors we hate — they are too much like University of California's."

There were seats for 1,000 at Tournament Park, but it soon became evident they wouldn't be enough. The two teams had ridden tallyhos in the parade, an introduction that stimulated the enthusiasm of many to see them "push and pull each other" on the field.

Tallyhos, 1901 automobiles known as Victorias, and farm wagons carried people on the narrow road to Tournament Park. Hundreds came afoot, kicking up dust. It was Pasadena's worst traffic snarl to date. For hours the crowd waited for the lone gate to Tournament Park to open. There was one policeman, H. L. Van Schaick, and a few ticket handlers in charge of controlling the mob. Finally, at 2 p.m., Van Schaick climbed to the top of the high board fence and shouted: "Ladies and gentlemen: may I have your attention! You are to line up single file and march through the gate in orderly manner."

About twenty lines formed, however, and each claimed it had the right to go through the gate first. The snarl was checked temporarily when the gate was closed. But a boy was hoisted to the top of the fence and he wriggled over. Another followed. And another. Then came the stampede. The fence became alive with bodies bobbing up, over, and down. First come, first served, was the public policy during the rush to

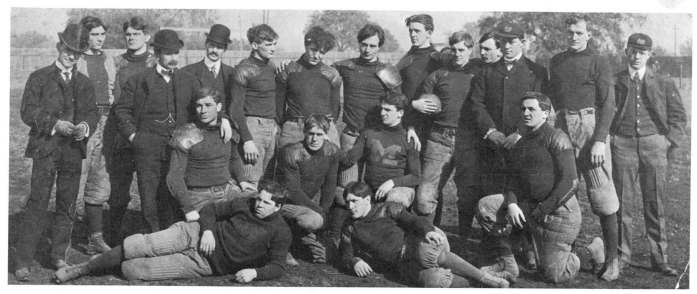

MICHIGAN'S POINT-A-MINUTE MACHINE, WINNER OF THE FIRST FOOTBALL GAME IN ROSE BOWL HISTORY

the stands; the crowd overflowed around the playing field, with hundreds more perched atop the fences. It was estimated that 8,500 witnessed the game between Michigan and Stanford, the first football game in Rose Bowl history.

Michigan couldn't pierce the Stanford line early in the game and a punting duel developed between Sweeley of Michigan, who kicked twenty-one times, and Fisher, McGilvray, and Traeger of Stanford.

Then Michigan's great star, Willie Heston, wrote his name into Rose Bowl history. He broke away for a 21-yard run that put Michigan on Stanford's 8 yard line, from where fullback Neil Snow charged over for the first touchdown in Tournament of Roses history. Before the action

THE 1902 STANFORD PLAYERS, WHO LOST 49-0

NEIL SNOW OF MICHIGAN

was ended, Michigan had rolled up a 49-0 victory on eight touchdowns (five points each), one field goal (five points), and four conversions (one point each).

While Heston was Michigan's superstar, with nearly 200 yards gained, there were other greats in the game. Michigan had Dan McGugin at left guard; he later was famous as coach at Vanderbilt. Left end Redden for Michigan scored two touchdowns on 25-yard punt returns. Sweeley stood out with his punting. Al Herrnstein, a great ball-carrier, won the respect of Stanford, and fullback Snow scored five times.

Stanford's lineup included tackle Bill Traeger, who was later to become sheriff of Los Angeles County, and left guard W. K. Roosevelt, a second cousin of Theodore Roosevelt. Early in the game Roosevelt hobbled over to R. S. Fisher, captain of the Stanford team, and said, "Something is broken in my leg."

"Stay with it!" snapped Fisher.

"You bet I will," replied the Stanford guard with true Rooseveltian grit. He dragged himself back to the line of scrimmage and played fifteen more minutes. Finally, he had to leave the game with a broken leg and fractured ribs.

One of the first newspaper stories reporting a Tournament of Roses football game also was one of the funniest. The Pasadena *News* reported the game as follows: "Several thousand Dutchmen and Britishers engage in several years of bloody fighting for the possession of a government and don't get an encore. Twenty-two college striplings argue for an hour over the progress along the ground of an inflated pig's hide, and law-abiding citizens bound up and down on the seats of their trousers, while demure maidens hammer plug hats down over the ears of their escorts with parasols."

1903

The stampede before the game may have had something to do with the decision of Tournament of Roses officials to abandon the idea of an intersectional football game after one try. President Charles Coleman and his aides had difficulty anyway in negotiating for teams. Nobody wanted to play the Michigan powerhouse again. The 1903 festival went back to the old format of general sports events, with a polo match drawing a small crowd of 2,000. Coleman did succeed in bringing one big attraction to Pasadena during his lone year at the helm. A large group of Navajo Indians came with their band from Arizona, set up camp at Tournament Park, and attracted hundreds of curious people. Needless to say, they were also a popular feature of the parade.

The Hotel Green float in the 1903 parade, a four-horse tallyho all red and green with flowers, was filled with pretty girls in big red picture hats and dainty summer gowns. As they passed the reviewing stand, each girl released a red toy balloon from under her parasol, dotting the sky with small red balls.

1904

When Charles D. Daggett took over the presidency in 1904, he called a meeting of the Tournament committee and declared, "Gentlemen, our beloved founder, Mr. Holder, has a wonderful idea. I will let him tell you about it."

Holder arose and said: "You have read the new best-seller, *Ben Hur.* That book gives us the idea we need for our festival. Let us stage a true Roman chariot race. It will make modern history."

The Tournament members cheered. They hadn't dreamed anything so exciting could be a part of their great festival. The world had to take notice now.

Ed Off, a courageous man who was director of the Tournament, said: "Yes, the world will notice. And I will race."

Race he did, though he was defeated by Mac Wiggins in the first Tournament chariot race in 1904.

Girls of Hotel Maryland, somewhat disappointed at having lost first prize to Hotel Green in 1903, showed their true feelings in 1904 by singing: "We want the prize, we want it bad, and if we fail, we'll feel sad." Apparently, the strategy worked, because they won in 1904.

The chariots weren't the only crowd-pleasers in 1904. Automobiles were a novelty, and driving was a tricky matter. To compare skills in handling the iron monsters, elimination contests of speed were held. Contestants drove over a given course, the one coming closest to driving at an average of four miles an hour winning a pair of women's gloves as a prize. There also was exhibition of control between horse-drawn vehicles and automobiles, in which each was driven at high speed and stopped at a given signal.

1905

Then came the memorable Tournament of Roses of 1905, the festival that became history for two reasons: Ed Off nearly lost his life in a wild chariot race that luckily avoided tragedy, and the Tournament named its first Rose Queen, Hallie Woods.

Miss Woods made her own gown and helped decorate the float upon which she rode in the parade. She had been chosen by her fellow students at Pasadena High School.

Bugler Ernest Crawford astounded the 1905 viewers by appearing in the parade in a suit in which leggings, coat, and hat were made entirely of flowers. The following description of the parade is taken from official Tournament archives: "Harry Zier's automobile was a dream of beauty. The scheme was a barge and the striking effect was made by covering the big touring car entirely with a frame, boat-shaped, so that not a bit of the running gear was visible. As if seated at the oars, the chauffeur and his friends sat amidst white carnations, dotted with red."

In 1905 the weather was so hot (76 degrees by mid-morning) that

HALLIE WOODS, FIRST
ROSE QUEEN

ED OFF, CHARIOT DRIVER
AND PRESIDENT

parade officials moved the automobile division from the rear to the No. 1 spot in the parade to prevent radiators from boiling over while the autos were trying to keep the slow pace of horse-drawn vehicles. The fire department rig was placed at the end of the parade so it would be in position for a quick getaway if necessary.

Ed Off went into the 1905 chariot race with memories of 1904. The following happened in 1904 before an audience of 6,500, according to a news account: "The race featured two authentic two-wheeled Roman chariots with teams of four horses lashed together to provide a tremendous picture of power. A tense hush fell over the crowd just before the start. The two lonely figures stood precariously in the small fragile chariots. Off, the novice with more enthusiasm than experience, met Wiggins, a veteran horseman from El Monte. The professional handling of the charging mounts by the latter was too much for the amateur. The race was no contest."

Off was determined to make good in 1905. He was matched against the widely known hotel man, D. M. Linnard. The popular Off got away to an early lead, but his beasts became unmanageable. Probably infuriated by gopher holes in the track, they roared around the curve; Off lost all control. Men shouted "Stop," girls screamed, women held handkerchiefs to their faces expecting at any moment to see the daring rider dashed to the ground and crushed to death beneath the horses' hoofs. But fortune smiled on the roses fete. A horseman astride a big bay came out of nowhere, hurriedly attempting the rescue. The crowd of 12,000 roared its approval when he succeeded in halting the runaway team. Following his narrow escape, Off attempted to bow before Queen Woods, who had viewed the scene from the royal box, but he collapsed into the arms of the man next to him.

1906

Off came back in 1906 to win a heat against a rider named Gaylord, but his horses wouldn't stop after crossing the finish line and Off was injured, ending his chariot-racing career but not his love for the Tournament. In 1907, Off succeeded Edwin D. Neff, who headed the Tournament in 1906, as president, the least honor the directors could bestow upon a man who had risked his life to make the Rose Festival a thrilling affair. No athlete in Pasadena roses history has had more right to say, "I tried."

The picnic atmosphere featured the concession of T. H. Cook of Los Angeles, who was granted the right to conduct a stand that featured "fortune telling birds, magic fish pond, and a doll race." Cook had to pay a $10 license fee. L. H. Lancaster had the food concession. He could sell sandwiches, soda water, and lemonade on condition he provide first-class sandwiches with meat and butter for ten cents each, a good cup of coffee with cream and sugar for five cents, and cigars at the same price and quality as offered downtown.

The 1906 Queen, Elsie Armitage, will go down in history as the queen with the largest court — twenty-four ladies-in-waiting. Altadena High School had the eye-stopper in the parade that year — a float representing a large man-of-war coasting on a sea of flowers.

QUEEN ELSIE ARMITAGE AND HER TWO DOZEN LADIES-IN-WAITING

JOAN WOODBURY

1907

In 1907 horse thieves raided many of the stables, and many rigs were stolen before they could be hitched for the parade.

Joan Hadenfeldt Woodbury, at the age of 35, became the first of two queens in Tournament of Roses history who was married when chosen. She lived to reach the age of 97, the oldest former queen at the time of her death in 1969.

"The mayor and city council came to me and asked me to be first queen under the official name of Tournament of Roses," she related, through her daughter, Joan Woodbury Wilcoxon of Cathedral City, California. "My husband built and was managing the Maryland Hotel at the time. I shall always cherish being asked to be the first Tournament of Roses queen under that official name. I designed my costume and the costumes of my court. I also designed my float. I made my own costume of white satin hand-painted with California poppies."

May Sutton Bundy returned each year to Pasadena to attend the former queens' luncheon, sponsored by the Occidental Life Insurance Company. Mrs. Woodbury also attended this function as long as it was held. "I enjoy coming back because I have felt it was such a beautiful gesture on the part of the people of Pasadena to name me queen," says Mrs. Bundy, former Wimbledon tennis champion, who reigned as Tournament queen in 1908, when George P. Carey opened his three-year term as president.

"Since my exposure to the Tournament of Roses many years ago, I have marveled at the many people involved, their handling of the many complicated details, and the use of great brain power, all blended to produce this wonderful festival," says Mrs. Bundy, who rates her most fruitful experience the opportunity to observe how efficiently people cooperated and blended their skills.

EXCITING, DANGEROUS ACTION—ONE OF THE CHARIOT RACES THAT THRILLED CROWDS IN EARLY TOURNAMENT COMPETITION

18

1908

MAY SUTTON

The festival of 1908 is remembered for many things. It was the first year parade officials had to be concerned about the height of wires above the parade route. Wires had to be elevated to let one high float pass. Another float, created by the Pasadena Merchants Association, got caught in the car tracks along Colorado; the flowery wheel had to be removed and a wheel of another color substituted to permit the float to continue its journey. Redondo Beach entered a most unusual float in the parade — a mammoth floral whale that spouted carnation perfume twenty-five feet in the air and opened a geranium-lined mouth. The Redondo Beach whale was forty-one feet long, and its mouth was eight feet wide. The mouth opened and closed as the huge creature wallowed down the street like a great denizen of the deep. Green magnolia leaves, 20,000 of them, made the whale look as though it had just left the water. Members of the Redondo Arrowhead Club, all in whaling costumes, marched beside the float carrying strings of freshly caught fish from Redondo Bay.

Redlands, famed for its orange groves, presented a gigantic orange eighty-six feet in circumference, created from three thousand ripe oranges. Altadena school entered a huge airship thirty-five feet long. All these were a part of the new age of spectacular floats.

In 1908 the trolley-line traffic from Los Angeles to Pasadena was so heavy it caused a temporary breakdown; there wasn't enough "juice" to operate so many cars. More than a hundred cars were on the rails between the two cities at the time. It was estimated that a thousand automobiles creaked into Pasadena, and at that early date there was a traffic jam on Pasadena streets.

Chariot-race rivalry reached a high point of intensity when a driver named Michel dueled C. C. West in the finals. They were neck and

MAYOR THOMAS EARLY AND THE CITY COUN-CIL RIDE IN THE 1908 PARADE

RUTH PALMER

neck down the stretch, West on the pole. Near the finish line, Michel drove in front of West's entry, knocking down two of his horses. West was named the winner on a foul.

1909

"We have sent thousands of posters to railroads for distribution in depots all the way to the east coast telling about our festival," said President Carey as the 1909 festival neared. The holdup of a stage-coach was re-created as part of the show that year. A crowd of 20,000 saw the chariot races won by West for his sponsor, Lucky Baldwin.

Ezra Meeker, pioneer traveler who crossed the continent with an ox team by the old Oregon Trail in 1852, and who repeated the trip in 1906, was a special attraction in 1910, driving an ox cart in the parade.

Individual floats became more spectacular also. In 1909, E. W. Knowlton used five hundred American Beauty roses to decorate a two-seated surrey drawn by two Arabian horses. Walter Raymond, owner of Hotel Raymond, decorated his automobile so that it resembled a huge sea shell.

1910

Mother Nature decreed that the 20th Anniversary festival in 1910 was to be a wet one — so wet that the chariot races had to be postponed a week. Tournament founders Holder and Rowland were grand marshals of the parade, which couldn't start until noon.

Dr. Rowland attracted attention aboard Prince Arthur as he led the parade. The magnificent horse wore a collar of red and white carnations, and tied to its front ankle was a garter of red and white ribbons, the Tournament colors.

ALHAMBRA, THE GATEWAY
TO THE SAN GABRIEL VALLEY
(1908 PARADE)

Pasadena's Tournament of Roses on New Year's Day.

1911

By 1911, when Frank G. Hogan took over the Tournament presidency for a year, the population of Pasadena had grown to 30,290.

"We haven't had a queen for two years. I think the practice should be revived," said Hogan, who came up with an idea for public voting for the queen; anyone who joined the association received a vote for a nominated queen. Ruth Palmer was elected queen for the 1911 festival. A second parade, a night affair, also was organized, staged by "The Komical Knights of the Karnival with King Kidder and Kween Karmencita."

1912

By 1912, 150,000 people were in Pasadena to see the parade as Edward T. Off returned to the presidency for a two-year term. Off did not have a queen for his court, but he did have the king of the airways. C. P. Rodgers, who had made an epic flight from the Atlantic to Pasadena, was named king of the festival. He flew over the entire parade route and dropped rose petals from the sky.

The promotion departments of the leading railroads already were taking advantage of the Tournament of Roses' drawing power as a travel attraction. The Salt Lake and Santa Fe lines printed folders which stressed that "The Tournament of Roses is like nothing else in the sun . . . it is a fiesta impossible to accomplish anywhere else in the world . . . it is Pasadena's New Year's gift to mankind."

1913

"What our festival needs is both a king and a queen," said the creative Off in 1913, and Jean French was named queen and Harrison P. Drumond became king. That year also there were an ostrich race and a race between an elephant and a camel at Tournament Park when interest in chariot racing started to dwindle. A collision in 1912, when the chariots of Albert Parsons and C. E. Post bumped in a nerve-tingling accident, suggested to sports fans that chariot racing was getting to be far too dangerous—the results were not of significance anywhere but in Pasadena and the news stories were brief. The sport had become too expensive. First prize seldom paid over $1,000, yet it was estimated by E. J. Levingood, a long-time competitor, that it cost $5,000 to train a team of horses for the event. Only Lucky Baldwin among the horse breeders had enough money to afford the luxury.

The ostrich race of 1913 was memorable. One of the riders was thrown from his mount in front of the judges' stand. In his subsequent attempt to capture the bird, he was kicked across the racecourse. For the next fifteen minutes, the ostrich kicked and scattered a half-dozen pursuing men before it was captured. In the elephant-camel race, the

FIRST KING AND QUEEN: HARRISON DRUMMOND AND JEAN FRENCH

ANITA BALDWIN'S PEACOCK FLOAT, CALLED BY MANY "THE MOST BEAUTIFUL FLOAT TO DATE"

elephant grabbed an early lead but stopped twenty feet from the finish line, refusing to budge. So his rider jumped off and goaded him across the line by prodding him from the rear.

1914

R. D. Davis became president in 1914, with Mable Seibert Loughry reigning as queen and Dr. F. C. E. Mattison as king. By now the horse-drawn floats were rapidly disappearing from the parade, and big cities like San Diego and Portland were entering floats. The outstanding feature of the Tournament's 25th Anniversary parade was Mrs. Anita Baldwin McClaughry (daughter of Lucky Baldwin) entering a huge white peacock mounted in an oak tree, a float using thousands of lilies of the valley, orchids, and white roses. The press about the country raved that this was the most beautiful float in history. The "Knights of the Rose," a booster group of fifty-four men in scarlet coats, riding horseback, made their first appearance. Although the United States hadn't yet entered the World War, thoughts of war and peace were evident. The Pasadena High School float featured Helen Marie Neilson as the goddess of liberty with her arms extended to the warring nations of Europe.

1915

In 1915 Mrs. McClaughry again entered a stunning float, the Santa Anita dove of peace, a gigantic floral bird with more than 500 lilies of the valley, 5,000 hot-house Killarney roses, 500 sprays of Stevia serulata, and 1,000 sprays of maidenhair fern. The bird was twenty-six feet long and had a wingspread of eleven feet.

While chariot-booster Off continued to praise his favorite sport as the greatest phenomenon since Rome ruled the world, the 1915 festival under the presidency of J. B. Coulston marked the last of the chariot races. Pasadena was not sure what its festival formula should be. The parade of 1915 featured the land of make-believe — fairytale characters and animals such as elephants, camels, lions, tigers, leopards. The Tournament began a queenless era, too — no queen for the next eight years.

"We'd better go back to football," advised co-founder Rowland, the ever-present advisor, and 1916 president Lewis H. Turner agreed as he set up a committee to land for Pasadena the biggest football game that could be scheduled — "so Pasadena can give the newspapermen from coast to coast something exciting to write about."

EARLY EQUESTRIAN
LEADER M. S. PASHGIAN
RIDES IN ELEGANCE, 1915

4
King Football Returns to Stay

GEORGE HALAS, 1919

THE EARLY nineteen-hundreds can be described as the Era of Search in the life of the Tournament of Roses — a search for the formula that would permanently establish the festival's true Granddaddy status as being first in all phases of activity, parade, and sports.

In the early years of the twentieth century, the parade evolved from the carriage and the decorated-automobile stage to the magical world of stunning flowered floats that eventually became mechanically powered and controlled.

During that same time, the enthusiastic experimenters in sports promotion tried everything from tug-of-war contests to chariot races. Then, after one stab at football in 1902, the Tournament fathers made the historic decision in 1916 that football had more combined local and national appeal as a festival feature than any other sport, and therein was born the permanent place of the New Year's Day bowl game in American life. Yes, Granddaddy became a man in 1916.

If the chariot races accomplished any purpose, they provided the impetus for the construction of wooden stands at Tournament Park, to the point that there were 25,000 seats for football fans by 1916. The solitary 1902 game had earned a profit of $3,161.86, and President Turner and his aides — men like W. L. Leishman who were coming forth with far-reaching football vision that eventually was to lead to the construction of today's Rose Bowl — had hopes of a solid financial enterprise when they invited Washington State and Brown to play the 1916 attraction. A heavy rainsorm, however, held the crowd to 7,000, and the Tournament lost $11,000 staging the game.

Discouragement could have thwarted the football idea right then, but men like Turner, Leishman, and others had foresight. They may not have completely envisioned the more than a million-and-a-half-dollar television income the Rose Bowl game produces today, besides three quarters of a million dollars at the gate, but as early as 1916 Pasadena's top businessmen knew that football would blend with their unusual parade of flowers to bring the Tournament of Roses story annually to the nation. This was the perfect formula, they believed. No promotion man was ever more correct.

24

LEWIS TURNER

FRITZ POLLARD

1916

In 1915 the honor of being marshal had gone to M. S. Pashgian, who had ridden in a dozen previous parades as an equestrian and was destined to appear another eighteen years before retiring. In 1916 the Tournament honored its co-founder, Dr. Rowland, by naming him grand marshal on the occasion that marked his retirement from the festival's active leadership.

The only event that didn't get dampened by rain in 1916 was the annual Tournament ball, held in the evening. It was customary in the early days to stage the ball at the conclusion of the New Year's Day activities. Yes, the folks a half-century back and more had stamina.

The Tournament of Roses parade was in its twenty-seventh year before bathing beauties made their appearance on a float. The young ladies, in "natty and alluring" bathing suits, rode on the 1916 Ocean Park float. What were those "alluring" suits like? They were all black, full-length arm-and-bloomer suits.

It was very wet and very cold at kickoff time when Washington State (6-0) faced visiting Brown (5-3-1). Brown's highly rated All-American, Fritz Pollard, was handicapped by the wet and cold, netting a mere 40 yards for the day. Washington State won 14-0, thanks to a hard-charging line that dominated in the mud.

Even at that early date, there was complaining that the best team in the East hadn't been secured. The Tournament fathers had tried to get the East's best, Syracuse, but that school balked at the long trip.

Howard Angus in the Los Angeles *Times* described the Washington State victory as follows: "The western backs, with five and six men ahead of them, literally tore the right side of the Brown line to shreds during the last half when all the scoring was done. Boone, Dietz, and Bangs, the Washington State backs, were practically unstoppable. It was seldom that they didn't reach the secondary defense before being downed. The interference caught the Brown men amidships and the men carrying the ball tore on, dragging two tacklers through the mud."

Referee Walter Eckersall praised Carl Dietz of Washington State for hitting the line faster than any back he had ever seen. A young man named Wallace Wade played guard for Brown and did a noble job trying to bust up the Cougar interference, but he, too, was trampled after a great effort. This wasn't the last of young Mr. Wade, however. Five times he was to lead a team into the Rose Bowl in later years, as a coach. Dick Hanley, another who went on to a great coaching career, at Northwestern, also played in the 1916 game for Washington State.

Perhaps no team "took home" more from its experience of coming to Pasadena than Washington State. While practicing in the Los Angeles area for the game against Brown, the players made $100 a day per man helping Hollywood film the movie, "Tom Brown of Harvard." It is rumored they pooled their earnings, bet on themselves, and went back to Pullman with big loot.

1917

The year 1917 will go down in Tournament of Roses history for two reasons: the parade became international in scope, with hotels from Yokohama and Manila, as well as American cities, entering massive floral floats; and second, western football prestige was established nationally for the first time when Oregon defeated Pennsylvania 14-0. While Brown the year before had been rated a secondary power in the east, Pennsylvania, with a strong 7-2 record, was considered one of the true strengths in the section of the country where the best football was supposed to have been played.

D. M. Linnard was president and Dr. C. D. Lockwood was grand marshal in 1917. It was a beautiful day with temperature at 86.

A model impersonating King Kamehameha III, former ruler of the Hawaiian Islands, escorted a float from the Mid-Pacific Carnival Association of Hawaii. Kamehameha rode horseback in full war costume and feather headdress. The float, an outrigger canoe formed of marigolds, smilax, and white carnations, was manned by four bronzed oarsmen and thirteen Hawaiian girls who threw thousands of pink and white carnations to the cheering crowd.

The crowd of 25,000 got its first thrill in the football game when Howard Berry of Penn got off a 50-yard punt early in the game. Fifty-yard punts were unheard of in the West. The fans watched it soar with something of the same awe that marks the viewing of a shot to the moon today. Little did the spectators realize that Oregon's Beckett and Montieth were to wind up with punting statistics that compared favorably with Berry's.

26

The Oregon backfield brothers, Shy and Hollis Huntington, soon proved their worth. Penn got the early breaks, however. A penalty saved Penn when Shy Huntington intercepted a pass and ran it back 25 yards. Penn recovered its own blocked drop kick by Berry to retain possession. Penn drove to the shadow of the goal posts with power and seemed to be ready to smash the ball into the end zone when "an error of judgment" (as described by Los Angeles *Times* writer Harry Williams) produced the turning point of the game. Instead of continuing the power drives, Penn's Quigley tried an end run to the right with two men providing interference. Oregon's left end, Mitchell, threw Quigley for a 10-yard loss, forcing a drop kick from the 29 which Quigley muffed as the Oregon line charged him.

This turn of events removed Oregon stage fright and discouraged Penn. Maxwell Stiles wrote: "Oregon gained confidence, not in Penn, but in Oregon."

After Berry failed in drop kicks of 41 and 36 yards, further depressing phenomena for the heavily favored easterners, Oregon drove to its first score in the third period, a 70-yard push after Shy Huntington intercepted a Penn pass. The Huntingtons made the big gains, with Shy passing to right end Tegert in the corner of the field for the score. The next touchdown came after another interception by Shy Huntington with Johnny Parsons breaking away 42 yards to the 1 yard line, where he was caught from behind by Berry. Shy then raced around end for the touchdown.

The quarterback for the Penn team was Bert Bell, who later in life became president of the National Football League. A Penn tackle was Lou Little, later a famed coach at Columbia who brought a team to the Rose Bowl and won. Oregon's two strong tackles, Beckett and Bartlett, outplayed Little in the 1917 thriller that forced eastern sports writers to admit good football had arrived west of the Rockies. Coach of this Oregon team that first established western football on the national scene was Hugo Bezdek, who came back in 1918 with the Mare Island Marines. They defeated Camp Lewis Army 19-7, when the Tournament of Roses turned to the military, marking the nation's involvement in the World War.

1918

B. O. KENDALL served the first of two terms as Tournament president in 1918; his grand marshal was Dr. Z. T. Malaby. Patriotism was the parade motif. Warship, tank, and flag floats, plus marching units representing patriotic groups, were featured in the parade.

President Kendall, A. L. Hamilton, chairman of the Pasadena City Commission, and William H. Veddar, chairman of the Pasadena Red Cross, had volunteered to President Woodrow Wilson to call off the parade. President Wilson replied that he did not see how a celebration of this type could hurt the government's war activities, and he suggested that the country's normal life should be continued in every way possible.

The largest crowd so far, estimated at 250,000, watched the 1918 parade on another very hot New Year's Day, 86 degrees. Because it was a "meatless day," in accord with Secretary of Commerce Herbert Hoover's meat-conservation edict, the hot dogs of the past gave way to tuna, minced egg, and other meatless sandwich concoctions.

There was no collegiate football, but military trainees were permitted to perform on camp teams as part of their rugged preparation for war. Kendall and his associates asked the military to provide the football attraction on New Year's Day to keep the nationally accepted Tournament game going and to take the country's mind off the hardships of staging a war.

W. L. ("Fox") Stanton, for many years identified with Caltech in Pasadena, returned to his former campus (Tournament Park) as coach of the Camp Lewis team. But his men were dominated by the men of Bezdek who featured "Jap" Brown at quarterback and Hollis Huntington (back for a second straight year) at fullback.

Clyde Bruckman wrote an interesting summary in the Los Angeles *Examiner* of the 19-7 Marine victory: "The mystic maze which Hugo Bezdek brought down from Mare Island in the disguise of a football team won as they were expected to win before a crowd of 25,000 fans. They won because they had the better team, the smoothest working combinations, led by Jap Brown, whose generalship throughout the struggle was superb. Always it was Brown and Hollis Huntington when the Marines made a drive. A year ago it was Shy Huntington who created a hero role, but yesterday it was brother Hollis who wrote his name large. Like a devastating tank he ripped through the entanglements of the Army defense. It was Hollis the unstoppable who carried the ball through the heart of the Army line. He made more yards than Hoyle has rules. He didn't have any more use for interference than a snake has for corn plasters. He was as easy to stop as a porcupine."

Army backs Romney and McKay were praised for performing great deeds behind a "line that leaked Marines," but the name McKay then couldn't perform the magic in Pasadena that USC's winning coach, Johnny (no relation), has attained in recent years.

Proof that football was toughening military personnel for war was offered in the Marine team's feat of playing the entire game without a substitution after right end Hobson went out with a shattered ankle after the first play of the game.

The Marines' Ambrose booted a 31-yard field goal to give his team a 3-0 lead. Romney ran end for 6 yards to put the Army ahead. Passes to Beckett and Sanderson set up a 5-yard sprint by Brown that put the Marines ahead to stay at 9-7. A thirty-two-yard run by Sanderson and a Huntington buck scored again, and Ambrose added a thirty-three-yard field goal.

PADDY DRISCOLL

1919

Kendall's "war term" was completed in 1919 when America celebrated the end of the World War with the theme "Victorious Peace" in the Tournament parade. The sun seemed to shine for the occasion. It was a warm beautiful day in Pasadena, but much of the nation was blizzard-bound. Returning servicemen were guests of Pasadena. "Welcome Home" signs were prevalent everywhere in the city. The flower crop was especially abundant, and the floats had a beauty that made all viewers gay and happy.

Actually, the Marines lost to "The Wasp."

The Wasp was Paddy Driscoll, out of Northwestern, who put on the following show for the 27,000 spectators:

Returned punts for 115 yards, an average of 12.6.

Gained 34 yards net from scrimmage while rushing.

Punted six times for a 43.5 yard average, one of the punts going 60 yards and another 50.

Completed four of eight passes for 77 yards, one for 45 yards and a touchdown.

Drop-kicked a 30-yard field goal.

Caught a pass to set up a touchdown.

Ran the whole show magnificently as Navy's quarterback.

Les Barnard, former great Minneapolis high school football coach, who retired to Orange, California, and who played for Great Lakes, recalls: "I used to admire watching Driscoll practice field-goal kicking. He would stand on the 50-yard line and drop-kick one ball through one goal post, then turn around and drop-kick another ball through the goal post on the other side of the field."

Another Navy star was George Halas, who became the founder of the Chicago Bears and was a National Football League pioneer. It was he who caught Driscoll's 45-yard touchdown pass. Charley Bachman, later to become famous as football coach at Michigan State, played in the strong Navy line.

Halas, who was dragged down from behind after a 77-yard run with an intercepted pass, often has said, "Playing in the Rose Bowl was one of the greatest thrills of my life."

Maxwell Stiles wrote this of Halas: "The Great Lakes right end was one of the most superb players ever seen in the Pasadena gridiron classic. His work in getting down under punts and dropping the safety man in his tracks has never been exceeded."

5

A Wonder of Our Times – The Living Float

ISABELLA COLEMAN, 1971

1920

THE WAR was over, the Tournament of Roses had been established as America's prime New Year's classic, and Pasadena was solidly on its way in 1920 to becoming the capital city of the festive world each January 1.

The 31st annual parade was significant because it marked the end of the horse-drawn era. It was in 1901 that mechanization began with the entry of six automobiles. Soon thereafter the floats were motor-driven. Each succeeding year saw fewer horse-drawn entries. From 1920 on, as a result of the trend begun at the turn of the century, the motor-driven float, a wonder of modern times, took over completely.

America never sees in any other parade the imagination of animation, flower beauty, and breath-taking replicas that millions come to see each January 1 in Pasadena. Actually, thousands start lining Colorado Boulevard the afternoon before, setting up sleeping quarters on the curb or sitting all night in camp chairs, sometimes even on sofas, in order to get a "50-yard-line seat" for the two-and-a-half-hour spectacle. Color television now beams the picture of this classic around the globe. This is Americana in joy and artistry.

Pasadena has the largest parade floats in the world — also the most original. Floats for the Tournament cost as high as $30,000. The average expenditure is about $15,000. Most of the floats are built by the "Pasadena method," a technique developed over the years. It is required that every float in the parade be completely decorated with fresh flowers and plant material.

Early floats were built by amateur groups, but today the competition is so keen only the professional builder and some talented amateurs have the know-how, skill, and equipment to create these competitive magical displays.

The professional firms that construct virtually all of the floats are Miller Brothers, Mrs. Isabella and Dr. Sam Coleman, Inc., Taylor and

Associates, Donald Bent Parade Floats, Herrin-Preston, Rick Chapman's Festival Artists, and Valley Decorating Company.

The basic construction of the floats occurs in the company plants, located in the Pasadena area. Several weeks before the parade, the floats are transferred to Tournament of Roses "huts" where they are finished, the major finishing task being the application of fresh flowers.

An artist such as Everett Fish of Valley Decorating Company develops the float blueprints once he is informed of the theme of the parade. He designs and creates a painting of the float as it will look, then the salesmen of the company, men like Valley's Mike Lawrence or Dick Hubbard, sell the project to the contest entrant, usually a firm, community, or organization. Once the decorating company receives the order to construct the float, work begins in midsummer.

The frame usually is the chassis of a stripped-down automobile or a truck with the wheels extended to make possible a float approximately 55 feet long, 20 feet wide, and 17 feet high. The shaping of the design is done with pipes, steel strips, chicken wire, and plastic materials. The next process is the "cocooning," which is applied by spray to form the coat for the flowers.

When asked to suggest the best formula for designing championship floats, Fish declared, "I find the SWAG System most effective." Asked to explain what SWAG stood for, Fish replied, "Scientific wild-assed guessing system."

Electric and gasoline engines provide the power for floats. Electronically operated mechanisms make it possible for flowery eyes to blink, arms to move, and generally any movement of parts the project requires. Usually there are at least two operators under each float, at least one provided with "seeing eyes" by periscope or some small opening in the construction. Artist Fish recalls building one float where the driver had to lie on his side in a small compartment just a foot above the pavement. A float driver receives approximately $50 for the day. He earns it.

Rick Chapman of Festival Artists of Pasadena, one of the Tournament float builders, has many memories of his experiences as a driver. Now twenty-eight years old, Chapman became involved in Tournament activities at the age of fourteen and began a float-driving stint at the age of sixteen. He knows what happens "down under" when one of these stunning wonders of the parade world moves down the avenue lined with viewers.

"The driver often has to work from cramped quarters in a part of the float where he can't see anything but the pink line on the pavement," says Chapman, who long has maintained that the line in the center of the pavement, the drivers' guideline, is all that need be seen.

"In modern float construction, it is almost impossible to put the driver in position to see," he explains. "So we give him a 'spotter,' a fellow who can be placed in some advantageous position under the foliage. Often this is in an area a considerable distance from the driver.

The man with the 'eyes' communicates with the driver either by telephone or, if he is close enough, through voice." Chapman's firm constructed one float in which the man with the "eyes" was forty-five feet from the driver. A telephone was used to communicate.

"I have preached for several years that the driver need not have vision of the parade route," says Chapman. "To prove it, I drove a float blindfolded. I listened to my observer and functioned accordingly as the driver. It worked very well. The driver has no depth perception in our modern floats, which are so low and have so much material that blocks vision. He is better off functioning by the advice of his spotter."

Chapman had a scare one year. He was driving a float that caught fire underneath. He had a fire extinguisher near the "cockpit" and the smudge was put out.

Chapman says a driver usually works from cramped position. The big problem is exhaust. "In our floats we have installed a system of exhaust blowers and fresh air pickup which is blown in."

Every float, he says, has two drivers—counting the "spotter." Chapman can't recall hearing of a driver ever failing by the "seeing eye" method.

Veteran drivers are calm and have no problems, he explains. "New drivers get shook up at first. It is quite an experience until you get accustomed to having someone else describe where you should manipulate your float."

Chapman says the future will create more stunning floats than ever before seen by man. "Floats will do more and more. Animation will develop much more than it has so far. All floats have an animation-control man now. In the future they may need several. I expect floats will divide and move in sections, then come together during a parade. Anything that will amaze will be the key to the future."

Chapman's firm insists upon having two sets of drivers for every float. "We use one crew to bring the float to the starting point and another to operate during the parade," says Chapman. "A man gets too tired staying up all night and then staying cramped during the parade. We want our operators fresh when the action starts. It's not precarious work, but it is trying under cramped conditions. A driver gets hot and he gets cold. He has to work with close synchronization with the rest of the crew. We want a man fresh for all of that."

Flower application begins forty-eight hours before the parade. This is an around-the-clock task. Students, various organizations, and volunteers provide the labor, usually as a money-raising venture for their group. To guide the workers, the cocooning usually is painted the exact color of the flowers to be applied.

A trio of distinguished persons judges the competing floats. They start their work two days before the parade, first studying all available information on the sixty floats, then making the rounds of the decorating sites to witness the final placement of flowers and checking to see that all regulations are observed. The final judging takes place at the South Orange Grove area where the floats are lined up before the parade. All riders and float personnel must be on their floats by 7 a.m., two hours before the start of the parade. The judges' decisions arc based on (1) beauty, (2) excellence of design and execution of theme, (3) originality, and (4) use of flowers and color harmony. There are fourteen major awards, the two major prizes being the Sweepstakes and the Grand Prize.

The Queen of Float Construction is Mrs. Isabella Coleman, a decorator of parade floats since 1909, who has been the recipient of more than 250 major awards. Her creations became so distinctive that her son left the practice of dentistry to carry on the work. The Isabella Coleman story is very much the story of the development of Tournament of Roses floats as the most stunning phenomenon in parade history — anywhere.

She started working on floats at Pasadena High School in 1904. That's when her enthusiasm for float creativity actually began, although she says her appetite for what was to become "her thing" really was stimulated in 1909 when she rode in the parade aboard the Maryland Hotel entry.

"It was fun. I wanted to do it again," she recalls.

"Why don't you enter your own horse and buggy?" her father asked as the 1910 Tournament of Roses neared.

"Can I?" she responded, petting her horse, Queen.

"Of course you can," said her father.

Isabella went to work to create her first float.

"In those days, people tied flowers to the wheels and body of the buggy with wire and string," she says. "I decided to fasten flowers

MRS. COLEMAN SUPERVISES CONSTRUCTION OF SWAN LAKE FLOAT

ISABELLA, 1919

in bunches instead. At the age of eighteen I was adventurous. I believed a bunch of flowers was prettier than a string. They didn't grow in strings. I wanted to make mine look real."

Isabella, her buggy with "bunched" flowers and proud Queen prancing in the lead, won second prize in the carriage division, and a career of float-making was on its way. Fate had a hand in this beginning, however. The excited Isabella went to bed early before New Year's 1910. During her dreams, the clouds opened up with a downpour. It was still raining when it was time to get up in very early morning.

"Go back to bed," her father said. "It's raining. There won't be a parade." But how could the anxious Isabella go back to sleep? She watched the skies, and the clouds broke up at 6 a.m. The parade wasn't doomed. And neither was her career.

"After getting second place, I kept on entering the parade," says Isabella. "Queen danced with her head high, and in the 1912 Tournament my float was judged the best horse-drawn vehicle. I recall the comment of some people, even though I was proud of the fact I had displayed roses with their full stems. 'You didn't win the prize. It was your horse,' they said. But the victory led to my first 'contracts.' In the 1913 parade, the realty board asked me to make up their float and I won first prize in the commercial division. My love for flowers was paying off. When I was a child in the buggy, when we lived in Honolulu, I always liked to play with flowers."

Isabella's fame spread quickly. In 1915 she won the Sweepstakes prize for the City of Los Angeles with her creation. When she was hired, one official said, "We expected a man. You are a girl. What do you intend to do for us?"

The 'girl' replied: "You want a streamer for your float. I will put every flower we grow in California in it."

"I lost $300 on my first float contract," confesses Mrs. Coleman. "I have always been a sucker for paying the top prices for flowers. I couldn't resist putting on the best."

Isabella's brother Matt was influential in getting the budding float-builder to try for one of the most remarkable jobs of her life — the building of a float for Aimee Semple McPherson, who wanted to display her Angelus Temple in the Rose Parade in 1925.

"I remember discussing the matter with her while I was eating a fudge sundae at the Biltmore Hotel," recalls Isabella. "She was a gracious lady, very charming and wonderful to work with. She told me to do the job for her, and we won first prize."

That float displayed the Angelus Temple above the flowers. Mrs. Coleman has many memories of Aimee McPherson. "She wanted to be just like anybody else in public. She would let her hair down, and few people would recognize her."

Mrs. Coleman said a development in float-making that was to become important to future beauty took place in 1929. "Instead of weaving the flowers, we started to paste them," she says. This made possible many lifelike creations, although the glue had to be perfected to prevent illness from "sniffing."

Mrs. Coleman is considered the original leader in float experimentation with engines and mechanical mysteries under flowers. She devised many special engines and contraptions. She is given credit for designing hidden cockpits.

"The next development in float-building was the trend to go low," says Mrs. Coleman. "This was the most important idea bringing the float down to pavement position, thus enabling people to see its beauty clearly. We used airplane wheels instead of the old high wheels. Then we worked on getting floats to be driven forward instead of backward. I take credit for that. The Tournament had a rule that three feet of space had to be open in front of the motor to prevent asphyxiation of anyone riding. I sought out mechanical help and we found a way to put the driver in front of the motor, and therefore the exhaust went out the back. Then came the age of animation, which was made possible with pulleys and gears."

Mrs. Coleman maintains, however, that the low chassis was the most important development in the history of float-building, and her hope upon retiring was that future floats would not go too high, for reasons of economy.

The use of vials to display flowers more realistically is another trend she helped develop. "Every float needs a climax," she says. "It is wrong to make them too cluttered." Mums are Mrs. Coleman's favorite flower to work with. Ironically, roses are the most difficult to work with, she has found. Roses wilt quickly — and they have thorns!

Another major development during her career was the wire frame and cocooning process for creating lifelike scenes. When it was possible to put the material on the frame with a "gun" or "blower" to form the background for the pasting of flowers, all the restrictions of the weaving days were past.

She cannot name her favorite float of all time. "There are so many I liked. The swan. The dragon. The peacock," she enthuses. "Every float needs a climax. I always tried for that. A float is a stage. You can do anything. The future is unlimited. Just so they don't go back to getting too high off the pavement. I want them to keep the floats low."

Born in 1892, just two years after the Tournament was created, Mrs. Coleman should know. She never experienced what it was like to lose. Always she had a winner. No float designer is likely to break her record.

The Coleman dynasty may continue long after her son also retires. Recently when visiting her granddaughter Cathy, Mrs. Coleman noticed the little girl was leading a Donald Duck.

"Look, Nanny," said Cathy. "I can make a float, too."

Lee Miller of Miller Brothers, a Temple City float-building firm, has memories of many striking floats his firm has constructed. But he rates the Kodak Grand Prize winner of a few years ago as his "most stunning."

"It was a giant float with turning panels," he says. "The revolving screen on top gave the viewers a constantly changing scene. It was breath-taking."

The Chrysler Corporation is one of the companies that annually has entered a major float in the Rose Parade. Chrysler also has been a major sponsor of the Rose Bowl Game telecast. Chrysler is a significant example of industry "teaming" with the Tournament of Roses annually in bringing to the public the message that Americans work and play together. The firm sponsored a portion of the CBS telecast of the parade for a few years, but recently it has concentrated on sponsorship of the Rose Bowl Game telecast with such companies as Gillette and Eastern Airlines.

Leading the way in Chrysler participation was J. R. ("Jack") Barlow, director of Chrysler advertising and sales promotion. The company's top management personnel annually came to Pasadena to witness the spectacle. Chrysler, which sponsored the Bob Hope Show, enjoyed a "double feature" at the Tournament in 1969, when Hope was grand marshal for a second time, the first being 1947.

Chrysler first entered a float in the Rose Parade in 1965, winning the Anniversary Award. Since then, other awards have been won by the firm, including the President's Trophy in 1969.

CHRYSLER'S 1965 WINNER: "BRITAIN CROWNS ELIZABETH II"

"Thanks for the Memory" said the Chrysler float in 1969, a tribute to Bob Hope, the grand marshal of the 80th Tournament of Roses. Fifty-five feet in length, the float was a beautiful bouquet of pastel-pink roses handsomely sculptured and artistically petaled with orchids. Riding this elegant entry were Dorothy Lamour, Rosemary Clooney, Barbara Eden, Lynda Bennett, and Jerry Colonna, all of whom were immediately recognized as long-time friends and associates of Bob throughout his colorful career.

The 1970 Chrysler entry, "The Eagle Has Wings," was a tribute to the Lunar Landing Missions of Apollo 11 and 12 and depicted the pride and camaraderie of all peoples around the world, represented by the flags of more than a hundred countries. The proud eagle of the United States was of carved styrofoam and decorated with white and gold gladiolus petals, tipped on in layers to achieve the soft fullness of feathers. The beak was decorated with satinlike tulip petals and the claws were made of scraped grapefruit rinds. The message between the banners in gold was from President Nixon's greeting to the astronauts when they raised the flag on the moon: "In one precious moment — united as one." The float effectively took part in the parade which had been headed by astronauts Charles Conrad Jr., Richard Gordon, and Alan Bean as grand marshals.

Eastman Kodak is another active participant in Tournament of Roses activity. Its 1970 float entry was "Holidays Are for Children." This float featured a geodetic spheroid. The equilateral pentagonal sides of the spheroid carried reproductions in flowers of color photographs showing children enjoying the various holidays, such as Christmas, Easter, Thanksgiving, and Halloween. Each pentagon was divided into five equal triangles and by complicated engineering they were all animated to simultaneously flip over the triangle, revealing another picture on the other side.

Eastman, through its Rose Bowl Game interest as the preserver in pictures of the excitement and drama of collegiate football competition, has closely allied itself to the American Football Coaches Association.

The Kodak All-American team is selected annually by the AFCA and honored by Kodak on a national television program. AFCA members also vote each year for the large college and college division Kodak coaches-of-the-year, with winners participating in a third phase of Kodak's football program — coaches' clinics.

Several members of the Kodak All-American team have participated in the Rose Bowl over the last ten years, among them O. J. Simpson, Bob Griese, Bubba Smith, Gary Beban, and George Webster.

The reasons for Kodak's wide participation in the collegiate football area are summed up by Wylie S. Robson, vice president and general manager, marketing:

"Football coaches are closely involved in the development of the character of several thousand young men each year. We at Kodak are pleased to be a part of the development of these individuals by providing teaching aids to coaches, just as we are proud to be a part of the alliance between sports and photography."

Many other nationally prominent firms and organizations participate in the Rose Parade, each with outstanding float entries. In 1971 this list included Al Malaikah Shrine Temple, American Hospital Association, Bakery and Confectionery Workers Union, Bank of America, Bekins Moving and Storage, Chrysler Corporation, Continental Airlines, Dr. Pepper Company, Eastman Kodak, Farmers Insurance Group, Florists Transworld Delivery Association, Hi-C Drinks, Huntington Sheraton Hotel, Knott's Berry Farm, Lutheran Laymen's league, Minnesota Metro Tourist Council, National Exchange Club, Native Sons and Daughters of the Golden West, Occidental Life of California, Odd Fellows and Rebekahs, Portland Rose Festival Association, Salvation Army, Soroptimist Federation of the Americas, Sunkist Growers, Treasure Tones Paints, and Union Oil of California.

The famed Clydesdales-led Anheuser-Busch float representing the City of St. Louis is an annual parade feature (see Chapter 36).

The Farmers Insurance Group is another prominent sponsor, and the story of Farmers Insurance Tournament activity is very much the story of R. M. Pittenger, the firm's vice president.

It was only natural that Pittenger likes a parade, particularly the Rose Parade. He is a showman and has a background in various fields of entertainment. He is known as Dick by his legion of friends — greats, near-greats, and unknowns. His friends include Bob Hope, Gen. Jimmy Doolittle, Senator George Murphy, and many of the governors of our fifty states. He is one of the hosts at the annual governors' conference.

FARMERS INSURANCE 1965 WINNER: "ARMED FORCES, HEADLINER OF THE YEAR"

Dick got exposure to Hollywood as a member of the publicity department at 20th Century-Fox Studios. He was what was known as a "plant man," getting photos of the stars into the metropolitan and suburban editions, and he was good at his craft.

While making the rounds of the desks in downtown Los Angeles, he stopped at the sports department of the Los Angeles *Times*. Sports Editor Bill Henry, who later became a Washington correspondent, had a problem—how to get the Times Sports Award Dinner off the ground. Dick had the answer—move it from the Times cafeteria to the Biltmore Bowl. It was an immediate success. That was the beginning of a lifelong friendship. When Bill passed away, the first person called by Mrs. Henry was Dick Pittenger.

Showmanship was in Pittenger's blood. He had the flair for it — and the creative urge. He became a member of the production hierarchy of Ken Murray's "Blackouts," which had an illustrious run in Hollywood. Pittenger had a lot to do with the rapid-fire format — one act right on top of another.

Being a family man, Dick began looking for more stable pursuits. He became vice president of the Farmers Insurance Group. He became involved in the National Safety Council, which needed exposure. Pittenger got the NSC to enter a float in the Rose Parade in 1960. The years immediately following were under the banner of the American Legion Post at Farmers. In 1964 the insurance concern was entered in Class E (business firms) .

Probably more than any other entrant, the Farmers Insurance entries have given impetus to having celebrities and personalities as float-riders. Dennis Day, Ann Blythe, Bob Hope, Bob Cummings, Steve Allen, and Lowell Thomas have appeared on the FIG entries. In 1964 Lowell Thomas was on the lovely float, "Seven Wonders of the World." Pretty queens also graced the float. The great commentator

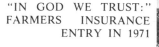

"IN GOD WE TRUST:" FARMERS INSURANCE ENTRY IN 1971

became ill during the earlier part of the procession and was taken to the hospital in the auto that was to have picked up all of the riders at Victory Park at the end of the parade. The auto, incidentally, had all of the clothes of the queens. Since it didn't show up at the procession's end, the pretty maidens attended the Rose Bowl game in parade costumes.

The Farmers VP, "once a showman always a showman," instituted a nation-wide contest for a queen for the Farmers Insurance float. Papers from every sector of the United States carried story after story about the contest, elimination, and winners. It is an annual part of the whole participation now, to the point where a national magazine carried the by-lined story of riding in the Rose Parade by the most recent queen.

In 1969 the Farmers entry was "Remember Hawaii." Once again, the flair for showmanship came to the fore. Dick staged a contest for identical twins to appear in the outrigger craft, appearing on each side of the main float structure — a twin on each side made it appear that one was seeing double on New Year's.

Just as the Tournament of Roses festival has been the American pioneer in New Year's Day presentations, the family of Walter and Cordelia Knott, creators and owners of the internationally famous Knott's Berry Farm in Buena Park, Californa, has participated in the Rose Parade to bring forth a message of pioneering, the American heritage, and patriotism.

Walter and Cordelia Knott first rode down Pasadena streets in 1921, a ride they repeated in the 1970 and 1971 Rose Parades under very different circumstances. In 1921, the Knott family appeared in Pasadena with all their possessions in an old dilapidated wagon drawn by two limping horses. They were aware of the stares, shouts, and whistling of Pasadena natives emerging from churches along the way. It was Sunday, but the Knotts had lost track of time during their three-week trek from the Mojave Desert where they had unsuccessfully homesteaded. The humiliating attention of the "city folk" was more than they could endure, until a gentleman approached in an automobile and informed them that the shaft of the buggy was dragging and in danger of collapse. It was this predicament that everyone had tried to call to their attention, and the Knotts were grateful for the kindness Pasadena people had shown toward them.

It was with spirit of love for people that Knott began his business career in Orange County. From a berry stand to Mrs. Knott's pies and chicken dinners grew a complex of several restaurants and eventually the creation of the Knott "Ghost Town" which tells the story of the West. His dream came true as he and his family advanced from sharecropper to entrepreneur, and his faith in the American way of life and fellow man spurred him on to expansion of Knott's Berry Farm to its present stage as one of the nation's most significant tourist attractions and amusement centers. To carry out the patriotic theme, he built a brick-by-brick reconstruction of Philadelphia's Independence Hall on his farm.

As his dream of creating Knott's Berry Farm as a display of Americana came true, Knott decided to relive his pioneer trip over the Pasadena streets by entering a float in the 1970 parade. He also wanted to bring the message to the entire world that America was the home of patriotism and opportunity. "July 4th" was the theme as the 1970 Knott's float in the Rose Parade featured a replica of Independence Hall made of chrysanthemums and carnations. Appearing on the float with Mr. and Mrs. Knott were Linda Lee Hall (Miss California), Lianne Fullmer (Miss Junior California), Terri Sonleitner (Miss Antelope Valley), Terri Susan Hall (Miss Sepulveda), Susan Culver (special guest from New York), and Patricia Fairbanks (Miss West Los Angeles).

In the second year of participation by Knott's Berry Farm in 1971, the theme was "Family Tales," with Mr. and Mrs. Knott shown retelling the tales of the West to their grandchildren. From the "scroll of memory," composed of gold and bronze chrysanthemums with detailed pictures painted with petals of various types of textured flowers, emerged the cavalcade envisioned by the children.

The great-granddaughters were portrayed by Jacqueline Haney (Little Miss California) and Elizabeth Haney (Wee Miss California) of the Miss Universe Pageant. The great-grandsons were portrayed by Johnnie Whitaker of CBS TV's Family Affair and Tod Starke of CBS-TV's Doris Day Show.

"My dreams for a greater and better America for all to enjoy have no end, and we await for more fulfullment to come," says Knott.

KNOTT'S "FAMILY TALES" DRAMATIZES
THE STORY OF THE WEST IN 1971

6
Granddaddy Is Born

W. L. LEISHMAN

A NEW HAVEN, CONN., and New York tailor who had become a community-minded Pasadena citizen, first as operator of an arts and crafts shop and then of a millwork and lumber establishment, ascended to the Tournament of Roses presidency in 1920. His name was W. L. Leishman; he was always neatly dressed, an imaginative and hard-working person blessed with foresight and interest in community good.

The name Leishman has become a significant one in Tournament history. W. L. Leishman inaugurated a new policy when he became president. The head of the Tournament always had ridden a horse at the head of the parade, but Leishman became the first president to ride in his own automobile. Leishman's car was decorated by ladies of the Eastern Star, and the driver of the car in the 1920 parade was Leishman's young son, Lathrop, who was destined to become president himself nineteen years later. In fact, the Leishman family through three generations has been active in Tournament affairs: Lathrop's sons, William and Robert, are active "Men in White" today, while Lathrop continues his contribution as chairman of the Rose Bowl Football Committee.

"I recall Dad sitting in the back seat alongside the oldest living president," recalls Lathrop of that time half a century ago. "They had tall silk hats."

The Tournament Park stands needed repairs during W. L.'s presidency. Lumberman Leishman knew the patchwork couldn't go on forever.

"Son," he said one day. "I am going to take you to my home town, New Haven, and show you the kind of stadium we should have here someday for our football games. I must go to Harvard to make a gold football award, and we will take a look at the Yale Bowl while in the East."

Lathrop accompanied his dad on the long railroad journey. When they returned, the younger Leishman recalls, many meetings were held

42

THE BIRTH OF THE ROSE BOWL: (ABOVE) W. L. LEISHMAN SHOWS PLANS TO SON, LATHROP; (BELOW) EXCAVATION PROCEEDS TO WHERE BOWL IS PARTIALLY FINISHED IN 1922

in the Leishman living room between W. L., architect Myron Hunt, and builder William A. Taylor.

"I'd peek through the keyhole and listen," recalls Lathrop. "They were talking about building a huge concrete stadium in Pasadena. It was thrilling conversation. Right then my interest in what today is the Rose Bowl was born. Dad always said Arroyo Seco, then just a barren area of rocks, was the place to build it."

The parade of 1920 was historic for more reasons than the switch of the president from horse to automobile. That year the Salvation Army band made its first appearance. This band has appeared in the parade every year since, the longest record of continuous participation.

The 1920 parade held a special meaning for the ladies of the WCTU. January 1 was the first day of observation of the Eighteenth Amendment, outlawing liquor. To celebrate the success of their long campaign in its behalf, the WCTU entered a float with "Victory" emblazoned on its side.

Big Bear Lake Tavern entered a novel float: a great mound of snow, surrounded by pine boughs and cones. Two pretty girls sat on a toboggan pelting viewers with real snowballs. However, the real surprise was a live bear cavorting on the snow bank. The Hotel Raymond entry was the only float still drawn by a team of horses, white ones; everything else was mechanized.

Attendance at the parade had grown to 200,000 people lining Colorado Boulevard.

Harvard was a football monarch in those days, and the mighty Crimson came to Pasadena with a 7-0 record, only a tie with Princeton marring its season. Oregon, with a 5-1 mark (it had lost to Washington State), was the western representative in the game at Tournament Park. Former Tournament game star Shy Huntington was the Oregon coach, and one of Oregon's stars was his brother Hollis, who piled up 122 yards rushing.

EDDIE CASEY

Harvard won a well-fought struggle, 7-6, a game that avenged eastern losses suffered by Brown and Penn in Pasadena. Coach Bob Fisher had Walter Camp's All-America selection Eddie Casey in his backfield, but it was speedy Fred Church who scored the touchdown and Arnold Horween who kicked the point that outscored the drop-kick field goals by Oregon's Steers and Manerud.

The smallest player ever to appear in the Pasadena classic, 128-pound Skeet Manerud came within one foot of succeeding with a 25-yard drop kick that would have won the game for Oregon. Harvard players were so sure the kick was good they banged their helmets to the turf, and the scoreboard custodian already had put up a big "9" for Oregon.

Church, who had replaced Ralph Horween in the Harvard back-

ACTION IN CALIFORNIA'S
JANUARY HEAT AS
HARVARD WINS OVER
OREGON 7-6

field, broke away in the second period, a 12-yard sprint in which he outran his interference. When he reached the end zone near the corner, he cut sharply toward the goal posts and crossed the goal line in the center of the field, a smart piece of work because the kick for point had to be made from a point directly opposite the spot where the touchdown was made. Thus Arnold Horween's kick was made easier.

The 30,000 seats in Tournament Park sold for 65 cents each.

In October 1969, the Boston Harvard Club paid tribute to the one and probably only Harvard appearance in the Rose Bowl. The little group of survivors of the great 1919 Harvard team held their fiftieth anniversary dinner. They recalled how Yale men, although Yale was traditionally Harvard's bitter enemy, refused to reveal any secrets about the Harvard team to Oregon. The East was represented by Harvard, Yale men decided, and there would be vindication for the Ivy League.

Old-timers from Harvard like R. Minturn ("Duke") Sedgwick, great left tackle, recalled that a few days before the game Douglas Fairbanks gave the Harvard players a tour of the movie set where he was making a picture. He and Charlie Chaplin were subsequently invited to sit on the Harvard bench during the game — which they did. Sedgwick remembered also that Jack Dempsey sat in the Harvard cheering section at the game. Sedgwick was heavyweight boxing champion at Harvard, and Dempsey's being there meant something to him.

Sedgwick declared: "I remember Oregon had one play in which the quarterback would lie prone on the ground as though injured, while his teammates clustered around him. When one teammate would inquire, 'Are you all right?' he would hand the ball to a back who would start to run down the field with it."

Sedgwick said all the Harvard players lost ten pounds or more in the heat.

1921

One hundred floats were in the 1921 Tournament of Roses parade, among them the Pasadena Elks Lodge float, a freight train in miniature composed of a locomotive, tender, box car, and caboose. The luncheon clubs of Pasadena Rotary and Kiwanis also had floats for the first time.

However, the big news of the day was the 41,500 crowd that flooded into Tournament Park. President Leishman and his aides looked at the mob, and W. L. turned to the man who was to be next year's president, J. J. Mitchell, and remarked, "We can't go on much longer like this. Soon there won't be enough lumber in the city to seat them. We've got to get our new stadium started."

California's first "Wonder Team" gained a decisive triumph over Ohio State, 28-0, which swung the Coast football pendulum southward. Until this great feat, it was believed that the Pacific Northwest was the stronghold of western football.

California, coached by Andy Smith, came in with an 8-0 mark; Ohio State, coached by J. W. ("Doc") Wilce, was 7-0. The passing combination of Harry ("Hoge") Workman to All-American Pete Stinchcomb had established Ohio State as the favorite, although Californians were wild about a young man named Harold Muller.

Charles Paddock, the great United States Olympic sprinter who wrote sports for the Pasadena *Star-News,* said, "Muller did everything a great end should do. He covered punts so swiftly, he often beat the ball to the receiver. He caught every pass that was thrown to him. His passing, too, was phenomenal."

Paddock told of a play in which Muller caught a trick flip behind the line from Pesky Sprott and then completed a long spiral to Brodie Stephens in the end zone. There resulted one of the arguments of all time, regarding the distance of the pass. Maxwell Stiles, after considerable research, came up with the figure of fifty-three yards, after the Spalding record book originally claimed seventy.

"It's my recollection that the play started on Ohio State's 38-yard line," Sprott told George T. Davis of the Los Angeles *Herald Express.* "I handled the ball some 10 yards back of the line of scrimmage before flipping it to Muller, who dropped back another 15 yards before throwing it to Stephens on the goal line."

The play uncorked when fullback Archie Nesbet pretended he was injured. Then, in unison with his mates, he suddenly jumped into the line as the center, not the fullback. This bewildered Ohio State, which stood up and watched. Nesbet snapped the ball to Sprott, who flipped it back to Muller. Then Muller, after retreating, let fly to Stephens.

1922

When J. J. Mitchell became president in 1922, Leishman concentrated on efforts to assure the construction of the bowl in Arroyo

BRICK MULLER

THE ROSE BOWL, 1970

PRESIDENT-ELECT RICHARD M. NIXON, GOVERNOR RONALD REAGAN OF CALIFORNIA, WITH THEIR LADIES AND THEIR ESCORT, CROSS THE FIELD AT THE ROSE BOWL IN 1969

THE TOURNAMENT OF ROSES PARADE MOVING
DOWN COLORADO BOULEVARD

PASADENA CITY COLLEGE LANCER BAND, THE
OFFICIAL BAND OF THE TOURNAMENT OF
ROSES

LONG BEACH MOUNTED POLICE POSSE IN 1971
PARADE, THEIR 25th APPEARANCE

ST. LOUIS FLOAT, 1970: "HOLIDAY AT BUSCH GARDENS"

BEKINS MOVING AND STORAGE FLOAT, 1970: "INDIAN FESTIVAL," WINNER OF THE PRESIDENT'S TROPHY

FLORISTS TRANSWORLD DELIVERY ASSOCIA-
TION FLOAT, 1971: "THE BIRDS AND THE
BEES"

BARBARA TRISLER AND GEORGE PUTNAM,
PERENNIAL EQUESTRIAN FAVORITES

EQUESTRIAN UNIT LED BY MARSHAL BILL
CROOK

Seco. Money appeared to be the big problem, but when 40,000 braved a rain to attend the game at Tournament Park between California, in its return appearance, and Washington and Jefferson, a game that showed a gross of $170,000, financing became less difficult.

California was held to a 0-0 tie by W and J, but there was no deadlock about what Pasadena was going to do about a stadium.

The city acquired the land. The Tournament agreed to raise the money for the construction. After the stadium was built, the Tournament would deed the stadium to the city, and the city, in turn, would lease the stadium back to the Tournament for ninety days each year. The Tournament financed the project by offering 210 box seats for a period of ten years at $100 each. Another 5,000 seats were sold for five years for $50 each.

The original stadium was a horseshoe with 57,000 seats, the south end open. The cost was $272,198.26.

Harlan Hall, whose nickname was "Dusty," dusted off a name that was to become historic: the Rose Bowl. He came up with the idea while he was a Pasadena *Star-News* reporter loaned out to the Tournament to serve as a press agent.

W and J was no softie. H. G. Salsinger of the Detroit *News* gave the tip-off that California hadn't contracted to play a humpty when he told how Coach Earle ("Greasy") Neale had to telegraph the players to come back to school when the Pasadena bid was accepted.

They certainly came to life in the game, the last battle ever staged at Tournament Park. It was played on January 2 because New Year's Day fell on Sunday. W and J never made a substitution in the game.

"All I know about Washington and Jefferson is that they are both dead," said one anonymous sports writer. He probably ate his words after the performance of W and J, a school with just 450 students.

Muller of California was suffering from boils and carbuncles on his neck and he had a knee injury. Thus he couldn't start. When he was called into the game in the second quarter, replacing Bob Berkey, he was met by a chorus of seemingly awed W and J voices.

"So this is the great Brick Muller!" said little end Herb Kopf of the visitors. "We are deeply impressed. We are humble in the presence of the great Muller. May I introduce myself?"

Sawed-off Kopf stepped up to Muller and wiped his muddy hands on Muller's jersey. Then all the W and J players did the same thing while the rain beat down on the playing field.

Liberty magazine's Norman Sper said he was present in Greasy Neale's hotel room the night before when the coach planned the mud-rubbing episode with Captain Russell Stein.

Paul Lowry, Los Angeles *Times* sports writer, credited tackle Stein with the strategy that stopped California's attack. "His method was simple," wrote Lowry. "He sensed the play and simply flopped on the ball. The stuff was off then, and Cal had to try it all over again."

7

The Four Horsemen

KNUTE ROCKNE

1923

As W. L. LEISHMAN proudly stood on the turf in the new Rose Bowl horseshoe anxiously waiting for the Penn State team to appear for its game with Southern California on January 1, 1923, he remarked, "Some day this will be a complete saucer like the Yale Bowl. The way people are jamming up the roads trying to get here today, I know we will have to expand."

Leishman's prophecy came true in 1928 when the open south end of the structure was closed, adding another 19,000 seats to make the capacity 76,000.

Pasadena was a proud city during the 1923 Tournament. It was celebrating its fiftieth year, and, of course, the new stadium symbolized Pasadena's growth.

The crowd viewing the parade was estimated at 300,000.

"We brought in 100,000 people ourselves," said an official of Pacific Electric Railway.

Tournament president Mitchell had named Hollywood film star May McAvoy queen. Her pictures were popularly attended in theaters everywhere; hence thousands came to Pasadena to see May in person during the parade.

Though Penn State had been chosen in April to represent the East in the Rose Bowl's first New Year's attraction, they still couldn't get to the game on time. In fact, Penn State had troubles from the moment that California, first choice of the Tournament people to represent the West, refused to play the Nittany Lions. Southern California, the substitute selection, then defeated Penn State 14-3.

U.S.C., with a season record of 8-1, was coached by Elmer ("Gloomy Gus") Henderson. Penn State, 6-3-1, was coached under the iron hand of Hugo Bezdek, who was making his third Pasadena appearance. He had led Oregon to victory over Penn in 1917 and Mare Island over Camp Lewis in 1918.

Bezdek will be remembered for his late arrival in keeping his 1923 Rose Bowl date and a subsequent argument and near fistfight with Henderson for keeping the Trojans waiting. Hugo hadn't liked it that newspapermen insisted upon watching his practice sessions.

MAY McAVOY, ROSE QUEEN
AND FILM STAR

"I'll let you in the first few minutes of each practice, but no pictures," said Bezdek, who suspected someone wanted to pass along his secrets to U.S.C.

A Los Angeles *Examiner* photographer refused to be denied. When Bezdek was roaring, "My team cannot be photographed in formation," the *Examiner* camerman placed his camera on the side lines and stood beside it with his hands in his pockets. However, each time the Penn State team came within range, the cameraman's right foot moved just enought to click the shutter. Penn State pictures appeared all over the *Examiner* sports page the next day.

The game was scheduled to start at 2:15 on New Year's Day, immediately after dedication ceremonies. A football game had been played in the Rose Bowl in October when California downed U.S.C. 12-0, hence the Tournament's game could not claim to be the first. But it can claim that it was one of the most spirited, mainly because of the Bezdek-Henderson argument that broke out when the Penn State bus didn't arrive on the scene until 2:30.

Gloomy Gus was waiting by the Penn State dressing room while his team anxiously squirmed in its quarters.

"Where've you been?" roared Henderson to Bezdek.

"We got caught in the traffic jam trying to get here," said Bezdek.

"You tried to stall so we would get itchy. Futhermore, you wanted the sun to lower, believing you'd have a better chance when it's cool," said Henderson.

"You're a liar," shouted Bezdek, according to Mark Kelly's story in the *Examiner*.

"You're a lot of bunk," said Henderson.

"Remove your glasses," replied Bezdek.

Just when it appeared fists were ready to fly, listeners stepped between the men.

"We're not going to come out on the field until all those people back on the roads who paid to see the game are in their seats," said Bezdek.

The game finally started at 3:05 and finished "by the light of the moon." Sports writers and telegraph operators had to strike matches to complete their stories.

Penn State took the lead when "Light Horse" Harry Wilson mousetrapped his way for several large gains to set up a field goal by Mike Palm. Leo Calland, captain of the Trojans, then shifted his defense to stop the Penn State attack.

U.S.C. had to survive the disappointment of a freak mishap before it took command offensively. Fullback Gordon Campbell powered the ball in following recovery of a fumble. Then Roy ("Bullet") Baker advanced the pigskin to the 1-yard line. While the huge crowd held its breath to witness the touchdown-to-be, the ball did not come back to the Trojan ball-carrier but sailed in the other direction, landing in the end zone. A Penn State defender fell on it for a touchback.

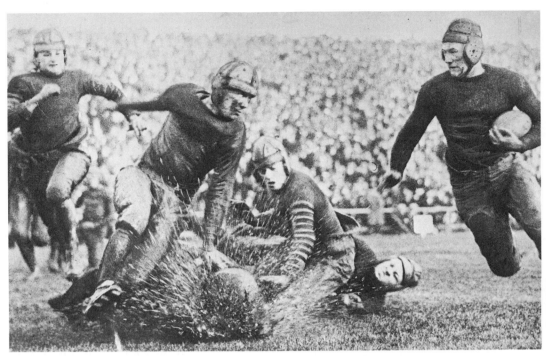

IN THE RAIN, RUSS
STEIN BLOCKS FOR
ERICSON OF W AND J
AGAINST CALIFORNIA

HUGO BEZDEK

GUS HENDERSON

Henderson, who wrote his own story of the game in the *Examiner*, explained: "Lindley, playing center for U.S.C., ordinarily snaps the ball directly back of him. This time the play called for a sideways pass-back to a backfield man who was crouched close to the line of scrimmage near the right end of the line. Lindley snapped the ball in the correct direction, but as our line heaved forward, the pigskin hit someone's heel and careened over the Penn State goal line."

U.S.C. steadily battered the easterners after that, however. Howard ("Hobo") Kincaid, one of the greatest blockers ever to play in the Rose Bowl, led Gordon Campbell and Baker to steady gains. Baker was a bulldog with the ball, but U.S.C. needed a freak play to score.

U.S.C. did more than throw the football to get its touchdown. It threw a man! The ball was thrown by Bullet Baker. The man was thrown by himself. The man was miniature Harold Galloway.

When U.S.C.'s ground attack was stopped on the Penn State 10, Baker threw a flat pass to the left, never more than shoulder-high, but it was far from the intended receiver. From nowhere, it seemed, a human meteor (Galloway) flew through the air. He skidded along, looked up, and saw the ball coming to him. It fell into his arms as he was hit on the 2-yard line. He was knocked out, but he held the pigskin in a death grip. Two plays later, Campbell scored on a delayed buck. Campbell and Baker took turns punching for the second touchdown.

While all of this was going on in 1923, a lad named Max Colwell was the Pasadena High School correspondent for the Pasadena *Post*. It was Colwell's job to report parade descriptions of the school floats for the newspaper. Little did he know then that this would lead to

50

his becoming the successful manager of the Tournament of Roses many years later, after he had pursued an active Pasadena reporting career.

1924

W. F. Creller became Tournament president in 1924. His parade featured two parts — the usual colorful floats in one section, and the Elks Lodges of California in the other section. The Grand Exalted ruler of the Elks, James G. McFarland, was a distinguished visitor.

"Our most stunning float annually should be selected to set it apart from the rest," said Creller, and the Sweepstakes Prize was initiated. Glendale's entry was the winner that year, an achievement often repeated in the years that followed.

The Tournament discovered its role as a football promoter was getting difficult, especially with various members of the association having favorites at team-selection time. A significant decision was reached by President Creller and his board of directors. They would let the colleges control the administration of the Rose Bowl Game, a policy practiced successfully ever since.

The United States Naval Academy accepted a bid to play in the 1924 game even before the football season started. Washington wasn't named the western representative until early December.

Larry ("Moon") Mullins, a Notre Dame star of the future, made the first long run of his career before the Navy-Washington game. He was chased the length of the field by policemen after crashing the gate. The South Pasadena kid was cheered loudly by the huge throng.

The 14-14 tie was history-making for several reasons: Navy com-

51

pleted its first fourteen passes; the tackling was so savage that Alan Shapley of Navy and Elmer Tesreau of Washington had to be carried off the field; and Les Sherman of Navy kicked two conversions with a broken toe. Tesreau went into the game with his leg heavily taped because of a serious outbreak of boils. His coach, Enoch Bagshaw, tried to keep him out of the game but he refused to remain idle.

The crowd was only 40,000 for this game because Navy, which had received its share of the game cut in tickets, made the mistake of distributing many of its tickets among the fleet, harbored in Long Beach. The admiral in command ordered the fleet to sea on December 31, and hundreds of tickets were offered to the public by a sound car circling the stadium.

Navy, 5-1-2 going into the game and coached by Bob Folwell, stunned Washington with its opening passing attack, featuring Alan Shapley aerials to Ira Mckee. Then a pass from McKee to Cullen scored. George Wilson, the Washington star, tied it up with a twisting run. A McKee-to-Cullen bomb set up a Navy go-ahead touchdown by McKee. But Washington tied it up with a trick play. On fourth down on the Navy 12-yard line, the Huskies lined up with an unbalanced formation. Bryan, Washington left guard, was at left end and therefore an eligible receiver. Nobody bothered to cover him, and he caught a pass from Abel to score. Washington had a late chance to win, but a field-goal try by Ziel missed the goal by a yard or two.

1925

In 1925 the American Legion was honored in the parade with its national commander, James A. Drain, present.

Massed colors led the American Legion division, which was loudly cheered all along the parade route. In contrast to the youthful step of the marching World War veterans, a group of old-timers from the Grand Army of the Republic rode in a special car with their fife-and-drum corps. One lone marcher, J. V. Fickes, represented the Spanish-

SLEEPY JIM CROWLEY
BREAKS INTO THE OPEN
FOR NOTRE DAME IN 1925
VICTORY

ERNIE NEVERS

American War. To qualify as a "floral exhibit," Fickes trimmed his old knapsack with posies.

The parade was a whopper — three hours of floats and marching units. Evangelist Aimee Semple McPherson's Angelus Temple float won the Sweepstakes Prize.

The Angelus Temple float broke Glendale's hold on the Sweepstakes with what was estimated to be the most costly float ever built up to that time. This float, typifying the broadcasting of the gospel by radio, cost up to $4,000 to construct. Today many floats cost more than six times that figure. A radio tower of snow-white carnations stood atop a miniature replica of the Angelus Temple in Echo Park. From it was broadcast an evangelical New Year's greeting.

The Salvation Army entered its first float in Tournament history. Its band, of course, had been marching since 1920 in the festival.

Pasadena had its second married queen that year, Mrs. Margaret Scoville, who had been Pasadena Christmas Mother and was asked to continue for the Tournament festivities.

However, the 1925 Tournament of Roses will forever be remembered most for the presence of Knute Rockne, the Four Horsemen, and Notre Dame's great undefeated gridiron machine. The Irish defeated Stanford 27-10, Stanford also going into the fray undefeated although tied once by California.

The 53,000 spectators came early to see Rockne match wits with Glenn Scobie ("Pop") Warner. They did not go home disappointed.

Stanford took the lead on a seventeen-yard place kick by Murray Cuddeback. The crowd believed in the invincibility of Elmer Layden, Jim Crowley, Harry Stuhldreher, and Don Miller. But the throng also

THE FOUR HORSEMEN: DON MILLER, ELMER LAYDEN, JIM CROWLEY, HARRY STUHLDREHER

POP WARNER

had faith in Ernie Nevers of Stanford. Could Stanford's great blond-haired Nevers counter the dread raiders of the Apocalypse?

Rockne started his "shock troops" but quickly jerked them because Stanford had so much fury. A fumble of the only pass from center that had come back to the Four Horsemen, a bobble by Miller, was recovered by Stanford's right tackle, Johnston, to set up Cuddeback's kick.

Shortly thereafter, Notre Dame took over on its own 20-yard line.

"Will the Four Horsemen start to ride?" thought the thousands looking on. The tension was like Babe Ruth coming to bat. Everybody expected Ruth to hit a home run each time he stepped to the plate, and those who were rooting against him sort of hoped against themselves that he would — just so they could say they saw him do it.

So it was when Adam Walsh, the Hollywood high school boy who had come home as captain and center for the Irish, bent down over the ball. The light cavalry behind him shifted into the Notre Dame box. Stuhldreher barked his signal. Into the big Red line Layden lashed with the sting of a whip. Layden was not like Nevers, the bone-crusher. Elmer was slithery and slender, fast, agile, and smart. He weighed only 165 pounds, not much for a fullback. The Layden knife stabbed sharply and rapidly, but it drew no blood.

Stuhldreher again barked signals and Notre Dame shifted in unison. This time it was Sleepy Jim's turn, and Crowley was far from sleepy. He swung to the left side of Stanford's line with great speed. His escort, Miller and Layden, picked him up. Each of the Four Horseman was a blocker as well as a runner. No matter which man had the ball, before him were three galloping shadows who carved out a downfield path.

Out of the line came others to join the convoy set up for 155-pound Crowley. There were Chuck Collins and Ed Huntsinger, Joe Bach and Edgar ("Rip") Miller, John Weibel, Noble Kizer, and Walsh.

That moment may have presented the most beautiful bit of downfield interference ever to be seen in Rose Bowl history.

Crowley hadn't gone ten yards before the crowd, electrified, was on its feet. Like pressing a button, excitement erupted throughout the Bowl. There they go — the Four Horsemen and the Seven Mules! Rockne's raiders are on the prowl! The raid is on!

Here, there, and everywhere between the Notre Dame 20-yard line and midfield, the light streamlined men in black shirts were playing billiard shots off the men in red.

Somebody at last brought Crowley down on the Notre Dame 49-yard line. The twenty-seven yard run had seared Stanford's defense.

Two plays later, Crowley made another first down on Stanford's 39 after a cutback away from Ted and Harry Shipkey, brother combination on the left side of Stanford's line. Stuhldreher then passed to Miller, to the 20-yard line. Miller shook off tacklers to skirt left end to the 9.

Led by Ted Shipkey and Johnston, the Stanford line held, and on fourth down Ted Shipkey rushed Stuhldreher, who was trying to pass. The ball glanced sideways off the Irish quarterback's fingers and was grounded. Time was taken out for Stuhldreher, who had his ankle taped. Later it was learned that a bone or two had been fractured. But these players refused to let injury keep them out of the action. Playing in the Rose Bowl game, Jim Lawson had one leg in a brace and Ernie Nevers had both legs so tightly bandaged after his recovery from two broken ankles that the circulation was all but shut off.

Following a short Stanford punt, Notre Dame took over again on the enemy's 32-yard line. The Four Horsemen zoomed to the 7-yard line as the quarter ended. Two plays later, Layden hit center for the touchdown, the only score that Notre Dame earned on straight, rushing football. Crowley's try for extra point was blocked by Swan, Stanford's left guard, and the score was 6-3.

Soon, Layden set Stanford back on its heels with a punt that traveled seventy-two yards over the Stanford goal line. Nevers then started hammering. He became a crashing wild man. Following up a fourteen-yard end-around gain by Lawson, Nevers punched the ball to Notre Dame's 31-yard line. On fourth down and six to go, quarterback Solomon called for Nevers to throw a flat pass to the right, intended for Ted Shipkey. Nevers did not get protection. Layden sensed the play. He streaked in front of Shipkey and pulled off a volleyball play. The pass was too high for him. Instead of trying to intercept it cleanly, he tapped it toward the Stanford goal line. Layden then ran under the ball as it came down five to ten yards away and caught it. Aided by the blocking of Huntsinger, Layden sped sixty yards down the side lines to score, and Crowley kicked the extra point to make the score 13-3.

Stanford came right back. The bulling rushes of Nevers, the end sweeps of Ted Shipkey, and some amazingly accurate passes by Nevers advanced the ball deep into Notre Dame territory. Warner was pulling a fast one on Rockne. The Irish had been expecting straight power, for which the Warner system was famous. Stanford, however, mixed things up, with Lawson and Shipkey end-arounds a real trouble for Notre Dame.

Nevers hit Solomon successfully for a twenty-five-yard gain, and Solly was away for an apparent touchdown when he was dragged down from behind by Notre Dame's Collins. Walsh then recovered a fumble by Stanford's Kelly on the 17 as the half ended.

Cuddeback narrowly missed field-goal kicks from the 32- and 45-yard lines before a fifty-yard punt by Layden was lost in the sun as Solomon tried to catch it. The ball slipped through Solomon's hands and seemingly was transferred into a greased pig. Solly slapped at the "animal," grabbed at it, and tried to fall on it. Each time the "pig" got away. Just as Solly thought he had it cornered and was about to put salt on its tail, he saw a pair of hands reach down out of the sun.

The hands belonged to Ed Huntsinger, and Huntsinger belonged to Notre Dame. He picked up the "pig" by the throat and hotfooted twenty yards into the end zone. Crowley's kick made it 20-3.

Nevers then had his greatest moments.

Ernie intercepted a Stuhldreher pass and was brought down on the Irish 39. The powerful blond blasted for steady gains, each time with Walsh's arms wrapped around him in vain. Finally, Walker rifled a pass to Ted Shipkey for the touchdown, and Cuddeback kicked the extra point.

In the fourth quarter, Baker intercepted Crowley's pass and ran it to the Irish 31. Nevers carried half the Irish team on his back to the 18, after Ted Shipkey had fought around end for five. Nevers bulled for a first down on the 6. On fourth down, Nevers was stopped on the goal line. Did he score? Many said yes, many said no.

"He went over!" shouted Warner as he ran up to an official near the side lines.

"No, he wasn't!" yelled back referee Ed Thorp, who put the ball on the 6-inch line and turned it over to Notre Dame.

The play was the basis for argument for years. Long after the game was history, the Four Horsemen were in Hollywood making the motion picture *The Spirit of Notre Dame,* with J. Farrell McDonald playing Knute Rockne. After a day's shooting of football scenes, the men were in the dressing rooms of Loyola University. George T. Davis, sports editor of the Los Angeles *Evening Express* and the most loyal of Nevers' boosters, started to argue with Layden, Crowley, and Miller about the Nevers "touchdown."

"I still say Nevers carried the ball over the line," roared Davis. "I was sitting right up there on the 10-yard line looking at the play through high-powered glasses."

"Last time we had this argument, you were on the 50-yard line," said Crowley.

"I have moved down forty yards in all these years," admitted George. "Next time I see you I will be opposite the goal line. But no matter where I was, Nevers was over the goal line."

"I say he didn't score," barked back Layden.

"That's right, he didn't," said a dapper little guy who had just entered the room. Davis gave the little fellow in the business suit a withering look.

"And where were you sitting?" asked Davis belligerently.

"On his neck!" replied the little man—who just happened to be Stuhldreher.

The Stanford football team battled back after being denied Nevers' touchdown, only to have Crowley intercept a Nevers pass on Notre Dame's 10. Layden punted out, and Stanford threatened once more. Nevers tried the flat pass again, received little protection, and Layden reached up for an easy interception. Elmer raced seventy yards for the game's final touchdown. Crowley's kick made it 27-10. Stanford out-gained Notre Dame in yardage, 298 to 179. But it was the scoreboard that told who really won.

Three of the Four Horsemen (Stuhldreher had passed on to his reward) had a reunion in Dallas before the Notre Dame-Texas Cotton Bowl Game in 1970.

They recalled their Rose Bowl experience.

"We spent two weeks getting from South Bend to Pasadena," said Crowley. "Rockne got very irritable because he felt the players gorged themselves out of condition. We went by bus by way of New Orleans, Houston, and Tucson, and everywhere we stopped people feted us. I remember at Houston we stuffed ourselves so much on oysters we couldn't move. Finally we got to Tucson, which was a cow town then. The Rock made us stay there a week. But he told us to be careful about reaching for a handerchief or billfold in our pockets. He said somebody might interpret it as a draw and we might get shot. Rock caught me and Ed Huntsinger at 9:55 p.m., five minutes before curfew time, buying Christmas cards in a store. He told us to get to our rooms and the next day to head for home. But Adam Walsh pleaded our case and we were allowed to remain on the team. At the start of the game, Huntsinger recovered a fumble and ran for a touchdown. I ran up to my buddy and said, 'Isn't it a good thing Rock didn't make us go home?' "

Crowley added he didn't remember Rock making a pregame speech before the Rose Bowl Game.

"Naw, because you were asleep," countered Miller.

Crowley remembered that, because of the many interceptions by Layden, sports writers wrote the game's best pass combination was Nevers of Stanford to Layden of Notre Dame.

1925 PARADE SCENE, DOWNTOWN PASADENA

8

The Age of Dixie

JOHNNY MACK BROWN

1926

PRESIDENT HARRY M. TICKNOR possibly received the first inkling his 1926 parade was jinxed when police officer John Fox was knocked down and trampled by a horse during the procession. The accident occurred at Colorado and Raymond when the horse became frightened. Fox suffered a wrenched back and spinal injuries.

Mrs. C. W. Bowen, age 51, was watching the parade from a brick parapet on a building twenty-five feet above the sidewalk at 127 West Colorado. She fell from the three-foot ledge and was killed as the parade went by.

Then, as the floats reached the corner of Madison and Colorado, the most tragic occurrence in the history of the Tournament of Roses stunned the community.

Two women died from injuries and 236 people were treated at Pasadena Hospital after a section of a wooden viewing stand collapsed on the southeast corner of the intersection. Dr. Daniel F. Fox, pastor of the First Congregational Church, suffered severe bruises about his head and face.

The stand landslided screaming people into the debris. Mrs. Edgar M. Weill, seated in the stand across the street, described the scene: "The front rows of the stand seemed to slip slowly from under the seats. The whole stand, gathering momentum, slowly sank into a shapeless pile of lumber amidst shouts and wails of the injured and the terrified. It was like a snow slide. It sank slowly at first and then gathered speed."

Many of the injured were treated on the scene, and scores were rushed to the hospital, where emergency quarters were set up. Many of the injured were carried into the Presbyterian Church across the street as volunteer doctors offered aid. The police and fire departments helped to control the crowd and prevent further panic.

Mrs. Caroline Sherman, 50, of Long Beach died of shock, and Mrs. Bessie S. Borich, 65, Los Angeles, succumbed to injuries.

The accident led to a city investigation, after the coroner's jury ruled improper construction of stands and carelessness in inspection.

FAY LANPHIER

HARRY TICKNOR

Strict construction rules were adopted for the future, including insistence on all-steel frames for all bleachers along the parade route. There have been no tragedies since the safety precautions were put into effect.

Ticknor's 1926 Tournament of Roses became historic for several other reasons. That was the year of the first radio broadcast of a Rose Bowl Game, with Pasadena sports writer and ex-Olympic track star Charlie Paddock doing the announcing. Only the year before the first wirephoto had been transmitted from a Rose Bowl Game. Miss America, Fay Lanphier, was named Tournament Queen.

The parade featured re-creations of the famed floats of the past. This also was one of the most beautiful floral parades to date. Appropriately, Miss Lanphier rode a float decorated with American Beauty roses.

Alabama launched the "Age of Dixie" in the Rose Bowl with a 20-19 triumph over Washington that was acclaimed by many the Rose Bowl's greatest game, a rating challenged by several subsequent thrillers. The victory climaxed a ten-game unbeaten record; Washington suffered its first loss in eleven games. Johnny Mack Brown, one of the Alabama stars, stepped from the game into a Hollywood movie career.

Besides Brown, Alabama featured "Pooley" Hubert, Grant Gillis, and three solid linemen named Buckler, Holmes, and Jones. Washington stayed in the game mainly because of the running brilliance of George Wilson, described by Maxwell Stiles as the hardest running back developed on the West Coast, who played only thirty-eight minutes because of injuries. During that short time, Washington scored three touchdowns and gained 300 yards. During the twenty-two minutes Wilson was on the sidelines, Washington gained only 17 yards and failed to score. Wilson wound up the day with 134 yards alone in fifteen thrusts, and he completed five passes for 77 yards. He was a terror on defense and one of his punts traveled sixty-two yards.

The game matched Wallace Wade as Alabama coach against Enoch Bagshaw of Washington. While such accepted experts as Paul Lowry of the Los Angeles *Times* astutely rated the game as a duel between Wilson and Hubert, both All-Americans in his opinion, Wilson himself praised Brown. "That Mack Brown was all they said of him and more," declared Wilson. "He was about the fastest man in a football suit I have ever bumped up against. Hubert was good too."

George Varnell, head linesman, who also was a Seattle newspaperman, said, "Johnny Mack Brown has the sweetest pair of feet I have ever seen."

Brown gained fifteen yards around end on the first running play of the game. Wilson stopped the drive by intercepting Winslett's pass, and Washington slashed fifty-four yards for its first touchdown with Patton driving the final foot. Guttormsen's try for goal failed and Washington led 6-0.

WALLACE WADE

Wilson was knocked out tackling Winslett on a Statue of Liberty play. Bravely he remained in the game and punted a sixty-two-yarder that set up a second Washington touchdown after Wilson made the longest run of the day, a thirty-two-yarder. A Wilson pass to substitute end Cole scored the touchdown. The play that was eventually to mean defeat for Washington then occurred, as Guttormsen's drop kick hit the crossbar and bounced back.

After Wilson was knocked out a second time and forced to leave the game, Alabama got going in the second quarter. However, Louis Tesreau, Wilson's replacement, made a great tackle of Brown on the last play of the half to thwart a possible Alabama touchdown catch and keep the score at 12-0 going into intermission.

Alabama stormed over the goal line early in the third quarter after a short Tesreau punt, with Hubert and Pooley ripping for big gains. Hubert went over and Buckler added the point.

Brown then caught a long pass from Gillis and raced the final twenty-five yards for a touchdown. Buckler converted via place kick again, and the visitors from the South went ahead 14-12.

A fumble by Louis Tesreau was recovered by Ennis of Alabama

WALLACE WADE ADVISES ALABAMA PLAYERS ON SIDELINES

60

GEORGE WILSON

on the Husky 38. Brown caught a pass from Hubert on the 3 and stepped ino the end zone, but Buckler's try for extra point was blocked.

When Alabama threatened to score again, Coach Bagshaw sent the previously injured Wilson back into the game. This stimulated Washington, and the Huskies took the ball on downs on their 12-yard line. Wilson launched a resurgence by running seventeen yards out of punt formation. Patton made a long run and Wilson started passing and smashing for gains, his twenty-seven-yard aerial to Guttormsen producing a touchdown. Cook, a reserve, received the call to try the extra point this time, and his kick was good, to bring Washington within one point of Alabama at 20-19. After an exchange of interceptions, the game ended.

Brown virtually ran right out of the stadium to Hollywood where he played opposite Mary Pickford in *Coquette* a few months later. A Washington substitute tackle named Herman Brix went on to Olympic fame in the 1932 Berlin Games, where he placed second in the shot-put. He, too, became a movie star under the name Bruce Bennett, and under his own name succeeded Johnny Weissmuller as one of the Tarzans of the screen.

ALABAMA LAUNCHES PASS PLAY AGAINST WASHINGTON

61

9

"Roses Are in Bloom"

ONE-EYE CONNOLLY

Oh the crimson of each sunset
And the glowing pink of dawn,
Royal colors of the roses
Holding court upon the lawn.
Oh the joy, the smiles, the fragrance
Of a land that knows no gloom,
Just a peaceful sun-kissed heaven
When the roses·are in bloom.

Those are words from the official Tournament of Roses song, "Roses Are in Bloom," written by Francesca Falk Miller of Chicago and put to music by composer Carrie Jacobs Bond during the second year of Ticknor's three-year term as Tournament president. The song was introduced to the world during the 1927 Tournament, which also is noted for the first national radio broadcast of the Rose Bowl Game. Graham MacNamee, who admired the mountains above the stadium only to call them incorrectly the mighty Sierra Nevadas when they are really the San Gabriels, was the first national broadcasting network announcer to broadcast from the Rose Bowl. The parade also was described over coast-to-coast radio. "Songs in Flowers" was the motif.

1927

Czechoslovakia was the first foreign nation to make an entry in the parade. The Beverly Hills float was the Sweepstakes winner. The theme of this float was "Sitting on Top of the World," with Madge Bellamy of films gracing the entry. Another movie star, Hoot Gibson of the westerns, rode his horse alongside.

Each float portrayed some famous song. Newspapers of the day reported that the sight of girls' legs proved shocking to some spectators.

The 1927 Tournament gained added stature in the world of gridiron style. The Stanford team showed up wearing silk pants!

Though the 1927 Tournament did not have a queen, it had a king of tricks. He was "Tricky Dick" Hyland of Stanford, who got the

62

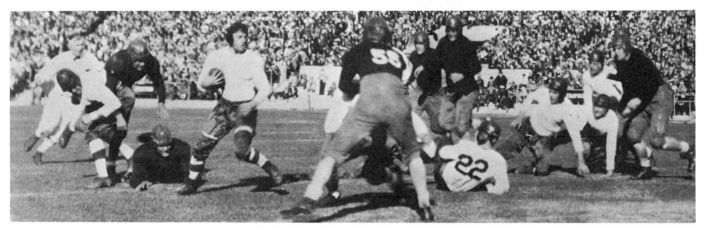

DICK HYLAND CARRIES PIGSKIN FOR STANFORD

FREDDIE PICKARD

block of the day from the goal posts during undefeated Stanford's 7-7 tie with undefeated Alabama. When Hyland scooted into the end zone while returning a punt, a pursuing Alabama player ran smack into the posts and knocked himself out. This helped Hyland escape.

Wallace Wade was tricky, too. The great Alabama coach, who was destined to bring Alabama and Duke teams to Pasadena four times before getting beaten, came strategically prepared.

Braven Dyer, for years a leading writer for the Los Angeles *Times*, told the story of how Alabama got its tie by securing the ball on Stanford's 14-yard line as a result of a blocked kick, relying on straight power to get into the end zone, and then using trickery to assure the extra point.

"After the touchdown came Herschell (Rosy) Caldwell's part in the drama," wrote Dyer. "What with our recent one-point margin games in these parts, we confess that we felt downright sorry for Rosy as he got ready to try for the lone digit. However, Alabama had made sure of the shot some time ago, Coach Wade giving the boys a play which ought to work. Getting their signal in the huddle, the Crimson athletes went up into the line. Captain Barnes hesitated a moment, stood up and then repeated his signals. Stanford naturally relaxed a bit. The Redskins took their eyes off the ball to watch Barnes. Just as the Cards let down, Gordon Holmes, Alabama center, shot the pigskin back to Winslett. Caldwell kicked it between the posts. Rosy wasn't rushed, and Stanford didn't come near blocking it."

Stanford took the lead in the first quarter on a twenty-yard pass gain from George Bogue to Ed Walker for a touchdown. Bogue kicked the extra point for Pop Warner's team.

Clark Pearce, Alabama center, blocked the kick of Frankie Wilton that set up Alabama's late score. Jimmy Johnson, out with a shoulder dislocation for a year, was inserted by Wade to inspire the Alabama team and help them punch over for the touchdown.

The game wasn't highly praised in the press for its excellence. Scribe Mark Kelly called it "frowsy football."

Ted Shipkey, Stanford's All-American end, wound up with very impressive statistics. He carried on two end-arounds, one of them for twenty-three yards. He caught five passes. He recovered two fumbles. He was a defensive fortress. In two Rose Bowl appearances, he accumulated twelve catches, scored two touchdowns, and saved many — against very tough opposition (Notre Dame and Alabama). Maxwell Stiles rated his Bowl work among the greatest ever in Pasadena.

Fred Pickard of Alabama was named player of the game.

1928

Gate-crashing star One-Eye Connolly, who always insisted there wasn't a prominent sports event in America that he couldn't see without having a ticket, was thrown out of the Rose Bowl seven times in twenty minutes when Stanford met Pittsburgh in 1928. When Connolly finally succeeded in gaining entry, he scurried up to sportscaster Mc-Namee and shouted into the mike, "I'm here — I want Tex Rickard to know his fights aren't the only shows I attend."

The 7-6 victory by twice-beaten Stanford over previously undefeated Pittsburgh is a story of a coach's faith in one of his athletes.

Frankie Wilton had been the goat of the game the year before because his punt was blocked to give Alabama a tie.

That was just the beginning of Wilton's growth of horns. In the Southern California game during the regular season, he fumbled to give the Trojans a chance to score.

Wilton fumbled again to set up Pittsburgh's touchdown in the Bowl. Jimmy Hagan of the Panthers scooped it up and ran seventeen yards to score. Although substitute Stanford tackle Walt Heinicke blocked the try for point by Pittsburgh's Booth, the 6 points on the Pittsburgh side of the scoreboard looked very big.

Wilton felt deep depression over the fact he again had made the mistake that was costing his team the Rose Bowl Game. His only thought of hope "If Pop Warner will let me stay in the game, maybe I can do something to make up for what I have done wrong."

ONE-EYE CONNOLLY
CRASHES ROSE BOWL

64

Warner stuck with his disconsolate young man. Pop proved to be a real Pop. He didn't send in a substitute for Wilton when Pittsburgh kicked off to Stanford in the third quarter with the Indians needing to rebound from a 6-0 deficit.

Biff Hoffman's running, catches by Sims and Worden, a timely scamper of four yards by Wilton, and a guard-around trick run by Seraphim Post gave Stanford a first down on the 8. In three shots, Hoffman, Wilton, and Hoffman made six. It was fourth and two for a touchdown. Spud Lewis, at quarterback in place of Murphy, called a play in which Hoffman threw a short flat pass to Sims on the line of scrimmage. Sims got possession of the ball, tried frantically to find a way through the Golden Panthers, and suddenly was hit with a jolt. He fumbled.

The ball bounded off to the left, and right then fate squared the books with Wilton. Fate rewarded Warner for keeping his faith in a depressed boy. The ball came directly to Wilton who took it away from three Panthers who also had a shot at it, and blasted into the end zone for the tying touchdown.

Hoffman kicked the goal and Stanford won 7-6 before a crowd that was up to 70,000 following this stage in the construction of the bowl.

Even losing coach Jock Sutherland admired his adversary's staying with a kid when he was down — a historic example of a coach having faith and a boy overcoming odds.

Pasadena had a mighty parade that year, a parade that excitingly carried out the theme "States and Nations in Flowers." The parade covered almost five miles. Glendale's float was a sensation — an eighty-five-foot-long smoke-breathing dragon.

Harriet Sterling, Tournament Queen, played the role of "Statue of Liberty" aboard her float, and the Pasadena Pigeon Club float released pigeons at intervals from wooden cages, much to the delight of youngsters.

HARRIET B. STERLING AS THE "STATUE OF LIBERTY," 1928

10
The Run that Stunned the Nation

ROY RIEGELS

1929

PRESIDENT LESLIE B. HENRY always could say, "When I headed the Tournament of Roses, the event really became famous. Roy Riegels ran the wrong way."

Yes, the Riegels scamper in the direction of his opponents' goal line is one of the best-remembered events ever to occur in the world of athletics.

Other things happened during Henry's one-year term in the Tournament office. The first post-parade exhibit of floats was staged at the Pasadena City Hall. Today this public viewing of the moving wonders of the flower world is one of the most popular features for Pasadena visitors at Victory Park, which is located near Paloma Street and Sierra Madre Boulevard where the parade concludes.

A crowd of 850,000 watched the 1929 parade, and by then twenty-two grandstands had been constructed along the Orange Grove and Colorado parade route.

The California-Georgia Tech football game attracted a crowd of 71,000, who paid $270,000 to see Tech win 8-7. The Tournament of Roses was in position after the game to pay off the Rose Bowl mortgage. Many communities throughout the nation today, heavily in debt after construction of stadiums costing up to thirty or forty million dollars, wish they could balance their books so quickly.

Because the Tournament of Roses deeded the huge structure to the city, and because all improvements have been financed from receipts of the game, citizens of Pasadena have not had to pay taxes to possess one of the world's most famous stadiums and enjoy first hand one of the world's greatest festivals. Only the routine upkeep of the Rose Bowl is taken from civic funds, a mere crumb of money in the over-all city budget.

The communities of Glendale and Beverly Hills were staging a duel for parade sweepstakes honors that rivaled the football classic for competitive intensity in the late twenties and early thirties. Beverly Hills won the top parade award in 1927 and 1928, but Glendale sprang forth with the "Lady of Shalott" in the 1928 parade. It pre-

66

sented a castle of yellow and red mums plus a barge carrying "Elaine" surrounded by banks of pink, red, and yellow roses. The "stream" was created with white sweet peas. Beverly Hills came back with victory in 1930, only to have Glendale "rally" in 1931.

The sun was so hot in 1928 it melted all the snow on the Camp Baldy float, but the Baldy youngsters came prepared. They threw papier-mâché snowballs at the crowd.

California had lost one game and tied one when it faced undefeated Georgia Tech in the often-discussed 1929 game.

The score was 0-0 in the second quarter when a pass from California halfback Benny Lom to his other halfback, Barr, slipped through the latter's finger tips on the goal line. The ball went over to Tech on the 20-yard line. "Stumpy" Thomason of Tech made a nice gain around left end, but he fumbled when hit by Lom. The ball bounced into the hands of California center Riegels on the 35-yard line of the Yellow Jacket team.

Riegels headed for the Tech goal, then suddenly wheeled to elude Thomason and started in the opposite direction toward his own goal line. Instinctively, other California players began to take out other Georgia Tech players, laying them low all over the field. California blocking was superb, so magnificent nobody put a hand on Riegels.

Lom sensed a mistake was taking place. He took off after Riegels. Lom yelled at the top of his voice for Roy to stop, but the roar of the crowd made it impossible for Riegels to hear the commands. Lom overtook Riegels near the goal line. He grasped the runaway with a desperate reach that connected with Riegels' wrist on the 1-yard line. With one mighty twist, just in time, Lom swung Riegels around. But before Riegels could head back in the correct direction, he was bounced to the earth by Tech's Frank Waddey on the 1-yard line.

This forced California to call for a punt to get out of trouble. Lom tried to kick out from deep in his end zone, but Tech's Vance Maree, a giant tackle, leaped high to block the ball with his hands. The last man to touch the ball as it bounced out of the end zone was California's Breckenridge. Referee Herb Dana ruled the play a safety and two points for Georgia Tech.

The Los Angeles *Times* carried this report of Riegels' reaction to his mistake, which actually produced the margin of California defeat:

"Roy Riegels, captain-elect of the California varsity, was heart-broken last night over his now-famous play in the Georgia Tech game. He declared that he had no excuses to make, that he was merely mixed up in his directions and that the first he knew anything was wrong was when Lom grabbed him by the arm on the goal line. Riegels' splendid play in the second half bears out this statement. No man, battered as some of the southern writers insinuate Riegels was, could come back and play the football that Riegels did. Lom said he sensed that Riegels was out of step the second he turned around."

Riegels became a silent man for a time after the incident. Seldom was he seen at football functions anywhere. However, time healed his wounds. Riegels returned to the Rose Bowl in 1969 to assist in the making of a film highlighting the greatest moments of college football's first hundred years.

Riegels, who operates a successful fertilizer business in upstate Woodland, California, says this today: "My philosophy to any young person who makes a mistake is that all isn't lost. I gained true understanding of life from my Rose Bowl mistake. I learned you can bounce back from a misfortune and view it as just something adverse that happened to you. At first it bothered me any time I heard the words 'wrong way,' but what happened doesn't bother me any more. I am happy I could play in the Rose Bowl and play hard. I got wrestled to the ground that day, but I haven't been knocked off my feet since. I am fortunate to have played football and had the experience of competing in the Rose Bowl. It is one of my richest memories even though I did goof. There isn't so much I remember about the historic play except that I would like to correct one misconception. I did hear Benny shout as I neared my goal line. So I slowed down as I looked back at him. He would never have caught me if I hadn't."

After the 1929 game, Georgia Tech All-American center Peter Pund, who played opposite Riegels, said: "That was a tough break for Riegels. But don't ever get the idea he isn't a wonderful center. He is the best center I have played against all year. He's a battler,

ROY RIEGELS RUNS WRONG WAY—THE MOST FAMOUS PLAY IN ROSE BOWL HISTORY

68

and he never quit. Some boys might have folded up under the situation, but Riegels didn't. I admire him for it."

The Riegels run so overshadowed other events that took place in the 1929 game that it is only justice that the others be recorded here.

Coach Nibs Price and his California team had to solve a unique backfield alignment devised by Tech coach William Alexander. The Tech quarterback stood with his back to the center. He received the ball between his legs and tossed it to his backs for straight and split bucks. Some people called it the "crap-shooters formation."

Lom could be famous today for winning the game, not for stopping Riegels. He recovered a fumble by "Father" Lumpkin, Tech fullback, and ran 60 yards for a touchdown. The play was called back because referee Dana said he blew his whistle before the fumble.

One time during the game, somebody kicked the air out of the football and it went flat.

Georgia Tech took an 8-0 lead in the third quarter when Warner Mizell gained thirty yards around right end and Thomason broke through left tackle and reversed his field to go fifteen yards for a touchdown. Thomason's conversion attempt was low and wide.

Historians hardly bother to record that Riegels blocked a Tech punt to start California on a drive that was climaxed by a long pass from Lom to Captain Phillips, a short clutch pass from Lom to a sub named Eisan, and then a scoring pass from Lom to Phillips. Barr kicked the extra point, but California still lost 8-7.

"WHAT HAVE I DONE?" PONDERS ROY RIEGELS

11
The Tournament Band Is Born

ALBERT EINSTEIN

1930

A PICKUP BAND made up of alumni and ROTC students played "Onward Christian Soldiers" at Pasadena Junior College when a director named Audre Stong decided to shake things up.

"What our school needs is an all-student band trained for marching and concert," said Stong, who borrowed instruments, solicited volunters to patch up old uniforms, and recruited music-minded students who were willing to "blow the depression out of our lives."

That was in late 1929; by January 1, 1930, Stong's group felt qualified to make an appearance in the Tournament of Roses parade. When the Caltech band failed to make an appearance that day, the PJC band won the hearts of the Tournament officials by volunteering to split up and form two bands, one filling the PJC spot and the other substituting for Caltech.

Stong had trained his performers well and they were very popular in the 1930 parade, so pleasing that a few months later parade chairman Charles Cobb extended the official invitation to Stong and his student musicians to become the official Tournament band.

"We put a lot of tricks into our marches, and we developed ten-minute concerts for the many pauses in the parade," said Stong, who retired as director twenty years later. To this day, Pasadena City College, as the school now is called, has enjoyed the honor of having the official Tournament of Roses band.

"A highlight of our experiences came in 1931 when we did the entire halftime show in the Rose Bowl," said Stong. "We had a large book the height of the goal posts, and we turned the pages of Rose Bowl history as we enacted the Tournament highlights. For years we represented the visiting teams when they came to the Rose Bowl, and we made many trips to other cities as the Tournament of Roses representative."

Radio was on a coast-to-coast network basis by then, and newsreels made Pasadena a major stop.

C. Hal Reynolds served the first of his two years as president in 1930. Holly Halsted reigned as Queen, and Mayor James ("Sunny

C. HAL REYNOLDS

JAMES ROLPH

HOLLY HALSTED

Jim") Rolph of San Francisco was brought in to be grand marshal.

"I think our grand marshal always should be some celebrity the world wants to see," said Reynolds, enunciating a policy that was adopted annually. "We also need to extend our line of march," he said. "The world wants to see this spectacle, so let's let 'em see it."

Miss Halsted, now Mrs. Frank S. Balthis of Newport Beach, California, and wife of an appellate court justice, gave the following account at 1970 Tournament time of her reign as Queen:

"With the year 1930 began a new concept of queen selection. Before that time, queens had been chosen for national prominence. For example, Fay Lanphier had been Miss America and May McAvoy was in the movies.

"Harlan Hall was secretary of the Tournament and Bill Dunkerley was secretary of the Chamber of Commerce. Mrs. Mills was president of the women's division of the Tournament. The offices were housed in the old Green Hotel facing on South Raymond.

"Harlan Hall and his committee conceived the idea of a young woman becoming queen who had a keen interest in the Tournament, whose family had been pioneers in early Pasadena, and who had been working closely with the board of directors.

"I had been working on publicity in addition to secretarial work, and I had worked for the Tournament of Roses for three years or so. And so it was that Holly Halsted, who had graduated from Pasadena High School in 1925, who had attended U.C.L.A., and who had become engaged to Frank S. Balthis, then attending Harvard Law School, was chosen to be queen.

"At first I was reluctant to accept the role of queen, but my family, especially my father and fiancé, urged me to do so. I have never regretted my decision, as the associations and friendships through the years have given me much pleasure. My father passed away in April of my year as queen. I have always been happy that he could see my float pass the Elks Club on Colorado where he sat with my husband-to-be and my family, with the exception of my sister who rode on the float with me as my attendant. She is Mrs. Paul G. Bryan (Gabrielle) whose husband is prominent in Tournament activities.

"I believe the thrill of making 'the curve' of Orange Grove and Colorado, facing the broad sweep of Colorado Boulevard and hearing the familiar voices of friends calling my name, and the experience of having a 'mike' shoved into view asking me how it felt to be queen was a very high moment in my life. Later, I was married in my queen's gown."

Beverly Hills won the Sweepstakes Prize with its "End of the Rainbow" entry, depicting a huge heart opening under a rainbow.

The Glendale floats in this era, which were consistent winners, were designed by L. H. Chobe. While preparing for the 1930 parade, Chobe's health failed and he underwent a serious throat operation. He still managed to work out the design, communicating with his asso-

RUSS SAUNDERS

ERNIE PINCKERT, 1971

ciates by written messages when he became unable to talk. Just before the float "Gold Rush of '98" was ready to move, Chobe's doctor told him he couldn't travel under any circumstances, but later the doctor relented and personally drove the designer to Pasadena under police escort. Returned home after learning Glendale had won its fifteenth gold cup as theme winner, Chobe was happy. But he had witnessed his last triumph. Ten days later he passed away.

The 1930 Rose Bowl game is remembered mainly because it introduced Howard Harding Jones to the Bowl world. When his great high-scoring team trounced previously undefeated Pittsburgh, coached by Dr. John ("Jock") Sutherland, 47-14, it marked the first of five victorious teams Jones was to take to the Bowl.

U.S.C.'s star was "Racehorse Russ" Saunders. On the first scrimmage play of the game, Toby Uansa, one of Pittsburgh's four All-Americans, cut between Francis Tappaan, U.S.C.'s left end, and Bob Hall, left tackle. Behind a wall of interference, Uansa broke into the open and streaked toward the Trojan goal line. Saunders, knocked down at the start of the play, got up and gave chase. One of the more thrilling foot races in Rose Bowl annals took place. Saunders caught him on the U.S.C. 14-yard line to bring to a halt what then was the Rose Bowl's longest to run from scrimmage, sixty-nine yards.

"Let us pray," implored a U.S.C. cheer leader.

Another U.S.C. star, Ernie Pinckert, answered the Trojan prayers by knocking down a fourth-down Pittsburgh pass to end that threat.

Saunders then started raising his arm. He completed a fifty-five-yard pass play to Harry Edelson for a touchdown. A twenty-five-yard pass to Pinckert scored again. Swivel-hipped substitute quarterback Marshall Duffield ran the score up to 26-0 at halftime before Saunders returned to connect with Edelson for another touchdown. Three Saunders passes and three touchdowns: that was good percentage. Saunders also was true with his next two passes, to run his completion streak to five, even though they didn't produce touchdowns.

"I want to praise Saunders for picking their defense apart," said Jones after the game. "Their great fullback Pug Parkinson played close to stop our running, and Saunders passed over him. Saunders is as good as any back I have ever coached."

Sutherland joined in the praise. "Saunders is the greatest back I have seen since Glenn Presnell . . . they rate with the great backs of all time," said the Pittsburgh coach.

"Never have I seen a game so dominated by the forward pass," declared Pop Warner.

"Every time Saunders hit us, we almost caved in under his drive," said Parkinson.

"I couldn't find any weak spots in the Pitt line, but sure found them in their backfield," grinned Saunders.

Braven Dyer in the *Times* wrote: "The outstanding lineman on the field was Garrett Arbelbide, who made tackles from front and rear,

GENERAL C. S. FARNSWORTH

MARY LOU WADDELL

knocked down interference with abandon, and rushed Pitt's passers so relentlessly that they must have wondered whether or not he had wings the way he came flying through the air."

"Pinckert was the most vicious tackler on the field. When he smacked them they stayed smacked," said Dick Hyland in the Los Angeles *Examiner*.

1931

Glendale returned to the sweepstakes pinnacle in the 1931 parade, with its float depicting "The Olympic Games," which were to come to Los Angeles in 1932. The float featured a discus thrower and a runner, constructed of chrysanthemums. The touching factor in this Glendale triumph was the fact that the float was designed by the widow of L. H. Chobe, the great designer who had died earlier in the year.

Gen. C. S. Farnsworth was the grand marshal, the last grand marshal to ride horseback. He rode atop a pure-blooded Arabian stallion named Jadaan which had been the mount of Rudolph Valentino in some of the movie idol's films.

Dr. Albert Einstein was honored by the Tournament. He remained in seclusion and watched the parade from the private office of a bank president. Einstein said later, "This was one of the most delightful days I have experienced."

In time for the 1931 football game, the last of the construction wood was removed from the Rose Bowl and the Bowl's seating capacity was increased to 86,000.

The queen was Mary Lou Waddell.

Missing was Harold A. Parker. The official Tournament photographer for twenty-eight years had died a few months before.

The Washington State Cougars had won the Pacific Coast Conference championship, and Alabama had won all of its nine games during the season, so they were matched for the Bowl feature.

Coach Babe Hollingberry of the Cougars came up with the bright psychological stunt of trying to outdo the Crimson of Alabama, appearing on the field with his men dressed completely in red from head to foot. Their helmets were red, their jerseys were red, their pants were red, their socks were red, their shoes were red, and — by dusk — their faces were red. Wallace Wade's invaders won 24-0.

The Cougars, who preferred to visit the orange groves instead of the movie studios, burned their uniforms before returning to Pullman.

Alabama was a cold, skilled machine. Wade shifted his lineup around to get the best combination for every possible situation; and Jimmy ("Hurry") Cain at the controls called a variety of bewildering plays. Alabama scored three quick touchdowns and added a field goal. Washington State got only as far as Alabama's 1-yard line.

Glenn ("Turk") Edwards and Mel Hein gave Washington State plenty of "oomph" in the line, but the Cougar backfield, especially on defense, was not up to reaping Hurry Cain. Monk Campbell spun

BABE HOLLINGBERRY

away from Cougar tacklers as if they were kittens. Fred Sington of Alabama, an All-American tackle every pound of him, dueled Edwards every minute, although West Coast writers concluded Edwards was the master this day.

Cain averaged forty-six-yards with six punts, truly a great kicking performance. But the game was won because Alabama's attack was too much. "The vaunted defense of the Western champions crumbled like the walls of Jericho," wrote Royal Brougham in the Seattle *Post Intelligencer*. Brougham added, "The freckle-necked southern gentleman won this game with his noodle. He used shock troops to give him time to dissect his opponents' strengths and weaknesses, then he sent his regulars in to win the game."

Maxwell Stiles wrote in the *Examiner*: "Washington State was like a trout in the rapids. The trout knew that he was in a lot of running water, but he didn't know where it was coming from."

Braven Dyer wrote: "Cain found Elmer Schwartz drawn in close backing up the line and other Cougar backs playing well up, so he called upon Jimmy Moore to fling the pigskin."

Moore started the scoring in the second quarter with 43 yards of skywriting to Flash Suther. A spectacular catch by Smith set up a touchdown smash by Campbell, who soon raced forty-three yards for another touchdown. A thirty-yard field goal by "Ears" Whitworth completed the scoring.

The victory was Alabama's third straight in the Bowl. Yes, this was the Age of Dixie.

ROSE BOWL ENLARGED FOR 1931 GAME

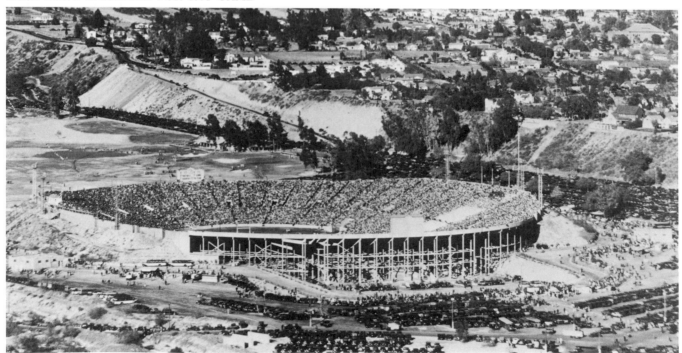

74

12
Queens, Horses, and Bands

WHAT'S A PARADE without pretty girls, peppy bands, and beautiful horses?

The Tournament of Roses long has known that these are the ingredients for America's most famous marching classic — along with the startling floats, of course, that have brought their floral artistry into the hearts of admirers throughout the world.

The world concurs that the Tournament has the perfect formula for a parade — sixty floats, twenty-one bands, forty equestrian units, pretty girls, hundreds of coordinated, enthusiastic working Tournament members, and millions of viewers — all of this in synchronization over a five-and-a-half-mile route in one of America's most beautiful communities in the foothills of the San Gabriel Mountains on a sunny, brisk morning.

This is California. This is Pasadena. This is America.

No parade better presents pulchritude in its most stunning form, happy principals aboard the gorgeous floats, some of them professional models, others winners of community beauty contests, others students or representatives of organizations and groups.

Of course, amid all of this feminine grace and warmth, the main attraction is the Tournament of Roses Queen and her court of princesses.

Originally, only young ladies attending Pasadena City College were eligible for this honor. Today the selection is made from all girls between the ages of seventeen and twenty-one who attend school in the Pasadena City College district. The contestant must have a C average in her studies, carry a full classroom schedule, and be unmarried.

"We look for the typical girl-next-door," said Ralph Helpbringer, 1970 Queen Selection Committee chairman. "We do not try to select a Miss America. We do not run a bathing-suit or talent contest. We try to pick a queen who has natural personality, projection, capacity to captivate and glitter, bloom and light up. We do not look for bodies and legs. We look for that girl with a quick flash of personality. We study how she acts on her feet, how she will handle situations when she is the hostess for people and teams."

Helpbringer said the Tournament of Roses annually has found what it has been looking for.

How is the Queen chosen?

A series of eliminations, in which a board of judges meets several times with the contestants, reduces the original field of about 350 entrants to 150 and then lesser numbers until finally there are seven. One girl is chosen Queen from that group, with the other six maintaining the rank of princess in her court. Until the final seven are chosen, all contestants are known only by number. They are interviewed, asked to make extemporaneous statements and appearances, and made to react to sudden situations. Factors in the judging (the selection committeemen keep scorecards) are appearance, carriage, complexion, teeth, personality, poise, projection, photogenic qualities, spontaneity, and figure.

"I would say poise is the first thing we look for," explained Helpbringer. "We will ask a candidate to walk to us. We will ask her a question. Her glitter, general response, and capability to react is closely observed by each of the nine judges. We aren't demanding scholastic answers or trained responses. We look for her normal feelings and capacity to respond. It is amazing how the winners stand out and how uniform our agreement when we check our scorecards and compare notes in our final decision-making. The girls who score high in the beginning usually stay there."

Helpbringer summed up the satisfaction that comes to a typical, devoted Tournament volunteer when he said: "My biggest reward is one of seeing these young women develop as wonderful persons in such a short time. In two or three months, a member of the court makes the transformation from a girl to a lady. The transformation is remarkable. Parents have told me they can't believe the change in their personality and poise. Seeing this happen and knowing what wonderful young ladies come out of this experience is most gratifying."

The horse, the faithful steed that originally brought man to the attractive land that now is California, always has been a major Tournament of Roses parade attraction — first pulling the floral buggies and later stepping to music in its equine glory.

The value of horses, equipment, and costumes in any one parade has been placed in excess of three million dollars. There are forty equestrian units, composed of approximately 225 riders, who spend up to $2,000 for each of their costumes. The average investment in silver-mounted trappings is $10,000 per saddle or horse.

Merton E. Goddard, chairman of the 1970 Equestrian Committee, is responsible for this popular phase of the parade.

"We try to show the western horse at his finest," said Eldon Fairbanks, Goddard's equestrian director. The Equestrian Committee at-

QUEEN JUDGING—THE SEARCH FOR
POISE, RESPONSE, PERSONALITY, AND
BEAUTY

tempts to have a cross section of the popular breeds represented. The palomino, with its silver tack, perhaps has been the most popular. Others include matched Morgans, Arabians, and pintos.

The horses do not have to be registered, although each mount must be of outstanding quality. Each entrant must pay all expenses involved in the appearance—shipping, feeding, stabling, and rider expense. It is believed the cost runs to $1,000 per entry.

Fairbanks receives hundreds of entry requests each year. Although a large number of requests must be turned down, several new horses and riders replace old equestrians each year.

"We try to improve the parade each year," said Fairbanks. "We look for new blood constantly. We remain considerate of the faithful riders who have continued to keep abreast of the changing times with new and better horses, tack, and costumes. Many riders have been with us ten to twenty years."

The horses in any year are valued higher than all the floats. It is believed the stock alone is worth $1,750,000; the floats cost about $1,000,000.

A special horseshoe is used to prevent slipping. The shoe is made with barium and is welded to the regular shoe. A rubber shoe was tried but discarded because of slipping when the pavement is wet.

There is no judging of the horses as there is for the floats. The equestrians are not in competition. Each rider in the parade receives a floral rosette, which includes the date and parade information, as a memento for the owner's trophy case.

Fairbanks said the Tournament hopes to have the Spanish Riding Academy of Vienna with its famous Lipizzan horses in a future parade. More floral neck pieces also will mark future equestrian appearances.

Many western movie and television stars and actors are among the notables who ride in the Rose Parade each January 1. Los Angeles Sheriff Eugene Biscailuz, Leo Carrillo, Monty Montana, and many others have appeared on mounts in the line of march.

Among other prominent riders have been the Con Davis family from San Diego, Alex and Phyllis Madonna and their daughter Cathie from San Luis Obispo, Willard and Dorothy Beanland from Hidden Hills, Lee Harbottle of Monrovia, Dr. Vernon Scott of Bradbury, R. Allen Burton from High Point, N. C., H. W. ("Buck") Hinson of Lee's Summit, Missouri, and Edna Fagan of Chatsworth.

An Arabian horse group led by Pearl Larson of Sunnymead riding El Rahnason, great Arabian champion, is an annual feature.

Richard Saukko has ridden Traveler, the U.S.C. Trojans' white mascot, annually since his school started going to the Rose Bowl with regularity.

Aaron G. Olmsted, an organ architect and builder in Hartford, Connecticut, told how he became a regular rider in the parade.

"For many years I watched this parade back East," he said. "In 1965, I received an invitation from Eldon Fairbanks to ride in the event. To one from the East such an invitation was a great honor and privilege. So, in 1965, I flew out to Pasadena for my first ride, borrowing equipment from helpful friends. Eldon asked my wife and me to ride in 1966, and again friends gave us a helping hand. In 1969, my daughter enjoyed her first ride with me. In 1970, a real treat for all of us was our family group of four participating. In 1971, we went back to a matched pair and rode with Monty Montana.

"Having paraded for years on the East Coast and all over the country, I can truthfully say the Rose Bowl parade is the greatest of all."

Barbara Trisler of El Monte, California, is an example of a rising young equestrian who has found happiness and success riding in the Tournament of Roses parade. She developed the skill of her Morgan albino mare, Misty, who once was given up by horsemen as too difficult to handle, and in 1971 she was the marshal of one section of the parade and was honored with a CBS interview conducted by Bob Barker. Miss Trisler's costume was a Spanish-style dress made of fifty yards of white lace with sequins and a sash of red velvet. Barbara designed and sewed it herself.

"I worked with Misty for a year, knowing I could win her confidence and transform her from a problem horse to a parade winner," she said.

Miss Trisler had never ridden in a parade anywhere until she was invited to ride at Monterey Park in 1966 with a borrowed costume. In the twelve major community parades in which Barbara has ridden, she has taken first prize seven times and second three times. One of her riding partners is Abe Schiller of Las Vegas, Nevada, who rides Honeybee.

Ruth Thompson of Crabtree, Oregon, riding Snow White, a pink-skinned albino, has been a popular recent addition. Gale Knaus annually comes in from Lee's Summit, Missouri, with Lullabye Skipper. Missouri horse-show champion Courageous Star is ridden by T. B. Smith of Prairie Home. Chief Eagle Friend of Arizona, is a popular rider. Dr. E. W. Paul of Osceola, Iowa, brings his horse in a trailer to Pasadena for a parade appearance each year.

Chief Eagle Friend is a blood brother of the famous Chief First to Fly, Joshua Wetsit, representing the Assiniboin Indians. In 1968, Chief Eagle Friend was invited to ride in the Tournament Parade to represent the American Indian. This he did as marshal of his equestrian unit, the first time the American Indian has been represented in the parade. He has participated in the parade each year since, riding the double-registered appaloosa stallion, The Wheel, owned by Darwin Waite of Phoenix, Arizona.

Among all these stars, one that Tournament viewers always cheer is George Putnam, the popular Los Angeles television news commentator, who has appeared fifteen straight years astride his famed palomino, Diamond.

In an interview with the author of this book, Putnam made vivid the story of the equestrian's participation in the parade.

"I consider it a great privilege to be included in the line of march in this — the most spectacular, colorful, best publicized parade in all the world," Putnam said.

"Strangely, there are those who make sport of the fact that I — a news reporter-commentator — participate. Among these are members of my own immediate family. But hell, it's as natural as it was for Leo Carrillo, Gene Biscailuz, and a host of others.

"All year long, we face a camera and microphone in a locked-in, sterile studio situation — then, comes New Year's Day, and the rare opportunity to look at these wonderful fellow Americans face to face and get a reaction — good, bad, or indifferent — but damn well a reaction!

"There are so few things that are still typically American — and the Tournament of Roses Parade is one of them.

"I am vastly appreciative of this opportunity, and I will share it with my daughter, Jil, 13. She, too, loves the horses, the out-of-doors, and the thrills that are part of the parade."

Putnam was asked a series of questions and gave the following answers. It may be of interest to give the interview verbatim:

Q. How did you get started in equestrian activity?

A. Being a farm boy from Minnesota who worked with horses from ten years of age on up, it was natural that I should later ride rodeos in Montana, American saddle horses in Central Park, New York, in Long Island, and parades in southern California. When the invitation came to participate, I jumped at the opportunity, and soon found myself a breeder of palominos. One year I rode in twenty Southland parades, acting as grand marshal in most of them. Then came my involvement in the breeding of thoroughbreds. I now have a total of eighty — fifteen currently in training at local tracks. Our best currently is the filly Bold Jil. She is a stakes winner, with a tremendous potential.

Q. How much is your investment in horses, equipment?

A. My two palominos are worth perhaps $5,000 each, although I wouldn't take $25,000 for Diamond, who is now fifteen, and with whom I have participated in most of my years parading. The two silver outfits are worth approximately $40,000 to $50,000. They are becoming more valuable each year, because the craftsmanship involved is fast becoming non-existent. Also, moving the horses requires trucks, trailers, and tack.

Q. How do you train a horse for parade activity?

A. Diamond was trained by George Ryan. Phantom was trained

by Gayle Lowe. After the basics are learned at the ranch, we begin with one of the less involved parades — smaller parades such as those at the outlying communities. This familiarizes the horse and the rider with traffic and other distractions.

Q. What is your immediate activity like prior to the parade, such as grooming the horse, etc.? Does the horse rest the night before? Where do you keep him? Is he bathed and combed the night before, etc.?

A. Few people realize the involved procedure in preparing horses for a parade of such importance as the Tournament of Roses. We keep ours in the pasture — they thrive on it. Two days prior to the parade, the horse is clipped, bathed repeatedly; the tail and mane are bleached, the horse is blanketed and kept in a stall. It takes at least six hours' work.

Q. What is your satisfaction in 'marching'?

A. In being able to do something well, other than broadcasting the news for which I have been known for thirty-six years. And to enjoy a ride which is becoming a rare luxury because of the press of two full hours of news, its preparation Monday through Friday, and running the ranch and racing stable.

Q. What are the problems while riding your horse in the parade?

A. The ever-present worry that a thoughtless parent will shove a baby carriage, go-cart, or toddler in the path of a skittish horse. The average person doesn't realize that a horse — unlike a dog — explodes under certain circumstances — a loud noise or sudden movement, or an unfamiliar object. A horse has tremendous strength, and bolts easily. If the average parade-watcher could only realize the danger involved, he or she would be more cautious around an animal of such potential. Also, pavement is an unnatural footing, and it's necessary to exert extreme caution when it's wet.

Q. Is the horse hard to control? Does he react to the crowd?

A. As I said earlier, loud noises (such as firecrackers, the crash of a drum, shrill sounds, fluttering canopies and pennants) — all these and more, which I'd rather not discuss because it might give trouble-makers some ideas, might startle the horse.

Q. Do you recognize friends in the crowd?

A It's always a thrill to have watchers call out your name, repeat such by-words as 'See you at ten, see you then' or 'And that's the up-to-the-minute news, up to the minute, that's all the news' — or 'George sent me' — or 'Say Hi to Pete, Tom, and Rona,' or 'How's Bold Jil?,' and so forth. You'd have to be a fool not to enjoy such exchanges. And I do recognize friends in the crowd.

Q. Does the horse need special shoes?

A. Yes. The horses are shod with barium, which is a substance preventing skidding on pavement. It is added to the toe and heels of the shoes by an expert shoer who specializes in this kind of work.

Q. Is it tiring to go the route?

A. It is both exhilarating and enervating, but I wouldn't miss it for the world. And I shudder to think of the day when I'll be too damned old to wave back at all those wonderful people. And after the parade come two hour-long news reports. It's a full day, but a rewarding one.

Q. Any interesting experience or incident you especially recall from your parade participation?

A. The thrill of riding for the last time with Leo Carrillo and Gene Biscailuz. Welcoming the *Bonanza* cast on their first ride, and predicting they would be an absolute sensation (which they are) on TV. Meeting and riding with Hopalong Cassidy (Bill Boyd) and Gene Autry, Roy Rogers, and Rex Allen.

I'll never forget the near disaster of the 1968 Tournament of Roses parade. My ranch manager, Al Rowland, drove Diamond in from the ranch in one of our three-horse trailers. When he arrived and we prepared to open the trailer, I couldn't find Diamond. Further examination led to the discovery of Diamond in the front compartment, out of sight and flat on the floor. He had fallen down en route, cut himself, and there my beautiful horse lay in blood and manure. Closer examination showed that he had suffered only a surface cut — nothing serious — and after washing him up and walking him out of it, we were able to make the parade. Since then, we have discovered he has claustrophobia and must have two stalls all by himself, and must never be tied in the trailer. Such are the ways of the aging parade horse — and rider.

Near disaster also threatened an earlier ride when the balloon man came too close, and Diamond threw a fit. On another occasion, he refused to cross over a small trickle of water. It was necessary to dismount and lead him. This is a real challenge in that the silver is stiff and weighty, and scrambling back on the horse is a challenge.

The most embarrassing moment was the time the horse refused to take the bit. Everyone and his brother gathered around to offer words of advice. Finally, we conquered the beast when my associate offered him some feed. He reached for it, opened his mouth, in went the bit, the bridle was buckled. I mounted, and the parade was on, concluded Putnam.

Another talented rider is Belle Starr of Burbank, California, who has ridden in the Tournament Parade for four years, two years as a unit marshal. She is typical of the many riders who participate for enjoyment and love of her sport. She shows quarter horses in parades and shows in California. She has participated in the Santa Barbara Fiesta, the Phoenix Rodeo of Rodeos parade, and many California events. Tournament riders take part each year out of pure enjoyment of having participated, and hundreds of equestrians can be cited in this category. It is one of the most devoted groups annually in the

Tournament Parade — and one that typifies California and the West.

The story of the parade in general is one that A. Byrd Christian of Pasadena, one of the fourteen hundred Tournament members serving on various committees, described as "a great American display of cooperation between the men who handle the details of parade direction and the hundreds of participants." Christian is a typical Tournament worker. He was on the U.S.C. football squad as a practice-field scrub during two seasons when the Trojans made it to the Rose Bowl. Byrd didn't get to suit up for those games, but here he is working among the fourteen hundred who give "their all" to make the festival a success. "This is the only activity of such major scope I know where members pay dues to get a chance to work hard without financial remuneration and wind up feeling they were totally rewarded in the form of self-satisfaction," said Christian, a statement thirteen hundred and ninety-nine others in the Tournament family would ditto.

Ralph Helpbringer, who was Float Construction chairman in 1964, recalled an episode that illustrates the philosophy of the Tournament membership that the "show must go on" no matter what the problem.

"En route to the starting point of the parade, at 4:30 in the morning, a float picked up a piece of steel which pierced the radiator of the motor," said Helpbringer. "The float was out of the parade if another radiator from the same model engine couldn't be found. I sent one of my committeemen out to get a radiator. Now this isn't easy at 4:30 a.m.

"He left with determination to succeed in his mission. Several blocks away he found a car with the exact radiator needed. He and other committeemen stripped the radiator from the car, left a note telling of their intention to replace it after the parade, hurried to the float, and made the substitution. The float was back in the parade just in time for the start. After the parade, we were contacted by the owner of the car who graciously forgave us and said, 'I won't charge you anything. Just bring my radiator back and re-install it.'

"Another time a float jumped the curve at about the same hour. We needed a dolly to jack it up for repair. The committeemen went on the search for a dolly and found it under a jacked-up house in South Pasadena. They called the house-mover and asked him if they could use the dolly. He got mad. He said, 'I'm mad only because you got me up this early. Why didn't you steal it and ask me later if it was okay?'"

Girls may be pretty, horses may be striking, floats may be stunning, and men may be ingenious, but the one ingredient no parade could be without is the marching band.

One of the more interesting phases of Tournament of Roses activity centers around the community excitement, the individual joys, and the displays of Americana that are imbedded in the annual appearance of twenty-one bands in the giant parade.

The unsung heroes of each Tournament are the members of the one band invited to the parade that never gets to play. "Each year we have a back-up band standing by, in case through some emergency one of the twenty-one bands in the parade can't show," said Harvey Christen, chairman of the Band Committee. "In 1970 the Santa Ana band was ready, even as late as 6 in the morning, to appear if we called them. The year before it was the Santa Monica City College band. These are real heroes who prove how much sacrifice and American spirit go into a Tournament of Roses parade."

Forty-one years on the staff of Lockheed Aircraft in Burbank, that company's senior employee in active service, Christen often has referred to the band story as one of the most representative of true American spirit in the entire Tournament picture.

"Some three hundred bands apply to play in our parade each year," said Christen. "They await our answer just like a football team anxiously awaits a bid to a Bowl game. They work hard to get to Pasadena and they do such a marvelous job while they are here."

The Tournament is committed to certain bands for annual appearances, based on tradition, past loyalties, and early allegiance to the Tournament. The Pasadena City College band long has been the official Tournament band; it returns annually. The Marine Band from El Toro has been in the parade over fifty years and commands the respect of all viewers and participants. Same for the Salvation Army Band. The competing conferences in the football game each have a band in the parade. The Toppers, a marching jazz outfit, originally came in as representatives of the musicians' union during an early labor dispute and have been invited back with popular approval each year. The McDonald All-American Band, which selects two playing members from each state in nation-wide high school band competitions, is a regular feature. San Diego County, the Los Angeles City Schools District, the Long Beach area, and Glendale-Burbank, on an alternating basis, through traditional appearance, are regulars.

"These bands have qualified because of legitimate reasons of tradition and long-time contribution," said Christen. "The Marines set the tempo of our parade. The world stands and cheers when they go by. Long-time respect exists for the Salvation Army. They have been so much a part of our parade — entering a float, providing a band, and even serving doughnuts and coffee up and down the parade route throughout the night. The Toppers are something to admire. Here is a group that plays together only once in a year. You see these musicians come in after midnight from their respective individual jobs. They are weary but eager. They start practicing their numbers, and a few hours later they are big hits in the parade. The McDonald Band does a wonderful work in our school band program around the country, providing the All-American player selection honors for bandsmen that we have in football. Its director, Paul Lavalle, known as the 1970

John Philip Sousa and who directs the Radio City Music Hall orchestra, does wonderful work, as does the McDonald Corporation for paying the way of these musicians to New York for rehearsals and then to the Tournament in Pasadena. The people in San Diego, Los Angeles, Long Beach, and Burbank-Glendale have organized programs to provide a worthy representative each year. In 1970 Los Angeles came up with the Locke High School Band through a contest conducted by John Deichman, and this is a great story. The Locke students had to raise thousands of dollars for their new uniforms and they just managed to get the money needed by Tournament time. How proud those kids were!"

Christen pointed out that, after the "regulars" are chosen each year, there is room in the parade for only ten more bands, which are selected by the Tournament Band Committee from the long list of applicants. The committeemen screen the qualifications of the applicants and make their decision based on these investigations of talent.

"We have not selected a Pasadena area high school band because we already have a Pasadena representative in the official City College Band," said Christen. "But we realize deserving bands in the Pasadena area would like to appear, and perhaps we can, in the future, devise a system of adding one or more regular bands from the Pasadena City College district, a plan similar to the Queen selection expansion."

The thrill for Band Committee members, according to Christen, is the moment the selected applicants are telephoned to inform them they are invited to the Rose Parade. The joyful response is heartwarming. Christen has heard many a "God bless you" on the other end of the line.

Each band that plays in the Tournament pays its own expenses to Pasadena. In many cases, this runs from $25,000 to $40,000. In nearly all cases, the money is raised by school and community projects.

Christen recalled many interesting stories. The La Crosse, Wisconsin, State College Band raised $40,000; then while the group was in Pasadena, the proud city raised another $40,000 for future use of the band. The Burlington, Ontario, band had many projects for expense-money raising, including the "kidnapping" of a city official for "ransom." A strike of traffic-control operators at the Burlington airport was dispensed with just long enough to let the school band's plane get off the ground.

When Christen informed Kenneth R. Force, director of the Port Chester, New York, High School band that it was invited, Force replied, "Send me a wire immediately so I can appear before our townspeople at a rally tonight and tell them the good news officially. We need a lift like this." (Port Chester, incidentally, is Ed Sullivan's school.) Merchants in that community pledged a portion of their receipts for one day to help pay the band's expenses. Uniforms worn by the bandsmen were models of those worn by the Buckingham Palace Guard in England — and made by the same company.

When John L. Alexander, director of the La Crosse Marching Chiefs, received the invitation, he wired back: "Thanks for making this the best year in about 230 kids' lives." The same kind of response came from Clifford Watkins, who directed the South Carolina State College Band in a successful display of marching "perpetual motion" down Colorado Boulevard in Pasadena.

Jerry T. Hanszen, director of the "Roughneck" marching band of White Oak, Texas, a coast-to-coast award-winning band that also won the NBC pre-parade band contest in Pasadena, didn't have too many financial worries in financing the trip. The school has several active oil wells on the campus. This band was one of the most popular ever with parade-goers.

With Tournament committeeman Al Embree, owner of a bus company, aiding in arrangements, nearly all visiting bands enjoy a busy week in Pasadena. They make other appearances, including Disneyland, where they earn a free day of rides by playing in the holiday parade at the great amusement center.

The Marshalltown, Iowa, High School band brought a special thrill to Tournament publicist Sam Akers in 1970, because Marshalltown was his boyhood community. George Bolinger, veteran Lafayette, Indiana, sports writer, told how Akers had his problems, however.

"Akers now believes in miracles," wrote Bolinger in his sports column. "Sam was a bit shaken when his schoolday pals called him from Marshalltown and said they needed 177 tickets for the Rose Bowl game. They refused to listen to Sam's plea that this was impossible. 'We're on our way to Pasadena,' they wired Akers.

"Just an hour before the delegation was to arrive in Pasadena to get their tickets from their old friend, the Tournament of Roses office received notice from the summer White House in San Clemente, California, that President Nixon would not come to the game, and his 150 tickets previously reserved were released. Akers received a big break from Max Colwell, the Tournament manager. He let Akers have them for the Marshalltown group, and even solicited 27 more from other Tournament members. Yes, Akers will forever believe in miracles."

Other experiences of the Marshalltown band, as told by director Armon Adams, typically represent what other bands enjoy on their trip to Pasadena. A report from Adams relates the story of the visiting band given a chance to march and play in America's most famous festival. (See back of book for a listing of the bands that have played in the Tournament of Roses during the past twenty years).

Said Adams:

"Though it may in this instance be telling of a specific group of young people from just one community, I can't help but feel it expresses the thoughts and feelings of hundreds, perhaps thousands, of others who have in the past and will in the future share this experience and of many, many towns and cities who have worked and sacrificed to make it all possible.

"I am now in my 26th year as a band director and I can say from my own standpoint that this was the biggest thrill in the entire career. I am positive our band members share my feeling, so here goes —

"It was late in July when the telephone rang, bringing the invitation from the music chairman of the Tournament of Roses Association, and since good news travels fast in our town, within three hours I believe half of our community had word of our good fortune. We were asked for a definite answer of acceptance within a week, so a meeting of all band parents was called for two nights later, and by that time, a local travel agency had chartered a jet, reserved hotel rooms for us in Anaheim, and had estimated an expense of $44,000 for us for the entire trip of five days and nights. This estimate almost hit right on the nose — we went over it just slightly. At our parents' meeting we gave all of the details, asking them to underwrite the cost of the trip for us, and we decided to start fund-raising, the parents to pay only the amount we failed to raise. Not a single vote was cast against accepting the invitation.

"We then chose co-chairmen for the fund-raising, all of the parents were put on committees, and everyone went to work. Carnivals, suppers, auto races, movies, bumper stickers, Rose Bowl pens, dances, all sorts of business promotions, car washes, slave auctions, card parties — every way imaginable was used to raise the necessary amount, and as it turned out, we raised $48,000, even having money left over to put into our band uniform fund. The parents didn't have to contribute a cent and it was figured in such a way that a student could make the entire trip without a cent in his pocket if he so wished. This included transportation, meals, admissions, rides, and even the Rose Bowl game.

"We scheduled extra rehearsals for every Sunday afternoon and Wednesday night. Sunday afternoon would find us marching five and six miles to get in shape for the long parade. The students were so eager that we had no attendance problems and for three months everything else in the community became secondary.

"Finally the big day arrived. On a Sunday morning four buses took us the 45 miles to Des Moines to the airport and we boarded the biggest commercial plane in operation at that time. All of our equipment had been sent ahead by trucks the day before, and it was loaded onto the plane by the time we arrived. There were 198 people in our total party, 162 of whom were marching band members. Fourteen were chaperones, and the others making the trip were friends of the band, including two cameramen and two reporters. We took along a TV cameraman from Des Moines to send back pictures and news and also to make us a documentary film which we wanted to keep as a memento.

"We left Des Moines in eight degree weather surrounded by snow and fog and 2 hours and 45 minutes later we landed in the sunshine in Los Angeles. The plane trip was fabulous. Many of our students had never flown before and the pilots gave us a running account of where we were and what to watch for. They even turned and banked the plane, first to one side and then to the other, to give everyone a perfect view. We were met at the airport by our host from the Tournament of Roses and by two gentlemen from Long Beach where we were to play a concert on Monday night.

"By 4 p.m. on Sunday afternoon we were checked into the Charter House and Saga hotels and then everyone visited Disneyland for about six hours. Bedtime was 11 o'clock, and at 7 a.m. the following morning we used 14 rolls of masking tape to line off a huge parking lot near our hotels and rehearsed for the NBC band review which we had been invited to participate in the following morning. Then at 9 a.m. we went back to Disneyland, which, by the way, was just across the street from us, and until 3 p.m. everyone had a ball.

"By 4 p.m. we had returned to the hotels to don uniforms and then back to Disneyland we marched to appear in a parade with 75,000 people watching. Back to the hotel for dinner and then a bus trip to Long Beach for a night concert for the Iowa Association there.

"On Tuesday morning we participated in the NBC band review, which was taped in Pasadena to be shown just prior to the Rose Parade on New Year's morning. We were very happy to place second in competition with nine other very fine marching bands and we finished the day with a tour of Farmers' Market.

"Wednesday morning was used to tour Universal Studios and, after a lunch back at the hotel, off we went to Marineland for the afternoon. The entire day was most interesting and the rides on the freeways proved quite a contrast to our 25- and 30-mile speed limit at home.

"It was early to bed on Wednesday night, 9:30 to be exact, as we were to be called at 3:45 a.m. the next morning to give us plenty of time to get to crowded Pasadena for the parade. As we stepped uniformly onto Orange Grove Boulevard, we found it almost beyond description. People, people, people for as far as we could see, and all aches and tired muscles were quickly forgotten as this most enthusiastic crowd gave us a lift we never could have imagined. There could never be another experience to equal ours of the next six miles. We played almost constantly with applause ringing from both sides, and one of our members was later to remark that his biggest thrill came when he realized as we turned off of Colorado Boulevard and looked up into the mountains in the distance that we were playing 'This Is My Country.'

"A fine box-lunch awaited us at the end of the parade and then we were rushed by police escort quickly across town to the Rose Bowl where we thoroughly enjoyed the football game and the accompanying spectacle. At last — back to our hotel, and we dined, danced, swam, and watched TV until midnight, not really wanting to realize that in the morning it would all end.

"Still, there was more to come. We packed our equipment and by Friday noon had boarded our plane once more for the flight back. We had never once given thought to what a stir all of our activities was causing back home and, when we touched down in Des Moines, who should meet us but the governor of the State of Iowa. After pictures and interviews, we were again led by police escort back to Marshalltown, where a large turnout awaited us in our high school gym for a welcome home. The mayor declared the entire month 'Bobcat Month,' and at last we returned to our homes, only to spend another several hours looking at the pictures and news releases which had filled our home-town newspapers during our absence. Truly, we felt like celebrities.

"For the following month or so, we enjoyed many telegrams, letters, and phone calls from all over the United States, congratulating us on our appearance in the NBC review and in the Tournament of Roses Parade.

"And now, the anticipation, the excitement, the thrills — all the experiences are over. Yet — not really. A million memories are ours forever. Snapshots, slides, and movies let us relive those five days and nights over and over. Perhaps as the years go by it will all become even more glamorous to us, as things sometimes have a way of doing. We can even yet seem to feel the thrust of the powerful jets as we are lifted far above Des Moines and headed toward California, and the noise of the crowd along Orange Grove and Colorado Boulevards still rings in our ears. And on each New Year's morning for many years to come, as we sit in front of our TV sets watching the splendor of the parade in Pasadena, with countless millions of others, we will thrill to the snap of music and to the precision of the march of twenty-one or so uniformed bands. But for 162 former central Iowa musicians, yet another band with heads held high and with white banner proudly waving out front will step smartly across the screen—The Bobcat Marching Band of Marshalltown, Iowa."

13
Year of the Olympics

SAN MARINO FLOAT, 1932

1932

THE STORY of the Tournament was sent to all parts of the world in 1932 when short-wave radio broadcasts of the activities were initiated. It was fitting that the world should receive the descriptions of the beautiful floats because, in the year that the Olympics were held in Los Angeles, the parade theme in Pasadena was "Nations and Games in Flowers."

William May Garland, who played an important role in the Los Angeles Olympics effort, was the grand marshal. Tournament president starting a two-year term was D. E. McDaneld.

A U.C.L.A. freshman, Myrta Olmsted, was chosen to ride in the parade as Queen of the Tournament's salute to the Olympiad.

Each float represented a country participating in the games, of which there were fifty-seven. San Marino's float, the Sweepstakes winner, a tribute to Australia, was a barge drawn by a huge floral lyrebird.

U.S.C.'s great football team had ended Notre Dame's twenty-five-game winning streak, 16-14, to qualify as the West's representative in the Rose Bowl against Bernie Bierman's Tulane team, which had an 11-0 record. Howard Jones' great machine had lost its season opener to St. Mary's, but as the season went along the tempo of crushing Trojan victories increased to the point where Georgia was trounced 60-0 in the final game.

The Trojans had six men who were named on one or more All-American teams — tackle Ernie Smith, guards Johnny Baker and Aaron ("Rosy") Rosenberg, halfback Ernie Pinckert, and quarterbacks Orv Mohler and Gaius Shaver.

Tulane didn't play dead for the great Trojans. Wop Glover made a 59-yard run, overtaken finally by Pinckert. The Trojans retaliated with a march that produced the game's first touchdown, scored by end Ray Sparling who dropped back into halfback position. Baker kicked the point and U.S.C. was ahead 7-0.

The score remained 7-0 until both teams erupted in the third quarter. Pinckert scored two touchdowns through the great Jerry Dalrymple's territory at right end, the touchdowns coming on runs of

HOWARD JONES

BERNIE BIERMAN

thirty and twenty-three yards. In Dalrymple's defense, it should be remembered he had suffered a kidney injury in an earlier game and was handicapped by protective padding that required frequent re-adjusting. Captain Stan Williamson of U.S.C. demonstrated fine sportsmanship when Dalrymple used more than his allotted time out. "Let him have all the time he needs," Williamson told referee Herb Dana. Not a Tulane player touched Pinckert on either run as U.S.C. combined masterful trickery and blocking. Jones moved his men around so completely that Tulane was bewildered.

Glover got a bee in his pants, however, and executed some runs for Tulane that set up a touchdown pass from Don Zimmerman to Haynes. Zimmerman's try for extra point was blocked. A Zimmerman pass to Dalrymple set up a scoring chance; Dalrymple batted the pass in the air and caught it as it started downward. Glover then skirted end for the touchdown. Pinckert knocked down a Tulane pass in the attempt for an extra point. The final score was U.S.C. 21, Tulane 12.

Bierman said, "U.S.C. has more power than any team I have ever seen." The Trojan performance perhaps whetted Bierman's appetite for power, because when he went to his alma mater, Minnesota, to become head coach the following season, he developed some of the most bruising power teams in college football history.

Pop Warner was impressed by the lateral passing in the game. "This verifies what many coaches have felt is an effective way to advance the ball," said Warner. "We will see much more of it in years to come."

"It was Pinckert's last game and he went out in glory," commented Paul Lowry in the Los Angeles *Times*.

ERNIE PINCKERT POWERS
FOR U.S.C.

14
"America's Sweetheart"

MARY PICKFORD

CHARLES BUDDY ROGERS wrote to the author on September 15, 1969:

Dear Mr. Hendrickson:

Please forgive the long delay in replying to your letter of July 25 addressed to Mrs. Rogers. Mrs. Rogers has not been as strong as we would like her to be, making it difficult to promptly follow through on all the letters we receive.

However, today I again read your letter to her and she gave me the following information. Her participation in the Tournament of Roses should have been one of the happiest experiences in her life, but, unfortunately, it was one of her saddest days, owing to the fact that her beloved brother, Jack Pickford, was desperately ill and fighting for his life at the very moment. Although her heart was breaking, Mary was waving and smiling to the millions of people.

Her motivation for accepting the role was a complete dedication to California and its people. She was happy to be part of this important annual pageantry of beauty.

1933

During the 1933 Tournament Parade, Mary Pickford, "America's Sweetheart," rode in a coach drawn by four white horses with reins and harness of white satin. The famous film star was garbed in white, and, with the floral decorations predominantly of the same hue, presented an unforgettable picture at the head of the parade as grand marshal.

Miss Pickford was the first woman ever to be Tournament grand marshal, and she was the first Hollywood figure to accept the parade's most honored role. People swarmed into Pasadena to see her in person.

But the hundreds of thousands of people who waved with gestures of love to their "Sweetheart" never knew the tragedy that hid behind her smile, as Buddy Rogers revealed in his letter thirty-six years later.

The Queen of the 1933 Tournament was Dorothy Edwards of Covina, California, who resides today in Kettering, Ohio, and is the wife of Joseph A. Conlon. Miss Edwards was one of the first queens

MARY PICKFORD ACKNOWLEDGES CROWD'S GREETINGS FROM HER COACH

selected through the system that exists today, in which students in Pasadena area schools compete for the honor.

"One afternoon early in November, 1932," she recalled, "I received a notice that the dean of women at Pasadena City College wanted to see me in her office. I found twelve other bewildered girls reporting in the same office. We were all a little frightened, thinking we might have done something wrong. The dean told us that we were the thirteen girls selected as the queen's court for the Tournament of Roses — the queen still to be selected, with the other twelve to become ladies in waiting. We had been selected by a committee of faculty and student-body leaders. We were told we were to go to a luncheon a few days later at the Huntington Hotel, at which time there would be judges who would select one of us as queen.

"The luncheon day came and we had an exhausting but exciting and wonderful afternoon with all of those interesting men. We visited with them all during the delicious luncheon. We had many individual pictures taken. We walked around the pool and garden area while they made movies of each girl. Then — we sat for what seemed like hours while the judges went off by themselves to discuss the contestants and make their decision.

"Finally, Mr. McDaneld came over to us and made a wonderful warm speech telling us that he was sorry we had to wait in anxiety for so long, but it had been a very difficult decision to make and that he wished he could make all of us queens but they had decided upon Dorothy Edwards.

D. E. McDANELD AND QUEEN DOROTHY EDWARDS (LEFT)

WILLIAM MAY GARLAND GARLANDED BY PASADENA GREETERS (RIGHT)

"You can imagine the deep emotion a girl of 19 felt after hearing words like that. I was so happy, and the other twelve girls were so sweet and complimentary towards me. Covina gave me the title 'Queen Dot.' The whole area seemed to enter into the fun and excitement which I and my family were experiencing — and we were proud of our community as well as ourselves.

"One of my big thrills was when the Los Angeles Breakfast Club hosted me as their honored guest along with Johnny Weissmuller, Jackie Cooper, and Leo Carrillo. I made a newsreel with Mary Pickford at Paramount Studios in Hollywood, which was exciting, too. What a charming person she is!

"Then came New Year's Day — 'Fairyland in Flowers.' It was a beautiful day. It was such a thrill to rule over such a magnificent pageant and to ride along the parade route and see and hear my friends calling out to me from the grandstands, high buildings, etc. After several hours along the route, our float turned into Tournament Park, where I was escorted by Mr. McDaneld to a special viewing box. My parents sat behind me, and I remember so well the 'tears of joy' in their eyes as they were living this wonderful experience right along with me.

"Every New Year's Day, no matter where we are, my husband treats me like a queen all day, and I have a ringside seat in front of our color TV to view the wonderful coverage which our networks give us of the entire pageant.

"What do I believe was my gain from taking part? It made me realize what a lucky girl I really was, and it made me feel very humble, as I did not feel that I deserved such an honor. I tried to be sweet and gracious and to set a good example for many girls who had looked up to me. Secondly, it taught me that all people are just the same no matter what their title or job might be. A college girl, such as I was, is no different or no better than anyone else just because she has the title of queen. After it was all over, I became the same girl again — no change. This philosophy has remained with me."

The nation was in the throes of depression in 1933, and it took remarkable fortitude by the men of the Tournament of Roses to plan a parade under such circumstance. The result was a significant achievement, summed up in the words of a Los Angeles *Times* reporter who wrote:

"Whatever economists may think of existing conditions will be belied by the great parade, for there is no depression in the world of flowers, nor in the spirit of Pasadenans and their neighbors in other Southern California cities who have contributed entries for the dazzling pageant."

Glendale won the Sweepstakes Prize in 1933 with its float "Hansel and Gretel."

Cotton Warburton turned U.S.C.'s victory over Pittsburgh into a

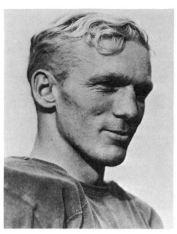

COTTON WARBURTON

35-0 runaway before 84,000 spectators who came to see the struggle between the two undefeated elevens. Weighing only 145 pounds, Warburton scored two touchdowns as Howard Jones' team wore down Jock Sutherland's men and romped for twenty-one points in the final period.

Braven Dyer wrote in the *Times:* "Nobody in his right mind will say there was that much difference between the two teams. The Panthers were beset by a series of unfortunate circumstances."

A fifty-yard pass from Homer Griffith to Ford Palmer put U.S.C. on the scoreboard in the first period. Bill Henry described the play in the *Times:* "As the ball arched high in the air, Pitt's safety man Sebastian set himself to knock it down in the end zone. Palmer came charging in from his left at top speed, and he and the ball hit Sebastian at the same time. Both players were a couple of feet off the ground. There was a brief but decisive wrestling match in mid-air. Palmer, perhaps aided by the impetus of his run, wrenched the leather away from Sebastian and lit in the end zone for the game's first score. Mr. Sebastian and the 84,000 people were surprised, and they were still gasping when Ernie Smith's suitcase-size shoe nudged the pill squarely between the posts for the first of four perfect placements for the day."

Pitt stalwarts in the game included Warren ("Heza") Heller, Charles Hartwig, Joe Skladany, and Ted Dailey. Heller was a great runner, and Skladany, the Czechoslovakian sensation at end, was in U.S.C.'s backfield constantly raising havoc.

The cotton-topped Warburton made his presence felt first defensively before he broke loose offensively. He stopped Pitt runner Weisenbaugh in a last-man save after the Pitt bruiser had gained 32 yards. This stop signaled the end of Pitt's chances.

Fumbles were costly to Pitt after that. The Panthers tried to rip Warburton's shirt off in an attempt to stop him, but the little speedster was too much as he carried the ball twenty-two times for eighty-seven yards.

15
The Great Flood

LOU LITTLE

1934

WHEN TOURNAMENT PRESIDENT George S. Parker invited top naval officer Admiral William Sims to be grand marshal in 1934, he demonstrated foresight. The parade theme was "Tales of the Seven Seas." How appropriate to have a admiral present with a "wet" parade theme! The rainstorm that fell during the forty-eight hours before the parade will never be forgotten. Twelve inches of water fell on Pasadena. The Rose Bowl field was flooded and scores of homes were washed away. The Pasadena Fire Department worked feverishly with pumps to get the water off the field, and only 35,000 fans braved the elements to be present when Columbia defeated Stanford 7-0.

Admiral Sims nearly missed the parade. He was guest of honor at dinner on the Navy flagship, U.S.S. *Pennsylvania,* on New Year's Eve and the storm was so violent that orders were given for him to remain on board. The Admiral demanded to be transported ashore. "I'm going to lead the parade if I have to swim every inch of the way, and my fleet will be in good formation even if every ship is floating."

Only nine times in the eighty-one-year history of the Tournament has rain interfered. The scorecard of moisture reads as follows: 1895, rain for a week before the parade; 1899, drizzle; 1906, rain at start of parade only; 1910, rain stops at noon; 1916, rain at game time; 1922, rain during game; 1934, a flood; 1937, a downpour the evening before the parade caused alarm but did not interfere with the parade; 1955, heavy rain during the game.

The fact that prohibition had just been thrown out by the voters, together with the parade's "Seven Seas" theme, prompted William Dunkerley, executive secretary of the Tournament, to quip: "Pasadena just went wet for the first time in history. It adopted Seven Seas as a parade theme, then turned the keys of the City over to all admirals of the fleet, and then, just to make the admirals feel at home, nature sent a flood on which to float the floats."

In addition to Sims, there were sixteen other ranking naval officers present. President and Mrs. Herbert Hoover also were there. Spurning an umbrella provided for him in the reviewing stand, the ex-President sat in a green slicker, rain dripping from his hat, as the floats sloshed

96

down the parade route. Four bands failed to show. Some bands rode in buses. The popular song played was "It Ain't Gonna Rain No More."

The 1934 Tournament also is historic because of a parade ruling making it compulsory for all horse entrants to have silver-mounted trappings. In addition, the riders were obligated to outfit themselves in Spanish costumes. These restrictions improved the general appearance of the equestrian divisions which annually are a feature of the parade.

Long Beach won the 1934 Sweepstakes award with its float "The White Swan," the giant swan constructed out of white carnations. Treva Scott was queen. Appropriately, the Long Beach float represented that city as "Queen of the Beaches." Girls riding aboard were garbed as mermaids.

The football game presented Stanford's "Vow Boys" coached by Claude E. ("Tiny") Thornhill against Lou Little's Columbia eleven. The Stanford team got the name "Vow Boys" when as freshmen the gridders vowed they would never lose to U.S.C., a vow they kept even though it took them three years as a unit to win a Rose Bowl game. In those three years, they had three tries at it. This team had Bob ("Horse") Reynolds, who played every minute of three Rose Bowl games, Bobby Grayson, who carried 152 yards against Columbia, great ends Monk Moscrip and Keith Topping, and right guard Bill Corbus, quarterback Frank Alustiza, and blocking back Bones Hamilton.

The major failing of this great three-year machine was its inability to field its full strength with any regularity. Often it played at 50 per cent of efficiency.

Damon Runyon, the accepted authority among eastern sports

ADMIRAL SIMS
GREETS TREVA SCOTT

LONG BEACH WINS 1934 PARADE AWARD
WITH WHITE SWAN CREATION

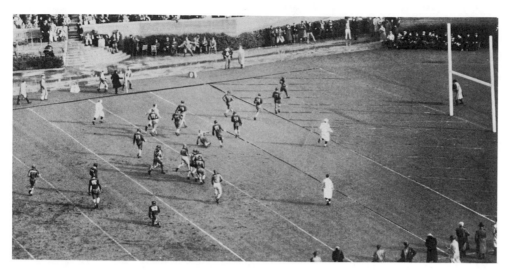

UNTOUCHED, AL BARABAS
OF COLUMBIA SCORES
ON KF79

writers, had ballyhooed Columbia, a team with a 7-1 record, over Stanford, 8-1-1. Stanford made him look good by fumbling eight times.

Columbia won the game in the second quarter on a skillfully executed hidden-ball play in which everybody but the Stanford waterboy made a dive for quarterback Cliff Montgomery while Al Barabas, like a sneak thief at night, slipped unseen around the Indians' right end for seventeen yards and the game's only touchdown. It was a play that moved Jack James, Los Angeles sports writer, to quote the Book of John, "Now Barabbas was a robber." The Columbia team lined up in single-wing formation strong to the right with an unbalanced line. Montgomery was directly back of center, with Barabas to his right. Cliff received the ball from center and midway in a spin handed it to Barabas. Then he completed his spin, pretended to hand the ball to Brominski, the Columbia right halfback, and then headed for the hole between the Stanford left tackle and left end. These two gentlemen, not daring to take a chance on Montgomery's not having the ball (which he pretended to have tucked deep under his chest), stayed where they were to check Montgomery.

Meanwhile, Brominski, also pretending to have the ball, charged over the Stanford right tackle. The purpose of this decoy was to pull Keith Topping in after Brominski, and the Stanford right end, a sophomore, fell for it. Bones Hamilton, the Stanford right half, also charged in after Brominski but was blocked out.

All this time, Barabas held his hands on his hips and gave an imitation of a man who did not have the football in his "pocket." He moved to his left far to the outside. Maxwell Stiles wrote, "When he reached the 15-yard line he stopped to chat with the little old lady who was selling red apples." Barabas had time to breeze laughingly over the goal line untouched and undetected. Newell Wilder converted and Columbia won 7-0. Stanford had chances, but always something happened, like a fumble or muffed play.

Bob Foote, writing in the Pasadena *Star-News,* credited Herb Kopf,

Little's assistant, for the victory. "The Lions knew they could win because Kopf was present," wrote Foote. "Kopf had helped pull the same trick when he was on the Washington and Jefferson team that tied California here 12 years ago. The very presence of Kopf with the Columbia bunch as a living reminder of what could be done was invaluable."

1935

Harold Lloyd, the movie comedian, was the grand marshal in 1935. Lloyd was no stranger to the parade. Each year he had pursued his hobby of photographing the various floats. This time the photographers of the world photographed him.

The person with the most unforgettable memories of the 1935 Tournament, however, was Queen Muriel Cowan, now Muriel Cowan Moore of Chino, California.

"I can still inhale the fragrance of the roses," declared Mrs. Moore. "One of my fond memories is receiving a letter from two boys in Shanghai. It seemed almost unbelievable that people so far away could hear about our parade. At the game I recall Dixie Howell of Alabama thumbing his nose at the Stanford team as he ran down the field for a touchdown. In the front portion of our float were several round balls of chrysanthemums about six to eight inches in diameter. These were hung from wires that came up like a fountain and they bounced like crazy as we went down the street. Eventually, much to our dismay, two of them bounced merrily down the street."

Muriel had an interesting experience when selected queen that illustrates the "thrills and spills" in queen competition.

"I was informed I was queen before the others," she said. "They wanted to make the pictures of the selection real. Unfortunately, one of the photographers was the boyfriend of one of the princesses. I had been cautioned not to reveal any information. The photographer's princess gave us the third degree. When it came my turn to deny what I knew, and when it came my turn to cross my heart that it wasn't me, I pretended confusion as to which was my right hand and she passed me by."

HAROLD LLOYD, MURIEL COWAN, AND C. ELMER ANDERSON

Miss Cowan may have been the only queen candidate in Tournament history to be selected while wearing a baggy skirt, a sweater, roll-over wool socks, and tennis shoes.

"The twenty-seven princesses were notified that we would be judged when we returned to school from our Thanksgiving vacation. We were told to wear dressy clothes and high heels. I got the day of judging mixed up and appeared in my old clothes. I was a standout. Maybe that's why I won," grins Mrs. Moore today.

The 1935 president was C. Elmer Anderson, who served two years. The 1935 Sweepstakes winner was Santa Barbara's "The Jay and The Peacock," a floral depiction of seven peacocks which turned from side to side. Seven men inside the sixty-five-foot-long float manipulated the moving birds and were in continual communication by built-in telephones.

The year made Tournament history because it marked the addition of commercial floats to the parade, although Tournament officials made certain there would be "no advertising."

Sports writer Mark Kelly told the story of the 1935 game, in which Alabama defeated Stanford's "Vow Boys," when he wrote: "Open that page once more in the Book of Football Revelation and add under the names of Dorais to Rockne, Wyman to Baston, and Friedman to Oosterbaan, those of Howell to Hutson. The latter should top the list of two-man combinations in football to make history."

Grantland Rice wrote: "Dixie Howell, the human howitzer from Hartford, Alabama, blasted the Rose Bowl dreams of Stanford with one of the greatest all-around exhibitions that football has ever known. The slender stripling, weighing 161 pounds, led a passing, kicking, and running attack that beat a big game Stanford team, 29-13, as 85,000 sat beneath a blue California sky and saw the sunny atmosphere full of flying footballs thrown from Howell's rifle-shot hand into Don Hutson's waiting arms."

DON HUTSON, PHYLLIS BROOKS, AND DIXIE HOWELL POSE FOR PUBLICITY

Howard Jones said the passing was the best he had ever seen.

Writer Kelly added: "Then like arrows from Robin Hood's trusty bow, there shot from Howell's unerring hand a stream of passes the like of which have never been seen in football on the Coast. Zing, zing, zing! They whizzed through the air and found their mark in the massive paws of Hutson and Bryant, Bama ends."

Howell completed nine of twelve passes for 160 yards, and he punted six times for an average of 44.8 yards. Hutson caught six of eight passes thrown to him for 164 yards and two touchdowns, little Joe Riley sharing some of the passing with Howell.

Bobby Grayson blasted for Stanford's opening 7-0 lead, after a recovery of an Alabama fumble by ball-hawking Keith Topping set up the score. Monk Moscrip kicked goal.

Dixie then started his passing show to set up his five-yard scoring bolt through the middle which ended in a startling somersault into the end zone. Riley Smith's conversion miss left the score 7-6 Stanford. Howell's passes led to a twenty-two-yard field goal by Riley Smith that put Alabama ahead 9-7. Howell ran sixty-seven yards for a touchdown, the play that produced the gesture the queen mentioned as being memorable. After this run, Smith's kick made it 16-7. Riley, who replaced the tired Howell, beat the halftime gun with a fifty-four-yard aerial shot to Hutson for a touchdown. Hutson's extra-point try failed.

Stanford opened the third quarter with a drive that was climaxed with a twelve-yard end run for the touchdown by Van Dellen. Moscrip missed the extra point, to leave the score 22-13. An interception ruined another Stanford drive, a turn of events that ignited another Howell-to-Hutson bomb that left the final score 29-13 after Smith kicked the point.

FRANK THOMAS,
ALABAMA COACH

16
Yippee!
Texas Invades

LEO CARRILLO

1936

THE TOURNAMENT of 1936 will go down in history as the beginning of the Rose Bowl sellout era that still exists. The credit for the greatest boom in ticket sales the Rose Bowl had experienced must be accorded the state of Texas. More than 200,000 requests for tickets to the Stanford-Southern Methodist game were turned down when the 84,784 seats in the Bowl were gobbled up by an invasion of excited Texas folk who made the Pasadena trip a crusade. Pasadena hospitality was extended to the point that Texas Governor James V. Allred was invited to be grand marshal. Ex-President Herbert Hoover was among the dignitaries who came for the big game.

The Stanford "Vow Boys" finally won a Rose Bowl game, 7-0, over the Mustangs from Texas who came in with a 12-0 season record only to fizzle out. S.M.U. had been a Southland favorite ever since Coach Matty Bell's team, led by All-American halfback Bobby Wilson and his cheer-leading sweetheart Betty Bailey, put on a show in a midseason 21-0 triumph over U.C.L.A. Then the Mustangs defeated T.C.U. in Fort Worth 20-14 to qualify for the Rose Bowl trip, the big play that beat Sammy Baugh and his teammates being a sensational catch by Wilson of a Bob Finley pass. Stanford was forced by public demand to invite Southern Methodist to be its opponent in Pasadena, January 1.

Keith Topping played a tremendous defensive game at end for Stanford. Backfield men Bill Paulman, Bobby Grayson, and Bones Hamilton were more than a match for S.M.U.'s Wilson. The Vow Boys, twice beaten in Pasadena, made another vow — never to lose another Rose Bowl game. They made good, finally.

The game was generally described as drab, but Pete Bruneau in the Los Angeles *Daily News* wrote a pert story. He nominated Stanford's Topping as "an honorary member of the S.M.U. backfield." Dick Hyland decreed the game wasn't an upset — "Stanford for once played 60 minutes like it always was capable of playing." Braven Dyer wrote: "I doubt if anybody ever saw greater end play than Keith Topping or Monk Moscrip revealed. It is questionable if there is a better tackle in the country than Bob Reynolds was this day. And if any center ever

BARBARA NICHOLS

NANCY BUMPUS

CHERYL WALKER

hit harder and more consistently than Wes Muller, he must have been arrested for mayhem." Bob Cronin in the *Daily News* said, "Coach Tiny Thornhill must have equipped Topping and Moscrip with kangaroo springs."

A quick kick by Stanford's Bill Paulman traveled sixty-two-yards to the Mustang 10. After S.M.U. punted back, Stanford moved in. Paulman plowed for the score, and Moscrip kicked goal. That was the first quarter, and that was the game.

South Pasadena produced the Sweepstakes winner in the parade with its float "Louis and Marie Antoinette."

Barbara Nichols was the queen. She is Mrs. William Field of Rolling Hills, California, today and has six children.

1937

A rainstorm struck the night before the 1937 Tournament, the downpour tearing open the roof of a huge tent where the floats were housed and being decorated. The faithful workers refused to stop their decorating, however, and the parade, which had a theme, "Romance in Flowers," went off on schedule. The parade was shortened this year with the accent on making the presentations more beautiful than ever. Santa Barbara responded with a stunning creation called "Omar Khayyam," presenting a Persian garden in violent colors. The huge throngs along the parade route gasped at the spectacular presentation, which won the Sweepstakes award.

Equestrians returned as grand marshals during the 1937 regime of Tournament president Cyril Bennett and the 1938 regime of president George S. Campbell. California's beloved native son and noted law officer, Sheriff Eugene Biscailuz, was the grand marshal in 1937. The year following, Leo Carrillo, familiar movie figure, descendant of one of the early Spanish California families, and expert horseman, consented to serve. He had ridden in the parade for some time and his appearance was to be a parade feature for years to come.

SOUTH PASADENA'S 1936 FLOAT WINNER

STANFORD'S VOW BOYS: BONES HAMILTON, BILL PAULMAN, BOBBY GRAYSON, JIMMY COFFIS

MATTY BELL

BOBBY LA RUE ELUDES WASHINGTON TACKLER

BOB REYNOLDS, WHO PLAYED
IN THREE BOWL GAMES

MARSHALL GOLDBERG ON THE LOOSE FOR PITT

DON HENSLEY INTERCEPTS
FOR PITT

WALTER MERRILL (48) CLEARS 'EM
OUT FOR ALABAMA

J. V. ALLRED

EUGENE BISCAILUZ

CYRIL BENNETT

Queen was Nancy Bumpus, who today is Mrs. John W. Johnson of Show Low, Arizona, where Nancy runs a real-estate business and her husband an insurance agency.

Andy Castle, a parade judge in 1936, came back "from the dead" during the 1937 parade. Castle suffered a heart attack while seated in the distinguished-guest section of the stands as the parade started. Grand marshal Bicailuz, upon hearing the news that Andy was feared dead, a report broadcast over the radio, ordered a sheriff's motorcycle escort to rush his friend Castle to Hollywood Presbyterian Hospital. Castle was treated at the hospital, where he recovered from the heart attack. "My wife had heard over the radio that I passed away," said Castle, who celebrated his eightieth birthday in 1971. "I believe I am the only person to truly come back from the dead during a Tournament of Roses parade."

The San Gabriel Mountains back of Pasadena had been snow-sprinkled the day before the 1937 parade to provide a most striking setting for the festivities.

Pittsburgh and Washington had identical 7-1-1 records going into the 1937 game, but Pittsburgh was unpopular because of previous defeats in Pasadena. Stung by criticism, the Panthers of Dr. Sutherland, who had worked hard in San Bernardino for two weeks to get ready, walloped the Huskies 21-0.

Straight power, featuring Bobby LaRue, Frank Patrick, and Marshall Goldberg as runners, and blockers Michelosen, Daddio, Matisi, Glassford, Hensley, Daniell, Hoffman, and Chickerneo, proved too much for the Huskies. LaRue wound up with 199 yards for fifteen carries, as Patrick scored twice and Bill Daddio once.

1938

The 1938 Tournament will go down in history for producing Alabama's first Rose Bowl defeat after four previous conquering invasions. California, coached by Leonard B. ("Stub") Allison, blanked the Crimson Tide 13-0.

The 1938 Tournament also is known for opening the door of movie fame to Queen Cheryl Walker, who signed a contract with Paramount the day after the parade and starred in the popular film *Stage Door Canteen* three years later. Cheryl is Mrs. Tway Walter Andrews today and lives in Alhambra, California.

"I was impressed with the reaction of P.C.C. students the day after the newspapers announced my selection as Rose Queen," recalled Mrs. Andrews. "They would stare or look over their shoulders while passing in the corridors. When entering a classroom all would stand and applaud. I thought, 'This for me?' I was just a modest kid and quite overwhelmed with the attention. I believe my most interesting experience was riding the Queen's float on New Year's Day. The response, warmth, and enthusiasm of the thousands of people lining the streets was most impressive. Never at any time during the campus

FIRST BIG FLOAT, SANTA BARBARA, 1936

WILL ROGERS FLOAT

GEORGE S. CAMPBELL

eliminations to select the queen did I feel I would be chosen. Even when the judges arrived at my home to inform my mother, I could not believe it. As a result of the publicity, I received my film opportunity. I never ceased to be amazed, after all these years, how people still remember that I was the 1938 Rose Queen."

The Burbank city schools won the Sweepstakes float award in the parade with a "Playland Fantasies" theme.

Vic Botari scored both of California's touchdowns in the second and third quarters of the football game. Sam Chapman, who became a major league baseball star, kicked one extra point.

Allison found Botari among the campus scrubs and, when he was moved up to the varsity, victories started coming. Chapman was the team's blocking specialist. The quarterback was John ("Jelly Belly") Meek, who was neither jelly-bellied nor meek. He not only was a great blocker like Chapman, but also backed up the line alongside 215-pound Bob Herwig, who was a better center in the Rose Bowl than the great Mel Hein of an earlier Washington State team the day they played. Herwig became a war hero, even surviving a Japanese sniper's bullet that made a hole in his helmet. Other great California players that day were Vard Stockton, Dave Anderson, and Perry Schwartz.

Mrs. Bob Herwig wrote a game story for the Oakland *Tribune* and Los Angeles *Examiner*. She told how nervous the players were before the game: "The poor kids had all the symptoms of a man about to walk the last mile to the electric chair — mouth dry, dripping perspiration, stomach empty, legs tired." Under the pen name Kathleen Winsor, Mrs. Herwig wrote another famed piece of literature, the book *Forever Amber*.

Mark Hellinger of the *Examiner* wrote: "Alabama had a pass and prayer. California has a pass and power."

Grantland Rice blamed Alabama's troubles on four fumbles, all of which California recovered. Coach Frank Thomas said, "This California team was tough. That Bottari — oooohhhh."

Jack James in the *Examiner* refused to go along with claims this California winner was "The Second Wonder Team." James more correctly described the Bears as "The Businesslike Team," which played the game without fussing around.

17

The Second Leishman

LATHROP LEISHMAN

1939

LATHROP K. LEISHMAN lost out in a bid for presidency of the United States Junior Chamber of Commerce.

"I figured I wasn't a big-time boy. So I decided to stick with being a home-town boy," he said.

"Lay," as he's known to his friends in Pasadena and throughout the United States, was destined to become an active Tournament man from the day he peeked through the keyhole and listened to his father, William L. Leishman, and companions plan a "Yale Bowl" for Pasadena.

Lay became Tournament president for the 1939 festival, the 50th Anniversary of the world's premier New Year's Day classic.

"I decided there was no name in America as big as Shirley Temple, the child movie star," said Lay, who was president at the young age of thirty-five. "So I decided she should be our grand marshal — if we could get her."

Leishman visited the Temple family at the film studio to ask them to accept the invitation.

"It was a big moment when her parents said, 'yes'," Leishman recalled. "Their main concern was her security. They wanted to be certain that she would be safe."

Leishman secured the promise of Sheriff Eugene Biscailuz to provide a sheriff's posse that would surround Shirley's float. A secondary major protective step was taken. A large plastic bubble to protect against inclement weather was constructed over the spot on the float where Shirley was to ride, but it wasn't needed.

When Shirley first heard from her parents that she could be the grand marshal, the child star beamed with complete Shirley Temple charm.

"Oh goodie!" she said. "Will I get to wear a badge?"

"You bet you will," said Leishman. Bill Dunkerley, manager of the Tournament, had a giant badge more than a foot long specially made for the young film star.

"Shirley liked it when she heard the siren when we took her to

LATHROP LEISHMAN
GIVES SHIRLEY TEMPLE
HER BADGE

the Tournament luncheon," said Lay. "After the parade, she asked me to have the policemen blow the siren."

Miss Temple was loudly cheered during the parade, and she smiled back with typical sweetness.

When Culver City's "Wizard of Oz" float passed, Shirley said, "Look, Mother, it seems like fairyland."

After the parade was over, Shirley commented, "I liked everything and everybody. Riding in the parade was the greatest thing I've ever done."

"The Temples were most cooperative people in every way," said Lay. "Shirley didn't go to the football game, but she was a true grand marshal of distinction in every way during her visit to Pasadena."

Leishman, who is active to this day in Tournament affairs as chairman of the Football Committee, which conducts the Tournament's duties in administration of the Rose Bowl Game and maintains all relationships with the collegiate world, looks back with satisfaction at Miss Temple's role during his term as president.

Leishman's imagination and promotional skill, as demonstrated in his selection of the only child ever to serve as Tournament grand marshal, has often been demonstrated in his thirty years of Tournament service. Leishman has been a dominant force in preserving harmonious relationship between the colleges and the Tournament. He also has planned and negotiated improvements in the Rose Bowl.

"My gain from more than thirty years of active work in the Tournament has been (1) being part of a successful venture, (2) working with great people in the Tournament, (3) knowing great people in

BARBARA DOUGALL

110

THE QUEEN'S COURT, 1969: (LEFT TO RIGHT) JANICE YOWE, VIRGINIA WALTER, CAROL LONDON, QUEEN PAMELA ANICICH, NANCY HENNO, JANICE FULLER, SYLVIA PEEBLES

THE QUEEN'S COURT, 1970: DEBORAH CARROLL, REBECCA GONZALES, VICKI TSUJIMOTO, QUEEN PAMELA TEDESCO, DIXIE WHATLEY, CHRISTINA NURCHES, PATRICE HIGHTOWER

CHIEF EAGLE FRIEND RIDING HIS HORSE, THE WHEEL

TWO 1970 PRIZE-WINNING FLOATS: "GEORGIAN HOLIDAY," WHICH WON THE NATIONAL TROPHY FOR GEORGIA (ABOVE); AND "HOLIDAY IN MEXICO," WINNER OF THE AMBASSADOR'S AWARD FOR THE REPUBLIC OF MEXICO (BELOW)

TWO BANK OF AMERICA FLOATS: "GREAT DAYS IN AMERICA," 1970 (ABOVE); AND "WHEN I GROW UP," 1971 (BELOW)

(ABOVE) CITY OF LOS ANGELES' 1970 FLOAT,
"FESTIVAL OF THE FLOWERS," SWEEPSTAKES
WINNER; AND (BELOW) UNION OIL'S 1970 EN-
TRY, "INDONESIAN HOLIDAY"

JAY JACKSON (ABOVE), WHO HAS SEEN A ROSE
BOWL GAME FOR EVERY YEAR HE HAS LIVED;
BELLE STARR (RIGHT), EQUESTRIAN MARSHAL

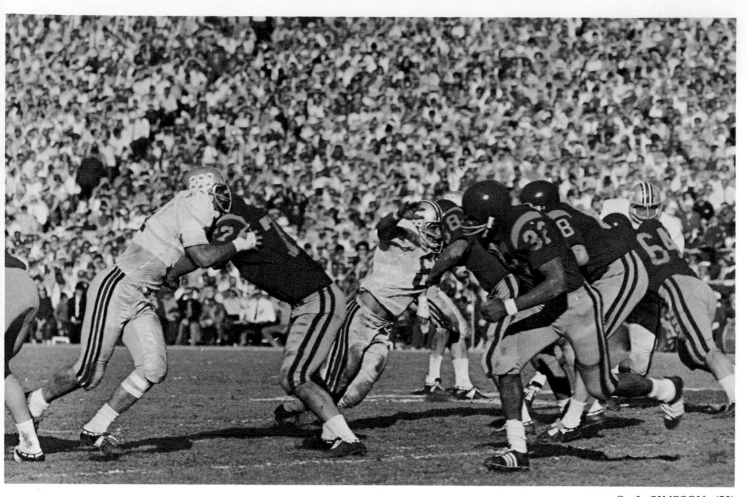

O. J. SIMPSON (32)

JOE HENDRICKSON AND O. J.

IN 1970, GUNN (83) OF U.S.C. GRABS MANDICH
OF MICHIGAN AS JENSEN BACKS UP THE PLAY
(ABOVE); U.S.C.'s JONES HANDS OFF (BELOW)

BURBANK

TALLY HO

BURBANK'S
FLOWERED COACH,
A SWEEPSTAKES
WINNER

the college ranks, and (4) having had the satisfaction of being in some real good fights and coming out with winners," stated Lay. "As a businessman I have gained an insight in collegiate sports and community cooperation that has made life fun, challenging, and exciting." The in-fighting of which Leishman spoke will be discussed in later pages, when some of the crucial moments of Rose Bowl negotiations and other crises are traced.

Harlan Loud, a lifetime associate of Leishman's in community activities, served as chairman of the Football Committee in 1939. Loud became Tournament president the next year.

"Golden Memories" was selected as the theme of the 50th Anniversary Tournament. When he announced the theme, Leishman said, "It was chosen because the development of Southern California, the progress of the West, the advances in science, music, art, and literature, as well as many other achievements of man, have been so closely linked with the Tournament of Roses throughout the past half century."

The competition for queen featured twin candidates — Laurine and Eileen Clark — but the winner was Barbara Dougall.

THE LAST SUPPER DEPICTED IN FLOWERS,
LAGUNA BEACH ENTRY, 1939

DOYLE NAVE

"When we moved to Pasadena from Pueblo, Colorado, Barbara was only one year old," recalled Mrs. William Dougall, her mother. "I remember holding her on my shoulders so she could view the parade, and I said, 'Barbara, someday you will be queen.' "

Miss Dougall is Mrs. Clifford Ward, Jr., today, and the Wards live in Altadena. Mr. Ward has served on various Tournament committees. When Barbara reigned, her crown of amber and diamond crystals was designed so it could be dismantled into three bracelets, a set of earrings, and brooches for her court.

On December 31 the first telecast of a special event from the Tournament of Roses took place when station W6XAO of Los Angeles, with Don Lee the commentator, described the New Year's Eve preparations of the royal court.

One of the most impressive floats in Tournament history was entered by artists of Laguna Beach. It portrayed "The Last Supper" in an exquisite blending of natural flowers. From the sixty-three floats in the parade, Burbank had the Sweepstakes winner. Union Oil Company stunned the audience with a float depicting Will Rogers. A riderless horse, head bowed, with a flag below, told a story of a great American.

The Golden Anniversary Tournament presented a "prologue," a special pre-parade division presented with the assistance of the Valley Hunt Club, founders of the parade fifty years earlier. As nearly as possible, mounted huntsmen with their hounds, tallyhos, surreys, and an old Pasadena Fire Department engine from 1890 formed an eye-watering treat for old-timers. Bands played music from the 1890 era. A small group of bandsmen in tight-fitting pants and waistcoats, carrying a banner which read "Pasadena Volunteers — 1888," paid tribute to the Valley Hunt Club with strains sounded through handlebar moustaches.

Maxwell Stiles was the first to tell the complete, true story of how Southern California defeated Duke 7-3 before 92,000 in the 1939 Rose Bowl game. It is one of the most amusing of football's many legends.

"The man who told me the inside story of the strange events that made it possible for Doyle Nave of U.S.C. to come off the bench, throw four passes to 'Antelope Al' Krueger that won the game, is Ensign Joe Wilensky of the U. S. Navy, former Trojan running guard and tackle and an assistant coach at U.S.C. in the 1938 season," wrote Stiles. But Wilensky did not dare tell the story until six years after the game.

The climax was set up when fullback Bobby Peoples took a short pass from quarterback Grenville Lansdell and put the ball on Duke's 34-yard line with less than two minutes left to play. Duke had gone ahead on a twenty-three-yard field goal by Tony Ruffa at the start of the final quarter.

Braven Dyer, the popular *Times* writer, was among those who had

AL KRUEGER

started for the exits to get a jump on the homeward rush when the big story unfolded. Ironically, it had been Dyer who had editorially urged Coach Howard Jones to "give my boy Doyle Nave a chance." Nave had played only twenty-eight minutes during the season while Grenville Lansdell, Mickey Anderson, and Ollie Day had alternated at quarterback. Dyer had written that Nave, too, deserved a chance to earn a letter as long as the quarterback job was such a community project.

Jones had admitted Nave could pass, but the coach insisted that young Doyle lacked the all-around skills he demanded of his quarterback.

While Nave's champion Dyer was gaining a motor escort to get to his office to write his story, Wilensky was manning the telephone on the bench, relaying the messages of assistant coaches Sam Barry, Bob McNeish, and Julie Bescos, who had been observing the action high above in the press box.

Suddenly Wilensky got an idea. He decided to take a chance to do something to pull out victory. He knew that the coaches above already had left the press box and were on their way to join the team. Nobody had scored a point all season against the great Duke line. "Our only chance is to get Nave in there to pass," thought Wilensky. "He has the arm to hit Krueger and dent this great Duke defense."

Wilensky snatched the phone.

"Yes," he shouted so everybody on the bench could hear. "Yes, yes — I get it. I'll tell him right away."

Wilensky slammed the receiver on the hook and excitedly nudged assistant coach Bill Hunter.

"The word is to send in Nave and have him throw to Krueger," said Wilensky to Hunter, who in turn passed it on to Jones. Nave didn't wait for Jones to respond. He leaped off the bench and rushed into the game. Jones did not stop him. Nick Pappas, also from the Navy, who helped Jones with the coaching and today is a member of the U.S.C. athletic administration staff, verifies that this is the true story of how Nave got into the game.

Duke played a "prevent" defense, all but one man drifting back to cover the receivers. Nave was rushed by only one man.

"Just fade back with the ball and throw it to me when I give you the sign by waving my arms, no matter where I go," Krueger, also a substitute, said to Nave.

Nave followed instructions perfectly. He faded deep on each of his four successes to Krueger. He eluded the rusher, Duke's E. L. Bailey, and waited for Krueger to jockey the great Eric ("The Red") Tipton.

The first pass gained thirteen yards to put the ball on the 26 (U.S.C. had been penalized five yards for an extra time-out when Nave went in). When Krueger was open, the throw was like a second baseman firing to first. Another strike put the ball on the 17. The next pass lost two yards. On the payoff pass, Krueger shook off Tipton with a sudden stop, then raced to the corner of the end zone where he danced up and down with his arms high in the air. Nave was back on the 31 by then, but he let fly. Krueger caught it easily for a touchdown. Phil Gaspar kicked the point with a minute remaining, and a perfect Duke season was ruined.

U.S.C. had many stars that day, including tackle Ray George, who was adjudged the best lineman on the field. However, even considering the heroics of Nave and Krueger, the lieutenant from the Navy must go down as the man who won that game with his imagination.

Dr. Norman Topping, chancellor of U.S.C., who was president of the school on New Year's Day 1939, will never forget that game.

"I was dying. They had given me up," said Topping. "They had given up on me. I was in quarantine in a hospital. No visitors, not even my wife. I had Rocky Mountain Spotted Fever, running a temperature of 105. I wasn't aware of much else, but I asked for a radio to listen to the Rose Bowl game between U.S.C. and Duke. They said it was impossible. I insisted, demanding that they grant my last request. They brought me a radio. And then when Doyle Nave threw those passes to Al Krueger to beat Duke in the final minute, something remarkable happened. A miracle. It did more for me than any medicine. My temperature immediately started going down. I recovered. I also won $50 on the game."

AL KRUEGER CATCHES DOYLE NAVE'S WINNING PASS

18
Confessions of a Queen

MARGARET HUNTLEY

DURING THE PRESIDENCY of Harlan Loud in 1940, Margaret Huntley was named Queen.

Miss Huntley, today Mrs. Robert Main of Orangevale, California, near Sacramento, is the happy mother of four children who raise quarter horses on their ranch for a hobby.

Mrs. Main's recollections of her experiences as a queen in the Tournament of Roses describe the feeling of a typical Pasadena girl who has emerged from the pack to gain sudden fame and a whirlwind trip through fantasyland.

These are Queen Huntley's words:

"It has been thirty years since I participated in Pasadena's legendary Tournament of Roses pageantry. Having lived in Pasadena from age five on, I watched the parade every New Year's Day; the Rose Queen with her glamour and beauty was the acme of my dreams. I planned to grow up and be Rose Queen, then become a movie star and make lots of money so I could become a missionary and help all the people in darkest Africa. So much for puritan Pasadena. Unfortunately for such girlhood dreams, I grew fast and tall. At age 14 I reluctantly gave up the queen dream. (I eventually became the tallest queen in decade. They came as tall or taller after me, but for years I was the giant.) The pleasant problem of boys had arrived and I decided to become a great writer, send the money to Africa, stay home myself, get married, and have four children.

"In the fall of 1939 it was still compulsory at P.C.C. to walk before the Tournament judges during your gym period, else I would never have entered the queen contest. I became more and more surprised as my name continued in the tryouts, until an experience on the Civic Auditorium stage. About fifty girls were present and we were called to the footlights in groups of seven. Suddenly I realized I was being called every time. Could this mean I was to be queen?

"As I watched the judges closely, I saw that they were watching me just as closely. Rather matter-of-factly, I accepted the idea that I was to be queen. With relative calm, I told my fiance, Bob Main, and we began to plan my school and church activities accordingly. Katherine Kester had chosen me for her student director of 'Sing Nowell' that year, and I hated to give that up. So calm was I that the night the judges were to come and notify the new queen of her selection, Bob and I went to a show.

"Although initially calm and sure of fate's hand in all of this, the thrill of being the admired center of everything eventually began to get to me. I was conscious of not having read Emily Post, of not having the right kind or enough clothes, and of not being comfortable with the new awareness that I was very, very tall. I used to watch Mrs. Harlan Loud and Mrs. Harold Hines closely to see what fork they used when Bob got Emily Post from the library, and I practically memorized it.

"I was impressed by the dedication of the Tournament members. I was impressed by the beautiful homes and the gracious people who took me into their hearts. I was impressed by the rewards a naive little girl received. Some reporters irked me. I said the next reporter who asked me to raise my skirt or pose in a bathing suit was going to get thrown out. I was impressed by the overwhelming movie contract offers. It did not matter, apparently, if I could not act. 'Just sign here honey and we'll get the world at your feet.' My girlhood dreams were coming true. But I looked into Bob's blue eyes and said 'No thanks.'

"The coronation ceremony and ball were tremendous. I felt scared and humble, yet sure of myself, as I waited for that venetian blind to open and rise. I'd memorized the entire script for the coronation, and when dear Harlan Loud forgot his lines, I raised the huge bouquet of roses to cover my lips and gave him his cues.

"The let down experience of going back to school on January 2 was difficult and led me to establish the Queen's Club to help future girls over that particular hump.

"In my queen fan mail lies the story I most frequently recollect. A small regiment of French soldiers sent me a long letter and a picture of about forty of them holding my colored newspaper picture. They asked me to be their 'Marianne.' We wrote several times back and forth. I sent each of them a small picture of their American 'sister.' They went twenty-two miles to find a typewriter with which to type their letters to me. Then Hitler crossed the Maginot Line and I never heard from my French pals again.

"What motivated me to accept the role as queen? It never occurred to me to refuse. What was my gain? Achieving some healthy realism for my idealistic young self . . . from the moment Dodge offered me a blue convertible to pose in a bathing suit, I realized a face and a body were gifts and a fact of life, so what else was new? There was also a brain, which was more challenging to be developed because it could not be seen."

19
The Age of Negotiation

CHARLIE McCARTHY AND
EDGAR BERGEN

HARLAN LOUD may have forgotten his lines during the 1940 Tournament coronation, but he never forgot how to cooperate and negotiate with university administrative and athletic authorities. Neither did men like Leishman, C. Hal Reynolds, John Biggar, Louis R. Vincenti, and others in the Tournament family.

It was this "Tournament Plan" for understanding collegiate problems and collegiate people, while at the same time helping the academic colony to see the festival's point of view, that brought the marriage between campus and community which assured a healthy relationship and successful New Year's Day football promotion.

The Tournament of Roses never has assumed that the colleges must play in Pasadena's nationally famous game. There were days when the colleges, at least many of them, didn't think they should get involved in post-season football games on grounds of commercialization and overemphasis.

It was at the meetings of the NCAA, the national governing body for college athletics, and at various conference meetings of Pacific Coast schools, that Pasadena people laid the groundwork for present amiable relations. Understanding and respect grew during those days of mutual faith-building between Pasadenans Leishman, Loud, Reynolds, Vincenti, Biggar, Nicholas, Hahn, Dorn, and college leaders like Hugh Willett, Wilbur Johns, Bill Hunter, Al Masters, Bill Ackerman, Vic O. Schmidt, L. W. St. John, Kenneth L. ("Tug") Wilson, and on to the modern groups which include collegiate leaders like Bill Reed, Tom Hamilton, Walter Byers, J. D. Morgan, Jess Hill, among many others.

These meetings determined how promoter and participant would "cut up the pie" and keep the "table" crumb-free so that Bowl football participation would prosper equally amid campus regulations and community ambitions.

Loud looks back at several highlights of his active days of Tournament leadership, including his presidency in 1940, with a feeling that the opportunity to know prominent athletic people and faculty

MR. AND MRS. HARLAN LOUD WEAR
BROAD SMILES IN PARADE

men better was one of his biggest rewards. He also lists high in his gains friendships with Tournament faithfuls like Leishman, Colwell, and others. Loud still has a blanket he received from Ted Payseur, then athletic director at Northwestern, one of his most honored tokens of friendship between Tournament and university. While serving on the Tournament Football Committee in 1938 and again from 1942 to 1950, Loud attended many conference and NCAA meetings with Leishman and others, at which decisions were formulated that established the pattern of today's Bowl-campus relationships.

1940

More than half the world was at war when the 1940 Tournament was staged. The theme of that Tournament was "20th Century in Flowers," which depicted peace, progress, and love of nature. Emphasized in the parade were such projects as Boulder Dam, progress in transportation and in the air, art and literature as represented by the Huntington Library, and astronomy, represented by the Mt. Wilson Observatory. Santa Barbara won the Sweepstakes with a scene in

CHARLIE WHISPERS TO MARGARET
HUNTLEY AS BERGEN LISTENS

AFRICA COMES TO THE PASADENA PARADE VIA EL MONTE

flowers of three modern racing sloops rounding a weather marker.

Charlie McCarthy was in his heyday as a headliner of the airways, so Loud invited Edgar Bergen and his famed dummy to serve as grand marshals. Charlie snapped back many a "Hi" to his thousands of admirers along the parade route; he never had a bigger smile. Charlie was so tired when the day was over, Bergen reported, that he was placed in a trunk and didn't move for days.

Malicious, one of the most popular horses ever to run at nearby Santa Anita race track, walked the length of the parade with special shoes protecting his tender racing hoofs. The horse, famed for his great stretch runs, drew thunderous applause.

Tennessee, with twenty-three straight victories, was the obvious eastern representative in the 1940 game, U.S.C. and U.C.L.A. played to a tie in their final game, but U.S.C. won the vote of the Pacific Conference, which had contracted, during the early negotiations and meetings mentioned previously, to have one of its member teams appear annually in the Rose Bowl.

U.S.C.'s 14-0 triumph over Tennessee marked Howard Jones' fifth victory in the Rose Bowl — and his last. Before he could produce another great team, he passed on.

"With his passing, there ended an era of football in the West," wrote Maxwell Stiles. "No man ever brought so much gridiron glory to the southern section of California. No man ever gave more of himself to the game he loved. To him, football was the first bright rays of dawn, the noonday sky, and the stars that shine by night. To him, football was a creed and he kept it clean and pure. Good sportsmanship and perfect execution of assignments on the field of play were

BOB NEYLAND

AMBROSE SCHINDLER

sacred, and woe to any player on his team who failed to measure up to the fullest degree by either standard."

Major Bob Neyland's Tennessee team brought to Pasadena such proven greats as All-American guards Ed Molinsky and Bob Suffridge, All-American quarterback George Cafego, and All-American halfback Bobby Foxx.

However, Jones faced them with guards Harry Smith and Ben Sohn, who outplayed the Tennessee pair; tailback Granny Lansdell and Ambrose Schindler, who outplayed the injured Cafego; blocking backs Joe Shell and Bob Hoffman, who outplayed Foxx; best ends of the day Bill Fisk and Bob Winslow, top tackles Stoecker and Gaspar, and an excellent center in Ed Dempsey.

By playing almost perfect football, Jones' team scored the first points Tennessee had yielded in a 10-0 season and ended a Vol streak that extended beyond the previous year. Major Neyland told Bob Hunter of the *Examiner,* "We were badly beaten by a superior team."

Cafego had a bad knee and carried only six times for 8 yards. His replacement, Johnny Butler, troubled U.S.C. considerably, but nobody was going to do too well, as Cafego explained it to Hunter. "I couldn't have done any good against those big guys anyway," said Cafego.

The whimsical Henry McLemore of the United Press summed up the hopelessness of Tennessee's case with these words: "They raise them rugged out here. Perhaps nature sees that they do so in order that they will be able to withstand earthquakes, unusual weather, and the taste of the water that comes out of the taps. There is a lesson to be learned from this Rose Bowl game. There is no sense in betting on a team that buys its clothes in the boys' department to beat a team that has to shave twice a day and is fitted for suits in the adult or grown-up section."

Ned Cronin of the *News* wrote that Schindler ran with his knees clear up around his chin. Dick Hyland in the *Times* called the Vol line a sieve. Shell's blocking for U.S.C. drew heavy praise in the press.

After getting to the 22 of the Vols early, only to be thwarted when Lansdell slipped on fourth down, Schindler started ripping and carrying tacklers in a manner that brought him the tag of "Desperate Amby." Schindler bowled over Suffridge for the touchdown and Jimmy Jones, later killed in the war, kicked the point.

Tennessee retaliated in the fourth quarter, but Bartholomew fumbled on U.S.C.'s 15, where Engle recovered for the winners. Sub halfback Engle caught a key pass, and Schindler passed to Al Krueger of Nave-to-Krueger fame for the touchdown. Gaspar kicked goal.

120

20

"T" Is Served in the Bowl

CLARK SHAUGHNESSY

1941

WHILE A YOUNG DRIVER of a float in the 1941 parade will always remember that year as the occasion he "discovered" his wife-to-be, it also will go down in history that Clark Shaughnessy of Stanford "sold" the T-formation to the football fans of the country during a stunning 21-13 victory his Stanford magicians scored over Nebraska.

Charles ("Chuck") Rubsamen, through a driver's keyhole underneath one of the parade's magnificent floats, admired the beauty and charm of Queen Sally Stanton on the float just ahead as she received the plaudits of the spectators. Rubsamen wasted no time in getting acquainted with Queen Sally, accomplishing his first meeting fourteen days later. They became engaged, then married, and today the couple has two children. Now Chuck annually shows his gratitude for the contribution the Tournament made in his life by serving on the Queen Selection Committee.

Mrs. Rubsamen, meanwhile, has been closely associated with space-exploration projects as a math assistant at Pasadena's Jet Propulsion Laboratory, where much of America's capability for landing men on the moon was developed.

To the Rubsamens, the Pasadena Freeway is known as "Mama's Freeway," because Queen Sally cut the ribbon when this link with Los Angeles was opened.

Sally's road to victory in the 1941 Tournament Queen contest wasn't an easy one. Her name accidentally was left off the list of candidates for the final tryout, and a stern doorkeeper was going to bar her from entering until she persuaded him to let her pass. She passed so well she became the winner.

The "America in Flowers" theme brought out the patriotism of the country in float designs in the parade headed by Tournament president J. W. McCall, Jr., with Pasadena Mayor E. O. Nay serving as grand marshal.

Eleven months before Pearl Harbor was bombed, the Central Japan Association entry of "Cherry Blossom Time in Washington" proved a popular parade feature. Winner of the Theme Prize, the

121

BIFF JONES

FRANKIE ALBERT

Japanese float showed the U.S. Capitol made of thousands of white chrysanthemums, with a flag done in red and white carnations. Five American-born girls of Japanese ancestry sat under a grove of cherry trees.

The band music throughout the parade was almost entirely of patriotic nature, with the shadow of war hanging heavy, although the ASCAP dispute of 1941 prevented radio listeners from hearing it. To enable the parade to be broadcast, Tournament officials had to research music libraries for tunes old enough for their copyright to have expired. At several points along the parade where radio microphones were located, the bands switched from their regular music to older tunes acceptable to ASCAP.

Shaughnessy, before his death in 1970, rated the backfield of Frankie Albert, halfbacks Pete Kmetovic and Hugh Gallarneau, and fullback Norm Standlee one of the greatest of all time in American football history. He also rated the 1941 Rose Bowl clash among the greatest games.

Biff Jones's Nebraska team came in with a 8-1 record, but Stanford's 9-0 team served up too much "T." The skillful execution of Shaughnessy's T-formation combination of pitchouts sold this type of football to the college world. The style of play became the rage of the country.

Nebraska rolled in to go ahead 7-0 when fullback Vike Francis galloped through like a wild horse. While Stanford concentrated on stopping the reverses of Butch Luther, the Husker running star in previous games, Jones took advantage with the Francis spinner play that featured a fake to Luther and a Francis shot into the line.

Stanford revised its defense and quickly struck with a retaliatory touchdown, gained through a combination of T-formation tricks that stunned the crowd. Gallarneau scored and Albert kicked the point.

A Nebraska quick kick was lost by Kmetovic in the sun. He touched the ball and it was recovered by a substitute Nebraska halfback named Allen Zikmund on Stanford's 33. Herman Rohrig passed over Gallarneau's head to Zikmund for the touchdown, although

J. W. McCALL AND QUEEN SALLY STANTON GREET E. O. NAY

122

STANFORD'S "T" BOYS

Stanford center Lindskog blocked the try for point to leave the score 13-7 Nebraska. (Rohrig is Big Ten commissioner of officials today.)

The passing and running of Albert, the speed of Kmetovic, and finally a pass from Albert to Gallarneau, who eluded Zikmund and Rohrig, then produced a touchdown. Albert's successful placement put Stanford ahead 14-13.

There was only one touchdown in the entire second half, but that one score was the coup de grace and the greatest single play of the game. Nebraska had made a magnificent goal-line stand in the third quarter and had taken the ball on downs on the 2-inch line.

"Hippity" Hopp, standing deep in the end zone, punted. The ball was caught by Kmetovic on the Nebraska 39 near the side line. Pete took four or five steps to his left and, just as he succeeded in drawing most of the Husker team over after him, turned and cut sharply back to his right. He began to pick up blockers. Dick Palmer cut down George Knight and Francis. Francis was hit so hard he did a pinwheel somersault high into the air and was knocked cold when his head hit the turf. Chuck Taylor, athletic director today at Stanford, put a block on one of the last Huskers remaining on his feet. Kmetovic, meanwhile, swivel-hipped his way behind the crushing blocking and finally beat Luther, who made a futile dive as Pete zipped into the end zone. Shaughnessy called the punt return the greatest he had ever seen from the standpoint of complete team response.

VIKE FRANCIS

When the game was over, a convinced Jones told Al Wolf of the Los Angeles *Times*: "Go tell Clark Shaugnessy I'll buy him 120 acres of fine corn land if he'll tell me where we can get a Frankie Albert. That kid had too much pass, too much kick, too much noodle for us."

Pearl Harbor was bombed on December 7, 1941.

1942

The Pasadena Tournament of Roses parade was cancelled in the interest of public security as the nation launched into war against

DUKE STADIUM, THE ROSE
BOWL OF 1942

Japan. The country was asked to create a parade in bonds instead of flowers. This was the idea of Lee Merriman, Pasadena newspaper editor.

Then one of the most cooperative ventures in the history of any festival took place when enterprising citizens in Durham, N.C., co-operated with Pasadenans in switching the Rose Bowl game to the University on the suggestion of Wallace Wade, Duke coach, after his undefeated Blue Devils were picked to meet Oregon State, which had a 7-2 record. While the United States government "blacked out" the West Coast for security reasons, it was generally believed the Rose Bowl series should continue for the benefit of public morale.

Duke authorities increased the seating capacity of their stadium from 35,000 to 56,000 in slightly more than two weeks.

Bob Hunter, Los Angeles *Herald-Examiner* sports writer who had been on an eastern football assignment for his newspaper, served as an unofficial Pasadena representative in Durham for two weeks before the transplanted Rose Bowl game. "My paper told me to rush to Durham," said Hunter. "I attended luncheons and civic affairs, and I found myself in the position of a Pasadena ambassador. They even had me at the depot with the official welcoming committee when the real Tournament of Roses representatives arrived in Durham. I had the time of my life."

LON STINER

Maxwell Stiles wrote: "The village was dressed up for what Sid Feder of the Associated Press described, 'The Big Party.' It was like a breathing thing, symbolic of the nation's defiance of its enemies in their foul efforts to choke out the life and free ways of a stalwart and resolute American people. Initiative — that is the America we saw in the playing of this game on the far side of a continent from where it had originally been scheduled. Initiative, too, was Oregon State's amazing team that entered the stadium 4 to 1 underdogs against the finest Duke team in history. Coach Lon Stiner's Beavers had been regarded as only the best of a sorry lot of Pacific Coast Conference teams."

The score was 14-14 when the big play was executed. Oregon

ROBERT H. McCURDY

KAY KYSER

DOLORES BRUBACH

State had the ball, second down and eight to go, on its own 32-yard line late in the third quarter. Bob Dethman threw a pass forty yards downfield that Gene Gray caught on the Duke 28-yard line as Duke's Moffat Storer, a sub halfback, charged in. The Duke man dove forward and Gray went into a dance before turning for the goal line. Storer fell on his face and Gray went into the end zone. Score: 20-14.

This touchdown won the game even though Don Durdan of Oregon State was tackled later behind his goal for a safety, leaving the final score at 20-16.

Durdan, the star halfback for the Beavers, who gained only 54 yards from scrimmage compared to 129 for Duke's great All-American, Steve Lach, held the crowd spellbound with his left-handed passing and left-footed punting. Duke fans mobbed Durdan for his genius. It took Durdan half an hour to get through the crowd to his dressing room. Durdan averaged 44.4 yards for eight kicks, Lach a 47.1 yard average for the same number, both outstanding records in the rain. Why Duke fans thought Durdan's kicking was better than Lach's has not been explained, except that Durdan's team won.

Kay Kyser, the band leader, served as grand marshal of the parade that never was, and President Robert M. McCurdy had to wait a few years to ride down Colorado Boulevard.

"I stand out from all other grand marshals because I never got to lead the parade," said James K. Kyser in a letter of recollection written in 1969. "That's my story. There is nothing more to tell."

President McCurdy looked back at his experience at the helm of the Tournament with these words: "I installed the first electric scoreboard in the Rose Bowl. Otherwise, my big satisfaction remains in the fact that I am one of the lifetime directors of our fine organization."

Dolores Brubach was the queen who did not have a parade, but she eventually had the thrill of riding aboard a float sponsored by Occidental Life Insurance in 1956. Now Mrs. H. Eugene Chase, she lives in Claremont, California.

In Queen Brubach's "Victory Court," Helen Creahan was princess of the armed services, Patricia Lee princess of agriculture for defense, Clare Blackwell princess of health and welfare, Doris Burns princess of defense stamps and bonds, Patricia Wiseman princess of industry for defense, and Barbara Forbush princess of civilian defense.

It was a cold day and a sad one in Pasadena that January 1. Queen Dolores and her victory court drove quietly down Colorado Boulevard unnoticed by the few pedestrians on the deserted street. Sixteen members of the Tournament of Roses band gathered at a war memorial flagpole where Orange Grove and Colorado intersect. Led by Jack McLeod, they formed a "V for Victory" and marched down Colorado playing military songs and singing "Stout-Hearted Men."

In the dining room of the Huntington Hotel that afternoon, Queen Dolores and her court were guests of honor at a display of thirty-three miniatures of floats that would have been in the parade had one been held.

The queen of the 1942 Tournament also had this dominant memory: "I spent a few moments in an empty Rose Bowl with Don Wilson and numerous sportscasters broadcasting on a coast-to-coast hook-up at halftime, and we ended by singing 'Auld Lang Syne.' "

Bill Login of Pasadena, who has published the *Tournament of Roses Pictorial* for the past forty-three years, recalls how the game was transferred to Duke.

"President McCurdy had called a meeting at the then Vista del Arroyo Hotel when the Oregon State-Duke matchup was made," Login told Margaret Stovall of the Pasadena *Star-News*. "We were checking the lineup for the game when the Army's West Coast headquarters announced on the radio there would be no Rose Bowl game while this war was on.

"Hal Reynolds, who was at the meeting, called the general in San Francisco, and then Percy Lacey, the Oregon State manager, got on the phone. They wanted to know if they couldn't have the game for just 5,000 people. The general said no. They wanted to know if they could have it just for the press. The general said no — no game; period!

"The meeting broke up with a decision to send a delegation to San Francisco. When they came back with no satisfaction, McCurdy suggested they have the game at Duke. We had 80,000 tickets that had to be cut up and burned to keep them from scalpers. Meanwhile, they decided we could use the programs, of which we had about one-third printed. My aide, Tommy Kyser, and I lived at the shop for three days finishing the programs and cutting up the tickets. Union Pacific helped us get the programs across the country. We got them to the stadium just before the gate opened."

1943

Mildred Miller was the queen in 1943 as the blackout of Tournament parade activities continued. A resident of Chamblu, Georgia, she is now Mildred Miller Stevens. Her interests include raising Tennessee walking horses and breeding gamecocks.

James K. Ingham was the 1943 president, and Governor Earl Warren of California was named grand marshal, as the Tournament continued to elect officers and maintain its organizational format.

Though the parade was banned, the game was permitted in the Rose Bowl to focus attention on the theme "Parade of War Bonds." Communities entered a contest to win prizes by selling the most war bonds. Honolulu won the sweepstakes with a quota of $4,350,000 in bonds sold. A total of $65,887,857 was raised.

The story of the 1943 Tournament is wrapped into the life of the University of Georgia players who never doubted the theme of the restricted festival: "We're In It to Win." Maxwell Stiles told it as follows:

MILDRED MILLER

126

JAMES K. INGHAM

FRANKIE SINKWICH

"On the warm evening of August 30, 1945, there was a strange reunion of three men who two and a half years before shared the major role in the glory that goes with a Rose Bowl victory.

"The three men were "Fireball" Frankie Sinkwich, Charley Trippi, and George Poschner of the University of Georgia. On New Year's Day, 1943, these three men, with considerable help from Van and Lamarr Davis, right end and right halfback, respectively, and from Willard (Red)) Boyd, a sub tackle who blocked a punt for a safety, contributed the most to Georgia's 9-0 victory over UCLA in the first Pasadena game won by a southern team in eight years. Georgia, coached by Wallace Butts, had a 10-1 record compared to the 7-3 mark of Edwin (Babe) Horrell's U.C.L.A. team.

"Sinkwich, in and out of the game six times while nursing two sprained ankles, scored the game's only touchdown. Trippi, the sensational sophomore, was a bright Rose Bowl star. Poschner, at left end, had been a power offensively and defensively.

"On this humid night of August 30, 1945, the three 'met' again. The scene was a bed at the Lawson General Hospital in Atlanta. One young man smiled as he listened to a radio broadcast of a game being played at Soldier Field in Chicago, Green Bay vs. the College All Stars. It was a game in which Sgt. Charley Trippi played so well that 200 of the 206 newspapermen voted for him as the outstanding player of the All Star squad. It was a game when Pvt. Frankie Sinkwich received from Commissioner Elmer Layden the most valuable player trophy of the National Football League for 1944.

"As he listened, the young man on the bed fumbled for a medal that had been lying on a little table beside his radio. Attached to the medal was a ribbon with a broad blue band down its middle, edged on either side by a pin-stripe of white and a slightly wider one of red.

"This was the Distinguished Service Cross, the nation's second highest military decoration. It, too, was a newly won trophy. It had been presented on this day by Brig. Gen. William Sheep, commander of the hospital, to the man on the bed. It was presented for gallantry in action in the Battle of the Bulge. There at Kohlhutte, France, on January 8, 1945, at the end of a one-man charge, Lt. George W. Poschner lay unattended on a frozen battlefield for two days.

"Now he was in the hospital with both legs and part of his right hand gone, but with memories that were rich. With a grim grin of irony, he recalled by himself how two sprained and swollen ankles had kept Fireball Frankie Sinkwich from tearing the UCLA line apart but did not prevent him from completing three passes or from scoring the game's only touchdown. He recalled how it was the Sinkwich ankle injuries that had given Trippi the chance to make his mark.

"The young man on the bed resolved that what Sinkwich did that New Year's Day on two bad ankles, he, George Poschner, would do in the future on those mechanical legs the docs had promised soon would be his."

21
Hardy Days

A. A. STAGG

1944

THE 1944 "PARADE" was a token affair — three decorated autos, one carrying Tournament President Frank M. Brooks, one carrying Queen Naomi Riordan, and the third carrying Grand Marshal Amos Alonzo Stagg, the grand old man of American football.

Wartime travel restrictions forced the Rose Bowl game to be an all-West Coast affair in which Southern California, 7-2, coached by Jeff Cravath, defeated Washington, 4-0, coached by Ralph ("Pest") Welch. The score in the big upset was 29-0.

Cravath was accorded the distinction of bringing a team back farther from midseason failure than any coach ever to lead a team into the Rose Bowl. U.S.C. had lost to March Field 35-0, a team Washington had had beaten 27-7. Nobody believed Cravath had a chance against Welch.

Cravath, however, had a young quarterback named Jim Hardy and a captain and guard named Norm Verry. Both were "verry" good.

Against Washington in 1944, Hardy contributed the first half of a remarkable two-game exhibition of passing, punting, and signal-calling that stands out in all-time Rose Bowl annals. In that game, Hardy equaled the Russ Saunders record of passing for three touchdowns. Against Tennessee a year later, he threw passes for two more and scored one himself.

Verry, out for the regular season with leg injuries, dragged his injuries with him into the Rose Bowl and played what Cravath described as "the greatest defensive game of guard the Bowl ever saw." Helping Verry murder the Washington offense were Bill Gray, center, and John Ferraro, All-American tackle.

"You'll have to put that boy Norman Verry on the all-time Rose Bowl team someplace, somehow," wrote Rube Samuelsen, known by many as Mr. Rose Bowl, in the Pasadena *Star-News*.

Bob Hebert in the Los Angeles *Daily News* said, "Jeff Cravath's magnificent coaching job was reflected in every move of the Trojans."

Al Wolf in the Los Angeles *Times* said, "Southern Cal never again will be a Rose Bowl underdog."

128

FRANK BROOKS

NAOMI RIORDAN

MARY RUTTE

"Washington never got beyond Troy's 28," reported Bob Hunter in the Los Angeles *Examiner.*

Maxwell Stiles wrote, "Only one other guard ranks in all-time Rose Bowl class with Verry. He is John (Baby Grand) Scafide of Tulane."

Morton Moss in the *Examiner* reported Cravath's speech to the Trojans in the dressing room after the game. Cravath said. "This day will always remain as a great memory for all of you fellows. I know you have made a former coach who has passed on very happy (he referred to Howard Jones)."

Cravath revealed the following inside story to George Davis, *Herald-Express:* "The Washington coaches kept talking so much about Sam Robinson's and Al Akins' passing that I thought they were overplaying their hands to conceal the weakness that none of them was effective in that department. So, acting on this hunch, I changed our pass defense on Thursday while working out in the gymnasium from a man-to-man to a zone, and I'm certainly happy that I did."

Washington completed only five passes out of nineteen, three intercepted.

Naomi Riordan, now Mrs. Martin Carey of Darien, Conn., later made up for her lack of Tournament exposure because of the wartime curtailed activities. She became a national figure in television commercials, and acted in plays on Broadway.

1945

The 1945 Tournament marked the fourth consecutive no-parade year, because of the war, but Tournament president Max H. Turner gave a luncheon at the Huntington Hotel before the football game to honor dignitaries like former president Herbert Hoover, who was grand marshal, and Queen Mary Rutte, today Mrs. Victor Wallace of Austin, Texas.

Max Colwell's dominant memory of Hoover's visit to Pasadena is the President's thank-you to the citizens of Pasadena, who had given him the biggest majority in the polls that Hoover had received in any city in the United States. "I am deeply gratified," said Mr. Hoover.

U.S.C.'s Rose Bowl theme was "Hold a Victory So Hardy Won." Little did the selectors of that theme realize that Mr. Hardy again was to provide the passing impetus for a 25-0 U.S.C. triumph over Tennessee.

Coach Jim Barnhill's young Tennessee team came in with a 7-0-1 record compared to the 7-0-2 mark of Cravath's Trojans. Wartime-depleted rosters produced this situation during the game: at one time Tennessee had seven starting freshmen and three sophomores on the field against U.S.C. when Cravath was using two halfbacks (Blake Headley and Ben Schlegel) who had not played one minute of varsity football in their lives.

DON BURNSIDE OF U.S.C.

The game also produced the quickest touchdown in Rose Bowl history — and the latest. The Trojans scored their first touchdown 1 minute and 50 seconds after the opening kickoff when Jim Callanan scooted in with a punt blocked by John Ferraro. The Trojans scored in the last seconds of the game on a touchdown pass from Hardy to Doug MacLachlan, who had to fight off scores of youngsters already storming the field to rip down the goal posts. No Rose Bowl receiver ever caught a pass among so many bodies.

Hardy also may have been the only player ever to run directly to the dressing room while making a play. On the try for extra point, he called a running play so he could keep the football for a lifetime trophy. Once downed, he got up and ran through the tunnel before the mob could get to him.

Rube Samuelsen wrote in the Pasadena *Star-News* that Hardy's quarterbacking, in the opinion of Chick Meehan, former Syracuse mentor, was on a par with the best of Sid Luckman of the Chicago Bears.

"Hardy must be rated with the all-time Rose Bowl greats," said Al Wolf in the Los Angeles *Times*.

"Hardy played despite a stomach disorder and a temperature. He had the flu," said Gus Vignolle in the *Examiner*.

BLAKE HEADLEY OF U.S.C.
CARRIES A HOT POTATO

130

CANDY FOR HERBERT HOOVER FROM MAX TURNER (LEFT) AND MANAGER WILLIAM DUNKERLEY

Coach Jeff Cravath confided to Al Santoro, *Examiner* sports editor: "Hardy was the greatest T-formation quarterback I have ever seen in action."

Bob Hunter wrote in the *Examiner:* "This was the fifth straight Rose Bowl game in which U.S.C. kept the opposition from crossing its goal line."

Coach Jim Barnhill of Tennessee told George T. Davis of the *Herald Express:* "We were outclassed."

1945 marked the beginning of Stella Morrill's career with the Tournament. She has been the secretary to the Tournament manager since that date and today is Max Colwell's efficient "Gal Friday." Stella has seniority in years of service among all present Tournament staffers.

"Through all these years, one thing has never changed," she said. "The volunteer Tournament workers today function with the same devotion and spirit of cooperation that the volunteers had when I started. This perpetuation of attitude is something a person admires while seeing it operate day after day and year after year."

Sam Akers, Tournament publicist, summed up Stella's role in the Festival's annual success story as follows: "She is a tremendous organizer with great capacity for volume of activity. She is a great lady of dignity."

STELLA MORRILL, 1945

1946

All good things must end, and U.S.C. suffered its first defeat in nine Rose Bowl appearances in the 1946 game when Cravath's Trojans succumbed to Frank Thomas's Alabama team 34-14.

"U.S.C. was the sorriest looking eleven that ever stumbled, fumbled, and groped its way through a game in the Rose Bowl," stated Maxwell Stiles, who admitted the victory by Alabama (9-0) was not as much of a surprise as the manner in which they won over U.S.C., which had come to the game 7-3. Harry Gilmer was expected to do it with passes, but he threw only a dozen and completed just four. Alabama tore the Trojans apart. Gilmer ran for 116 yards himself.

131

TED TANNEHILL

ADMIRAL WILLIAM F. HALSEY

PATRICIA AUMAN

Troy did have some standouts, however. Ted Tannehill was a defensive demon with six tackles in the first half and more to come. Punters Jerry Bowman and Verl Lillywhite averaged 47.8 yards on six punts, three each. Ironically, Alabama averaged only 19.8 yards on four punts. Both figures were Rose Bowl records. U.S.C. had only a 6-yard net rushing, another record. Its 41 yards on total offense also was an all-time low for one team.

As if those statistics aren't startling enough, U.S.C. permitted Alabama to score more points in this one game than eight other teams combined could score against Troy in the Bowl.

Ned Cronin of the Los Angeles *Daily News* perhaps best described the trend of the game when he wrote: "The ushers were having trouble finding places in the stands for guys wearing white jerseys and red helmets who were constantly being thrown up there by the Alabamans."

The Trojans had one distinction. They had the biggest player on the field. He was 320-pound Jay Perrin in the line, one of the few Trojans to play well enough to get some praise in the papers the next day. Jack Musick and Harry Adelman also were given satisfactory grades, but Al Wolf of the *Times* pointed out nobody should have expected anything good because "The Trojans had stunk out the joint most of the season."

The football game was not the event that Californians like to remember from the 1946 Tournament.

Throughout the nation, the important news was that the war had ended. V-J Day had been proclaimed in August 1945. The 1946 parade theme, therefore, was "Victory, Unity, and Peace." Admiral William F. Halsey was the grand marshal.

With five stately "task forces" moving behind him, the stately admiral set the pattern for a parade which symbolized what he and other American fighting men had fought for and won. When asked what he thought while leading the parade, Halsey said, "I thought about all those other New Year's Days — the tough ones — that led up to this." The admiral had declined to ride a white horse offered him, claiming his equestrian prowess had been greatly overrated.

Long Beach won the Sweepstakes float award in the parade with a floral replica of the aircraft carrier "Shangri-La." The raising of the flag at Iwo Jima also was presented on a float.

The four presidents who were denied the opportunity to ride in the paradeless Tournaments — Robert M. McCurdy, James K. Ingham, Frank M. Brooks, and Max Turner — rode in decorated cars along with 1946 president Charles A. Strutt.

Equestrians were granted permission to wear western outfits.

The queen in 1946 was Patricia Auman, today Mrs. Charles Richards of Bellevue, Nebraska.

132

22
Marriage with the Big Ten

BOB HOPE

1947

THE 1921 FOOTBALL game between California and Ohio State provided the first stimulus for the modern pact between the Pacific Eight Conference and the Big Ten, today the most logical, financially soundest, and most popular agreement between two conferences that exists in the post-season collegiate gridiron world.

Howard Lucas, president of the Ohio State Alumni Association of Los Angeles, in response to the clamor from Big Ten alumni clubs to put a Big Ten team in the Rose Bowl, wired an invitation on behalf of the Tournament of Roses committee to L. W. St. John, Ohio State athletic director, asking him to send his championship 1920 football team to the Pasadena game.

St. John secured the permission of President William Oxley Thompson of Ohio State and the Buckeye faculty to place the matter before the Big Ten Conference for acceptance. After the urging of Professor Thomas E. French of Ohio State, faculty representative, the Big Ten permitted Ohio State to accept the Rose Bowl invitation.

As previously related in these pages, Ohio State lost 28-0. On June 2, 1921, official action against post-season games was taken by the Big Ten. Although many informal invitations were issued by Rose Bowl spokesmen, no Big Ten team was permitted to play in Pasadena for the next twenty-six years. Faculties in the Big Ten remained firm that the football season was long enough and should end with the completion of the regular schedule. The matter was brought up each year at Big Ten meetings, however. Major John L. Griffith, commissioner of the Big Ten, was a strong advocate of a rule change that would permit Big Ten participation in the Pasadena game — and the item was on the agenda when Kenneth L. ("Tug") Wilson became Big Ten commissioner in 1945.

Meanwhile, as the wrangling over prospective January 1 opponents increased in Pasadena, with almost everybody having his favorite nomination, the wise decision of Tournament of Roses officials to put the negotiations and administration of the Rose Bowl game into the hands of the Pacific Coast Conference and the competing schools was made preceding the 1924 game between Navy and Washington.

Although there were many crises in the early years of this arrangement, crises accentuated by internal problems and eventual break-up of the conference itself, the decision to let the colleges administer the staging of the game has long proved to be successful.

"Early Tournament presidents who possessed strong interest in Rose Bowl relationships with Pacific Coast Conference athletic leaders were Jack Mitchell, Les Henry, and C. Hal Reynolds," said Lathrop Leishman. "The year I was vice president, Reynolds told me to pick a companion and go to the Conference meeting at Monterey and do all I could to tell them about us and learn more understanding of them. Harlan Loud was my companion. To this day, I have been going to Conference meetings and NCAA meetings. The spirit of cooperation that exists between our people and their people is one of the richest rewards of being a Tournament of Roses football committeeman."

Through all negotiations for years, Lou Vincenti "was a good thinker and planner," said Leishman in stating that Vincenti, representing the Tournament, and Ralph Aigler, Michigan faculty man, "hit it off" during the early negotiations with the Big Ten.

Leishman remembered Bill Hunter, Al Masters, and St. John as three of the negotiators who "wielded the big stick" in the negotiations to get the Big Ten to agree to a pact with the West for an annual Rose Bowl game.

In his book, *The Big Ten,* Commissioner Wilson picks up the story:

TUG WILSON

When I succeeded Griffith in 1945, I sincerely felt the question of Rose Bowl participation should be settled once and for all. The directors of the conference at that time were Doug Mills of Illinois, Zora Clevenger of Indiana, E. G. Schroeder of Iowa, Fritz Crisler of Michigan, Frank G. McCormick of Minnesota, Ted Payseur of Northwestern, L. W. St. John of Ohio State, Guy J. Mackey of Purdue, and Harry Stuhldreher of Wisconsin.

No commissioner ever started with a better group of directors and faculty representatives than I did in 1945. The big job would be selling the game to the faculties. A careful study was made showing how we could insure there'd be practically no absences from classes by the participants. This meant that the Pacific Coast and the Big Ten would have to agree on a definite starting time for Rose Bowl practice, that a Big Ten team should not depart for the West Coast until classes had adjourned for the holidays.

A second major point for us was that no member of the Big Ten could go out two years in a row. This was to meet the argument that one school might monopolize the Rose Bowl game by

134

a long winning streak. It was also agreed that the conference proceeds of the game would be divided into twelve equal shares, each member of the conference to receive one share, the participating team to receive two shares plus its traveling budget, and the conference to receive one share.

This was the first time that Bowl receipts had ever been distributed evenly among the members of any conference. Thus, no team could get wealthy by the assignment.

I would be remiss if I did not mention the wonderful support given me by members of the faculty representatives: Ralph W. Aigler of Michigan, whose skill and enthusiasm in helping to sell his colleagues was tremendous; Frank E. Richart of Illinois, William R. Breneman of Indiana, Karl E. Leib of Iowa, Henry Rottschafer of Minnesota, Dr. G. R. Lindquist of Northwestern, James E. Pollard and Wendell Postle of Ohio State, Vern C. Freeman of Purdue, and Dr. William F. Lorenz of Wisconsin.

At the special meeting of the faculty representatives and directors on September 1, 1946, the deadlock which had existed for twenty-six years was ended by a favorable vote for a five-year agreement with the Pacific Coast Intercollegiate Conference permitting a Big Ten team to play a Pacific Coast team in the January 1, 1947, Rose Bowl game.

At the first meeting of the Rose Bowl committees from the two conferences, it looked like the agreement might never be signed. The Pacific Coast Conference didn't like our no-repeat provision. They wanted our champion each year. There was a lot of controversy over the number of tickets to be allocated to the Big Ten, which was finally set at 12,500 tickets. Other provisions were hammered out, item by item, until agreement was met and the contract approved by both conferences.

The uniting of these two great conferences was not received with much enthusiasm on the Coast by the sports writers. They wanted the agreement to be postponed a year so that Army, which had one of its greatest teams, could appear in the Rose Bowl. Many caustic things were said about both conferences. Following the end of the football season, Illinois was selected as our representative and the Pacific Coast named UCLA.

Illinois, although conference champion, had lost games to Notre Dame and Indiana, and there was some West Coast suspicion that the Illini weren't exactly a glamour club. In fact, critics on the West Coast bluntly referred to them as second rate. UCLA immediately was installed as a heavy favorite, but the damage had already been done to the West Coast cause.

Illinois read all the papers calling them a second place club, and the Illini were really ready. As commissioner, I had opportunity to sense the feeling that had been created against the start of the Rose Bowl pact when I spoke briefly at the Los

Angeles *Times* sports awards dinner. It was my bad luck to follow a young football player named Glenn Davis. A California boy, he was the star of the grand team from West Point that year, and he was receiving an award as the best college football player in the country. When he spoke, he said it had always been his hope to play in the Rose Bowl.

I was actually booed when I was introduced as the next speaker. At first, I was tempted to sit down, but I finally waited until they quieted down. I told them Illinois was not a second class team and that the conference had worked hard on this pact with the Pacific Coast for many years. I even stuck my neck out by saying I thought Illinois would take care of the situation.

Looking back at the crises precipitated by West Coast fervor for Army as the invited opponent for the 1947 Rose Bowl game, Leishman said, "All of us were very severely criticized, but 'our horrible mistake' in the eyes of our critics became a lasting contribution to our present Rose Bowl success."

What Leishman meant was that the Rose Bowl now has the most secure line-up each year, pitting two great sections of the United States against each other in a contest with national appeal, appeal that in 1970 produced a television contract in excess of a million and a half dollars.

"During our troubles with the West Coast public prior to the 1947 game, Tournament President Bill Welsh stood by us," added Leishman.

Although the pact with the Big Ten has produced one popular sellout after another and the Rose Bowl annually enjoys the highest television ratings in all sports, along with the World Series and Super Bowl pro football game, Leishman and his football committee have faced some criticism each year from some West Coast fans who ask for the open invitation system "so Alabama and teams like that can return." The Leishman reply that cannot be contradicted has been: "We have the top game, and our pact with the Big Ten has made it possible. There is no doubt connected with our promotion. We know what we have and who we are dealing with. We are most happy with the arrangement."

And most successful!

The game between Illinois and U.C.L.A. was not the only significant happening in the 1947 Tournament.

The parade was telecast locally for the first time and viewed in Los Angeles on the seven-inch screens then available. Bob Hope made his first of two appearances as grand marshal. A "queen mother" was named for the parade, and the selectee, Maudie Prickett, said, "What a pleasant way to get a family of seven lovely daughters."

A tradition in the "Holiday of Flowers" parade was begun when

the Long Beach Mounted Police rode at the head of the procession. Each of the thirty riders, all on matched palominos, held aloft the colors of the United States, a practice that has been continued by this group annually.

Bob Roberts roller-skated the entire five miles of the parade at the head of the Los Angeles Rams band.

Grand prize winner among the floats was Van de Kamp's "Tulip Day in Holland." The entire deck of the float was made up of more than 5,000 multicolored tulips placed in rows to give the appearance of a tulip field. Each tulip was placed in an individual vase, similar to a test tube.

Norma Christopher was chosen Queen. When President Welsh came to her home to notify her of her honor, he said, "We are taking your title of princess away from you." Miss Christopher was temporarily stunned. Then Welsh said, "We are giving you the title of queen instead."

"I was thrilled beyond words," said Norma, who today is Mrs. Don Winton. (She met her husband when he was commissioned to do a portrait of her as Rose Queen. They were married a year later.) When asked to select her most exciting experience as Queen, Norma replied: "I feel like a little child in a candy store, asked to choose one kind of candy over all the others, all delicious. When I entered the contest, all I really wanted to get was tickets to the coronation and ball that went to the final twenty-five girls." Norma said that during the final judging she remained very quiet while the other six girls were more animated. "I have often thought that the judges may have taken my shyness for poise," she said.

Norma stated she would always associate the Tournament with dignity, beauty, and wholesomeness.

"My gain?" she concluded. "Unforgettable memories, the privilege of being part of the Tournament the rest of my life, a new confidence and poise because of the experience . . . and my husband."

National radio shows originated at the Tournament scene. Kay

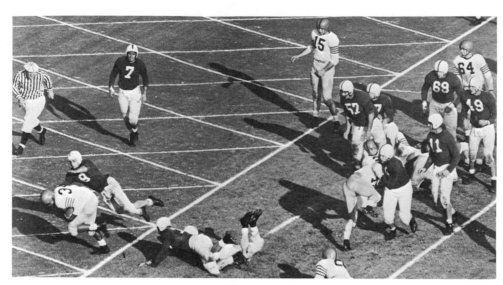

PAUL PATTERSON SCORES
FOR ILLINOIS

RAY ELIOT

Kyser described the Queen-selection festivities on an NBC-KFI broadcast. Bob Hope broadcast his Pepsodent Show from the Pasadena Playhouse.

"This will be my first game from a 50-yard-line seat," said Hope. "Last year I had a dollar ticket."

"Dollar ticket? Where did you sit?" Queen Norma asked Hope.

"I didn't. . . . I was 86th in line for the telescope at Griffith Observatory."

When Hope accepted Welsh's invitation to be grand marshal, he wrote to Welsh as follows: "I haven't told a soul about it, except my wife, which means nobody knows a thing about it now except the whole San Fernando Valley."

After the January 1 festivities were over, Hope said, "For those who were driving to Pasadena it was a Tournament of Fenders. They picked me to be grand marshal because they wanted a movie star and the uniform wouldn't fit Lassie. The beautiful girls looked so sweet — blushing red from excitement and turning blue from cold."

Hope left his football tickets at home in the early morning rush and had to "crash the gate." Actually, Welsh came to the rescue and told the ushers to let him through.

No team ever played more inspired football in the Rose Bowl than Illinois, coached by Ray Eliot, in trouncing U.C.L.A. 45-14. Illinois had Claude ("Buddy") Young, Julius Rykovich, Paul Patterson, Russ Steger, and Perry Moss. Illinois rushed 326 yards and had 23 first downs. Records fell all over the place. Little Al Hoisch of U.C.L.A. was coach Bert LaBrucherie's star. Weighing only 139 pounds, second to Oregon's 128-pound Skeet Manerud among the mighty midgets of the Arroyo Seco, Hoisch returned an Illinois kickoff 102 yards to become the first Rose Bowl player ever to return a kickoff to a touchdown. He just missed returning another for a touchdown, needing one more block after going 51 yards. He averaged 44.5 yards for four kickoff returns.

AL HOISCH RETURNS
KICKOFF 102 YARDS
FOR U.S.C.

BERT LaBRUCHERIE

U.C.L.A.'s record was 10-0 going into the game. Illinois' was 7-2. In the Illinois lineup were the Agase brothers, Alex and Lou, who went on to fame as coaches and pro players.

"Illinois turned out to be the best all-around team in the Bowl since U.S.C. slugged Pitt 35-0 in 1933," wrote Sid Ziff in the *Valley Times.*

Paul Zimmerman in the Los Angeles *Times* said: "The Illini almost washed the Uclans out of the sun-drenched stadium."

"Today Illinois was one of the greatest teams in Illinois football history," said Wilfrid Smith of the Chicago *Tribune.*

"The boys from Westwood went too far. They should have stopped off at Forest Lawn," declared Ned Cronin in the *Daily News.*

"What running by Julius Rykovich," said Al Santoro in the *Examiner.* "Call him Orange Julius."

On their first series of the game, the Illini scored, a long pass from Moss to Rykovich setting up an eventual scoring plunge by Rykovich; Don Maechtle missed the extra point. A pass from Ernie Case to Hoisch set up a retaliatory touchdown by U.C.L.A., which gave the Bruins a 7-6 lead when Case kicked goal.

A clever play put Illinois ahead to stay. Case had been refusing to kick to Illinois' fleet little sprinter, Young. The Illinois team, therefore, had been denied a chance to spring Mr. Five by Five into the open where his speed and dipsy-do were effective. So off a spread formation, Moss flipped the ball back to Young, who was lined up quite deep in the backfield. This gave Young a chance to move as the blockers waited for the Bruins to rush and then picked them up. Young ran sixteen zany yards to set up a touchdown he himself scored on a few plays later. The merry rout was on. Young wound up with 103 yards and Rykovich with 107.

23
The Golden West

GENERAL OMAR BRADLEY

1948

THE TOURNAMENT theme in 1948 was "The Golden West."

That's the way the Big Ten found it as it went about the task of panning gold in the Rose Bowl.

Fritz Crisler brought in his Michigan football team and it duplicated the feat of Fielding Yost's 1902 Pasadena troop. Michigan defeated U.S.C. 49-0.

When Bo Schembechler of Michigan and Johnny McKay of U.S.C. were reminded of this rout just before the meeting of the same schools in the 1970 game, each answered, "I doubt if any of our present personnel was born then. I doubt if our boys will suffer much pain over what happened in 1948."

Louis Vincenti, the man who had so much to do with negotiations between the Pacific Coast Conference and the Big Ten, was Tournament president in 1948. General Omar Bradley was grand marshal. Virginia Goodhue was the queen; she became a professional model after her reign. Today Virginia is Mrs. Donald Hess of San Gabriel, California.

The floats in the 1948 parade utilized more animated figures and puppets. Yes, the age of Walt Disney had come. San Francisco won the Sweepstakes award, since ingenuity was vying with beauty as the No. 1 asset of the big spectacle. The cable car, of course, was San Francisco's feature "personality." The car, about three quarters the size of an actual cable car, even turned around on a replica of the Powell Street turntable.

The maize and blue of Michigan in the 1948 game could be the greatest team ever to play in the Rose Bowl. It swirled and aerialed its giddy way down the arroyo like a midwestern cyclone.

Led by a magnificent All-American halfback named Robert Chappuis and a whirling dervish fullback named Jack Weisenburger, it blew down the University of Southern California varsity 49-0.

Chappuis and Weisenburger, the latter handling the ball one way or another on almost every play, got plenty of help. The charge of coach Crisler's unstoppable line, the pursuit of the entire defensive

LOUIS VINCENTI

VIRGINIA GOODHUE

platoon in gang-tackling the hapless and helpless Trojans, set standards of excellence not seen at Pasadena since that day in 1902 when the first game was played.

Stanford in 1902, also a 49-0 loser to Michigan, had little to offer in resistance, for that was long before the awakening to the true potential of American football in the West. It was before the day of the forward pass. It was a day when touchdowns and field goals each counted 5 points, and it was a day when Michigan scored eight touchdowns, four conversions, and one field goal before the game was mercifully cut short by ten minutes because of darkness.

Southern California came to Pasadena in 1948 with a Rose Bowl record of eight victories and a lone defeat (to Alabama in 1946). The team had lost but one game during the 1947 season, to Notre Dame by a score of 38-7. So the Trojans were caught right in the middle of Michigan's feud with Notre Dame for the 1947 national championship, because Michigan set out to better what the Fighting Irish under Frank Leahy had done to Troy.

Michigan achieved its objective, but afterward coach Jeff Cravath and most of his Trojans claimed Notre Dame had hit harder and was better than Michigan. Notre Dame played power football against U.S.C. Michigan employed speed, deception, that whirling fullback as its ball-handler — and the forward pass.

Stanford held out for twenty-three minutes against Willie Heston, Neil Snow, and others of Michigan's earlier "Point A Minute Team." U.S.C. gave up its first touchdown after nine minutes of the first quarter. Weisenburger went over facing backward from one foot out, and Jim Brieske booted the first of his seven extra points — a Rose Bowl record.

Weisenburger scored two more later on, each on a one-yard plunge. Chappuis passed eleven yards to Bump Elliott and eighteen to quarterback Howard Yerges for two scores. Yerges passed twenty-eight to Dick Rifenberg for the final score, and Henry Fonde, who had replaced Chappuis, rang the bell when he passed forty-five to Gene Derricotte.

Chappuis, who must rank high among the all-time Rose Bowl halfbacks, figured in six key plays leading up to or scoring five of Michigan's seven touchdowns. His pass to Rifenberg, who lateraled to Bruce Hilkene for sixteen yards to the U.S.C. 10, was the key play in the first score. His pass to Bobby Mann for fifteen on the Trojan 11 set up the second. He passed eighteen yards to Yerges for a score and set up another with a thirty-eight-yard run around right end, the longest run of the game.

Dick Hyland wrote next day in the Los Angeles *Times* that Chappuis "looked every bit as good as Dixie Howell did when he gave Stanford a passing lesson a dozen years ago. His receivers, all of them, were great, making almost unbelievable grabs."

BOB CHAPPUIS

JACK WEISENBURGER

Chappuis and Weisenburger shared rushing honors, each with 91 yards net. Chappuis also had 188 by air.

Meanwhile, Crisler's alert smashing defense held U.S.C. to 91 yards net running and 42 passing. Only twice did the Trojans penetrate beyond the midfield stripe, once to the Michigan 46. The other time they had a sustained drive of 75 yards, every inch of it on the ground, from their own 12 to Michigan's 13. Then, on a second down, quarterback George Murphy went to the air and his pass was intercepted by Dick Kempthorne.

Maybe Bob Hunter said it best in the Los Angeles *Examiner:* "The Trojans stood up on one play — the playing of the National Anthem."

It took Cravath's men twenty-four minutes to make their first down. Michigan players agreed with Crisler that U.S.C.'s best man was Paul Cleary, a very good end. Center Walt McCormick also came in for praise.

Braven Dyer had it pretty well summed up in the opening sentence of his lead story in the *Times:* "Well, it wasn't as bad as we expected; it was worse."

Vincent X. Flaherty in the *Examiner:* "A terrible thing happened here this afternoon. They threw the Trojans to the Wolverines in full view of 93,000 horror-stricken onlookers. And it shall go down in history as the most macabre spectacle ever beheld since they fed the Christians to the lions rare. And by golly, it was awful . . . the Wolverines gave U.S.C. the worst defeat in the history of the school . . .

"Michigan more than lived up to all of the lofty things said about it. It is a truly wonderful football team — and not only that, but a football squad of really good football players that just about defies comparison."

From Ned Cronin in the Los Angeles *Daily News:* "University of Southern California's football club needs one of two things, and possibly both. Reading from left to right, they are: (1) a couple of barrels of plasma, and/or (2) a new matchmaker. The one they've got is going to get somebody killed if they don't get him out of there."

A young man named Tommy Walker, the place-kicker on the Trojan football team, suited up for the 1948 Rose Bowl game, but he had to wait several years to actually "play" in the famed saucer.

When the Trojans ran out on the field on January 1, 1948, Walker was sure his lifetime ambition to compete in the Rose Bowl game was about to be realized.

"I didn't march with the band that day," grinned Walker. "It was all football with me. My big dream coming true. But we got trampled by Michigan 49-0. So I didn't get a chance to kick a point. In the last minute, Jeff Cravath, our coach, decided to give everybody the thrill of seeing action. I was about the last one to get sent in. However, because I normally didn't do anything but kick points, I didn't wear any shoulder pads. Frantically, the trainer tried to get pads on me, but just when he pulled the jersey over my head the final gun went off. So I didn't get in."

That's chapter one in the Rose Bowl life of Walker. In the 1955 game between U.S.C. and Ohio State, Walker returned as program director of the Trojan band. His tendencies toward spectaculars already were evident. The U.S.C. band staged a gala halftime show in the rain. The field was wet and muddy — and Walker's halftime activities left more than a few footprints on the soggy gridiron. When Woody Hayes returned for the third quarter with his team and saw the condition of the field, the Buckeye coach became furious. "People come to see the football game, not the bands," he shouted.

Walker gained one triumph that day, however. During the parade, a float ahead of the Trojan band broke down just as the U.S.C. musicians approached the national television camera area. "We were on the air for twelve minutes before they could get the parade going again," chuckled Walker.

The versatile Trojan returned to the Rose Bowl on July 4, 1970, as the promoter of a giant fireworks show. He called it the biggest fireworks display in the country. "The Rose Bowl deserves the best," he said.

1949

In the official program for the 1949 Tournament of Roses, California's Governor Earl Warren wrote the following:

"Here in this day's events you will find much that reflects the spirit of California — much that embodies the will to grow and develop that has brought our state such progress in less than a hundred years. California is proud of the tradition fostered by this great annual event. Here on New Year's Day we strive to give emphasis to the American spirit of teamwork, good will, and fair play with the hope that it will become dominant in our approach to all our problems during the year to come."

Nobody has better stated the spirit of the Tournament of Roses. It is fitting, therefore, that Warren was to return for the second time as grand marshal in 1955; Richard Nixon and Bob Hope are the only others to serve as grand marshal twice.

"The Tournament of Roses is made possible only through the cooperation of all people of Southern California," added Tournament president Harold C. Schaffer in an official statement marking Pasadena's extension of its community hand to its neighbors in making the Tournament "as much America as the soda in our corner drug stores."

Perry Brown, national commander of the American Legion, was the 1949 grand marshal. Brown was a veteran of two world wars. In the first he was gassed and seriously wounded. He became the Legion's foremost advocate of a "peace through strength," preaching the folly of unpreparedness.

The Marine Band from San Diego was very popular that year with the viewers.

The theme "Childhood Memories" lent itself to many novel and beautiful floats, with Long Beach's entry "Fairy Queen" capturing the

PERRY BROWN

143

HAROLD SCHAFFER CROWNS
QUEEN VIRGINIA BOWER

Sweepstakes. Other outstanding floats were "Circus Days," a series of small floats hitched together, representing animal cages with floral occupants, a large giraffe, and a calliope, all drawn by a floral elephant, and "The Barnyard," a typical barnyard scene with animated floral animals.

Queen Virginia Bower described most realistically how a queen feels when she travels the parade route.

"As we rode on our float down Colorado Boulevard, looking along the way, seeing all the cameras raised to people's eyes, it was a sight most difficult to describe adequately," said Miss Bower. "I smiled for so long (I truly felt like smiling) that when we arrived at the end of the parade route, I could not stop smiling. The muscles in my face wouldn't relax. That was a strange sensation, indeed."

A music student, Queen Virginia treasured the chance to sing on a Don Ameche national radio broadcast, and today in her life as Mrs. Paul Nichols of Walnut Creek, California, treasures the album of that broadcast.

When the judges came to her home for a final interview, Miss Bower said they wanted to know if she was left-handed or right-handed, because they needed a left-handed girl on the float to hold the roses. A few days later, President Schaffer called in person at her home with a bouquet of roses and said, "Princess no longer, but Queen Virginia." Miss Bower said many of the things she learned in a course on grooming, charm, and poise have been helpful to her throughout life.

That long way to go to Tipperary was never so far as the Northwestern varsity had to go in the purple twilight of January 1, 1949.

The day was dying in the west. It was 14-13 in favor of California, and the Wildcats from Evanston had between them and the goal line a fired-up California team, eighty-eight yards of embattled ground, and six minutes of time. It had to be done on the ground because Northwestern, which completed only one of four passes all afternoon, had no more aerial attack than Hannibal had to throw against Rome.

Unlike Hannibal, who was stopped by the Roman legions on the 5-yard line, Northwestern made it — made those eighty-eight yards

144

in three minutes and two seconds to leave 2:58 on the clock when they had achieved their 20 to 14 triumph in one of the Rose Bowl's most bitterly fought and controversial games.

Perhaps the Carthaginian conqueror was stopped for the reason that among the elephants that crossed the Alps with him there was no 165-pound Ed Tunnicliff at right half opposite the brilliant "Player of the Game," Frank Aschenbrenner.

Ed Tunnicliff, from Kewanee, Illinois, was not very big, but forevermore he was to be a *purple* elephant, Northwestern purple, dancing in the dreams and haunting the nightmares of Lynn ("Pappy") Waldorf.

For Pappy, who had previously coached twelve years at Northwestern, the nightmare began on the Wildcats' 12-yard line. California recovered a fumble by Tunnicliff as Northwestern put the ball in play at that spot with six minutes to go. But what many believed was a fast whistle by referee Jimmy Cain (Washington) nullified the recovery and Northwestern still had possession of the ball with no gain. Tunnicliff didn't have the ball when he landed head first, but the whistle had been blown.

It was at this moment that Northwestern completed its only successful pass of the game, seventeen yards from Aschenbrenner to Don Stonesifer, to put the ball on the 'Cat 29. Then reserve fullback Gasper Perricone raced fifteen to the 44.

Waldorf sent in Norm Pressley to replace his starting left end, Frank Van Deren. Mae West would have liked Van Deren, for he was a man who took his time. He swam off the field like a slow boat to China and before he crossed the side line by the bench of the Golden Bears, quarterback Don Burson had put the ball in play for Northwestern.

California was penalized five yards for having twelve men on the field. The penalty advanced the ball to the Bear 46, second down, with only a yard to go. It took Perricone three plays to make that vital first down, by inches, on the 45.

Aschenbrenner tried left end but made only two yards, to the 43. And so here it came — the only direct pass the Wildcats used

PAPPY WALDORF IN A CHEERFUL
DISCUSSION WITH JACKIE JENSEN

all afternoon, on a play they had used before but not while Tunnicliff was in the line-up. Coach Bob Voigts, a Waldorf product, had had his team practicing this play in Pasadena during the week before the game.

Although U.S.C. had used this or a very similar play during the 1948 season, when used, suddenly and unexpectedly, by Northwestern, it caught the Golden Bears by surprise and completely unprepared to meet it. The play had even fooled Wildcat defensive units in those workouts. The 'Cats had great confidence in this play if it were used at the right time.

That time was now.

There, in the chill of the late afternoon before a crowd that sat bundled in overcoats, the violet mists hanging heavy upon the surrounding hills, Tunnicliff received the direct pass and started off on his run through eerie air.

Tunnicliff went around his own right end as the California left wing, Pressley, came charging in too fast. The Kewanee Kid needed no blockers to swing around Pressley. But soon an escort picked him up as he raced down the side line forty-three yards to the winning touchdown.

Northwestern's first two scores came on a brilliant seventy-three-yard run by Aschenbrenner and a one-yard plunge by fullback Art Murakowski, the legality of which has never been completely ascertained to the satisfaction of everybody.

Aschenbrenner's run set a new Rose Bowl record for distance on a dash from scrimmage. Murakowski's was unique in that he fumbled the ball, and every photograph taken of the play shows the ball falling off his left hip while both his feet are still on the field of play.

Referee Cain raised his arms to signal a touchdown after field judge Jay Berwanger (Chicago's all-time great) had signaled to him

DISPUTED TOUCHDOWN: DID ART MURAKOWSKI CROSS THE GOAL LINE BEFORE HE FUMBLED?

that Murakowski had poked the nose of the ball beyond the goal line before the fumble. This decision is disputed by every photographic evidence there is, but camera angles are deceiving and Waldorf said if it was a score in the eyes of Berwanger that was good enough for him. The only thing that is certain about this play is that, when Murakowski himself crossed the goal line, the ball was falling to the ground like a hot pumpkin. It is also certain that Jim Farrar missed the extra point, so the Northwestern lead was only 13-7.

There was even an argument over who recovered the ball in the end zone after Murakowski's fumble. Both Will Lotter of California and George Maddock of Northwestern claimed to have done so.

Aschenbrenner's long scrimmage run in the first quarter got the Midwest representative off to a 7-0 lead. Aschenbrenner went over his own right tackle, twisted away from Paul Keckley, and went all the way, as tackle Steve Sawle, after going down while blocking one defender, got up and took out two more on the play.

Soon after this Jackie Jensen, later to become an outstanding baseball player, made the third longest Rose Bowl run from scrimmage, sixty-seven yards, to the touchdown that made it 7-7. Jensen was injured on the second play of the third quarter and never returned, but his replacement at fullback, Frank Brunk, turned in an exceptional performance for an unkown junior.

Ray DeJong recovered a fumble by Don Burson, who was trying to pass on the Wildcat 44. Brunk began the drive with fourteen yards, then made first down on the 18, another on the 6 with a charge of thirteen yards over right tackle. Right halfback Jack Swaner scored from the 4 and Cal took the lead when Jim Cullom kicked goal. It was from this 13-14 deficit that Northwestern struck for victory in that final period.

Statistics released by the California team after the game had many inaccuracies, including one that had Burson, not Aschenbrenner, throwing the pass to Stonesifer.

Aschenbrenner gained 116 yards in ten plays and averaged better than 43 yards on six punts. He was clearly the "Player of the Game." Jensen gained 70 yards rushing, Swaner 79, Brunk 39, Bob Celeri 41, Tunnicliff 83, and Murakowski 39.

For the West, at least, it was better than the 49-0 shellacking one year earlier.

24
Survival Against Opposition

DRUMMOND McCUNN

THE BIG TEN-Pacific Coast Conference pact did not survive without difficulty.

After the 1949 game, Dr. J. Louis Morrill of Minnesota, an athletic faculty representative when he was at Ohio State before accepting the U of M presidency, spoke out against the pact. He said he wanted it discontinued.

"I will vote against renewal and I will use every possible means to influence other schools to ballot against the agreement," he said. He said he didn't like the pressure the pact put on coach or school.

Despite opposition like this, the pact survived until the Pacific Coast Conference dissolved it in the process of dissolving itself. Then a new five-school conference, called the Athletic Association of Western Universities, was formed. The Tournament made an agreement with the AAWU to supply the western antagonist. The Big Ten, meanwhile, left it up to its individual membership whether to accept an AAWU bid to be the eastern team each year. Ironically, Minnesota voted for the pact in 1953 and voted to accept the bid for the 1961 game, and Minnesota independently agreed to compete when Ohio State's faculty rejected the bid in 1962, Minnesota accepting as the substitute choice. This switch by the school that previously had opposed the pact led to a new signed agreement, which still stands, between the Big Ten and the AAWU prior to the 1963 game.

The financial success of the Rose Bowl game prompted a rash of other bowl activity. In 1951 at the NCAA convention at Dallas, a motion was brought to the floor to curtail extra-event participation such as bowl football play.

Leishman, William Nicholas, and John Biggar pleaded against such action. NCAA vice president A. C. Everest of the University of Washington made the famed "Mt. Everest Motion" to table curtailment. It was passed.

Out of this action came a plan to screen carefully all bowls and to grant NCAA sanction only to those bowls deemed within the format of NCAA specifications.

The Tournament of Roses also sent Leishman, Biggar, and

PAUL G. HOFFMAN RIDES THE GRAND
MARSHAL'S CAR

Nicholas to western campuses to plead the case for participation at Pasadena, a step that assured participation after presidents at a conference meeting at Riverside had voted for withdrawal.

1950

Drummond J. McCunn, assistant superintendent of Pasadena schools, was president of the Tournament for the 1950 game. Paul G. Hoffman, the Marshall Plan administrator, was grand marshal, and Marion Brown was queen.

A feature of the parade was "The Story of American Flags," a presentation of the banners that had flown over the country during great moments in the country's history. This and other displays carried out the parade theme, "Our American Heritage," and led to the Freedom Foundation at Valley Forge presenting the Freedom Award to the Pasadena festival. The award is one of the memories of which McCunn is most proud.

Long Beach won the Sweepstakes Prize in the parade with a float titled "Freedom."

A colorful float was "Showboat," a two-story Edison Company re-creation of a typical Mississippi river boat, with fifty real passengers. There was a floral water-wheel, and smoke came from the stacks. The float had to be operated with the assistance of an intercom system because the man who handled the gears and the man who steered were thirty feet apart. Between them were four other operators, two for the smoke effects and two to play the music. The paddle wheel revolved, churning up a wave of light and dark blue flowers.

Springfield, Illinois, entered a float which depicted Abraham Lincoln's birthplace and emphasized his ideals.

Under McCunn's administration a telephone system was installed along the parade route to control the movement of floats. Another innovation that year was the filming of the parade in color for showing at functions throughout the United States.

MARION BROWN

149

WESLEY FESLER

The parade trumpeter was Harold Cullinson, who blew the trumpet used by his father seventy-five years earlier as a coach guard for the Earl of Lonsdale in England.

Hollywood celebrities had an active part in the 1950 Tournament activities. James Stewart appeared at the Queen's breakfast. Bob Hope again broadcast his network radio show from Pasadena, and Edward Arnold did the narration at the coronation.

Grand marshal Hoffman gave this account of his experiences in Pasadena: "I was most impressed by the vast amount of work that went into the preparation of floats for the parade. I remember in particular one float on which there were 10,000 little glass tubes for 10,000 roses. My most interesting experience was riding down the street before a million and a half Americans. There was an element of excitement in it for me because several anonymous postcards had been received which stated that I would be bombed somewhere along the line of march. I rather assumed that if a serious effort was going to be made to bomb me, I wouldn't have been warned, but I couldn't fully erase from my mind the possibility."

Queen Marion Brown today has become Senora Miguel de Guajardo of Acapulco and Mexico City.

Miss Brown met her husband on a trip to Mexico City with 1951 Tournament president L. Clifford Kenworthy and Mrs. Kenworthy.

"After the Republic of Mexico entered the first float from outside the United States in our parade, Mrs. Kenworthy and I accompanied Queen Marion Brown to Mexico City to judge their Spring Festival of Flowers," said Kenworthy. "Several years later, she married a young fellow from Mexico City who was at that time attending U.C.L.A. He is the owner of extensive hotel properties in Mexico. They have a lovely home and family."

Until slightly more than two minutes before the final gun in the 1950 Rose Bowl game, some 100,936 football fans seated in the huge stadium believed that The Hague was a municipality located somewhere in the Netherlands devoted to peace. Quite suddenly all these people learned that The Hague was a fellow named James Hague from the town of Rocky River, Ohio, and he came equipped for war.

For it was this James Hague who booted a seventeen-yard field goal that gave Wes Fesler's Buckeyes a hard-won 17 to 14 victory over California before the largest crowd yet to see a Rose Bowl game.

Breaking the 14-14 deadlock Hague wound up a game in which the Ohioans had been much the superior team through most of the contest because of a freak incident that had just given Ohio possession deep in Golden Bear territory. Freak, that is, if you will agree that it is a bit unorthodox for a right-footed kicker being forced to punt, while on the run, with his left. The play put Pappy Waldorf's team in something of a pickle, since time was beginning to run out.

California was back on its own twenty-yard line after forcing Ohio State to punt. Fred ("Curley") Morrison, the outstanding player in the game, booted the ball into the end zone from the California 38.

Quarterback Bob Celeri, who previously had a punt blocked to set up an Ohio touchdown, called on fullback Pete Schabarum, who lost five yards. Soon on fourth down and fifteen to go, Cal had to kick.

Cal's first-string center, George Stathakis, was out of the game with an injury. His replacement, George ("Ozzie") Harris, had no experience whatever in passing the ball ten yards deep to a punter. All he'd ever done was hand it back to the quarterback in the usual T formation.

This was the time, the place, and the perfect cast for disaster. It wasn't long in coming.

Harris rolled the ball back along the ground to Celeri, who had no chance to kick from where he finally retrieved the rolling, tumbling ball. Buckeyes were swarming like bees down upon the hapless Celeri. All he could do was run, scampering out of the way as best he could.

At last, in desperation, Celeri applied his left foot to the ball, which promptly went out of bounds on the thirteen-yard line.

California stopped the Ohio charge, but the ball was close enough to enable Hague to make the rather easy field goal that cost California the game.

The Bears had taken a convincing drubbing. Ohio State had out-rushed them, 221 yards to 133. California gained 106 yards in the air to 34, but there was no consistency to Cal's aerial game. The Buckeye line dominated the trenches, blocked a punt, and opened holes in the line through which the big Morrison, later a star with the Cleveland Browns, gained 113 yards net in 25 carries. Halfback Jerry Krall, another star of the contest, rolled for 80 in 28 tries. Jim Monachino led California rushers with 87 yards in 13 tries, the most important of which was a forty-four-yard touchdown gallop on a pitchout from Celeri.

California scored the only touchdown in the first half, a second-quarter score that sent them into the mid-game break with a 7-0 lead. The touchdown was set up by a fifty-five-yard pass play to the Ohio 13, Frank Brunk making the catch though covered by three Buckeyes at the 30. He went on from there to the 13. Monachino scored on a seven-yard run that started with a pitchout from Celeri.

In the third period Ohio moved deep into Cal territory. On a crucial fourth down they pulled one of the neatest plays of the game. It was a reverse from Pandel Savic to Krall that ended with a jump pass to Ralph Anderson for seven yards and first down on the Bear 7.

Morrison burst through into the end zone. But then Curley slammed his helmet to the ground when officials ruled his progress had been stopped on the 3. Morrison came right back, got his touchdown, and Hague's conversion tied the count at 7-7.

Bill Trautwein, one of the most aggressive tackles who ever played at Pasadena, broke through and blocked a Celeri punt. Center Jack Lininger scooped up the bounding ball and ran some fifteen yards to the Cal 6.

Frank Humpert, Paul Baldwin, and Carl Van Hueit momentarily fought off the inevitable, but on fourth down Krall, working on a spinner, scooted through a sizeable opening at left tackle for the 14-7 touchdown.

Trautwein's dribble kickoff, a Wes Fesler trademark, was carried back seventeen yards to the Cal 42 by Schabarum. Later from the Buckeye 44, Schabarum applied a telling block on the pitchout from Celeri to Monachino as the latter whirled around the right flank. Big Jim Turner blocked out a threat to Monachino, and Jim ran home free. The score was 14-14 after Jim Cullom added the extra point.

It is noteworthy here that, shortly after this, Waldorf sent into the game Charley ("Boots") Erb, son of the quarterback of the famed California "Wonder Team" that had defeated Ohio State in 1921 at old Tournament Park, 28-0. Erb the Elder, the great brain of that earlier team, had caught three passes, thrown none. Erb the Younger threw two, one of which was intercepted.

Waldorf had this to say after the game: "You can't violate the oldest fundamental in football. Your punt game must be sound. Ours wasn't. You can't make the mistakes we did against a good team — and Ohio State IS a good team — and expect to survive.

"We made them — three big ones that cost us the works. There was the blocked kick, the intercepted pass and long runback by Vic Janowicz that led to Ohio's first touchdown, and the bad pass that led to Celeri's futile left-footed kick. They were the killers."

1951

ROBERT S. GRAY

The 1951 Tournament is historic for many reasons.

General Dwight D. Eisenhower, then president of Columbia University, had been selected by President Kenworthy to serve as grand marshal. However, because of his sudden return to military duty, he had to cancel his Pasadena visit. Robert Stewart Gray, a Marine private back from Korea, substituted for Ike.

The parade of 1951 also marked the first network telecast of that colorful event. It was transmitted by station KTTV of Los Angeles through microwave to KPIX, San Francisco, with Prudential the sponsor.

Peggy, the first Hollywood movie using the Tournament of Roses as a theme, was released, featuring Diana Lynn, Charles Coburn, and Rock Hudson. This story of the tribulations of a Pasadena City College coed who was secretly wed was shown in premiere at the Pasadena Civic Auditorium.

More than 100,000 orchids were flown in from Honolulu for the "Hawaiian Holiday" float. Monterey Park won the parade Sweepstakes with an Arabian Nights creation. The State of North Dakota

152

entered a novel float, depicting a table with a potato on each plate, and steam rising from the turkey.

Significantly embodying the theme of the 1951 parade was Union Oil's float, "Joyful Living." It featured a frozen pond of real ice covering three hundred square feet on which Canadian skating champion Helen Legge and other skaters performed.

Film star Bill Holden emceed the Queen's breakfast.

President Kenworthy described the Eisenhower withdrawal as marshal as follows:

"Mr. Eisenhower had accepted my invitation. He and Mrs. Eisenhower had come as far west as Denver to spend Christmas with Mrs. Eisenhower's family, the Dowds. I received a call from General Eisenhower telling me he had been ordered back into military service by President Harry Truman and was leaving immediately for Paris to set up the new SHAEF organization.

"He asked how he might help in getting someone to take his place on New Year's Day, and our final conclusion was that he would pick a 'buck private' from the rear ranks, wounded in Korea, to represent himself and all the armed forces in Korea. Consequently, Bob Gray arrived at Camp Pendleton where he was met by the Tournament officers, Pasadena city officials, the queen and her court. The queen and her court visited many of the wounded in the Camp Pendleton hospital, leaving television sets and boxes of oranges."

Private Gray had suffered machine gun injury in his left arm. When the order came to report to his commanding officer about the grand marshal's job, he was in such a dither that he wound up with his injured arm not in a sling but in a diaper grabbed from the maternity ward of the hospital.

President Kenworthy's dominant memory of his Tournament experience was this: "The United States Department of Commerce and the Department of Agriculture asked me to manage United States Fairs, which were held in the four major cities of India. In going to India and being there for several months and returning the rest of

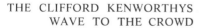
THE CLIFFORD KENWORTHYS
WAVE TO THE CROWD

153

ELEANOR PAYNE

the way around the world, I visited many cities and made contact with many people. Whenever I mentioned I was from Pasadena, the majority of the people immediately connected the Tournament of Roses with the city."

Kenworthy added, "I always have been impressed by the determination of everyone to work willingly for the Tournament without any compensation."

Kenworthy was one of those who recognized that it was too much to ask of a Chamber of Commerce staff to direct the activities of that organization and the Tournament of Roses also. The two staffs were intertwined in early days. When Bill Dunkerley and Jessie Ogston were worked to a frazzle handling the Chamber work from January to October and the Tournament work from October to January, Kenworthy, a former Chamber president, saw to it that the two offices were given separate staffs. "We decided both staffs should work in complete harmony, augmenting each other," said Kenworthy.

The queen in 1951 was Eleanor Payne, who became the wife of USAF Lt. Col. John Ford.

Mary Baker, who with her late husband Lynn Baker, New York advertising executive, coordinated the first Rose Parade network telecast, has many memories of Rose Parade televising since 1951. Currently account executive with Wolcott, Carlson & Company, the Tournament's public relations agency, Mrs. Baker annually is in the thick of activities that take place on Orange Grove and Colorado Boulevards each New Year's morning.

"The problem the first year was one of getting all of the features of a two-and-a-half-hour parade in a one-hour telecast," said Mrs. Baker.

"Our prime advertisers in the early years were Woolworths the first four years and Quaker Oats for nine years. The director of the show has a tougher job than the director of the telecast from the football game. He can't leave out a band or a float, and coordinating everything with the time slots isn't easy. We have had many tense moments in the telecasts. One year when Ronald Reagan was the commentator, somebody had neglected to arrange his transportation to the television booth on the corner of Orange Grove and Colorado. We couldn't get a cab anywhere, so we sent an ambulance after him and it got through the traffic beautifully.

"One New Year's, I had a dreadful experience. I left my duffel bag containing parade and game tickets for all of our parade advertisers in the lobby of the Beverly Hills Hotel where I was staying. I didn't notice my error until we tried to get through the traffic and I suddenly found I didn't have any credentials. However, Tournament officials pulled us out of the jam by issuing replacement tickets for the parade and game.

"I will never forget Jeanette MacDonald's year as a parade commentator. It must have been her first appearance as a live television commentator because she was very nervous and was having much difficulty with her contact glasses. We felt sorry for her because she was really in distress, but Gene Raymond picked up for the show beautifully.

"Of all our commentators through the years, Bess Myerson gets my vote as the most adept and most beautifully prepared for the role. She always had tremendous interest in the parade and had so much feeling for the role of bringing the story to the public. Vin Scully, the baseball broadcaster, did a marvelous job one year, too. He prepared himself so completely."

Scully, who is an NBC morning star on a quiz-stunt show titled "It Takes Two," quickly discovered it takes more than two to stage the Tournament of Roses. "I studied up on what the floats depicted," said Scully. "If a float featured swans, I tried to learn as much as I could about swans. If the float featured dragons, I read everything I could find about dragons. It helped me when the action started."

Mrs. Baker believes the future of Tournament parade telecasts lies in the policy of bringing the show to the public "as it is."

"I don't think the parade ever should be designed just to fit television," said Mrs. Baker. "Television should fit the parade."

Lynn Waldorf, a large, friendly bear of a man who could tell you all about how and why certain generals won or lost nearly all the bitter, bloody battles of the Civil War, sat in the Rose Bowl catacombs trying to explain a defeat of his own on January 1, 1951.

Pappy had become low man on the Rose Bowl totem pole. He had just become the first coach ever to lose three consecutive Pasadena contests, and the one he had just lost was one that his critics believed he should have won. Their stories the next few days reflect the thought that this defeat was of Pappy's own making.

The scoreboard read: Michigan 14, California 6.

It was rather generally agreed, especially by men from the Big Ten, that this was not one of Michigan's better teams. It had lost games that season to Michigan State, Army, and Illinois, and had been tied by Minnesota. California, though tied 7-7 by Stanford, came to Pasadena undefeated.

In the game program, Les Etter, Michigan's athletic publicity director, described the team he publicized as follows: "A tale of courage, of fortitude, and the ability to rise above handicaps that would have daunted lesser men — that's the story of the 1951 Michigan Rose Bowl team."

A great many people went to Pasadena that day believing that California would win.

Braven Dyer, in the Los Angeles *Times*, wrote the following lead: "Credit victory to Ortmann. Charge defeat to Waldorf."

Definitely, it was not one of Waldorf's better days. His team had left the field leading at half time, 6-0. It could have been 9-0 but

BEN OOSTERBAAN

for Pappy's failure to call for a field goal on fourth down on the Wolverine 4-yard line.

"If that situation doesn't call for a field goal then all I have ever learned about how to win football games is worthless," Dyer said later in his story of the game. "Particularly since Cal had missed the conversion. Six points in this day and age are nothing. Nine points at half could have won the game. Instead, Cal tried another line smash and lost the ball."

This happened just before the first half ended. In the second half, California stayed in its seven-diamond defense, which was picked apart by quarterback Charles Ortmann's passes, particularly a series of screen passes, and by the rugged rushing of fullback Donald Dufek.

First-half yardage and downs favored California, 192 to 65, and 10 to 2. It was Michigan, 226 to 52, and 15 to 2, in the second half.

Sid Ziff, in the Los Angeles *Mirror,* gave a fine report on how the insistent San Francisco writers kept pecking away at Waldorf in the dressing room:

" 'How come?' they put it right to him.

" 'We got licked by a better team,' said Pappy, squirming.

" 'Why did they have a better team?' the scribes insisted.

" 'You were there, you saw for yourself, didn't you?'

" 'If you had it to do all over again, what would you do?' they demanded.

" 'I prefer to look at the films before answering that,' Pappy said stubbornly.

" 'Do I get the idea you don't know what happened?' snapped Pappy's chief tormentor. Waldorf glared at the writer and passed over the remark."

Ziff gave credit to Michigan: "It had to get off the floor to win. Its second-half rally was about as fine a comeback as any team ever staged in a gridiron classic."

Cal, ahead by 6 points, set up a pass interception by Ray Solari, returning seven yards to the Michigan 39. Jim Marinos did a masterful job of hiding the ball behind exceptional protection. With time to spare he lofted the ball easily to end Bob Cummings who got behind Dufek, the defending left half. Cummings took the ball on the 5 and bowled into the end zone as Dufek tackled him from behind. Cal didn't call that play again all day! Les Richter's try for point was wide to the left.

The Golden Bears previously lost a touchdown when a seventy-three-yard run by Pete Schabarum was called on a backfield-in-motion penalty.

The third quarter was scoreless and there were only about twelve minutes to play when Michigan began its winning drive from its own 20. Ortmann completed six of eight strikes (one perfect shot dropped) for sixty-four of the eighty yards.

Ortmann was throwing them long and short. He was flicking screens. Dufek took one on the left wing and roared for fourteen big yards to Cal's 37 before he was nailed by Solari. Dufek bagged another first down and Ortmann hit Lowell Perry on the 15. Cal's line stopped Dufek at center, so Ortmann went upstairs again to hit Harry Allis on the 4. The Bears dug in and it took Dufek four plays to go over into the end zone. Allis converted and it was 7-6 with 5:37 to play.

Michigan's second touchdown was a gift. Marinos threw an incomplete pass and the Wolverines took over on the Cal 13. It was Dufek three and six, then Dufek around end from the 1-yard line and people started tearing down the goal posts.

There was a split vote as to who was the outstanding player. It was between Ortmann and Dufek, with it being acknowledged that Michigan's left tackle, Tom Johnson, was probably the best lineman.

Dufek moved into all-time Rose Bowl contention at fullback with 113 yards in 23 tries. Ortmann had a passing record of 15 for 19 for 146 yards.

25
Max Colwell

MAX COLWELL

1952

THE TOURNAMENT OF ROSES has had seven managers since the first one, A. J. Bertonneau, was named in 1916 and served until 1918.

Mrs. R. C. Bartow served from 1919 to 1923, followed by Malcolm Fraser 1924-1927, Harlan Hall 1928-1930, William Dunkerley 1931-1947, Theodore J. Brodhead 1948-1952. Eventfully, Max Colwell started in 1952. Colwell, a former Pasadena newspaper reporter, continues to this day in office.

Many people have been called "Mr. Rose Bowl" or "Mr. Tournament of Roses." Certainly nobody is more entitled to the honor than Colwell, although many are entitled to share the distinction with him.

Colwell is not a big man physically, and, unfortunately, his frame lessened a bit after he was slugged by some Manhattan ruffians while walking back to his hotel one evening on a business trip a few years ago. But Colwell always has been a vigorous, yet quietly efficient, operator during his many years as the guiding light of the Tournament of Roses.

"We have the greatest organization in the world," Colwell, who started as a working member, has declared. "The Tournament workers are dedicated people. Political influence means nothing in this organization; capacity to work and produce does. When we send out our notices of annual dues, 90 per cent of the checks are back in four days. The volunteer workers are the kings in our organization. I try to remain in the background. If I have been successful, it is because I have been able to give out the idea and let them run with it. Nobody can say we sift off the community's leadership. Our leaders are the leaders in other community operations. My biggest reward is working with volunteers and seeing the eagerness of these volunteers to do a job."

Colwell completed his term as president of the International Festivals Association in 1969, proof of the esteem in which he is held by his fellow festival managers around the world.

Max started his Tournament interest in 1922 when he was a correspondent for the Pasadena *Post* while he attended Pasadena High

158

School. He reported float descriptions during the Christmas holidays. He got to know the Tournament people well and soon became a member.

After Colwell's years of various committee jobs in the Tournament while he was a full-time city hall reporter for the Pasadena newspapers, William Nicholas, Tournament president-to-be for the 1953 festival, said, "Max, you would make a good manager." To that point, the Tournament manager had been the Chamber of Commerce executive also. Colwell was the first full-time Tournament manager with no other duties.

Leon Kingsley was the 1952 president before Colwell was named. Nancy True Thorne was the Queen.

The 1952 game is known for the convincing manner in which Illinois dished out a 40-7 whipping to Stanford, the sixth straight triumph by a Big Ten team over the West. It also was the occasion for the first nationwide telecast of a Rose Bowl game, Mel Allen doing the play-by-play.

Stanford, 9-1 in the season, led 7-6 at halftime over Illinois, 8-0-1. The Illini opened with a seventy-six-yard touchdown drive in six running plays by Pete Bachorous and Don Tate, including a forty-one-yard blast by Tate to the five from where Bachorous scored. Don Sanders blocked Sam Rebecca's try for extra point. Gary Kerkorian's passing sparked a retaliatory score by Stanford that put the Indians ahead. Kerkorian connected to Pasadena's own Harry Hugasian, Bill McColl, and Ron Cook before Hugasian scored from the 4. Kerkorian's extra point gave Stanford its lead.

Then came the Stanford collapse that jolted the West.

"A defensive halfback, a kid who seldom gets his name in the papers, lit the fire at a time when Stanford was heading for another touchdown in the third quarter and, in all probability, a lead which the Illini would not have overcome," wrote Braven Dyer in the *Times*. The young man Dyer pointed to was Stan Wallace, 6 3 sophomore, who intercepted a pass from Kerkorian aimed from midfield at Bill Storum, Stanford end. Wallace raced back to Stanford's twelve-yard line. Soon Tate took a pitchout and scored. Stanford wilted badly after that; Illinois crossed the goal line virtually every time it got the ball. Tate scored again, and touchdowns were added by John Karras, Don Stevens, and John Ryan. Illinois gained 371 yards runing and 73 passing in burying Stanford. Tate ran 150 yards himself in 20 carries.

"Stanford players had too many malteds in training camp at Arrowhead Springs," wrote Dick Hyland in the *Times*.

Stanford's Sam Morley said, "Illinois kept grabbing our shirts. They did some slugging and they used their elbows in the clinches. But they did it all very cleverly and got away with it."

Mel Durslag reported in the Los Angeles *Examiner* how Illinois turned the tide with a switch in strategy at intermission. Illinois coach

Ray Eliot told Durslag: "We changed our pass defense. We had to cover their hook passes near the side lines. So we moved our linebackers out and back about two yards. Of course, it helped that they lost Kerkorian in the third quarter."

Kerkorian, holding his aching back, gave Morton Moss of the *Examiner* a different version: "Our offense got stopped by the way they held up our ends on the line. They put two men on each of our ends, and often they couldn't get out of the line."

Bob Hunter in the *Examiner* praised Illinois' deep defenders, Herb Neathery, Al Brosky, and Wallace, for the victory. "Stanford expected to win with Kerkorian's passes," he said, "but they didn't take the trouble to say who would catch them. Illinois interceptions turned this game around."

"Stanford took such a beating the commotion must have shattered the seismograph at Cal Tech," reported Vincent X. Flaherty in the *Examiner*.

But perhaps the best line of all was written by Dyer: "The Illini refused to give the Rose Bowl back to the Indians."

Meanwhile, with the Big Ten-West Coast Rose Bowl pact having one more year to run before action on renewal by the competing conferences, the West Coast sports writers started to clamor for an end to the slaughter. Although Bill Leiser of the San Francisco *Chronicle* said, "You don't call a halt because you lose six in a row — you just go out and try to win the next one," the West shouted loudly as follows:

Tom Harmon, KNX sports director, Los Angeles — "Illinois refused to quit fighting as Stanford did, and Illinois figured out Stanford's weaknesses at halftime."

Dyer — "Unless football is de-emphasized in the Big Ten, I see little prospect for the West in Pasadena for the next two years."

L. H. Gregory, Portland *Oregonian* — "The only hope for the future that I can see is that, having fulfilled the Biblical prophecy of a seven-year famine, the Pacific Coast should now have seven good years to come."

George T. Davis, Los Angeles *Herald-Express* — "This is a case of the men playing the boys."

Prescott Sullivan, San Francisco *Examiner* — "If there is another Rose Bowl game next year, fair play would indicate that the Big Ten be given some kind of a handicap. A better or more humane idea might be to call the whole thing off. Big Ten football is too much for our boys."

Arch Ward, Chicago *Tribune* — "It took Stanford 11 years to land in the Rose Bowl but only 60 minutes to prove they should have stayed home. I can find no words of excuse for Chuck Taylor's troops."

Ray Haywood, Oakland *Tribune* — "With the Big Ten, football is a science. With us, it is a game."

Al Santoro, Los Angeles *Examiner* — "The Pacific Coast Conference men, who made the pact with the Big Ten, like the men who built

NANCY THORNE

the race tracks, certainly did not do it for our benefit. After six straight defeats, it would appear the PCC is a sucker who has not yet learned the old frontier adage: 'Never play a man at his own game.' "

A unique idea left the West with pleasant memories after the football game, however. The public liked it that seven of the country's Congressional Medal of Honor winners had been grand marshals. Major Carl L. Sitter, Capt. Lewis L. Millet, Lt. Stanley T. Adams, Lt. Thomas J. Hudner, Lt. Raymond Harvey, Sgt. Ernest R. Kouma, and Sgt. Joseph Rodriquez were cheered by the spectators viewing the parade. Two of the floats in the parade carried 20,000 roses each. The theme, "Dreams of the Future," gave an opportunity to the Southern California Floral Association to capture the Sweepstakes prize with one of the largest floats ever seen in the parade. It was entitled "Every Girl's Dream Comes True." There were rare fresh blooms depicting a Japanese garden on which floral butterflies alighted.

Queen Nancy True Thorne today is the wife of Dr. John F. Skinner of Newport Beach.

An award winner in the 1952 parade was the Minute Maid presentation of "World Peace" — a huge globe and arching rainbow surmounted by the dove of peace. Miss America of that year, Colleen Kay Hutchins, graced the beautiful presentation.

South Pasadena entered a float that produced many a laugh from the politically minded among the spectators. It showed a happy elephant striding into the White House while a glum donkey left by the back door. To show the city wasn't trying to sway political opinion, South Pasadena's float the next year was "A Bicycle Built for Two" — an elephant in the front seat and a donkey in the rear seat.

If the West was depressed over six straight football defeats, it had reason to rejoice when Tournament president-elect Nicholas named Colwell permanent manager of the festival, the beginning of an unbeaten string of successes that continues to this day.

SEVEN MEDAL OF HONOR WINNERS RECEIVE HEROES' WELCOME AS GRAND MARSHALS

Colwell believes the advent of television was the turning point in Tournament of Roses assured success. "I remember the first production man that NBC sent out here to supervise the Woolworth-sponsored televising of the parade," said Colwell. "He wore a loud checked sport coat and slacks. I recall asking him, 'Can't you afford a full suit of clothes?' " With television paying in excess of a reported million and a half dollars for the right to televise the football game today, Colwell speaks with more affection to the NBC help.

Colwell recalls how Roy Riegels' wrong-way run almost broke the Tournament financially. "We had a clipping service," said Colwell, "to see how well we were doing in publicity. After the Riegels run, the mailman brought sack after sack of clips mentioning the Rose Bowl. At ten cents a clip, it was very, very expensive."

Colwell tells an interesting story of how the Top Hat Band became a fixture in the parade. During the WPA days, the musicians' union insisted upon a union band playing to match the amateur high school musicians in the parade. One union band was paid four times to equalize four high school bands. The union band, the Top Hatters, became so popular they have continued to be an annual feature even though the original union deal no longer exists.

Colwell rates Dwight Eisenhower the most interesting personality in Tournament of Roses history. "He was natural amidst his greatness," says Colwell, who remembers having to keep a telephone installed at all times at Ike's bedside.

Among the minor crises recalled by Colwell were the time Dinah Shore's golden dress was scorched by the exhaust from the motor in her float, and when Steve Allen got lost trying to get to the parade.

When Colwell watches the parade or the football game, he is in communication at all times with Tournament authorities. He has a telephone under his grandstand seat.

"One day I called my wife at home just to ask her how she was. I wanted to make use of my phone," laughs Max.

Colwell, not so incidentally, owes to his Tournament association his finding his wife. Before Walter R. Hoefflin, Jr., became president in 1965, he sent some Tournament films to a nurse in Norway for showings at hospitals there. When he became president, Hoefflin invited the nurse, Kari, to come to Pasadena to see the festival she had helped present to the people in Norway. At a dinner in her honor at the Hoefflin home, the Tournament president invited Colwell to be present. It was love at first sight. The couple soon was married at the Tournament House.

26

Richard Nixon Comes to Pasadena

RICHARD NIXON, 1953

1953

"ROSE BOWL GAMES are kind of special to us. Pat and I had our first date at the Duke-U.S.C. game in 1939," said Richard Nixon, newly elected vice president of the United States, when he accepted the invitation of Tournament president William Nicholas to be grand marshal of the 1953 festival.

Nixon, who was raised in nearby Whittier, California, added: "I saw my first parade as a kid nine years old. We came real early that morning and sat along the curb."

Originally, Nicholas invited Dwight Eisenhower to be grand marshal.

"Actually, knowing that my term was coming in an election year, I decided to contact the heads of both the Democrat and Republican parties asking them to deliver as grand marshal the president-elect. I had a firm agreement from both parties," said Nicholas. "When Mr. Eisenhower was elected president, he agreed to fulfill the commitment. However, in late November he phoned me to say that he hadn't realized how much work was involved in getting ready to set up legislation and get ready for the new Congress which was meeting in early January. He suggested Vice President Nixon come to Pasadena in his place."

Nicholas had to send the invitation to Mexico City where Nixon was making a ceremonial appearance as the representative of the United States. Nicholas phoned down to Gene Biscailuz, former grand marshal, who was in Mexico City; Biscailuz relayed Nicholas' message to the vice president, and Nixon accepted.

Nicholas has many memories of Nixon's appearance at Pasadena, memories that prove that Nixon loved football long before the 1969 season when he attended the Texas-Arkansas game and crowned Texas national champion.

When Nicholas was going over the seating details for the honored guests at the game, the vice president's sister-in-law, having been delegated to represent the family, said, "Don't have Mother and Dad sitting in front of Dick at the game. He is a violent rooter. He would probably

WILLIAM NICHOLAS CROWNS LEAH FELAND

roll up his program and in the excitement knock Mom out by hitting her over the head. Please put Mom and Dad in the seats behind him."

This Nicholas did, and he was happy he listened to the advice.

"When the game started, he got excited," said Nicholas, who was seated next to the vice president. "He started bopping the people in front of him with his program. He really enjoyed the game. Afterward, he visited both dressing rooms before we returned to the Huntington Hotel."

Nicholas' tribute to the Tournament of Roses, after years of committee work, then the Tournament presidency, and now a Football Committee post, sums up the feelings of many men who have devoted their time and energy to making the Pasadena festival worthy of the respect it holds around the world. Nicholas expressed it this way:

"Ringling Brothers does not have the greatest show on earth. The Tournament of Roses has to be the greatest show of them all. I don't think there has been any president in the history of the Tournament who ever went into the organization and its various chairs with any thought of personal gain. It is a most remarkable organization when so many people on a volunteer basis will perform so many duties — the dollar value of this talent so much more than any organization could afford to buy. There is satisfaction in knowing that each year of the Tournament is greater than the previous year."

Mr. and Mrs. Nicholas were guests of the Mexican government in Mexico City, along with the Tournament Queen and her court. "Dean of Women Calkins of Muir High School was busy handling the seven lovely girls, who were being swept off their feet by the Latin lovers," said Nicholas.

He also had the experience of making a speech at the Mexico City Opera House when he received a scroll from the President of Mexico. But then the interpreter turned around during the ceremony and asked Nicholas, "What did you say?"

"Melody in Flowers" was the theme for the 1953 parade. The Anheuser-Busch Clydesdale horses, a popular feature each year thereafter, drew the St. Louis float which was entitled "Waiting for Robert E. Lee." Glendale won the Sweepstakes award. San Gabriel presented a float which needed a mermaid; 163 applications for the role had been received.

The "Song of India" float, a neighborhood entry, carried $10,000 worth of electronic equipment to operate the organ played by organist Korla Pandit, wearing an Indian turban.

The 101,500 spectators at the football game between U.S.C. and Wisconsin received an extra thrill in addition to the ending of the West's losing streak, which had reached six straight games. Robert Harold Sinclair of Fairbanks, Alaska, an amateur photographer, bailed out of a plane over the Bowl into the waiting arms of the police. He was trying for unique aerial shots of the game, he said, but he missed the stadium — and his pictures. He landed twenty feet outside Gate 9 at halftime. Police "arrested" him, then released him because there was no ordinance prohibiting what had happened.

U.S.C. defeated Wisconsin 7-0 when Rudy Bukich, substitute quarterback, threw a twenty-two-yard touchdown pass to Al ("Hoagy") Carmichael in the third quarter. Bukich had taken the place of U.S.C.'s All-American Jimmy Sears, whose leg was broken on the ninth play of the game. Sam Tsagalakis kicked the extra point. "I guess we should have passed more," said Jess Hill, U.S.C. coach, after the victory.

Hill became the first man to have played on and coached winning Rose Bowl teams. He had been a fullback on the 1929 U.S.C. team that defeated Pitt in the Rose Bowl. Since then he has been the athletic director during several U.S.C. Rose Bowl triumphs.

JESS HILL

Tsagalakis had the misfortune of seeing his field-goal attempt from the 23-yard line hit the crossbar. If the kick had been good, U.S.C. would have won 10-0.

"I almost sent in my great punter, Desmond Koch, to attempt the field goal," said Hill. "Sam had been good all year from inside the 25-yard line, although Koch was better from longer distances. I first called for Koch to go in but changed my mind when I saw the ball was inside the 25." But, one of the features of the game was a 72-yard punt by Koch.

Wisconsin put a great deal of pressure on U.S.C. after Alan Ameche, the bruising Badger fullback who gained 133 yards in twenty-eight carries, ran around end for fifty-four yards in the third quarter. He was caught by Frank Clayton, who was described by Sid Ziff of the Los Angeles *Mirror* as an "unknown hero."

"I have a confession to make," said Ziff. "I never even knew he was a member of the team. Jess Hill couldn't even remember in what games he had played. Some people thought this was a dull game, but it wasn't decided until the last twenty-four seconds, when a Wisconsin touchdown drive was stopped."

"The touchdown drive by Bukich, a total advance of 73 yards, happened when Troy's 'Wrecking Crew' took the ball away from the Badgers when Bob Hooks flopped on a fumble deep in Trojan territory," said Braven Dyer in the *Times.* Wrecking Crew? Troy is known for its great titles. The fans in the 1970 game were to see how the "Wild Bunch" did it.

Frank Finch of the *Times* was in the Trojan dressing room after the game and gathered these quotes from some of the winners:

Carmichael: "It was a beautiful pass..But it came to me so slowly I was afraid that some Wisconsin guy would pick it off. We first used that play in the U.C.L.A. game, but it didn't work that time. The maneuver called for the ends to cross and for the right halfback, who was me, to delay two counts before taking off. Then I swung wide and cut back to the middle."

Bukich: "Man, oh man! Did you see the protection I got from Lou Welsh, Ed Pucci, Don Stillwell, and Bob Cox? Except for one pass, I had all the time I needed to throw."

Jack Geyer, writing in the *Times,* said: "S.C. was as potent on the ground as an airplane. Victory came to the Trojans in the third quarter when they forgot what laughingly can be called a running attack and struck by air. Nixon's party won this year, too, after a long wait — 24 years, to be exact."

Marv Goux, later a member of Johnny McKay's coaching staff during U.S.C.'s four straight trips to the Rose Bowl from 1967 through 1970, was one of the stars of U.S.C.'s victory over Wisconsin, according to Dick Hyland in the *Times.* Goux, a linebacker, and his teammates like Charlie Ane and George Timberlake were the key men in stopping Wisconsin, whose game featured the running of Ameche and the passing of quarterback Jim Haluska.

Trojan guard Elmer Willhoite chose the day for his wedding to Mary McCallag of Pasadena. Ironically, he was put out of the game by referee Jack Sprenger for using his fist on defense.

"The official said I was using my fist but I wasn't," explained Elmer. "I was using my shoulder."

Leah Feland was chosen Queen of the 1953 festival. She is one of two queens in Tournament history later to become "Kings." She served as grand marshal of the San Jacinto parade in Texas and was escorted by Roland King. They were married a few months later. The 1959 Queen, Pamela Prather, became Mrs. John F. King after her reign.

Chilled by the 35 degree temperature at 5 a.m. when the parade participants reported to their floats, Queen Feland took no chances with the weather. Under the flowing regal white gown she wore were "long johns" for protection until the parade started at 9 a.m.

1954

BIGGIE MUNN

Biggie Munn, coach at Michigan State, later to become athletic director, had built up Spartan football from relative obscurity. His seven teams from 1947 through 1953 won 53 games, lost 9, and tied 2. He brought a team with an 8-1 record to the Rose Bowl in 1954, an opportunity that arose when the Big Ten renewed the pact with the Coast Conference for three more years, thanks to the deciding vote by Minnesota, his alma mater.

"You never tried to steal our players in our recruiting territory," Bernie Bierman once told Munn. To this day, Munn feels grateful to Minnesota for making his first Rose Bowl trip possible.

Munn used the strategy of chalking an "Off the Floor in '54" message on the cement of the dressing room to inspire his Spartans between halves. They proceeded to defeat Henry ("Red") Sanders' U.C.L.A. Bruins 28-20.

Sid Ziff in the Los Angeles *Mirror* called the Michigan State second half outburst "the greatest second half explosion in Rose Bowl history."

The Spartans scored two touchdowns in the third quarter and another in the fourth to rally from a 14-7 halftime deficit.

Max Stiles in the *Mirror* praised Munn and Sanders for playing the game under "the most cordial relations." Stiles said: "No two coaches ever did more, never went further out of their way to make friends than did Red and Biggie. They were constantly going overboard doing things for everybody. Nor did they glare coldly at one another, as rival mentors so often do. At the Pasadena Kickoff Luncheon yesterday they sat side by side, had their arms around one another much of the time, and patted each other on the back. There were no sour grapes of any kind, no beefs or bellows after the game."

Ziff said a photographer who broke into the Spartan dressing room after the game found Munn in tears as he emotionally thanked his team for the victory. Then he asked his men to kneel with him in silent prayer. Ziff called Munn's team the "Feather Merchants" because they were small and swift.

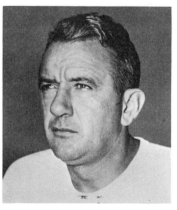

RED SANDERS

Sanders burst into the Michigan State dressing room and said to Munn: "Congratulations, Biggie. This was one of the cleanest and finest games I ever saw a team play. I still think we had a great team. You were just greater."

Ziff's story in the *Mirror* excellently summarized what happened:

"A Bruin lineman missed his block in the second quarter, and Ellis Duckett, Spartan left end, slashed through to hit the football as it was leaving the foot of Paul Cameron. Duckett scooped up the bouncing ball and carried it six yards into the end zone. The Bruins had led 14-0 at the time on a 12-yard pass from Cameron to Bill Stits and a plunge by Cameron plus two conversions by John Hermann.

"Michigan State went ahead 21-14 on touchdowns by the great LeRoy Bolden and equally great Bill Wells plus conversions by Evan Slonac in the third period. U.C.L.A. cut it to 21-20 early in the last quarter when Rommie Loudd took a 28-yard scoring pass from Cameron, although Hermann's conversion failed.

"Cameron punted the ball low and on the line to Wells in the fourth period. The kick was made to order for Wells. Cameron had kicked away from the mass of players on the right side. Wells had a running start down a clear alley along the west sidelines. He didn't stop running until he had reached the end zone 62 yards away. That made it 28-20 with the conversion.

"U.C.L.A. went into the game with a record of seven blocked punts against opponents. U.C.L.A. hadn't had a punt blocked. Yet, in the final analysis, it was the punting game that beat U.C.L.A. in the Rose Bowl."

Tommy Prothro, then U.C.L.A. assistant coach, now Los Angeles Rams and formerly U.C.L.A. head coach, said after the game, "Michigan State was the best team I have ever seen either as a player or coach. I would have called anyone insane if they had said before the game that we would lose on our kicking game."

Ex-U.S.C. coach Gloomy Gus Henderson said the Michigan State split-T, which spread out the U.C.L.A. defense, accounted for the victory. Jordan Olivar, Yale coach, said Munn won it when he switched from double wing and trap plays to the split-T.

Dick Hyland in the *Times* wrote: "The mothers of ancient Sparta advised their sons to return from the Persian wars with their shields or upon them. The Spartans held their shields and the field as the evening shadows lengthened."

Munn told Al Wolf of the *Times* that his team had worked hard on rushing the punter and Duckett's blocking of the Cameron punt was no accident.

The game produced an odd statistic according to modern standards. Michigan State tried only ten passes and completed two, both by Tom Yewcic, while sub Earl Morrall, destined later for pro fame, was zero for two. The Spartan passing yardage was a mere eleven. Michigan State ran for 218 yards, however. "That was our plan," said Munn.

The president of the Tournament in 1954 was Harry W. Hurry. He selected for his grand marshal a Korean war hero, General William F. Dean.

At the Kickoff Luncheon, General Dean said, "The Rose Bowl represents a field of battle to determine the caliber of football played in the Big Ten and Pacific Coast Conference. These two teams symbolize the heights of good sportsmanship and clean living. I have been a guest for over three years of a people who don't understand the meaning of good sportsmanship."

Fifteen years later, Dean looked back at his experience as grand

HARRY W. HURRY PRESENTS
PLAQUE TO GENERAL
WILLIAM F. DEAN

marshal. "I was impressed more than anything else during my partici-pation by the organization of the Pasadena Tournament of Roses Association and its Executive Committee. The dedication of the participating members was outstanding, and the staff setup was comparable to that I have been accustomed to in the military. My most interesting experience was in having the opportunity to meet Dr. John A. Hannah, Michigan State president. I was not able to see the parade in review, my only disappointment. I was taken to the temporary post office, after I had traveled the parade route, where I autographed special day covers. However, later I saw the parade in a news movie theater. My gain from participating in the Tournament was the opportunity to make friends with individuals I might never have met — friendships which have continued to this day."

Queen Barbara Schmidt, who later made many TV commercials for such firms as Kodak, Max Factor, Toni, and Colgate-Palmolive, and who met her husband Terry Mulligan when she was queen of the Los Angeles Home Show, recalled an interesting experience.

BARBARA SCHMIDT

"When I was eleven years old, having just moved from New York to California, Mother and I were passing the Civic Auditorium in Pasadena when we stopped to admire a beautiful young girl. She was wearing a resplendent gown, a shining crown was upon her head, and she was holding an armful of red roses. Many people surrounded her and photographers were taking her picture. She was the 1947 Rose Queen, Norma Christopher, and, of course, the first Rose Queen I had ever seen. Little did I know then that I would some day become a queen, too. It was a strange and happy coincidence that the traditional dinner honoring me as the new queen was held at Norma's home."

Queen Barbara added: "In competing for the role of queen of the Tournament of Roses, I was probably motivated by the dream of all girls to play a part in an enchanting fairy tale — a wonderous fantasy created and made real by the Tournament of Roses. The experience strengthened my belief in the goodness and graciousness of all people and the universal love of fun and beauty evidenced by the spectacle of this annual festival of flowers."

169

The theme of the parade was "Famous Books in Flowers," and Long Beach won the Sweepstakes with a float on which rode Miss France handing Miss America a deed to the Statue of Liberty. Myrna Hanson was the Miss America and Christine Martel the Miss France. They wore filmy evening gowns of white and stood under a canopy of blossoms.

Las Vegas came up with an imitation of a swimming pool in its float.

Six television channels carried the parade, and it was estimated that 67 per cent of Southern California's television sets were tuned in.

27

It Rains— Money and Water

EARL WARREN

MAX COLWELL declared that the most significant development in Tournament of Roses history was the growth of the festival's television and radio exposure.

Lathrop Leishman, as chairman of the Football Committee, has been involved in the negotiations with the networks. It is televising the football game that has produced the revenue in addition to the gate receipts. The parade has not been a revenue-producer from the networks, although the parade telecasts have been worldwide attention-getters.

Leishman recalled early negotiations with Lew Frost, NBC vice president in charge of West Coast operations.

"Our radio broadcasts started out noncommercial," said Leishman. "I recall telling Frost 'You couldn't pay us enough money.' When NBC offered $50,000 for the radio rights of the game while the Tournament was asking $60,000, the negotiations broke down, with the Tournament giving away the early broadcasts without commercials."

When television came along, the Tournament took bids on a year-to-year basis. Radio, at the time, was commanding about $100,000 yearly. CBS came up with a television bid of $210,000 and got the contract for a year. Then Tom Gallery, representing NBC sports events, outbid the rival, and long-range contracts started to be the vogue. The Tournament has remained with NBC, and, in Leishman's opinion and the opinion of most financiers, the policy has paid off. It is believed that current TV sponsors are paying in excess of a million and a half dollars for the Rose Bowl telecast each year. With another million dollars coming in from ticket sales and other sources at game time, the Rose Bowl game has grown to a two-and-a-half-million-dollar venture. So when fans at the game note "time outs" for TV commercials, they should realize why TV can command such interruption in the action.

One of the assuring trends of Tournament of Roses history has been the steady rise of gross revenue. The first games grossed only

171

HAPPY PAIR: ELMER
WILSON AND CHIEF
JUSTICE EARL WARREN

a few thousand dollars. The U.C.L.A.-Michigan State game of 1966 grossed $1,331,669, and the figure per game has gone up a million dollars since, a result of increased television revenue.

How is this money divided each year? In years of stadium improvements, the competing conferences each receive 37½ per cent with the sponsor or the Tournament of Roses receiving 25 per cent. In a normal year, the Tournament gets 15 per cent. In 1966, for example, the Big Ten received $506,925, the Athletic Association of Western Universities received $506,925, and the Tournament of Roses $246,365. The teams paid their own expenses out of their conference shares, the amount being about $75,000. Because the conferences divide up their receipts, each school received some $40,000 to $45,000. From its share, the Tournament of Roses paid all expenses for staging the game plus contributing to policing the city, $149,039. The amount of $44,000 also was taken out for payment against stadium improvement projects, leaving a balance of $52,370 profit to stay in Pasadena. Yes, that's what Pasadena keeps from a typical game. The figure is higher today because of increased television revenue, probably closer to $80,000.

In 1966, under the Tournament contract with the city of Pasadena, half of the $52,370 Pasadena share ($26,185) was turned over to the city treasury. The other half went into the Tournament of Roses trust fund under the joint jurisdiction of the Tournament and the city. This trust fund money is used for upkeep of Tournament buildings.

It is under an arrangement like this through the years that Pasadena has acquired a paid-up stadium that would cost $25,000,000 to

172

build today. The city government's records show it cost Pasadena about $61,434 above the amount received from the Tournament to carry out the policing and clean-up of the festival.

1955

Money isn't all that has rained upon the Tournament. When Elmer Wilson, for years a Pasadena promoter of musical events at Pasadena Civic Auditorium, was president of the Tournament in 1955, rain fell throughout New Year's Day.

Wilson told an interesting story of his experiences in the rain.

"My grand marshal, Chief Justice Earl Warren, and I got soaked riding down the parade route. A luncheon annually is held for the president and grand marshal at Brookside Park near the Rose Bowl. Enroute to that affair, we thought we would stop off at the home of C. Lewis Edwards, one of our Tournament executives. Lewis had a warm fire and a bracer for us, and it was so comfortable there that we remained longer than we anticipated. The secret service people, here to protect the Chief Justice, had received some false reports that efforts would be made against Warren's life during the parade, so all concerned with his safety were alarmed when he could not be located. Somehow nobody knew that we had gone to Edwards' home. When we showed up a bit late at Brookside for the luncheon, a search of the town already was in full force. Warren turned out to be quite a football fan. We sat through the entire game in the rain, and he loved every minute of it even though he was soaked to the skin."

"I have been an avid fan of the Tournament," said Warren. "I have attended thirty consecutive Tournaments over a period of years and perhaps ten others somewhere along the line prior to that time. The Tournament is a great public enterprise carried out with much dignity. For me it is always a happy occasion, particularly when the team from the West wins."

Wilson and Warren were not the only ones to get "lost" that day. The West Point band got lost during the parade and did not finish the route.

ROY ROGERS AND DALE EVANS CHAT WITH ELMER WILSON AND EARL WARREN

DINAH SHORE IN
THE 1955 PARADE

The Monterey Park float lost a wheel in the formation area. A parade committeeman climbed the fence of an auto-wrecking lot and returned with a wheel, which was then put on the float.

Tournament Manager Colwell had to solve a sudden crisis when the Shah of Iran, a guest of the Tournament, arrived with fourteen extra people in his party and accommodations at the parade and game had to be obtained.

A Miami *Herald* reporter, covering the Orange Bowl festivities before watching the Tournament of Roses Parade, wrote in his newspaper: "We had no fog, no smog, no pre-dawn frost, and no long underwear here in Miami to hide the loveliness of the parade beauties. In Pasadena, the parade and game spectators shivered in the rain and near-freezing temperature, while spectators huddled around fires, girls on floats compared colors of their long underwear, a far cry from the beauty that was Miami's."

Colwell, always one to come up with a good answer to any complaint, replied: "Okay, bud, we did have some rain on New Year's Day. But you are wrong about the long red flannels. Our girls just wished they had some."

Despite the weather problems on January 1, 1955, a manager of a world-wide travel service, Janes Mienna, made the following inquiry: "I would like to buy shares in the Rose Bowl. I would consider this an excellent investment."

Colwell had to reply, of course, that no shares in the Rose Bowl were available to any individual. The stadium was property of the City of Pasadena. "You should view with suspicion a person selling Rose Bowl stock as you would a person selling shares in City Hall," Colwell told Mienna.

Because many letters were received each year addressed to "Rose Bowl, Pasadena," Colwell asked Postmaster Ray Holmquist if there was an address for the famed Arroyo Seco stadium. The postmaster replied: "I can't supply you with any address. But I assure you any letters directed to it will be delivered to the Tournament offices."

The year 1955 marked the withdrawal from active Tournament participation of one of the most faithful workers in the festival's history — Dr. Russell E. Simpson. He had served fifty years, never in any higher post than a seat on the board of directors, though he held twenty different committee chairmanships.

John Biggar, Pasadena furniture merchant, who was treasurer of the Tournament, had a rosy face in 1955. Biggar had made a trip to Alaska to sign up some float entrants for the parade. When he returned, he was very optimistic about one particular entry he had been promised. He gave the name of his key Alaska contact to the parade committee chairman. Letter after letter was written to this party in Alaska to firm up the details of the entry. Finally, after an inquiry in Alaska, Biggar's "Alaska big shot" turned out to be a second assistant cook in a lumber camp.

CORDELIA AND WALTER KNOTT RIDE THE KNOTT'S BERRY FARM FLOAT, "JULY 4th," WIN-
NER OF THE 1970 PARADE ANNIVERSARY AWARD

UNIVERSAL STUDIOS' 1970 FLOAT, "ALL THE WORLD'S A STAGE"

(LEFT TO RIGHT) CHARLES L. CONRAD, JR., RICHARD F. GORDON, JR., AND ALAN L. BEAN,
SPACEMEN AND GRAND MARSHALS OF THE 1970 TOURNAMENT

BILLY GRAHAM (LEFT), 1971's GRAND MAR-
SHAL LAWRENCE WELK (BELOW), GRAND MAR-
SHAL IN 1972

HILLARY SHOCKLEY OF STANFORD TACKLED BY BEECROFT OF OHIO STATE IN THE 1971 ROSE BOWL GAME (ABOVE); JANKOWSKI (82) OF OHIO STATE TRIES TO ELUDE BARNES (29) OF STANFORD AS SAMPSON (91) CIRCLES IN FOR THE KILL (BELOW)

THE KNOTTS IN 1971 TELL "FAMILY TALES" OF THE AMERICAN PIONEERS TO ONE OF THEIR
OWN GREAT-GRANDCHILDREN AND TO JACQUELINE HANEY, LITTLE MISS CALIFORNIA,
AND JOHNNIE WHITAKER AND TOD STARKE, OF TV FAME (ABOVE); THE 1971 GRAND
PRIZE WINNER, FARMERS INSURANCE GROUP'S FLOAT. "CINDERELLA," A COMPLEX AND VERY
AIRY CONCEPTION

JOHN CABOT (ABOVE) AND VIRGIL WHITE (RIGHT), TOURNAMENT PRESIDENTS

GRANADA HILLS MARCHING BAND IN THE 1971 PARADE

THE 1971 COURT: JANET KAYE HAGEMEIER, CYNTHIA LEE COLEMAN, CHRISTINE MARIE HARTWELL, QUEEN KATHLEEN DENISE ARNETT, DEBBIE ANN GILMORE, PATRICIA HARTMAN BURCH, PAULA KAY HUBBARD

Starting in 1955, the Tournament of Roses contributed to the Olympic Fund by raising the price of Rose Bowl tickets 49 cents, from $5.50 to $5.99. The odd price was adopted because of an internal revenue order that no ticket could sell for an even $6.00. It had to be one cent less or one cent more.

Elmer Wilson, to this day, holds a most unusual distinction. He has witnessed every Rose Bowl game since the series began in 1916 after the 1902 "teaser." Wilson rates Jon Arnett of U.S.C. and Hopalong Cassady of Ohio State the two most exciting players he has seen in the long series, although the greatest players, in his opinion, were Ernie Nevers of Stanford and Russell Stein of Washington and Jefferson. "Stein, a giant tackle, called their signals," Wilson reminisces.

Another consecutive-game record has emerged, a record that may never be equalled by any other person. An eleven-year-old "businessman," Jay Jackson, of Double J Packaging Company, located near Pasadena, has set as his goal watching a Rose Bowl game every year of his life. When Jay was just a few months old, his father, Jack, took him to the Rose Bowl classic wrapped in a blanket — and Jay has attended the classic each year since. Jay also is the youngest "chairman of the board" of any company. His father named him to that post. Jay officially functions as an officer of the company in a public relations capacity.

Automobiles parked at the 1955 game chewed some $20,000 damage to the Brookside golf course adjacent to the Rose Bowl.

However, the rainstorm did not spoil either the parade or the game.

An actual aircraft, first in the Tournament's history, appeared on San Diego's float. It was a Convair XF-92A delta wing jet research

THE 1955 ROYAL CEREMONY: QUEEN MARILYN SMUIN AND PRESIDENT ELMER WILSON

interceptor covered with flowers. In its cockpit was Col. Royal Baker, Korea jet ace and supersonic test pilot.

Another parade first was the appearance of the U. S. Military Academy band from West Point. It was the first trip west of the Mississippi by a Cadet band.

A hometown hero was honored. Irv Noren, star outfielder for the New York Yankees, rode in his Yankee uniform on the Pasadena American Legion Post 13 entry, "Champions Are Made, Not Born."

Marilyn Smuin was 1955 Queen. The wife of Dr. Wells F. Martell today, she lives in Oxnard, California.

The crowd was over a million along the parade route and headlines in the newspapers described the spectacle as "glittering." The theme was "Familiar Sayings in Flowers." Again Long Beach won the Sweepstakes with a float entitled "A Thing of Beauty Is a Joy Forever."

That also could have been the motto of Woody Hayes and his Ohio State football team, which defeated U.S.C. 20-7 in the mud and rain.

WOODY HAYES

Never known for making the statements his opponents most want to hear, Hayes told Sid Ziff of the Los Angeles *Mirror:* "My coaches who sat in the press box said we would have beaten U.S.C. by a higher score on a dry field. They thought our men would have gone a little farther on every play."

Hayes also said, "There are about four, possibly five, teams in the Big Ten that could beat U.S.C. . . . Big Ten teams are better in the Rose Bowl because they are raised on tougher competition. . . . The bands should have been required to stay on the sidelines instead of putting on the show where we were going to play. I think bands are a fine thing, but they owe their popularity to football, not the other way around. If you don't believe that, invite the bands out to the Rose Bowl some year without the football teams and see how much of a crowd they would draw."

When U.S.C. coach Hill heard that Hayes believed at least four other Big Ten teams could have handled the Trojans, Hill retorted: "Is that so? Well, that's mighty generous of him. Just say for me I'd like to play Ohio State again on a dry field. The rain hurt us a lot. We planned to throw and rely on our speed. We were handcuffed both ways by the rain."

The Ohio State victory increased the howling in the West for an end to annual beatings in Pasadena. The Pacific Coast Conference was indulging in the luxury at that time of not permitting its champion to compete two years in a row, and scribes like Ziff shouted, "We should play our champion each year or get out. If we can't beat them with our best, we shouldn't try to do it with our second best."

U.C.L.A. was adjudged the best team in the West during the 1954 campaign, but was restricted by the PCC rule from going to Pasadena.

"Ohio State definitely is No. 1 in the nation," Hayes told Jack Tobin of the *Mirror*.

Braven Dyer in the *Times* described the 89,191 spectators at the game as "waterlogged lunatics." He described the playing conditions "the worst in Rose Bowl history."

Dave Legget, Ohio State quarterback, was loudly praised by most writers. He did not fumble the ball once in slipping it to Hopalong Cassady, Bob Watkins, and Dick Harkrader on quick opening shots which called for split-second timing. Marvelous Marv Goux was given most of the praise for what stop-work the Trojans of Jess Hill managed during the mudfest.

Paul Zimmerman of the *Times* wrote: "Drives of 77, 68, and 35 yards resulted in Ohio State's three touchdowns with Legget playing the feature role. He scored the first touchdown on a three-yard plunge on the second play of the second quarter, threw a 21-yard pass to Watkins for the second score only a half dozen plays later, and then flipped a pitchout to Harkrader for a nine-yard scoring run in the final period.

"Fumbles hurt U.S.C. Jim Contratto's second successive fumble fell into the ready hands of Jim Parker, and from this break Legget engineered his first touchdown drive. Most of the runs were to the outside on pitchouts. Legget set up the second touchdown when he latched on to Frank Hall's bobble."

Zimmerman described an Aramis Dandoy eighty-eight-yard touchdown punt return for U.S.C.'s only score as follows:

"There was little more than five minutes of the second quarter remaining when Dandoy cut loose with the most brilliant run of the afternoon to put the Trojans temporarily in striking distance.

"Hubert Bobo, back to kick, had to duck away from two charging Trojans and barely got the ball away. The punt was a line-drive affair that went 55 yards before Dandoy fielded the dribbling ball on his

14. The Trojan eluded two onrushing Buckeyes and fought his way to midfield where George Belotti, 231-pound tackle, served up the key block. The fleet Trojan did a neat job of eluding Bobo after that as he sped toward the end zone."

A fumble by Arnett, the most exciting Trojan runner other than Dandoy, set up another Ohio State scoring chance after Jon thrilled the crowd with a thirty-one-yard run to midfield. Bob Thornton recovered, and the Buckeyes punched goalward. The Trojans stopped them, however, and Arnett ran seventy yards before Cassady dragged him into the mud. When U.S.C. was stopped after that, Ohio State marched back to score the game's final touchdown.

28

Big Ten Dominance Continues

DUFFY DAUGHERTY

1956

THE TOURNAMENT of 1956 presented Charles E. Wilson, Secretary of Defense, as grand marshal.

It presented June Allyson-type Joan Culver as queen. Today Miss Culver is the wife of Dr. J. C. Warren of Costa Mesa, California.

The 1956 festival also presented Dr. Alfred L. Gerrie as president. He started Tournament work forty-five years previously as a youngster who received ten cents an hour for tying flowers on a float. Then he ran home to don an angel's costume to ride on the float.

The theme of the parade during Dr. Gerrie's year as president was "Pages from the Ages." Burbank won the Sweepstakes Prize with a float depicting the planets, sun, moon, and stars. Thousands of orchids, sweet peas, and rose petals were used.

At the parade Mrs. Mildred Bosteder and Mrs. Howard Willis of Pasadena introduced comfort to curbside parade-viewing. They brought a davenport to the sidewalk's edge and lived it up with food and drinks plus blankets to keep warm.

David Llewellyn of Los Angeles, who rode in the first Pasadena parade in 1890 and in every parade after that until 1956, appeared with his world champion palomino "One in a Million," the saddle and trimmings valued at an estimated $75,000.

Post Cereals' "I Love a Western" float created the illusion of a stagecoach and horses emerging from a television set as a family watched the show. Television Western stars Roy Rogers and Dale Evans added a realistic touch.

Occidental Life Insurance Company brought back memories to paradegoers with its "Tournament First Ladies" float, a tribute to Rose Queens of other years. Riding on the float were Hallie Woods McConnell, first Rose Queen (1905); Dolores Brubach Chase (1942), who did not get to ride in a parade that first month of World War II; and four other queens. Occidental, in fact, has made it a point to have the Rose Queen of the preceding year grace its annual float.

Another commercial float that attracted the youngsters was the Bakery and Confectionery Workers' "First Birthday Cake," with a

179

QUEEN JOAN CULVER

EQUESTRIAN DAVID LLEWELLYN

huge floral one-year-old child, his arms moving up and down as he huffed and puffed, trying to blow out the flame of a lone candle.

The big story in 1956, however, was the continuing Big Ten domination in the Rose Bowl. Duffy Daugherty's Michigan State team defeated U.C.L.A. 17-14 on a forty-one-yard field goal by Dave Kaiser with seven seconds left to play. This may have been the most dramatic field goal ever kicked in the Southland until the 1969 season when Ron Ayala of U.S.C. defeated Stanford with a field goal as the final gun cracked.

A series of penalties against U.C.L.A. had forced Ronnie Knox to punt from behind his goal line, thus setting the stage for Kaiser's clutch field goal when Michigan State, too, got bitten by the penalty bug.

Daugherty, a popular story-teller as well as a winning coach, revealed how a lost contact lens may have been the deciding factor in his 1956 triumph.

The score was 14-14.

"We had time for just one more play with the ball on U.C.L.A.'s 24-yard line and the clock stopped," said Daugherty. "Two of our kickers had previously missed field goal attempts. Our best kicker, Kaiser, had not been doing this chore for us during the latter part of the season due to a leg injury. He had not practiced kicking field goals for two months. I knew Kaiser had the ability to kick the ball forty-one yards, but the gamble was whether he could be accurate after so long a layoff.

"In addition, Kaiser normally wore contact lenses but did not have them available the day of the Rose Bowl game. He had lost one and didn't have the set. This meant he could not see the goal posts with any degree of clarity.

"I decided to let Dave make the kick. The lost contact lens was probably the reason he kept his head down and met the ball squarely. If he had had these lenses in his eyes, he might have let curiosity get the better of him. He might have looked up to see whether the kick was good.

"Immediately after the kick, Kaiser turned around and waited for the referee to make the signal. He did not follow the course of the ball through the air. It wasn't until he saw the referee's arms go up that he knew the kick had been true. His kick is one that every Spartan will long remember. Dave will go down in Michigan State football history as Golden Toe Kaiser."

Harvey Knox, stormy stepfather of U.C.L.A. tailback Ronnie, blamed Coach Red Sanders for the defeat.

"Kaiser's kick didn't beat U.C.L.A. Sanders blew the game in the second quarter," Harvey Knox told Melvin Durslag of the Los Angeles *Examiner*. He said Sanders overdid the running stuff when, with the score 7-0 in U.C.L.A.'s favor, he let Ronnie sit on the bench when Ronnie could have offered some run-pass variety to the Bruin attack, which had gained field position for a second touchdown possibility.

Vincent X. Flaherty of the *Examiner* said, "It was a good thing Kaiser made his kick when he did, because if it had been a second later the goal posts wouldn't have been there. Happy Michigan State rooters toppled them over as soon as the kick was signaled good."

Jim Decker of U.C.L.A. had intercepted a diagonal pass by Michigan State quarterback Earl Morrall on the Spartan 20 and carried it

DR. ALFRED L. GERRIE AND
CHARLES E. WILSON

to the 16 to set up U.C.L.A.'s first score early in the game. Sam Brown and Bob Davenport ripped for steady gains with Davenport going the final two yards to score. Jim Decker made it 7-0 with his conversion.

Nine minutes into the second quarter, Michigan State tied the score on an eighty-yard drive. Morrall passed thirteen yards to Clarence Peaks for the touchdown and Gerald Planutis kicked the point.

Early in the fourth quarter, Morrall lateraled to Peaks, who shot a long pass to tall John Lewis, who caught the ball on the 20 and ran in for a sixty-seven-yard touchdown play. Planutis again converted.

After nine minutes of the fourth quarter, U.C.L.A. moved fifty-six yards in five plays. Knox passed from midfield to Jim Decker on the Michigan State 16. Walter Kowalczyk pulled down Decker on the 7. Knox ploughed to the 2 from where Doug Peters went over on a dive. Decker's kick tied it 14-14.

Michigan State drove back until Hardiman Cureton and Steve Palmer led a Bruin stand that forced an unsuccessful Planutis field-goal try.

U.C.L.A. soon got into trouble and, rather than risk a safety so close to his own goal line, Knox tried to punt on second down; the ball didn't go far enough and the play eventually led to Kaiser's winning field goal.

"Tell the folks back home that the winter won't be so cold now," Daugherty told a Michigan writer.

1957

FOREST EVASHEVSKI

The West's football pact with the Big Ten received a jolt before the 1957 Tournament of Roses when the Pacific Coast Conference barred Washington, U.S.C., U.C.L.A., and California from playing in the Bowl because of infractions of conference rules. It also allowed many players in these universities to play in only five games, an action that reduced the strength of these teams and made it possible for Oregon State to win the PCC title and a Rose Bowl spot for the first time. Iowa won in the Big Ten and became the Beaver's opponent. The two had met in the first game of the season, Iowa winning by a point.

"It Gets Easier All the Time for Big Ten," shouted the headline in the Los Angeles *Mirror* after Forest Evashevski's Iowans defeated Tommy Prothro's Beavers 35-19.

"If this keeps up (10-1 for the Big Ten to date), the Humane Society will have to step in," commented Sid Ziff in the *Mirror*. Ziff summed up the West's latest defeat with "Pitiful line, miserable tackling, poor strategy. It all fits the weakest team we have ever sent into the Rose Bowl." Ziff accused Oregon State players of just grabbing Iowa tacklers instead of tackling them.

ANN MOSSBERG

Evashevski told reporters that Iowa won the game for Cal Jones, Iowa All-American tackle the year before who had been killed in a Canadian air crash.

"His spirit was in the back of our minds all day," said Ken Ploen, the Iowa quarterback who led the Hawkeye triumph. Braven Dyer of the *Times* called it a "Ploen beating."

Ploen completed nine of ten passes. He rushed for fifty-nine yards net. He opened the scoring with a forty-nine-yard run. Collins Hagler scored twice, once on a sixty-six-yard run.

Oregon State fumbled the ball away three times. Dick Hyland in the *Times* said, "The Black Bandits of Benton County turned out to be the most philanthropic group to perform in the Pasadena classic in years."

Prothro said, "Our first fumble and their first long run were very significant." He was referring to Beaver fullback Tom Berry's fumble to Iowa end Frank Gilliam on Iowa's 40 in the opening minute and Ploen's touchdown run five plays later.

"It beats me why the team that is rougher, tougher, and more aggressive always has to come from the Big Ten," said Maxwell Stiles in the *Mirror*. "Why can't our own men hit harder, run harder, just once in a while?"

Oregon State's best were Joe Francis, who ran seventy-three yards and completed ten of twelve passes; Sterling Hammack who caught four passes, one for a touchdown; and touchdown scorers Nub Beamer and Tom Berry.

Ann Mossberg was the Queen, Capt. Eddie Rickenbacker the grand marshal, and John S. Davidson the Tournament president for the 1957 festival, which had the theme "Famous Firsts in Flowers."

Queen Ann is today Mrs. Robert Hall, Jr., and lives in Hacienda Heights, California.

Indio, California, won the Sweepstakes with the float entitled "First Date Festival." It was an Arabian setting in delicate pastel-

EDDIE RICKENBACKER AND
JOHN S. DAVIDSON

shaded petals. Real dates in clusters were suspended from floral trees for which 20,000 orchids were used. Among the "firsts" depicted in the parade were "Baby's First Tooth" and the "First Satellite."

Two familiar parade features were missing in 1957. For the first time in some twenty years, Los Angeles County Sheriff Eugene Biscailuz didn't ride in the parade astride his palomino. The sheriff, suffering from eye injuries sustained in a grass fire, instead rode in a carriage. Dave Llewellyn became ill the last minute and missed his first parade as a rider since the Tournament had started in 1890.

1958

John Biggar became president of the Tournament for the 1958 festival. "I have always been impressed by the desire of the men in white to upgrade the quality of the floats," he said.

Biggar also has looked back at his 1951 one-night stands with Leishman and Nicholas traveling by railroad to Pacific Coast Conference schools when the question arose regarding continued participation in the Rose Bowl.

"Participation in this great civic event is the motivating force and success is the reward for taking part," said Biggar, who rated as his biggest thrill having the privilege of inviting Dr. Robert G. Sproul, University of California president, to be his grand marshal.

After his presidency, Biggar was to serve for many years on the Football Committee of the Tournament.

The Queen was Gertrude Wood, who was among the girls who had to survive a rain squall that broke up one of the judging sessions. Among Miss Wood's memories are appearances on George Gobel's network television show with Eddie Fisher. Today she lives in Los Gatos, California.

After the 1958 parade, William Ferrier, a television viewer from LaPorte, Indiana, wrote to Colwell: "Every American should see Washington, D. C., and the Tournament of Roses parade. The one

GERTRUDE WOOD

ROBERT GORDON SPROUL
AND JOHN H. BIGGAR

184

fills you with awe and the solidarity of our country. The other fills you with joy and respect for the Creator of all mankind and beautiful things."

"Daydreams in Flowers" was the 1958 theme. Burbank won the Sweepstakes award with a replica of the gold cup it had won two years before as the Sweepstakes winner.

Woody Hayes again became a winner when his Ohio State team defeated underdog Oregon 10-7 on a thirty-four-yard field goal by Don Sutherin in the fourth quarter. Oregon, however, was the team that won the hearts of the 98,202 spectators with a tremendous effort, after being given little credit before the battle started.

Not all sports writers on the Coast thought in advance that Ohio State would rout the Ducks. Bill Boni, Spokane sports editor who later was sports editor of the St. Paul *Dispatch-Pioneer Press,* predicted Oregon would lose by only three points.

Big Ten writers said after the game that they believed Oregon deserved to win the game. Bert McGrane of the Des Moines *Register* said: "Oregon tore a gaping hole in Big Ten prestige. They were all guts and all heart. They were another version of the Gas House Gang." Charles Johnson, sports editor of the Minneapolis *Star and Tribune,* added: "Ohio State had to fight for its football life and only one bad break kept Oregon from the upset of the season. Crabtree was a sensation. Oregon should have won. We hate to pull against our own territory, but we wish Oregon had won today."

Jim Schlemmer of the Akron *Beacon-Journal* said: "The Bucks were outplayed decisively. Oregon won everything but the score."

Kaye Kessler of the Columbus *Citizen* added: "This was a hell of a lot better Oregon team than I expected to see."

Cy Burick of the Dayton *News* declared: "You have to give Len Casanova a lot of credit for defensing Ohio State after seeing those pictures. Ohio State didn't give the ball away. That's why it won."

Oliver Kuechle of the Milwaukee *Journal,* who may be the only sports writer outside the state of California who has seen every game in the West-Big Ten series through 1970, stated: "I had written before coming to California that this would turn out to be the weakest defensive team the Big Ten had ever sent to the Rose Bowl. Oregon deserved to win and I'm sorry they lost. Oregon was well coached and took full advantage of Ohio State's defensive weaknesses."

John Dietrich of the Cleveland *Plain Dealer* concluded: "Ohio State was baffled to a standstill."

Francis Powers of the Chicago *Daily News* stated: "Oregon played 60 minutes of inspired football."

George Pasero of the Portland *Journal* commented: "It was no surprise to me that Oregon played so well. The Ducks have played some good games because they have real desire and have reacted to humiliation."

Sid Ziff of the *Mirror* concluded that Hayes' desire to let this team have some fun on its Rose Bowl trip nearly backfired. Ziff's observation may explain why Hayes was much tougher in denying his boys a good time when they returned in 1969. On the latter trip he wouldn't let the Buckeyes compete in the beef-eating contest at Lawry's Restaurant in Beverly Hills, where the two Rose Bowl teams annually eat it out in the "Beef Bowl." That hungry Buckeye team whipped U.S.C. and O. J. Simpson.

"Nobody can be humiliated like our boys were and take it," said Coach Len Casanova. "They were derided by everybody, but they showed 'em. In my mind, I have the best team in the country. It out-gutted everybody and came from nowhere. Our boys went out there to show the Los Angeles sports writers how wrong they were."

Oregon led in first downs, 21-19, and made the most yardage — 351 to 304. But Mr. Hayes came off a winner again.

"Sutherin was our star," said Woody. "He had a bad back and a bad leg, and he hadn't kicked for a long time until a week before the game because of his injuries."

"I was sure I would make it good," said Sutherin. "I didn't look up. It felt good. I didn't know it was good, though, until my holder, Frank Kremblas, jumped up and said, 'Thank God.'"

DON CLARK OF OHIO STATE FOLLOWS BLOCKER FRANK KREMBLAS

LEN CASANOVA

Ironically, Oregon had tried a field goal from the same spot earlier, but Jack Morris' effort was no good.

Ohio State took the opening kickoff and marched seventy-nine yards to a touchdown. After Bob White and Don Clark made steady gains, Kremblas passed thirty-seven yards to Jim Houston to the 2. Kremblas scored from there and added the extra point.

Oregon tied it up in the second quarter. This eighty-yard drive featured Crabtree pitchouts and keepers. A pitchout to Charley Tourville made a big gain deep in Ohio State territory. After a five-yard keeper put the ball on the 5, Crabtree pitched out to Jim Shanley, and Shanley went over untouched. Jack Morris' kick made it 7-7.

Oregon did not have to punt once during the game. There were no runbacks of the two Ohio State punts, since both went out of bounds.

Jack Crabtree was the star of the game as he quarterbacked the surprising Ducks' attack, completing ten of seventeen passes and contributing some effective running.

"We intercepted two passes and recovered two fumbles. We figure if we can get the ball four times on turnovers, we can win," said Hayes. "Oregon had good defense and its attack was pretty good. Oregon was better than its three losses during the year suggested and better than its twenty-point underdog role."

Ron Stover, Oregon end, caught ten passes during the game and was adjudged one of the finest receivers ever to play in Pasadena, but he made a most costly fumble and ruined Oregon's comeback chances. After Ohio State took the lead at 10-7 on Sutherin's kick in the first minute of the fourth period, Oregon set off on a recovery drive. Crabtree passed from midfield to Stover, who caught the ball on Ohio State's 24. When he was hit with force, the ball bounced away — and Ohio State's Joe Cannavino recovered. The Buckeyes then used up most of the remaining time with a typical Hayes ball-control style of game.

Walter O'Malley, owner of the Los Angeles Dodgers, who had just moved to the Coast from Brooklyn, saw the game and said, "The Rose Bowl looks like a good place for my ball team."

However, subsequent negotiations led to the Dodgers remaining at the Coliseum until O'Malley could build his own new stadium in Chavez Ravine.

29

First of the Pamelas— and a Fellow Named Jim

PAMELA PRATHER

1959

THE 1959 TOURNAMENT of Roses can be called the start of "The Pamela Decade."

Pamela Prather was Queen in 1959. In the next decade or so, two more young beauties named Pamela were to become queens — Pamela Anicich in 1969 and Pamela Dee Tedesco in 1970.

The 1959 game was the last in which the Big Ten enjoyed its long streak of football dominance. Since Iowa came out West in 1959 to drub California 38-12, the West has managed to stay very competitive in the inter-conference series, winning six of the next eleven games.

The Pacific Coast Conference was crumbling by the time the 1959 game rolled around. The wounds of the "purge" by the northern members hadn't healed, but schools like California were now permitted to play in the Rose Bowl. The feeling in the West among some PCC members was that the Conference ought to disband and give up the pact with the Big Ten. Meanwhile, the Big Ten got caught in a 5-5 vote for renewal of the pact; hence, it was left up to the individual Big Ten schools to negotiate with the West if they wished to compete in Pasadena on January 1.

Iowa, with a Big Ten champion under Forest Evashevski, was only too happy to invade and meet Pete Elliott's California team, which was led by Joe Kapp, destined to become the king of the National Professional League quarterbacks with the Minnesota Vikings in the 1969 season.

Evashevski and Elliott, outstanding athletes during great careers at Michigan, will go down in football history as two of the Rose Bowl's most distinctive coaches. Evashevski came out with a winner twice. Elliott has had the experience not only of playing in the Rose Bowl with Michigan in the 1948 game, but has coached on each side. Elliott lost in 1950 as a coach of the Western team (California), but he returned as a Big Ten mentor in 1964 to lead Illinois over Washington.

E. L. BARTLETT DANCES WITH QUEEN PAMELA PRATHER

PRESIDENT STANLEY K. BROWN AND PAMELA

The 1959 game was advertised as a battle of quarterbacks: Randy Duncan of Iowa *vs.* Kapp of California. Duncan didn't have to duel Kapp in any passing war. Iowa made 441 yards rushing out of 528 yards, with 298-pound Mac Lewis at guard opening holes for Bob Jeter and Willie Fleming, the star runners of the day.

Maxwell Stiles, in the Los Angeles *Mirror,* after the decisive Iowa victory, the twelfth by the Big Ten in thirteen games during the pact, commented: "Maybe it is just as well the Pacific Coast Conference is dying. That's one way to end the pain. Until we signed the pact with the Big Ten, I always thought Vassar.was located in the East. Now I'm not so sure." Further Stiles wrote: "Evashevski knew where Cal was weakest, at the tackles. That's where Iowa hit. As long as it worked (and the speedy Iowa backs whistled by while they worked), why change it?"

"I'm probably the lousiest-feeling winning coach in Rose Bowl history," Evashevski said after the game. He had the flu with a temperature of 101 the day before the game, and got up out of a sickbed to handle his team.

When Elliott told writers his California boys had worked hard on stopping Iowa's outside stuff and forced Iowa to go inside, Stiles commented: "That's like being happy if you don't lose all your money in the stock market. You lost it to the ponies instead."

Other remarks about the game:

Rube Samuelsen in the Pasadena *Star-News* — "You'd almost think National Football League champions played Citrus Junior College. Cal's lineman came across so straight that Iowa cross-blocked them silly."

Kapp to Elliott — "I let you down, coach."

Elliott — "Iowa could move the ball. If they're not great, they're close to it."

Bill Miller in the Pasadena *Star-News* — "Lewis brushed the Cal linemen aside like he was swatting flies."

Evashevski — "Films showed us our running game had to work from a spread. We have been able to hit the home run all year."

Duncan — "On the first play of the game I saw both of their linebackers line up deep. Then I knew our running game had to go."

California got a break at the start of the game when Bill Patton recovered a fumble by Fleming on Iowa's 36. But four plays made only four yards. Iowa opened with a seventeen-yard run by Jeter and had a touchdown in ten plays when Duncan sneaked over. A forty-one-yard run by Jeter and a Duncan pass to Jeff Langston for a touchdown made it 14-0, Bob Prescott kicking both points after touchdown, and the rout was on.

With the score 20-0 against Cal, Kapp's pitchout plays worked in a third-quarter drive that culminated with Jack Hart scoring. A thirty-seven-yard run by Fleming on a reverse and Jeter's eighty-one-yard sprint, however, really settled the issue. Fleming scored again before Kapp got a token touchdown pass to Jack Hart.

Jeter wound up with 194 yards for the day, to beat by 43 yards Bobby Grayson's total for Stanford in 1934.

Queen Pamela, now Mrs. John King, resides in Old Greenwich, Connecticut.

In addition to Iowa saluting itself that afternoon with a super performance, the Tournament of Roses saluted Alaska, the 49th and newest state. The parade theme was "Adventures in Flowers," and one of the more interesting adventures was South Pasadena's elephant, animated by eleven persons riding inside and unseen. Glendale won the Sweepstakes award, and Quaker Oats won the Grand Prize in the business division.

That the space age was just around the corner was evident in many of the floats. Long Beach's "Adventures in Universe" featured a rocket blast of white pompons. Gardena presented the "First Moon Shot," and San Gabriel came up with a portrayal of "A Visit to the Planet Earth."

E. L. Bob Bartlett, the newly elected senior Alaska senator, was the choice of Tournament president Stanley K. Brown for grand marshal. Lawyer Brown, still in practice in Pasadena, has a fond recollection of his experience in Merriam, Kansas, during his travels as the Tournament's president and emissary of good will.

"In my visit to the high school at Merriam, at an occasion when the 2,600 students were in convocation to receive various awards for past athletic and scholastic achievements, my presence had not been announced because the superintendent wanted to make it a surprise," recalled Brown. "In his introduction he said the President of the Tournament of Roses had come all the way from California to present the school with a picture of its band, which marched in the Tournament parade. For a moment there was complete silence, and

BEAUTIFUL WRIGLEY MANSION,
THE TOURNAMENT HOUSE

then the applause which ensued was in volume greater than I have experienced before or since. It made an everlasting impression."

Brown said he always had been a part of some form of civic, fraternal, patriotic, religious, or cultural activity, but he was especially interested in Tournament work because he believed it to be the greatest organization of its kind in the world.

"After twenty-five years of committee work and having gone through the various steps, I was honored by being selected for the presidency of the Tournament," Brown said. "The element that has impressed me most has been men working together, accomplishing wonders because they do not care who gets the individual credit."

1960

While the 1960 Tournament will be remembered most by sports fans because Jim Owens' Washington team stopped the Big Ten's winning streak with a 44-8 triumph over Wisconsin, Tournament president Raymond A. Dorn looks back with considerable pride on several accomplishments. Besides having Richard Nixon for his grand marshal (Nixon's second such visit), Dorn handled the negotiations for the gift of the William Wrigley mansion and gardens on South Orange Grove Boulevard to the city and the Tournament for use as a public park and Tournament headquarters. Today it is one of Pasadena's beauty spots, visited by thousands each year.

Dorn outlined the steps in the transaction:

"Shortly before taking office as president and after the death of Mrs. Wrigley, who had previously resided at the residence, I wrote to P. K. Wrigley in Chicago suggesting that, inasmuch as the old mansion was practically the starting point for the parade, he might like to consider it as a monument to his parents by donating the property for that purpose. After two trips out here by the trustees of the estate and two trips to Chicago on my part to negotiate the matter, the gift was made.

"Aside from the Wrigley mansion proving an ideal headquarters for the Tournament, I had a feeling then, and I think the intervening years have reaffirmed it, that South Orange Grove Boulevard one day would be completely improved with garden apartments and become the one large 'green spot' of our community."

Dorn recalled happy experiences with the Nixons:

"The Vice President was a very warm, cooperative grand marshal. Together with his wife Pat and their two daughters, he seemed to enjoy every minute of the activities, including viewing the float-building," declared Dorn.

"Pat and the two girls arrived on the scheduled time, but the Vice President was delayed in Washington because of negotiations he was conducting toward settling the steel strike. He was due to speak at the Kickoff Luncheon December 31, and it was touch and go whether he would make it. He arrived at the Rose Bowl area by helicopter and was driven to the Civic Auditorium, arriving just five minutes before he was due to speak. He proved to have a wealth of sports information which he disclosed in his talk. This was the first knowledge I had of his deep interest in sports.

"The membership tea and reception was scheduled to be held immediately following the Kickoff Luncheon, and we had been advised by the Vice President's Secret Service people that he would not attend the function. However, shortly after the tea had started, with some 450 members and their wives present, he showed up at the reception and stood there in the receiving line for a couple of hours shaking hands with everyone.

"On New Year's Eve, he and his family accompanied my family, including my daughter Andrea and son Gary, to view float-construction activities. Upon returning to the Huntington Hotel about midnight, my family and I were invited to the Nixon suite and enjoyed a toast to the New Year with them.

"When the daughters, Patricia and Julie, were asked whether they would like to ride in their father's official car down the parade route, their answer was, 'How can we see the parade if we ride in it?' So they sat in the stands."

To the question "Why do so many men seem anxious, irrespective of their social or financial status, to work long hours for the Tournament of Roses?" Dorn said:

RAY DORN AND RICHARD NIXON, 1960

"Because these fellows know the Tournament of Roses is bigger than anyone in it. It also offers an association with a great group of men. It provides a complete change of pace from their ordinary daily lives. And they can see each year where their efforts have developed a thing that is outstandingly successful and that has provided a few hours of enjoyment to millions of people throughout the world."

Dorn, a Pasadena real-estate developer, has also served on the Tournament Football Committee with Messrs. Lay Leishman, William Nicholas, and Stanley Hahn, all former presidents. These popular good-will ambassadors are known as the Tournament's "Four Horsemen."

Long Beach took the Sweepstakes trophy again in 1960; Occidental Life, always an active Tournament participant, won the Grand Prize. The theme of the parade was "Tall Tales and True."

A Minneapolis-born beauty, Margarethe Bertelson, was queen in 1960. She is the wife of Capt. Richard G. Knoblock, who, in 1969, was stationed in Okinawa.

RAY DORN CROWNS
MARGARETHE BERTELSON

A bleary-eyed football fan ambled into the Rose Bowl after the 1960 game had started. He looked up at the scoreboard and mumbled to his pal. "My gosh, Ed!" he said, his voice quivering in horror. "This is the Rose Bowl, not the Orange Bowl. I told you we were in the wrong place."

The Wisconsin team of Milt Bruhn also quickly discovered it was in the wrong place. Washington, led by Bob Schloredt, star quarterback who had only one eye, and halfback George Fleming, had a 17-0 lead before Wisconsin had made a first down.

Owens had worked his Huskies hard for this game and had removed the West's defeatist complex. He had his men fired up. They came believing they could win and knowing they had the weapons and the battle plan. That battle plan included the run-or-pass option work of quick-hitting Schloredt.

Don McKeta opened the scoring by taking a pass option from Schloredt and scoring from the 6 to climax a forty-eight-yard drive. Fleming kicked a thirty-six-yard field goal and Fleming returned a Jim Bakken punt fifty-three yards for a touchdown.

QUEEN MARGARETHE AND HER COURT AT THE ROSE BOWL GAME

TOM HAMILTON

BOB SCHLOREDT

After Tom Wiesner plunged over for Wisconsin, Lee Felkins took a Schloredt twenty-three-yard pass with a most sensational diving catch for a touchdown. Ray Jackson zipped over on a short gainer for another touchdown before Schloredt climaxed a ninety-two-yard march with his keeper for a score. Bob Hivner ended the scoring by completing a short pass to Don Millich for the final touchdown.

Dale Hackbart, Wisconsin star, was completely bottled up by the Washington defense. Schloredt, meanwhile, rushed twenty-one times for 81 yards and completed four of seven passes for 102 yards more.

Said Owens: "Our agility offset their weight edge. We made a lot over their strong side."

Bruhn, the Badger coach (and, incidentally, a former teammate of this author on the University of Minnesota baseball teams of 1933 and 1934), said: "They maneuvered us into a hole right off the bat and down went our spirit. As things went their way, we could see them getting higher and higher."

Rube Samuelsen wrote in the Pasadena *Star-News:* "When Washington went ahead 7-0, you knew then and there that New Year's Day belonged to the long-suffering Far West. You knew it because here was a team trained to the hilt for an all-out performance."

Tom Hamilton, the executive director of the newly formed Athletic Association of Western Universities, which was to replace the Pacific Coast Conference in Rose Bowl matters, said following the game: "The belief existing here, call it Big Tenitis, that the Big Ten is always superior, has been disproved. This Washington team is good. From now on, the Big Ten'd better be ready when New Year's Day comes around."

The AAWU, now called the Pac Eight, has proved the merit of Hamilton's warning.

Other statements of significance after the game:

Tug Wilson of the Big Ten: "I was impressed by Washington's speed."

Richard Nixon, who since has become a foremost American sports authority (ask Texas about 1969): "As a Californian, I'm delighted to see the West do so gosh-darned good."

194

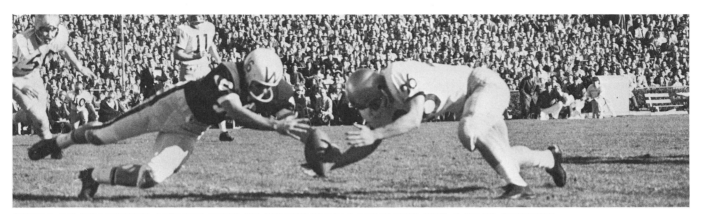

HOBBS OF WISCONSIN AND WOOTEN OF WASHINGTON SCRAMBLE FOR LOOSE PIGSKIN

Bruhn again: "Fleming's punt return hurt us. We had one good shot at him in their territory. Then he was gone. All we had to do was play some sound football, but Washington wouldn't let us."

The Big Ten was unable to agree on a contract with the AAWU after this game, but the Tournament of Roses allied itself with the AAWU, which was given authority to select its Rose Bowl foe until a pact could be negotiated. It was here that Minnesota again proved to be the saving factor in Big Ten-AAWU relations by agreeing to come for the 1961 game against Washington when it was riding high as national champion.

VICTORY RIDE FOR COACH JIM OWENS

30
Minnesota
Gets Repaid

WILLIAM F. QUINN

1961

WHAT DOES THE GOVERNOR of Hawaii have to say after coming to California to serve as grand marshal of the Tournament of Roses Parade?

Governor William F. Quinn, now president of the Dole Company in Honolulu, summed it up after leading the 1961 parade:

"I remember my participation in the Tournament of Roses with great pleasure. I was impressed most by the dedicated efforts of all those people who work an entire year to make the parade and all of the events surrounding the game so exciting and memorable. I don't know that I have ever encountered a civic group that pursued its objective with such intense vigor.

"All of my experiences were interesting. I nearly froze when I got up early in the morning to be interviewed on television. Naturally I could not wear a top coat, but I had borrowed some longies which I did wear. They were fine until the warmth of the hot sun started to beat down about eleven in the morning. I shall always be grateful to the unknown spectator at the parade who saw me squinting in the brightness and ran out to the car and handed me sun glasses to relieve the glare.

"At the Kickoff Luncheon honoring the competing coaches and teams, I had an experience which still gives me chills. Shortly before the event I had broken my glasses and had taken them to an oculist for repair. I am extremely myopic. During the luncheon, I was called up to say a few words. As you know, it is a stag lunch and the temptation might have been there to pass a ribald comment. Just as I was concluding my remarks, a messenger came with my glasses, and I put them on only to learn for the first time that I was on television without knowing it. As I say, anything could have happened.

"I was motivated to accept the role of grand marshal by the very pleasant personal call from Art Althouse, the president of the Tournament. His invitation was so cordial and the honor was so great that I felt I should accept."

In the Tournament Football Committee plan of always striving to

196

CAROLE WASHBURN

ARTHUR W. ALTHOUSE

make the Rose Bowl a finer place for this greatest of all bowl games, the $350,000 new press box, financed again through the cooperation of competing schools in a plan of selling advance tickets, was put into operation for the 1961 game.

"Ballads in Blossoms" was the theme for the parade. Burbank won the Sweepstakes award with its entry "Orchids in the Moonlight."

The Queen was Carole Washburn, who today is the wife of Dr. Robert Lumsden, orthopedic surgeon of the California Medical Center.

Gate receipts for the game surpassed a million dollars when 99,281 spectators saw Schloredt of Washington continue his Rose Bowl mastery by leading Owens' Huskies to a 17-0 first half lead over Minnesota, the nationally top-rated team. Washington held on in the second half to win 17-7.

Mannie Pineda wrote the following in the Pasadena *Star-News:* "No gophers ever dug themselves a deeper hole than did the Golden Gophers from Minnesota."

The game featured a battle of rooting sections. "We're No. 1," said Minnesota rooters. "Not for long!" answered the Washington side.

A childhood firecracker accident had blinded Schloredt in one eye early in life. But he was busy lighting Washington firecrackers this day. He also had returned to action after breaking a collarbone in mid-season. Much to the delight of West Coast fans, he overcame all handicaps.

Jordan Olivar, Yale's coach, said, "Schloredt had 'em dizzy. The Gophers were so thrown off stride in the first half that they didn't know what Washington was going to do."

Coach Owens of Washingon said, "I felt we would win from the time we started workouts for the game. We were determined to whip the national champions. We had to slug it out toe to toe this time. Last year against Wisconsin we gained early momentum and rode with it."

Schloredt said, "I learned a lot of football sitting on the bench half of this season."

Bob Hivner, a Washington star, said, "We had a feeling when we took the field that we had everything under control."

Owens added: "Hivner started us and Schloredt finished the job."

Murray Warmath, Minnesota coach, said, "We lost because of a couple of punts we didn't field and a couple of end sweeps we didn't turn. We were not tense. Washington was well prepared. We had evaluated Washington as a running team and didn't expect them to pass so much. We know what we did wrong but we don't know why."

Washington got the jump by gaining field-goal position through better punt play. George Fleming, with Hivner holding, made his kick good from the 34-yard line.

After Schloredt kicked dead on Minnesota's 8 and Sandy Stephens punted back, Washington drove in for a touchdown with sixty-two impressive yards of Schloredt's play-choosing. The big gainers were a twelve-yard pass from Schloredt to Ray Jackson, a nineteen-yard Jackson run through Minnesota's line and giants Tom Brown and Frank Brixuis, an eleven-yard dash by Charlie Mitchell after a pitch, and a pass from Schloredt to Brent Wooten.

Minnesota tried to retaliate but Washington repeated another long march with Schloredt the big gainer, once for thirty-one yards on a sneak. Schloredt scored to make it 17-0 at halftime, Fleming added the extra points.

Minnesota came back fighting after intermission and moved from the 26 to Washington's 35 where Roger Hagberg, strong-legged fullback, was stopped inches short of a first down by Jim Skaggs. Hivner fumbled and Bob Deagan recovered for Minnesota on the Washington 32. Soon Stephens climaxed some steady Gopher gaining by pitching out to Bill Munsey, who scored, with Jim Rogers adding the point.

Sandy Stephens, Gopher quarterback, said his team had had a date with ill fate. "It was just like the Purdue game," he said. "They got us in the hole and we couldn't take any chances. By the time we got started, it was too late."

Star of the victory, Schloredt had a date after the game with Queen Washburn and marriage was rumored in the newspapers. Matrimony never materialized, however.

1962

Ohio State won the Big Ten championship in the 1961 season and qualified to come to Pasadena if it cared to accept the bid of the AAWU. The Buckeye football team wanted to come, but the faculty said no. Riots erupted on the Buckeye campus and on High Street in Columbus.

Second place Minnesota, however, now the Tournament's friend after originally opposing the East-West pact, agreed to accept the bid to meet U.C.L.A. Coach Warmath, athletic director Ike Armstrong, and the Gopher administration wanted to make up for the 1961 muff. And the Gophers made good, too, in the 1962 game by trouncing Bill Barnes' Bruins 21-3. Stephens had a great day. Sandy tallied two touchdowns, completed seven of eleven passes, and ran for forty-six more yards.

The game was the first nationally televised in color.

Albert D. Rosellini, governor of Washington, was the grand marshal on the invitation of Pasadena Superior Court Judge H. Burton Noble, who was the Tournament president.

Rosellini declared after his experience: "The thing that impressed me most was the friendliness and enthusiasm of the people. I enjoyed the reception I received during the parade. I accepted the invitation because I wanted to be of help to one of the greatest pageants in the country, and I felt recognition would come to the State of Washington."

Judge Noble said: "I was impressed mostly during my twenty years of Tournament participation by the unselfishness of so many

ALBERT D. ROSELLINI

MARTHA SISSELL

people who had no expectation of receiving anything in return except satisfaction for a job well done. My most interesting experience was visiting authorities at the University of Minnesota. I do not wish to appear immodest in saying that the vice president of the school and athletic director Armstrong later told me that my visit was significant in the school's vote change in favor of Bowl participation."

Martha Sissell, today a school teacher in Los Angeles, was Queen of the 1962 Tournament. The theme of the parade was "Around The World With Flowers." The State of Washington entry was decorated with roses from fifty countries, and the Farmers Insurance float had blossoms from many distant lands. The Girl Scouts of America celebrated the organization's 50th anniversary with the entry "The Girl Scout Rose." Santa Monica paid tribute to the late Leo Carrillo, who had ridden in the parade for many years, with a floral likeness of the popular movie star entitled "Mr. California." San Diego was the Sweepstakes winner.

This author, writing in the Pasadena *Star-News,* wrote as follows about the game:

"A convincing, methodical victory for Minnesota. The quick and brutal Minnesota defense stopped the opening UCLA single wing lightning in time. Tenacious Minnesota then forced UCLA to make the mistakes. Sandy Stephens brilliantly called an inside-the-tackle grinding Minnesota T-offense sandwiched with key passes on opportune switches to pro spreads. It was the kind of game in which, if you were watching in Paducah, Kentucky, you could safely go into the kitchen and mix a New Year's evening tranquilizer without having to ask what happened upon your return. It was monotonous fun only for the Minnesota rooter. The Gophers punched and punched inside the tackles against a UCLA defense well prepared to watch the outside rollouts of Stephens. The big gaps were sugar plums for Sandy. His use of the reverse by his halfback and the middle socking of his fullback monopolized the clock and ground out yardage. His passes, when needed, were true. There have been few better demonstrations where a team won more perfectly as it planned. Flesh cannot match a machine."

MURRAY WARMATH

Coach Warmath said: "This was the most gratifying victory of my career and for the team. I am especially glad we won for the team's sake. Most of the men played in the Rose Bowl last year, and all they've heard for a year is how bad they were."

U.C.L.A. coach Barnes said: "We didn't throw enough single wing at them. We used too much garbage and made too many mistakes."

Sid Ziff in the Los Angeles *Mirror* wrote: "It was the old story of the Coast being overpowered and overmatched."

Bobby Bell of Minnesota, now a star in the line of the Kansas City Chiefs, said: "U.C.L.A. has a good line, but they better get rid of that single wing. You've got to run four yards to travel one. They've given up on it in the Big Ten."

H. BURTON NOBLE

BILL BARNES

Dick Cullum of the Minneapolis *Tribune* wrote: "The big rush put on the passer and the fine offensive play of the Minnesota line decided it."

Dick Gordon of the Minneapolis *Star* said: "A very hard hitting Gopher line proved superior."

Murray Olderman of the NEA added: "If ever the single wing looked archaic, this was it."

Bobby Smith of U.C.L.A. kicked a twenty-eight-yard field goal to open the scoring. A Minnesota recovery of a U.C.L.A. fumble on the Bruin 6 led to Stephens putting Minnesota ahead 7-3 with a short dash. Bill Munsey scored again for the Gophers on a short run capping a seventy-five-yard drive in the second quarter. Stephens rolled out to score at the end of an eighty-three-yard drive in the fourth period. Loechler kicked all the extra points.

Representatives of the AAUW (made up of California, Washington, Stanford, U.C.L.A., and U.S.C.) met with Big Ten authorities after the game to stimulate good feeling for a renewal of the pact that once existed between the Big Ten and the Pacific Coast Conference. It was agreed the Big Ten would maintain a no-repeat rule; the AAUW would send its champion each year.

The pact, for an indefinite period, was approved by both conferences during the year 1962, effective starting with the 1963 Rose Bowl game.

A veteran Tournament of Roses newspaper reporter, Dave Swaim of the Pasadena *Star-News,* recalled a reporting experience that was more interesting to him than any of his others.

"I was a reporter for the Los Angeles *Examiner* when Governor Rosellini was grand marshal," said Swaim. "The Los Angeles County Board of Supervisors, always generous with scrolls of honor to visiting notables, had a beautiful one made up for Rosellini, but never had a chance to present it because Rosellini's schedule was too full. He went home without it. A year and a half later, after my paper folded and while I was doing liaison work for Supervisor Warren M. Dorn, I discovered the unpresented scroll in Dorn's office. Since I was traveling north on a vacation trip that year — 1963 — I updated the scroll, got it duly signed, took it along with me, and made a formal presentation eighteen months late in the state house in Olympia, Washington."

31
The Space Age

RON VANDERKELEN

1963

THE TOURNAMENT OF ROSES in 1963 acknowleged the age of space in more ways than one.

In addition to Tournament president Stanley L. Hahn's selecting as grand marshal Dr. William H. Pickering of Pasadena's Jet Propulsion Laboratory, where many of this nation's space achievements originated, a floral replica of "Mariner," the satellite that traveled millions of miles in a fly-by of Venus, appeared in the parade. The parade theme was "Memorable Moments."

The City of Torrance had a float that depicted the coming United States trip to the moon, and Minute Maid told the Telstar story in flowers. When President Hahn and his family rode in a gaily decorated carriage, it was a reminder to parade viewers that the world hadn't always zipped about through space.

The football game also paid tribute to the wonders of space. U.S.C. quarterback Pete Beathard threw four passes for touchdowns, and Wisconsin quarterback Ron VanderKelen shattered records with 33 completions in 48 attempts as the Badgers rallied in near darkness to pull up within 42-37 of winner U.S.C.

The game took so long to play — because the officials apparently chose the occasion to seek the Emmy Award as actors — that Vander-Kelen hardly had time left in the evening to keep his date with Rose Queen Nancy Davis.

Paul Zimmerman wrote a stinging column in the Los Angeles *Times* condemning the officials for hamming it up before the television cameras. "Who were the boobs in striped shirts?" asked Zimmerman. The Times sports editor called the game the most magnificent offensive battle in the history of the Rose Bowl. Only the remarkable play of the two teams kept the officials from spoiling the contest, Zimmerman added, in condemning what he termed "over officiating."

U.S.C. was penalized 93 yards, Wisconsin 77.

"The game lasted only slightly less long than the War of 1812," said Jim Murray of the *Times*. "If the game had lasted one more quarter, they would have run into next year's Rose Bowl traffic. The game was

DR. WILLIAM H. PICKERING

STANLEY L. HAHN

like Russian roulette with all barrels loaded. U.S.C.'s pass defense was so poor they were lucky VanderKelen didn't score between the halves from the dressing room."

Rube Samuelsen of the Pasadena *Star-News* called VanderKelen's performance the finest one-man effort in Rose Bowl history. "Ernie Nevers and George Wilson have no choice but to move over," Rube said.

It required three hours and five minutes to reach the finish of the scoring duel in hazy darkness. The Rose Bowl lights were inadequate at that time. Anxious to protect the huge Rose Bowl television contract in the future, the Tournament of Roses Football Committee started a campaign for new bright lights for the Bowl, an improvement that was achieved in 1969.

The scoring show started when U.S.C. fullback Ben Wilson opened with a softening of the Badgers, who sent their linebackers keying on the Trojan man in motion. Beathard then threw a touchdown pass to Hal Bedsole, only to have it called back because the officials said Pete had run past the line of scrimmage. The Trojans then lined up quickly with tackle Ron Butcher at end. Butcher broke straight ahead in the hole left clear by the roaming linebackers and took a snappy thirteen-yard toss from Beathard for the first touchdown of the day.

"You had a premonition it was going to be a football spectacular when Southern Cal scored twice the first time it had the ball," said Bud Furillo in the Los Angeles *Herald-Examiner*.

A Badger passing show led to the Badgers tying the score on a plunge by Ralph Kurek, who had teamed with Lou Holland in catching the ball as Pat Richter, eleven-catch Badger end for the day, opened as a decoy.

A pass interception by U.S.C.'s Damon Bame initiated the next U.S.C. score, which was set up by a Willie Brown run and finally some Wilson smashes. A pass from Bill Nelsen to Willie Brown, who hauled it in over his shoulder with Jim Nettles on his back, was good for forty-five yards and set up a twenty-five-yard cutback by Ron Heller to make the score 21-7. Again it was a case of the Badger linebackers running in too many directions as they followed the Trojan man in motion. The Trojans had the men who could counter.

Just before the half, VanderKelen completed a bomb to Holland for a touchdown, but the officials ruled the Badgers guilty of clipping and called the play back. Milt Bruhn, Badger coach, was so disturbed by this call he protested to the officials as the teams left the field at intermission. Bruhn also accused the men in stripes of blowing a quick whistle which prevented a Badger recovery of a Nelsen fumble.

Bedsole made it 28-7 (Tom Lupo had a perfect six-for-six day in conversions) in the third quarter when he took a look-in pass from

PETE BEATHARD

MILT BRUHN

Beathard in the vacated linebacking zone and raced fifty-seven yards for a touchdown. A roll out of the pocket by VanderKelen was good for a seventeen-yard Badger touchdown. Badger placekicker Kroner also was perfect in conversions for the day with five for five. Bedsole then took the points back by leaping over Nettles in the corner of the end zone for a twenty-three-yard touchdown, one of the finest catches of Hal's career. U.S.C. had a 42-14 lead with less than a quarter to play after Lupo intercepted a pass and ran it to the Badger 14, from where Beathard tossed a touchdown strike to Fred Hill.

What happened in the next fourteen minutes made the finest quarter of football in Badger history. VanderKelen completed eight of ten passes in a drive to set up a thirteen-yard Holland touchdown at 3:19 of the quarter. After Wilson fumbled the ball to the Badgers on U.S.C.'s 29, VanderKelen hit Kroner with a touchdown pass.

In the semi-darkness the Trojans looked bewildered and blind as VanderKelen drilled completion after completion to Richter and others. On a pass from the 4, Brown made a big save by intercepting in the end zone. U.S.C. couldn't move, and a bad pass from center produced a safety. With the score now 42-30, VanderKelen completed a touchdown pass to Richter. There were still over two minutes left, but U.S.C. froze the ball after that, punting successfully on the last play of the game.

Wisconsin outgained U.S.C. 486 yards to 367 for the day, out-first-downed them 32-15, and had the champs groggy at the finish.

What happened to U.S.C.?

"We won. That's what happened," said U.S.C.'s Brown. "We relaxed when we got way ahead, but we still won. Why do people always want to downgrade the Trojans? We weren't supposed to win, remember?"

U.S.C.'s line coach Ray George said, "I don't understand. We worked our bellies off to win and nobody seems to appreciate it. We're tired, but not too tired to go out there and beat them all over again."

Johnny McKay, U.S.C. coach, merely commented: "We came in No. 1. They came in No. 2 and lost. That makes us still No. 1."

McKay said his team ran out of men for the tackle position because of injuries, and it started congratulating itself too early. "We also ran out of gas and couldn't get our tank filled up again."

Bruhn said: "I wasn't surprised by U.S.C.'s poor pass defense. U.S.C. had quickness though."

There were other than space exhibits featured in the 1963 parade before the football game. Santa Monica won the Sweepstakes with a depiction of "First Love," and the Quaker Oats float rendered a floral depiction of "The Birth of The Republic."

Queen Nancy Davis recalled "interestingly getting acquainted" with members of the football teams during the Tournament festivities.

NANCY DAVIS

"My date with quarterback Ron VanderKelen resulted from our becoming friends when we visited Disneyland," said Queen Nancy, who today is Mrs. Frank Maggio of Arcadia. "We went out for dinner after the game. We purposely went out of Pasadena so as not to be recognized. But we were found at Dino's on Sunset Strip. The morning papers ran the story 'King and Queen Together for Future Ruling,' which amused everyone but my boy friend. He was unaware of the date until the papers arrived. It was soon forgotten and forgiven."

Mrs. Maggio said her gain from Tournament participation was "learning to adapt to any situation."

Hahn, a pleasant, quiet, diplomatic individual, has made a major contribution to Tournament of Roses football negotiations through the years, Lay Leishman has often insisted. Hahn has known how to think with the educators, to deal with them and retain their good will.

32

Mr. Eisenhower Finally Comes to Pasadena

DWIGHT D. EISENHOWER

1964

AFTER THE TOURNAMENT had made two unsuccessful attempts to bring Dwight Eisenhower to Pasadena as grand marshal, though he had accepted the honor, President Hilles E. Bedell accomplished the feat of producing the ex-President of United States and Mrs. Eisenhower at the 1964 festival.

In fact, a family friendship between the Bedells and Eisenhowers that lasted throughout Ike's remaining years developed during the visit.

Five years later Bedell summarized it: "My dominant impressions of Mr. Eisenhower are these: He fit right in. He got into the spirit of the Tournament. He was impressed by the lack of politics in our operation. He spoke in short sentences and simple words. He seldom carried money with him. In his military and political life, he hadn't needed ready cash. He was warm to our children. He drove a golf cart with abandon."

Bedell and Ike carried on a correspondence after Ike's visit. The letters from Gettysburg and Washington came regularly, and the Bedells annually visited the Eisenhowers in Palm Springs. When Bedell suffered a heart ailment and faced open heart surgery, Eisenhower wrote: "Welcome to the club. If you submit to the rules set down by your doctors, you can live a long and useful life." The last letter Bedell ever received from Ike was written by his chief aide who reported Mr. Eisenhower was too weak to write but sent along his good wishes. In a stroke of fate that saddened Pasadena, Bedell also passed away in early 1970, the year after his friend Ike's death.

During the height of their friendship after the 1964 Tournament, Hilles recalled the Bedell youngsters being in San Francisco where Ike was making an appearance. When Ike encountered them in the hotel lobby, he remembered them and remarked, "I am very busy at this moment, but Mrs. Eisenhower would love to have you drop into our suite and say hello."

205

HILLES BEDELL

When the Bedells visited Gettysburg to receive the Freedom Foundation Award for the Tournament, they were guests of the Eisenhowers. When the Bedells' daughter Joan had her first child, Ike sent a telegram, "Welcome to this wonderful world."

One of the amusing episodes of Eisenhower's stay in Pasadena occurred when, prior to an engagement at the Tournament House, Ike retreated to the washroom for a few moments of silence away from the crowds. An old sliding door to the washroom, which he closed a little too abruptly, locked, and the former President of the United States was trapped inside. Bedell's son, serving as a guard, thinking Ike wanted the moments alone, turned away those who would come to his rescue because "Dad said Mr. Eisenhower shouldn't be disturbed."

Ike told Bedell during their appearances at Tournament events that "I can't turn down anybody who wants to talk to me or have my autograph." When a little boy was brushed aside by Secret Service agents as he sought an autograph, Ike shouted his Palm Springs address to the lad and said, "Write to me there."

Ike was particularly impressed by the Tournament directors' dinner, where each man introduced himself to the audience. "Everybody is equal here," Ike remarked.

During the parade, as he passed a group of wheel-chair viewers who were guests of the Tournament, Ike rose from his seat in his car and gave them the V for Victory sign with his fingers.

In Palm Springs, Bedell played golf with Ike. "He drove a golf cart like a maniac," grinned Hilles. "We came up to a green where I thought a man putting looked familiar. I said, 'Let's stop and watch if he sinks his putt.' Ike obliged. That man turned out to be Stanley Hahn, former president of the Tournament."

The ex-President of the United States had followed the Marine Band during the parade. He listened to the "Marine Corps Hymn" for miles and miles. After the parade, Ike wanted a brief rest before going to the football game. He was taken to the Pasadena armory where a cot was placed in a small room. Who should show up for a brief rehearsal? The Marine Band, of course, and what did they practice? "From the Halls of Montezuma." No rest for Mr. Eisenhower.

Tournament committeeman Frank Hardcastle, chairman of the Float Committee in 1970 but serving as a Tournament security man for Mr. Eisenhower during his 1964 visit, recalled an interesting experience.

"I was assigned to that task mainly because I was 6-4 tall and weighed 250," said Hardcastle. "President John Kennedy had been assassinated not long before, so all of us were especially anxious to provide top security for Mr. Eisenhower. In line with that duty, I was trying to guide the General through a crowd at the end of the

PETE ELLIOTT

parade route by placing my hands on his shoulders to better protect his back. In doing so, I leaned forward to ask that he keep moving. At that moment, his chief aide quickly stepped up to me and sternly admonished me by saying, 'Hey, don't handle the merchandise!' "

Later when he for the first time served on the Float Contruction Committee, which has the duty of checking to see that the sponsors' wishes are fulfilled, Hardcastle had another amusing experience.

"I pleaded continually with one float builder to correct a welding situation," said Hardcastle. "He ignored me. When the day of the maneuverability tests came (we took each float out of its decorating place and ran it around the block to test it), I waited in the doorway. As the float in question was being driven out, I stepped on it and jumped up and down above the welding point which had been questioned. Yes, all 250 pounds of me. Of course, the float broke in half. It was at this point that I was named 'Float Destruction' chairman."

The parade was "The Diamond Anniversary" event in Tournament history, the 75th anniversary of the festival. The game was thus the 50th. The parade theme was "Symbols of Freedom." Long Beach took the Sweepstakes with a float, "Diamond Jubilee." Occidental Life showed Betsy Ross and the making of the American flag with an impressive float, "First Symbol of Freedom."

Illinois defeated Washington 17-7 that afternoon.

"Illinois won the game the same way that Castro won Cuba — by a systematic liquidation," said Jim Murray in the Los Angeles *Times.* "Illinois was like Sonny Liston — not very smart — but they didn't have to be. I think they hurt Washington just shaking hands with them before the kickoff."

Paul Zimmerman of the *Times* called it "a rugged, hard-hitting contest that was utterly devoid of the spectacular. A crowd of 96,957 shirt-sleeved spectators basked in 85-degree weather to watch Pete Elliott's Illinois crash to a pair of touchdowns over the outclassed but determined Huskies in the second half after trailing 7-3 at intermission. Whatever chances coach Jim Owens' smaller, slower squad had were dissipated in the first five minutes when its star quarterback, Bill Douglas, was carried from the field with a knee dislocation. Bill's replacement, Bill Siler, who had been out all season with hepatitis, threw three interceptions, fumbled the ball twice, and generally had a discouraging afternoon."

In my Pasadena *Star-News* column, I wrote, "The anvil and the hammer ruled . . . a bigger and stronger Big Ten team wore down a well-prepared and highly stimulated Washington team that had everything but brawn, muscle — and good luck."

Coach Owens kept the press away for thirty-five minutes after the game. Then he said: "It hurt us to lose Douglas, but that was not the difference. We made too many mistakes and gave up the ball too often."

Harley Tinkham of the *Herald-Examiner,* by the way, correctly tabbed Illinois a 17-7 winner twenty-four hours in advance.

Washington started fast as Douglas picked the Illinois defense apart with pitchouts, short passes, and keepers to advance fifty-three yards to Illinois' 15. On a twelve-yard scamper around right end, Douglas was felled by Bill Pasko, who hit him from behind. Douglas was carried off the field.

Little Siler came in and moved the ball to the 10, but his short look-in pass was bobbled by Al Libke with Wylie Fox recovering for Illinois.

After keeping Illinois bottled the rest of the first period, Washington got back to Illinois' 18 where Siler fumbled and Fox recovered again. Then quarterback Fred Custardo of Illinois fumbled and John Stupey of Washington recovered on Illinois' 27. Siler passed to Joe Mancuso to the 6. On a pitchout, Dave Kopay ran wide, got a good block from Ron Medved, and scored. Medved kicked the point.

Just before the half, after Siler fumbled, Bruce Capel recovering, Jim Plankenhorn kicked a thirty-two-yard field goal that made the score 7-3.

An interception by George Donnelly gave Illinois the ball on Washington's 32 in the third quarter. Jim Warren soon scored on a pitchout from Mike Taliaferro, and Plankenhorn's conversion gave Illinois a 10-7 lead. Some fine plunging by Junior Coffey gave Washington a chance on the 9-yard line, but a Donnelly interception saved the day for the Big Ten team. An eighty-five-yard march by Illinois in the fourth quarter led to player-of-the-game Jim Grabowski scoring the insurance touchdown. Grabowski had a net of 125 yards for 22 carries for the day.

"Siler did a fine job. He played as well as he could under the circumstances," stated Owens.

Nancy Kneeland was the Rose Queen. When she graduated from Pasadena City College, she flew to the Philippines to become the bride of Lt. (j.g.) William J. Kish, who had 114 combat missions over North Vietnam. Today he is a pilot for Northwest Airlines.

DWIGHT EISENHOWER
IN PLEASANT COMPANY
WITH THE 1964 COURT

208

FRITZ CRISLER AND DAWN BAKER DISCUSS THE BIG GAME

GOLF'S ARNOLD PALMER AND HIS WIFE AT THE GAME

1965

Tournament President Walter R. Hoefflin, Jr., hospital administrator and sportsman, switched precedent by naming one of the world's leading sports figures, Arnold Palmer, grand marshal of the 1965 Tournament.

It proved to be a very popular choice. Arnie's Army came to the parade, which had the theme "Headlines in Flowers."

"It was a personal highlight for me to have Arnold Palmer as grand marshal," said Hoefflin, executive vice president of the Methodist Hospital of Southern California, in Arcadia. "It meant much to me to get acquainted with him, his adorable wife, and their two fine daughters. As far as I am concerned, Arnold made my year. Our close friendship continues. During each of his public appearances, he said just the right thing at the right time with absolutely no coaching."

Lakewood, California, won the Sweepstakes in the parade with the float "Parade of Roses."

The sports theme was further carried out when the St. Louis float featured World Series stars Bob Gibson and Tim McCarver. Chrysler depicted one of the era's great news events with a float entitled "Britain Crowns Queen Elizabeth The Second."

Dawn Baker was the Tournament Queen. Later she married Lt. (j.g.) Joseph E. Rogers. She began a career in radio broadcasting and has been active in community affairs in the Fresno area.

Hoefflin declared some of his most interesting experiences during his term in office came during his travels to present awards on behalf of the Tournament.

209

WALTER R. HOEFFLIN

"I was in Nashville to make a presentation to the Isaac Litton High School Band," Hoefflin recalled. "In making the presentation to Sammy Swor, the band director, I likened a band to a football team — great coaching, fine players, discipline, dedicated practice, etc. The director had come to Pasadena in November prior to the parade on January 1 to develop a 'band plan.' When the band was to be marching uphill, they would not be playing, etc. When I made this reference to a band being like a football team and when I made the presentation, the roof almost caved in with applause for Mr. Swor's band. Then I went to Prince George, Virginia, for another presentation. I made the same reference to great coaching, good players, and practice. Everyone in the auditorium laughed. When leaving the auditorium, I asked the high school principal if I had made a boo-boo or had said something. He replied, 'You sure did. Our football team hasn't won a game in six years.' "

Looking back at his experience, four years after the 1965 festival, Hoefflin gave this summary of his reactions to his role as Tournament president:

"It has long been my conviction that a person is on the pathway to a successful life when he does more for his community than the community does for him. There can be no question but that the Tournament of Roses is the greatest single community event in the world. To be intimately associated with it and to be a president of such a successful organization is a rare privilege. The hundreds of friends one makes during the experience is the greatest compensation a man can get from participation. These friendships are lifelong. This, of course, includes the close relationships with coaches, athletic directors, and faculty representatives of the 18 universities of the two competing conferences. No finer people can be found anywhere. Those of us closely associated keenly look forward to each December for 'Old Home Week.' "

Michigan crushed Oregon State 34-7 in the 1965 Rose Bowl game.

The following is from my *Star-News* column: "Michigan unleashed two break-away runners and a break-away pig in drubbing Oregon State. . . . Mel Anthony sprinted a record 84 yards and Carl Ward spurted 43. Those runs broke the game open . . . Michigan fans became so elated they released a speedy pig named Cleopatra. It was a fitting name because Anthony was the leading man of the day (three touchdowns). He fell on a blocked punt and his run was the longest in history, three yards longer than Iowa's Bob Jeter in 1959. Cleopatra ran the wrong way on her scoring dash. The fleet pig executed the most notable wrong way effort since Roy Riegels' famed mistake. After 'scoring,' Cleo tried to amend by coming back the right way. A fan made a diving tackle to halt the critter. If the fan came from Oregon State, he made the best Oregon State tackle of the day."

210

Paul Zimmerman wrote in the Los Angeles *Times,* "Coach Tommy Prothro's Beavers made one bold scoring move early in the second quarter and then promptly collapsed."

Sid Ziff in the *Times* stated: "The AAWU was asking for trouble when it picked Oregon State over U.S.C., and it got it. The Beavers were in over their heads. It wasn't a defeat. It was a disaster. Michigan should have been awarded a technical knockout."

Bill Becker of the New York *Times* summed it up: "It was a runaway after the halftime recess as armchair TV experts throughout the nation doubtlessly dozed off."

Coach Bump Elliott said Anthony's eighty-four-yard run was "the play that got us moving."

Anthony said, "I saw nothing but daylight after Carl Ward and John Henderson sprang me on that pitch-out."

Charlie Park of the Los Angeles *Times* said Prothro's Oregon State "Mad Dogs" on defense turned out to be the "Pooped Pooches."

Prothro summed up the game as he saw it: "Our offense did as well as we expected to do. But our defense didn't. We thought our best hope was to punt for field position and try to hold it."

The defeat, Prothro's second in the Rose Bowl as a head coach, didn't ruin his career beyond some immediate criticism in the press for punting on second and third down and presenting an unexciting offense. He was hired as U.C.L.A.'s new football coach as soon as J. D. Morgan, athletic director, could pry Tommy loose from the Beaver campus. And Prothro came back into the Rose Bowl on the next January 1 with one of the big upsets of the Big Ten pact when his Bruins upset national champion Michigan State.

COACH BUMP ELLIOTT HAS A TIP FOR BOB TIMBERLAKE

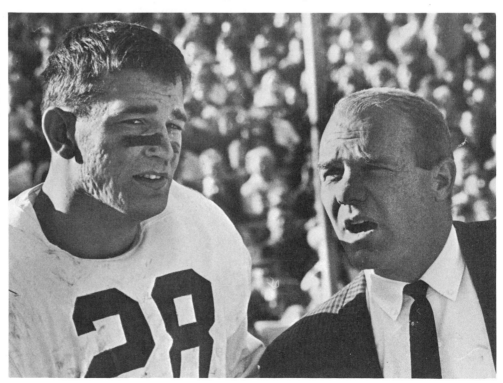

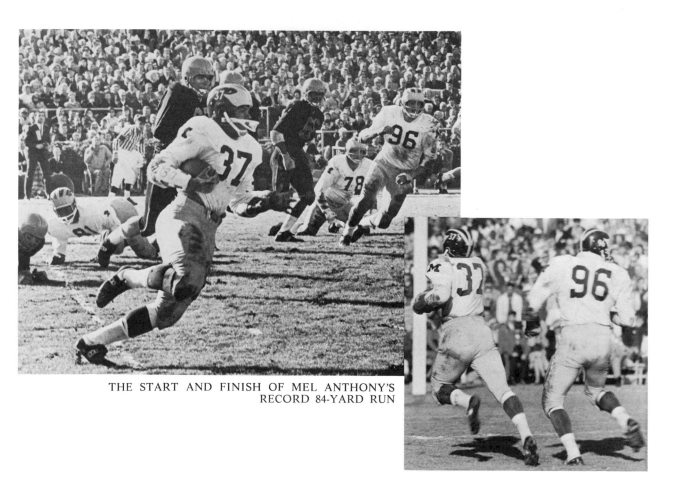

THE START AND FINISH OF MEL ANTHONY'S
RECORD 84-YARD RUN

Michigan gained 346 yards rushing and 83 more passing for 415 yards total, almost twice the yardage of Oregon State.

Sophomore quarterback Paul Brothers directed Oregon State eighty-four yards for the Beavers' early touchdown that gave Prothro's team a deceiving 7-0 lead. Brothers completed six of six passes in the drive. The receivers were Len Frketich, Bob Grim, Olvin Moreland, Cliff Watkins, and Doug McDougal. The latter's catch was for five yards and the touchdown. Steve Clark kicked the extra point.

Six minutes later, back on Michigan's 16, quarterback Bob Timberlake pitched out to Anthony. The fullback barreled over the right side, found the Oregon State secondary massed in tight, and reversed his field to score on an eighty-four-yard run. The Beavers still led, however, when Timberlake missed the extra point.

But Ward soon ended Oregon State hopes by going forty-three yards on a similar play. A two-point pass try by Timberlake failed, to leave the score 12-7 Michigan.

Michigan then completely sewed it up in the third quarter. Expert kicker Frketich was rushed by the Michigan horde while punting. Guard Bob Mielke blocked his kick and Anthony recovered on Oregon State's 15. Anthony scored five plays later. Timberlake ran right end for two points to make it 20-7. Anthony soon scored again on a short plunge after a seventy-eight-yard drive. Timberlake then scored on a twenty-four-yard keeper. It ended 34-7 after Rick Sygar's extra point.

212

33

Mickey Mouse Makes Good

TOMMY PROTHRO

1966

THE TOURNAMENT of 1966 will long be remembered by the midgets of the world.

Sicilian ponies, 27 inches tall, pulled a pumpkin carriage in the parade. Mickey Mouse, not a big guy in anything but public acceptance, led the parade and his creator, Walt Disney, served as grand marshal. And the mightiest of mighty mites, U.C.L.A.'s Bob Stiles, was the hero of the football game, a 14-12 victory over Michigan State, before 100,087 surprised spectators and millions watching on television, a game that will be remembered as long as football is played.

Bob Stiles was sunning himself on a sandy New Jersey beach in the summer of 1963. "We were sipping a bit of liquid refreshment," he told Dwain Esper of the Pasadena *Star-News.* "Suddenly this friend of mine said, 'Let's go to California.' So we did."

Michigan State football fans will forever wish he had "stood at home." Stiles was named the player of the game in U.C.L.A.'s victory as he "took it to 'em," to use his own words. Stiles was only 5'9" tall and not much over 170 pounds. He intercepted passes and finally made the big save that enabled U.C.L.A. to win.

The player of the game annually is determined by the board of the Helms Athletic Foundation, founded by Paul Helms and directed by W. R. ("Bill") Schroeder. The winner's picture is placed in the Rose Bowl Hall of Fame, and he is given a trophy, too. The Hall of Fame, formerly located between tunnels 1 and 28 in the Rose Bowl and visited by thousands of visitors to Pasadena each year, has been moved to the Tournament House.

The owner of the Pasadena Athletic Club, J. Randolph Richards, strong of physique and love for his community, was president for the 1966 Tournament.

"My most interesting experience had to do with getting Mr. Disney to serve as grand marshal," said Richards. "After he had given due consideration to my invitation, he stated that he couldn't think of anything more undesirable from his standpoint than to ride for two

WALT DISNEY AND MICKEY MOUSE BRING
CHEER TO THE 1966 PARADE

hours in parade doing nothing but trying to smile and wave to the crowd. However, he stated that if we would allow him to have twenty or thirty of his characters, such as Mickey Mouse, Donald Duck, and others, surround his car so that he could play with them, he would accept."

The million and a half spectators along the parade route loved every minute of Disney's appearance. The 100,087 in the Rose Bowl also got a kick out of U.C.L.A.'s Mickey Mouse, young Mr. Stiles.

Richards went to Lebanon and Japan on a trip around the world to recruit parade participants. Both countries agreed to appear in the parade which saluted the Disney theme "It's a Small World."

Richards explained: "The country of Lebanon, being extremely proud of its heritage in regard to the 'Cedars of Lebanon,' decided to tell the world through our parade of this great pride. The Tenri high school in Tenri, Japan, decided to send their great high school band to our parade to help solidify the friendly relations between our two countries."

Richards said that throughout his travels around the world he did not find one person who didn't know of Walt Disney.

Disney's response after his experience as grand marshal was: "I can think of no time in my life when I have been treated to nicer or more sincere hospitality."

The national flowers of twenty-one countries were flown to Pasadena for the parade.

Canada was well represented with the Vancouver Beefeater Band (it didn't pause to serve Bloody Marys), the Canadian Mounted Police, and floats from Calgary, Alberta, and from British Columbia. The State of Montana won the Sweepstakes Award.

The queen was pretty Carole Cota, who will forever make de-

214

J. RANDOLPH RICHARDS CROWNS
CAROLE COTA

voted Queen Selection Committee chairmen (like Ralph S. Help-bringer, 1970 Tournament) happy.

"This may sound crazy — but one of the things that impressed me most was that the selecting of the queen wasn't 'fixed,' " said Queen Carole. "I guess there is always going to be someone who can't believe that a really good thing can be honest — but it won't ever be me." Miss Cota, today Mrs. Frank A. Gelfuso of South Pasadena, added: "Every detail about the tryouts was so fair — and so much fun. Even those who didn't become a member of the court weren't really crushed. They just chalked it up as a 'groovy experience.' I can speak from experience because I had gotten as far as the 'last 25' the year previous to my selection as queen."

Among her memorable experiences was being chosen "Sweetheart of University of Indiana's Little 500," an event that takes place at the university two weeks before the Indianapolis 500-mile automobile race. The flight to Bloomington was Miss Cota's first trip on an airplane.

"Another fun time was going to Disneyland with both football teams," Queen Carole said. "Imagine being with both teams at the same time. Only a girl can appreciate those odds — 80 to 7. My court and I even touched Jack Jones."

Miss Cota will not be forgotten by the author's family. At the annual Coronation Ball, my wife's leopard coat got caught in one of the hooks on Miss Cota's coat, and for a few moments the two were Siamese twins.

A football empire was "blown up" the afternoon of January 1, 1966.

U.C.L.A.'s famed bomb plus its courage and never-say-die spirit defeated Michigan State 14-12 in one of the most exciting and dramatic of all Rose Bowl games. Prothro's often-ridiculed defense hung on in face of the late countercharge of the Spartans, who stormed

BOB STILES

back from a 14-0 deficit with two late touchdowns. Twice after these comeback scores by previously undefeated Michigan State did U.C.L.A.'s determined defense turn back two-point attempts.

Stiles, defensive left halfback for U.C.L.A., and Jim Colletto teamed up to make the super-save with thirty-one seconds left to play after Michigan State scored its second comeback touchdown.

After Steve Juday dove eight inches to score the touchdown that cut U.C.L.A.'s lead to 14-12, reserve Spartan quarterback Jim Raye, an expert of the pitchout, received Coach Duffy Daugherty's call to get the big two points. Raye started to his right, then flipped a pitchout to strong 212-pound Bob Apisa, who tried to skirt right end. Colletto came up to hit him, but Apisa's strength still had to be reckoned with. Stiles stormed in, leaped on Apisa's shoulders, and spun him back just as he was about to cross the line. The play was stopped inches short.

Stiles was knocked cold from the blow he took. He could not hear the cheers, but triumph was preserved for Stiles and his mates.

U.C.L.A. scored twice in the second quarter on one-yard dives into the line by the sophomore of the year, Gary Beban. The first touchdown was set up when U.C.L.A. recovered a fumbled punt by Spartan co-captain Don Japinga on the Spartan 6-yard line. John Erquiaga fell on the ball to give U.C.L.A. possession. Beban skirted left to the 1 and then bucked in. The second shocker was set up by Kurt Zimmerman's brilliant on-side kick-off, recovered by Dallas Grider, and the bomb that U.C.L.A. had learned to love when it had rallied over U.S.C. to gain the Rose Bowl bid. Beban fired a twenty-seven-yard strike to end Kurt Altenberg to Michigan State's 1 from where Beban dove over. Zimmerman kicked both extra points.

U.C.L.A.'s defense then asserted itself and rushed Steve Juday into trouble. Three times they took the ball away from Michigan State on fourth down stops. Three times they intercepted Juday passes when he was forced to throw hurriedly under pressure. Twice U.C.L.A. recovered fumbles.

The U.C.L.A. stalwarts up front were Colletto, Terry Donahue, John Richardson, Steve Butler, Alan Cleman, Erwin Dutcher, Dallas Grider, Jim Miller, and Jerry Klein.

With 6:38 of the game remaining, substitute Spartan quarterback Raye flipped a lateral to Apisa, which surprised U.C.L.A. Apisa lumbered thirty-eight yards to score. Juday tried to pass for two points on a fake, but reserve defensive end Klein mussed it up with a rush.

Juday and Raye alternated in directing another Spartan attack. Juday scored, and then came the great save by Stiles and Colletto.

"We needed every man to win," said Prothro.

"We just took it to them," said Stiles.

"We got tired of reading stories of pity," added Beban.

216

"We lost by inches," said Daugherty.

For Prothro, the victory was especially sweet because he had never won in the Bowl as player or coach, and he had always taken pride in coaching defense, yet it was his bomb attack, not his defense, that had been hailed before this day.

U.C.L.A. won, in the final analysis, because it had perfect command of the unexpected.

Rose Bowl football fans always ask: "What happens to the football tickets? Why can't we buy any?"

In the 1966 game distribution, the Tournament of Roses purchased 17,059 tickets, which it distributed principally to parade participants and Tournament members. There are 1,400 members who pay dues of from $10 to $25 each (the money used for administration expense) who are permitted to buy an allotted number of tickets based on rank and service.

The Big Ten in 1966 received 18,546 tickets for use by Michigan State and other Big Ten schools. Ten-year advance purchasers received 8,100 tickets. Press, radio, and TV statewide and nationally received 3,281 tickets. There was a public sale by lottery of 3,500 tickets.

This accounted for approximately half of the tickets. The other half was administered by the AAUW through the school that participated, which happened to be U.C.L.A. J. D. Morgan, athletic director at U.C.L.A., revealed that 22,000 tickets went to U.C.L.A. alumni and public season-ticket holders for U.C.L.A. games. A total of 17,000 went to faculty, rooters, school staff, and players at the school. Hospitals, service groups, and benefit groups received 4,500 tickets. Other conference schools got 3,800 tickets. U.C.L.A. sold the final 3,400 to special groups, such as hotels and public organizations.

34

Rose Bowl Put on U.S.C. Schedule

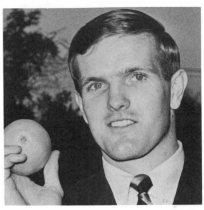

BOB GRIESE

1967

WHEN MICHIGAN Coach Bo Schembechler brought his Wolverines to Pasadena to play Johnny McKay's U.S.C. Trojans in the 1970 game, he said, "We are at a disadvantage. McKay has the Rose Bowl on U.S.C.'s schedule each year."

McKay started a Rose Bowl streak of four straight U.S.C. appearances with the game of 1967, in which Purdue came off a winner by one point.

U.S.C. defeated Indiana the next year, then succumbed to a great Ohio State team of sophomores before getting revenge on the Big Ten by out-lasting Michigan. Thus, in four straight tries, McKay's Rose Bowl record is 2-2, although his lifetime mark is 3-2 when the 1963 triumph over Wisconsin is counted in.

The year 1967 will go down as significant in the history of the Rose Bowl because it marked the occasion when Pasadena let the world know on which side it stood in the growing competition between professional and collegiate sports. Pasadena let it be known, clearly and firmly, that it was a college town.

The issue came up when pro football expressed strong interest in staging its first Super Bowl game between the champions of the National Football League and the new American Football League in Pasadena's huge structure.

The AAWU and the Big Ten, representing the collegiate world that had been in partnership with the Tournament of Roses in staging the Rose Bowl game, objected to this invasion. The Super Bowl game between the Green Bay Packers and the Kansas City Chiefs was to take place a week after the Rose Bowl game. The collegians objected that this pro classic would take away from the significance of the Rose Bowl game.

The Pasadena *Star-News* editorially supported the collegiate stand amid much popular demand in Pasadena for the second attraction which, pro supporters said, would bring a big rental fee to the city, attract more business, and make Pasadena the capital of pro football as well as collegiate.

After listening to the views of the colleges as expressed by J. D. Morgan of U.C.L.A., Jess Hill of U.S.C., and Admiral Tom Hamilton, commissioner of the AAWU, views that were loyally supported by the Football Committee representing the Tournament of Roses, *Star-News* publisher Ben Ridder said: "This newspaper supports the college point of view."

The *Star-News* printed a series of articles that clearly showed how the Super Bowl game on a Sunday would not bring in enough financial gain to the city of Pasadena to offset the danger of the colleges withdrawing from the Rose Bowl game. College authorities often have said that Ridder's stand was a most important act in cementing a warm and deep relationship between the college world and the city of Pasadena.

Hamilton's analysis of the problem created by the possible Super Bowl invasion influenced Ridder significantly.

"Speaking of the AAWU and its eight member institutions, we appreciate being asked to state our views on the matter as a non-voting partner in the Rose Bowl game. The schools feel fortunate that they have been able to participate the last fifty years and enjoy the relationships with the people of Pasadena. We have been working partners in building the Rose Bowl game.

"Last September, by a vote of conference chancellors and presidents, the conference went on record as opposing use of the Rose Bowl for the pro title game as proposed immediately after our New Year's game. The stand was explained to the Tournament of Roses Association.

"Pasadena has built an image of quality and class in its Rose Bowl presentation. We are anxious to see the cultural and unique community aspects of this game preserved with all aspects of commercialization minimized.

"The Rose Bowl game already is No. 1 in the national sports picture. You can't have two No. 1 games. One or the other has to become No. 2. An event as solid as the Rose Bowl game should not be subjected to that.

"If the pro game were permitted in the Rose Bowl at such proximity, we should have to take another look at our agreement to participate. We are proud of our top Nielsen television ratings, the annual sellout, and the general high recognition accorded our game. We would feel very much let down if this were damaged or diluted.

"The presentation of the Super Bowl game with tickets selling as high as $12 coming a week after our game, for which tickets sell for $7, would detract from the prestige of our event, which has been built up through long-time cooperation between the schools and Pasadena. We have also participated in the construction and improvement program of the stadium. Strong loyalty has existed on both sides. It would be unwise to create a situation in which our faculties and

INTERNATIONAL
GOOD WILL EXPRESSED
BY PRESIDENT
HENRY KEARNS
AND GRAND MARSHAL
THANAT KHOMAN

school administrators would be tempted to take a new look at our pact because of a change in the commercial environment."

William Reed, Big Ten Commissioner, expressed a similar attitude and pointed out that Big Ten participation in Pasadena had passed by only a 6-4 vote the last time it had come up.

The Super Bowl went to the Los Angeles Coliseum in 1967, to Miami the next two years, and to New Orleans in 1970. A policy was defined in Pasadena regarding future use of the Rose Bowl by pros — O. K. if at a time when it doesn't detract from the New Year's Day classic. Professional football in the stadium during August or September would meet with no opposition in Tournament or collegiate circles. Pro commissioner Pete Rozelle, too, has let it be known that professional football does not want to antagonize the collegiate world, which provides the National League and American League with talent in the collegiate player draft.

Henry Kearns, now president and chairman of the Export-Import Bank of the United States, was Tournament president in 1967. Kearns said he began his Tournament life as a driver of a float in the 1934 parade "when it was a little damp."

His next assignment came in 1937 as a member of the Traffic Committee, "when it was my responsibility to precede the parade and at certain intervals stop it to prevent gaps when the Santa Fe train went through east of Raymond Avenue."

Kearns worked his way up to the Tournament presidency.

"The significant thing that I have observed has been the friendliness and good cheer of the viewers of the parade and the participants," said Kearns. "I question that there is an event any place in the world where good will abounds to the extent that it does at the Tournament of Roses parade."

Participating in an event that brings joy and good will to millions of people everywhere has been Kearns' gain from thirty-three years as a Tournament worker, he declared.

Barbara Hewitt was the 1967 Queen. She married David Laughray of La Crescenta, California, and has been a model in the John Roberts School of Pasadena.

Kearns' grand marshal for the 1967 Tournament was Thanat Khoman, minister of foreign affairs of Thailand. This marked the first time the grand marshal's office was filled by someone from a foreign country.

The parade theme was "Travel Tales in Flowers" as the Tournament emphasized world-wide friendship. A float entitled "Around the World in Eighty Days" carried a baby pink elephant. South Pasadena won the Sweepstakes award with "A Voyage to Atlantis."

Members of the Congress of the United States (from 44 states that had participated in the New Year's Day events in Pasadena) paid tribute to the Tournament of Roses with laudatory statements entered in the Congressional Record.

Al Stewart's all-male Purdue glee club won the hearts of South-

QUEEN BARBARA HEWITT AND HER 1967 COURT

SCORING CATCH BY
U.S.C.'s ROD SHERMAN

land folks before the Purdue football team coached by Jack Mollen-kopf stood off the bid of McKay's Trojans.

A clear victory in statistics is all U.S.C. could claim after it was over, 323 yards to 244.

Rod Sherman of Pasadena, who played his high school football at Muir in the Rose Bowl, almost became the all-time Bowl hero when he got behind Purdue's George Catavolos to pull down a nineteen-yard pass from Troy Winslow for six points with two and a half minutes left to play, to reduce Purdue's lead to 14-13. Wearing goat horns for a brief second or two, Catavolos avenged his failure to prevent the pass to Sherman. When McKay gallantly refused to settle for a tie and ordered Winslow to "go for it," Catavolos stepped in front of the intended receiver Jim Lawrence to intercept Winslow's pass after a roll-out right option.

Purdue's fullback Perry Williams scored a touchdown in the second period and another in the third, each on a short but powerful blast. Bob Griese engineered the pass-and-run attacks that set up each of the scores. Griese had a day's passing record of ten for eighteen compared to Winslow's twelve for seventeen, and it was Griese's two perfect conversions that proved to be the margin of victory.

After two drives, Williams scored the first Purdue touchdown to make it 7-0. In the second period, the U.S.C. offense suddenly took charge, working up to two good scoring chances. Jim Lawrence ran thirty-nine yards with a pass and would have gone all the way if he hadn't stumbled at the start. In the second drive, good catches by Sherman and Lawrence plus blasts by Homer Williams, playing for the injured Mike Hull at this point, set up a touchdown by Don McCall.

U.S.C. stormed for a third drive before halftime intermission with the big runs being a sixteen-yarder by McCall and a thirty-five-yarder by Hull, both down the middle. Hull, too, stumbled or he would have gone all the way. A forty-two-yard field goal by Tim Rossovich was straight but was a couple of feet short.

Each team blew scoring chances in the third quarter before Griese connected on two passes to Bob Hurst to set up Williams' second touchdown run.

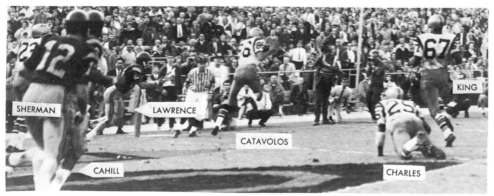

GEORGE CATAVOLOS OF PURDUE SAVES THE GAME WITH AN INTERCEPTION

SHERMAN   LAWRENCE   CATAVOLOS   KING   CHARLES   CAHILL

JOHNNY McKAY ORDERS HIS TROJANS TO SCORE

U.S.C. wanted a touchdown so badly in the fourth quarter it monopolized the ball twenty-six plays to Purdue's eight. A thirty-four-yard pass from Winslow to Sherman, who got beyond the stumbling Leroy Keyes, seemed to set up the scoring chance U.S.C. wanted, but then Winslow was thrown for a big loss. After Purdue punted, U.S.C. got the break it needed when Purdue roughed the U.S.C. punter. From there the challenging touchdown emerged.

However, young Mr. Catavolos with his big interception made good the promise of his mother, Mrs. Lou Catavolos of Chicago, that "someday George will be a hero." She uttered that statement when friends wanted her to name her son, born on V-E Day, Victor Edward in honor of the great day in American history. She said she would sell bonds in honor of the end of the war but she was going to stick to the Greek name of George.

Catavolos gave Bill Miller of the Pasadena *Star-News* this version of his save: "They had to go for two points in a game like this. And they had to throw because they couldn't run on us down there. John Charles, our other defensive halfback, broke up Sherman on his pass pattern. This enabled me to step in front of Lawrence to intercept. I was playing between Winslow and Sherman. When Charles took care of Sherman, I went behind and took care of Lawrence. He and I were the only ones left."

Coach Mollenkopf said: "I would have done the same thing. I would have tried for two."

Lawrence told Dwain Esper of the Pasadena *Star-News:* "I could almost feel the ball in my hands, it was so close. It was a perfect pass. Troy had me pegged all the way. But that Purdue fellow made a tremendous play."

McKay said: "We had no thought of playing for a tie. Even if we had tied it up, Purdue could have worked Griese's short passes to the side lines after we kicked off, and they could have moved within range of a field goal. We put Sherman, Lawrence, and Ray Cahill on the right side. Sherman and Cahill criss-crossed in the end zone and Lawrence flared to the right. Troy threw the ball perfectly, but that Catavolos played it beautifully."

Jim Murray wrote some very amusing paragraphs in the Los Angeles *Times*. "The Trojans died with their boots on and their guns out . . . Long after the game you could still hear the ghostly chorus of Wyatt Earp, Billy the Kid, Black Bart, and whoever else ever turned over a hole card with his life's earnings riding on it, shouting, 'That's the way boys. Don't die hiding in the closet' . . . Let the record show that the Trojan bet the hand, lost like men, smiled, pushed the chair back, and walked out the swinging doors like John Wayne. They showed up for the shoot-out."

Bud Furillo, *Herald-Examiner* sports editor, said: "John McKay, the ol' black-jack player, hit 13 and went broke in the Rose Bowl."

Mel Durslag wrote in the same newspaper: "McKay reasserted the old credo that if a man must go, he should go with honor."

Murray also wrote some comments about the bands in his *Times* column: "As a West Coaster, I'm getting good and bloody sick of the Big Ten Rose Bowl pact. Wait a minute! It's not the football team. We can handle them. It's show business where they are clobbering us. In football, we're five for twenty-one. In bands, they've shut us out. Purdue came out with a band that John Philip Sousa never dreamed of — plus they had four girls in sequins, balloons, smoke bombs, and more tubas than a hock shop on New Year's morning. The band had more people in it than the Washington Senators drew last season. I don't mean to take anything away from the poor kids at USC, but they looked like an Indian club act by comparison. 'What's the name of that combo?' asked the press box's Bud Tucker (San Gabriel Valley *Tribune)* as U.S.C.'s thin red line trickled out onto the field. Our colleges should start recruiting for Swiss bell ringers, not scatbacks, fiddlers, nor fullbacks."

Murray' comments did reveal that times had changed in the western newspaper fraternity. It wasn't too many years earlier that the cries were centered around Big Ten football being too tough. Men like Jim Owens, Tommy Prothro, and Johnny McKay changed all that.

35
O.J.

O. J. SIMPSON

1968

O. J. SIMPSON's boyhood dream was to play in the Rose Bowl. It remained his driving goal throughout his two-year U.S.C. playing career, an ambition he realized once as a winner and once as a loser.

When he transferred from San Francisco City College to become a Trojan, thereby surrendering a year of university eligibility, Simpson consoled his depressed future teammates after they suffered that disheartening 14-13 loss to Purdue in the 1967 classic: "Don't worry about it," O. J. told end Bob Miller in the dressing room after the game. "We will be back next year."

H. W. ("Hoot") Bragg was president of the Tournament when O. J. made his debut in the Arroyo saucer. "Hoot", a rosy-faced amiable Santa Claus type and a Los Angeles oil executive, had only one choice for his grand marshal—another affectionate person, Senator Everett Dirksen of Illinois. Although the senator's face was pale, his heart was glowing. Pasadena loved him.

The senator's heart perhaps got warmed a bit at Santa Anita race track one afternoon when Bragg decided they needed a recess from the round of official visitations. Bragg noted that the senator excused himself from their box after each race. Assuming Dirksen had been going to the parimutual window, Bragg remarked, "Having any luck, Senator?"

Dirksen appeared more jolly, it seemed to Bragg, after each return to the box. Thus, to cash in on some of his companion's good fortune, Bragg accompanied the grand marshal on his sojourn after the seventh race. As they passed the turf club's 'fountain of lively waters,' the bartender beamed, "Shall I mix you another one, Senator?"

Bragg was fascinated by Dirksen's affection for people. "We were running a little late to attend the Chrysler reception prior to the Big Ten dinner at the Palladium," recalled Bragg. "We stopped in front of the Palladium on Sunset Boulevard, and I warned the senator not to stop for autographs and the usual handshaking because we were due inside. He said, 'Fine, don't worry.' Then he got out of the car and walked to the glass ticket-sales window and shook hands with a gray-haired 60-year old gal. He said to her, 'Now put your mouth up to the round

GREETING TO PARADE VIEWERS FROM H. W. ("HOOT") BRAGG AND SENATOR EVERETT DIRKSEN (TOP LEFT); DIRKSEN DANCES WITH QUEEN LINDA STROTHER (TOP RIGHT); THE OFFICIAL TOURNAMENT FAMILY (ABOVE)

hole in the glass and give me a kiss.' She promptly did. This caused a great applause from the people milling around outside. Then Mr. Dirksen explained to his wife that the lady might live in Illinois someday and he needed a vote everywhere he could find it.

"I also recall a great evening after the Grand Marshal Ball in his honor at the Huntington when we attended a meatball party at the Overland Club. Since he was very tired, he suggested he stay only 30 minutes. We arrived at 10:15 p.m. and he was still visiting and exchanging stories with Maudie Prickett at 2:45 in the morning. Before leaving the party, the Senator shook hands with everyone and called them by their first and last names, which, in itself, is a pretty hard thing to do, especially after Overland Club hospitality."

Bragg said the senator was never off schedule during his entire stay in Pasadena and wrote all of his speeches on a cloth napkin with a felt pen about two minutes before giving them.

Bragg's appraisal after a week with Dirksen was: "He loved people. He had a spontaneity that was rare."

Bragg was a president with foresight. Five months before New Year's Day, at an annual guess-the-team contest gathering of Tournament people, "Hoot" predicted it would be Indiana against U.S.C. in the Rose Bowl. Johnny Pont's amazing Indiana "Cinderella Kids" made his prediction come true by staging a series of startling comebacks in Big Ten thrillers to qualify as national champion U.S.C.'s opponent on January 1. Each team had lost one game during the season.

The 79th annual Tournament of Roses was a special occasion, for it marked the first time the parade and game telecasts were beamed "live" by satellite to other parts of the world. Bragg had been cognizant of the international acceptance of the Tournament when he visited Thailand with Henry Kearns as guests of Thanat Khoman. During a garden reception, two hundred Thai children pasted flowers on a nearby wall to spell out, "Welcome, Pasadena Tournament of Roses."

Bragg's last memory of his Tournament experiences was this: "I was most impressed by the complete cooperation and sense of team play that is exhibited by the 1,400 members. I have seen attorneys (who I personally know probably earn in excess of $50,000 a year) work all night doing a simple job like moving traffic barricades and working with a partner who might be a service station operator or grocery clerk. The ability this group has to react to unpredictable emergencies is amazing."

INDIANA CHEER LEADERS

Bragg first rode in the Rose parade in 1914. He was a three-year-old boy riding on the Fire Department truck driven by his father. In 1929 he was an usher in the Rose Bowl. He threw a handful of tickets away in excitedly trying to gesture Roy Riegels when he ran the wrong way. Bragg has been a member of seventeen Tournament committees and chairman of six of them.

A chilly but clear day greeted Queen Linda Strother and her court for their reign on January 1, 1968, a day that will be remembered as "The Great Indiana Invasion." More than 20,000 Hoosier rooters came to Pasadena, their bright red dominating the west side of the Rose Bowl. The Hoosier red was not dominant on the field, however.

U.S.C., led by Simpson's superiority (he scored two touchdowns and gained 128 yards in 25 carries), turned back the young Indiana challengers, 14-3, in a performance that did not excite the experts.

Jim Murray wrote in the *Times:* "Well, Indiana finally sevened out . . . They had gone a long way without having to show their openers . . . The gambling gentlemen from Indiana U will have to turn in their gold-tipped canes and silver vests and join the working people for a while . . . It looked like the Trojans were swatting a fly with a telephone book. Their execution was fine if it was themselves they were

trying to execute . . . For U.S.C. to go into the locker room at halftime with a four-point lead was the biggest waste of manpower since Russia backed out of Finland."

The 102,946 spectators enjoyed the performance, however, while young Indiana quarterback Harry Gonso and his sophomore pals made the Trojans work to win. Paul Zimmerman of the *Times* praised the Trojan defense for the victory. "The U.S.C. defense shut off quarterback Gonso's option plays, adjusted to the sprint-out pass and Pont's belly series where the quarterback fakes to the fullback, slides along the line, and pitches back or keeps the ball," wrote Zimmerman in his last Rose Bowl story before retirement from a sports-writing career of eminence.

Veteran television commentator Paul Christman, himself a great player in his day, said after his first broadcast of a Rose Bowl game (the spectacle impressed him) that an injury to Gonso in the fourth quarter, when the Hoosiers were making a comeback bid, prevented a wild finish and denied Indiana a chance to take a shot at another dramatic victory.

The Trojans took advantage of the Hoosier strategy of keying on Simpson by mixing in the forward pass with more-than-usual use of fullback Dan Scott as a runner to the inside. The strategy paid off. Simpson scored twice on short runs, and the best the Hoosiers could get against the U.S.C. defense was a twenty-seven-yard field goal by Dave Kornowa. Simpson's longest run was fifteen yards, but this All-American's speed and durability fulfilled his reputation as one of the greatest runners ever to step on the Rose Bowl — or any other — turf.

"We knew Indiana had quick linebackers," said Trojan quarterback Steve Sogge, "so we figured if we ran Scott, who lines up directly in front of Simpson, we would gain an extra step. That extra step helped a lot."

Coach McKay excused what many thought was a mediocre Trojan performance. "The idea is to win," said the quick-speaking Trojan jester. "Five of our regulars were out at the start of the game because of injuries, and we lost two more during the action. Our replacement players had a hard time because of timing, but I think they adjusted very well."

Coach Pont of Indiana said his team did well against a champion. He thought his defense was the victim of bad field-position too frequently. He also praised Trojan defensive ends for keeping Gonso on the inside.

"I only wish we were quicker," concluded Gonso.

But this is only half of the story of the "O. J. Era" in the Rose Bowl.

1969

Trojan followers should have known, as January 1, 1969, approached, that there was trouble ahead when Ohio State's sophomore-studded team swept through a nine-game undefeated season and qualified to battle U.S.C., once tied by Notre Dame, for the national championship. Ohio State went into the game rated No. 1 at the polls, U.S.C. No. 2.

The big tipoff came the day before the game. Woody Hayes, Buckeye coach, who had never lost in Pasadena, appeared a half hour late at the Kiwanis Kickoff Luncheon. He was highly keyed and wanted to leave early. In fact, the program had to be readjusted to fit into his afternoon plans. He wanted to rejoin his team so he could drive the boys through one more practice, which he said they needed.

When it came his turn to speak, Hayes was asked what he feared most about U.S.C.

"Not a damn thing!" bellowed Woody.

The way the Buckeyes hit against the Trojans, Woody was correct. They didn't fear a damn thing.

President of the 1969 Tournament was Gleeson L. ("Tige") Payne, a handsome, tall athletic-looking insurance executive. Payne selected Bob Hope as his grand marshal for "A Time to Remember" milestone in the great history of Pasadena's famed classic.

"Thanks for the Memory" Hope was a popular choice. Bob hurried back from his annual Christmas tour of entertaining troops in Vietnam to join Payne in leading one of the most beautiful parades ever to pass down Pasadena's Colorado Boulevard.

"I think the most interesting happening of the day was Hope's automobile stalling half way in the parade route," recalled Payne. "He was one of Chrysler's top performers and was riding in a car specially built for the occasion." The traffic was heavy that morning. This made the Hopes late. They were to have arrived at Tournament House at 7 a.m. for breakfast. Bill Faith, public relations man for Hope, paced nervously to and fro in the driveway at the mansion

BOB HOPE AND GLEESON
L. ("TIGE") PAYNE AT GAME

when the hands of the clock pointed to eight o'clock. The entourage finally sped in the back driveway about ten minutes before the grand marshal's auto was to have rolled down the front concourse to Orange Grove.

There was excitement inside the former Wrigley mansion. Hope was being presented awards — one a desk set from a San Diego historical group. Out of nowhere came a man wearing tennis shoes, sweater, and a shirt open at the neck, who pushed his way up to the front and presented Bob with a putter.

With just minutes left before boarding the rose-covered auto, the TV crews were asking for the man of the hour. The interviews might have been hurried and harried, but the King of Laughter retained his professional calm, joking and kidding all of the way. He carried the putter with him. Microphones were still being thrust before him as the famed comedian got into the sleek white Chrysler Imperial.

The driver of the grand marshal's auto was Clarence ("Paddy") Padfield, who was neatly attired in his "men in white" suit of the Association. He stepped on the starter, but nothing happened. The battery had gone dead. Small wonder! Every conceivable contraption had been installed in the plush auto — TV set (so Bob could view the earlier Bowl games), radio receiver and transmitter, the latter being the device that made it possible for the honoree to talk to the world as he passed the NBC and CBS video and audio equipment.

A resourceful Tournament man ran down to the Orange Grove formation area, arranged for an emergency vehicle to come to the scene, and got the Imperial started with a jumper cable. Emitting a sigh of relief, Padfield drove onto the processional concourse. He kept the motor running. Bob Hope raised his right arm precisely at 8:45 a.m. and the parade got under way. The assembled one and one-half million spectators greeted the Hopes on this day of happiness. As Bob passed the networks' cameras, he said, "I would have been Rose Bowl Queen, but my wig fell off during the semifinals."

Everything went smoothly until the auto reached Holliston Avenue. The motor went dead. Full force upon the starter wouldn't turn the motor over. The battery had conked out completely. A driver of a truck on one of the abutting side streets offered to push or tow the immobile Imperial. He was discouraged from carrying through on his kind offer, for it would never do to have a smaller car coming to the aid of the majestic Chrysler Imperial.

Five teenagers, several of whom were barefooted and had long hair, offered to push the stricken vehicle. Their offer was accepted. All five put their shoulders to the task at hand. The first mile was easy, but after the turn north at Sierra Madre Boulevard it was uphill all the way. Meanwhile, Hope was delighting the spectators by pretending to use the putter as a club to get more effort out of the pushers. Finally, Hope himself got out of the car and lent his muscle as assistance to the fast fatiguing fivesome.

Arriving at Victory Park, Hope gave his Rose Bowl game tickets to the Good Samaritans, saying to President Payne, "We will sit with you at the game."

Imagine the surprise of Tournament Manager Max Colwell at the stadium when he saw the barefooted young men in the grand marshal's seats. He was further surprised when they said, "Bob Hope gave us the tickets."

The 80th Tournament, with Queen Pamela Anicich reigning, was staged on a beautiful, warm, summer-like day. Gaiety was the mood, after Hope had broken all pregame tensions with a rib-tickling talk at the Kickoff Luncheon the day before.

"It was nice of Tige Payne to recall my boxing career. I was known as Rembrandt Hope—I was on the canvas so much," said the comedian, who then added:

"I'll tell you one thing about my trip to Vietnam with Ann-Margret. After fourteen days with her, I deserve to be in the Tournament of Roses. I'm in full bloom. . . .

"You know Everett Dirksen was grand marshal last year. The parade will go faster this year. I don't have to sell albums. . . .

"They didn't need a float for Dirksen. They just frosted his hair. He looks as if he were electrocuted and lived. . . .

"It's a great honor to be grand marshal. Some of the past men honored were General Eisenhower, Chief Justice Warren, and Richard Nixon. I think I'll go to Whittier while I'm over this way and see the manger Nixon was born in. . . .

"And wasn't it great that our astronauts have just made it around the moon? It was the first American flight in weeks that wasn't hi-jacked. . . .

"Of course, we're all happy that the *Pueblo* crew was released. I

PAMELA ANICICH

thought LBJ made a mistake when he asked the Russians to help out when the crew was captured. That's like asking DeGaulle to name a good California wine. . . .

"I went over to look at the parade floats. The best one is a drinking man's float — Dean Martin on skates holding a bottle of four roses. . . .

"One good thing about the game tomorrow. We will be seeing students belting each other around, rather than the faculty. . . ."

Four of the great names of American intercollegiate football rode the National Football Foundation's float: Dr. Jerome ("Brud") Holland, Cornell; Ernie Nevers, Stanford; Fritz Crisler, Minnesota, Princeton, and Michigan; and Morley Drury of U.S.C. This was part of the Foundation's observance of football's 100th year. Television surveys claimed 98,000,000 people saw this float and the others in the parade, which was beamed via television to many parts of the world.

Floats from San Diego, City of Commerce, and San Gabriel depicted two hundred years since the beginning of California. Many organizations celebrated their birthdays with floats: Loyal Order of Moose, 80 years; DeMolay, 50 years; Odd Fellows and Rebekahs, 150 years; and National Restaurant Association, 50 years.

Richard Coy took over the directorship of the PCC Tournament band.

President Payne's final observations were these: "The thing that impressed me most about my experience, which included 50,000 miles of travel, was the unqualified acceptance of the Tournament of Roses. It is rare today to find any idea or event where acceptance is complete. This even attracts all ages and all races and eventually will be seen by everyone in the world. I was most impressed by the effort extended by the participants — especially the bands which go to such great efforts to raise money to be here on New Year's Day. This same effort is made by the community endeavors which present the non-commercial floats."

The world of horses continued in the 1969 parade just as it has in all Tournament parades. The Long Beach Mounted Police Posse again led the procession. Wearing red fezzes and white uniforms, the fifteen riders of the Al Malaikah Shrine Temple Silver Mounted Patrol appeared for the nineteenth consecutive year on matched palominos.

With the temperature in the high seventies, the Buckeyes of Ohio State, who had trained with hot blowers providing California conditions in their field house in Columbus, put on a tremendous display of hard hitting, solid football, and stamina to defeat Simpson, Sogge, and Company, 27-16, before 102,036 stunned spectators, including President-elect Nixon, who flew to the stadium via helicopter which landed on Brookside golf course west of the stadium.

At Nixon's side during the game was ex-coach of renown Bud

Wilkinson, appointed to the "cabinet" for the day as "minister of football." Nixon was so thrilled by the spectacle of seeing 100,000 American flags displayed during the singing of the National Anthem that he wrote a letter to Payne congratulating the Tournament for its patriotism.

The flags were secured and paid for through the efforts of three Pasadena men — Art Neff, Bob Mulvin, Marv Gray — and distributed by military personnel, Boy Scouts, and volunteers to every person who entered the stadium. Americans watching the telecast in foreign countries were thrilled.

Dick Cullum, accepted football authority from the Midwest and columnist for the Minneapolis *Tribune,* said before the game: "This isn't Indiana that USC is playing. Ohio State is a great football team. Watch out."

Cullum's analysis was *so* correct.

In my game comment in the Pasadena *Star-News,* I described Ohio State's victory as follows, after erroneously picking U.S.C. in advance to win:

"The Trojans, known as the 'Cardiac Kids,' for their many stirring comebacks during the season, died from a 'stroke' suffered shortly after the kickoff. The stroke resulted from a blow on the head inflicted by the powerful Ohio State Buckeyes and was aggravated by Trojan nervous tension. The Trojans apparently were in good health

O. J. SIMPSON, FULL SPEED AHEAD

O. J. SIMPSON SCORES ON 80-YARD RUN

with a 10-0 lead before they collapsed. They made a last gasp for life, but death was inevitable. A shot of 'football cocaine' administered by the officials gave U.S.C. one dying moment of breath in the form of a disputed touchdown when it was ruled Trojan end Sam Dickerson had equal possession of a Sogge pass with defender Mike Paluski before they and the ball went flying out of the end zone. Woody Hayes rushed to the death scene to charge cruel prolongation of life of a victim already doomed, but the end came peacefully and, for thousands of Ohio State rooters, without tears."

The Trojans paved the way for their doom, as Dwain Esper so perfectly described it in his Pasadena *Star-News* story, by throwing two costly interceptions on bids for touchdowns and by losing the ball three times on fumbles — five turnovers that reversed the trend of the game completely, despite another workhorse display of staying power by Simpson. In contrast, Ohio State had no interceptions and never lost the ball once on fumbles.

Simpson fumbled the ball away twice and Sogge once. Each threw it away on potential touchdown plays. One of Sogge's fumbles set up a Buckeye touchdown and one of Simpson's set up another. These mistakes offset a brilliant eighty-yard touchdown run by O. J., also his 171 yards gained while carrying the ball twenty-eight times and his eight pass catches that were good for 85 yards more. After a display of skill like this, it was sad for the Trojans to watch their Heisman Trophy hero suddenly come up with greasy fingers.

U.S.C.'s 10-0 lead on a twenty-one-yard Ron Ayala field goal and O. J.'s eighty-yard dash deteriorated when Ohio State got its inside running game functioning, a blasting attack that the Trojan defense could not stop. Sophomore quarterback Rex Kern earned player-of-the-game honors by directing and executing this attack as

234

GOOD PROTECTION AS REX KERN PASSES FOR
OHIO STATE

he ran and passed the Trojan defense into a state of futility. Big Ohio State ground-gainers were fullback Jim Otis and halfback Leophus Hayden. Simpson's great run, in which he broke off left tackle, cut back and outraced the Buckeye defense, was the last Trojan gem of the day.

A sixty-nine-yard Ohio comeback drive culminating in an Otis thrust for the score and a twenty-six-yard field goal by Jim Roman three seconds before the halftime gun tied it up and signaled a "Roman Holiday" after intermission.

As Simpson and Sogge took turns handing the ball to the Buck-

OHIO STATE'S LEO HAYDEN BURSTS PAST
U.S.C. TACKLERS

eyes, Ohio State scored again on a twenty-five-yard Roman field goal, a Kern touchdown pass to Hayden, and a sixteen-yard looper from Kern to Ray Gillian. Meanwhile, the Trojans blew scoring chances by throwing two interceptions before Sogge connected on a spiral to Dickerson for the disputed touchdown deep in the end zone. Joint possession, according to college football rules, becomes a touchdown for the offense if the receiver at least touches one foot in the end zone while retaining partial possession coming down. This Dickerson may have done, as substantiated by excellent Associated Press photos, although the fans thought they had witnessed nothing more than two players and the ball splurting out of the end zone. The play was the topic of argument for days, the touchdown small consolation for a Troy that had fallen in a jittery performance against a team that hit harder, forced mistakes, and came prepared to win.

"When you fumble deep in your own area, you get beat," said McKay. "Yes, they were hitting. It wasn't a game for girl scouts and cookie eaters. O. J. had a fine game, but it detracts when you fumble. He proved that a containing defense is not the key to stopping him."

Ohio State line coach Lou McCullough said his team set up its defense to avoid giving Simpson the cutback.

"U.S.C. took away our wide game," added Hayes. "But they did it at a price. We were able to curl our receivers around their front for passes and we were able to run inside. Even when we were down 10-0, I knew we could come back. I knew our offense would roll. And I also felt Simpson would not break away again."

"Tying before the halftime gun was a big lift for us. It gave us the momentum and it took that away from them," said Kern, who not only was player of the game, but also dated the Rose Queen, who soon decided to enroll at Ohio State.

"That's the first time I ever saw a touchdown when the ball was rolling on the ground," said Hayes, who couldn't forget the disputed U.S.C. touchdown.

Then Woody headed for Vietnam to show the troops the pictures of how Ohio State continued to be a power in the Rose Bowl.

"Yes," said Hayes, "we weren't afraid of a damn thing."

The Bank of America story is illustrative of the spirit that has guided corporations in their Tournament of Roses participation. It portrays how business firms and the Tournament have become successful partners.

In April 1905, A. P. Giannini formed the Bank of Italy. He had been with a savings and loan firm that believed loans were only to be made to affluent people, not the rank and file. But Giannini felt the little man should be helped, too, to add to the productivity of his country.

Right after the San Francisco earthquake in 1906, the Bank of Italy set up desks and tables on the sidewalk and began making loans. The bank's name was changed later to the Bank of America, which grew into a corporate entity with offices throughout the world and a roster of over 30,000 employes. The personal touch remained.

About 1961, Herb Speth, Bank of America vice president in Pasadena, began looking for a project that would reflect the bank's image of community involvement. While watching the New Year's Day parade, this longtime booster of Pasadena and its activities exclaimed, "This may be it."

He talked with George Banse, vice president in charge of the bank's Pasadena area operations, who for years has been a Tournament committeeman.

It was learned that Class E (business firms) would be the category in which Bank of America would be listed. This class is limited to twelve entries, and there was a waiting list. Meanwhile, Speth consulted with Louis B. Lundborg, retired as chairman of the board; president Rudolph Peterson, and the man next in line to become president, A. W. Clausen. Also lending their enthusiasm and support to the undertaking were C. H. Baumhefner, vice chairman of the board and cashier, and Charles R. Stuart, Jr., vice president in charge of advertising and marketing. The new chairman of the board is C. J. Medberry.

It was in 1967 that the Tournament of Roses, having an opening in the Class E division, sent an invitation to the Bank of America to participate in the Rose Parade with a float entry.

The Bank of America team swung into action. Charles Stuart headed up the effort at the bank's San Francisco headquarters. Herb Speth was the on-the-spot contact in Pasadena. With the theme of the 1968 parade being "Wonderful World of Adventure," Lee Miller created a popular float titled "A Child's World of Adventure."

Emmett Glanz, Jr., public relations man, was detailed to tell the world about the entry, giving particular emphasis to photo and story placement where there are Bank of America offices, including other countries. Copy sent abroad was in the native language of the country. Stories went to cities and countries throughout Europe, Asia, Africa, South America, and North America. Every employee and depositor received a mailing piece telling about the float.

In 1969, with the theme "A Time to Remember," the Bank of America entered "The First Prom."

"Great Days of America" was the float title in 1970 when the motif was "Holidays Around the World." The bank sent Frances Malmgren, the company's publication editor, to Pasadena a week ahead of New Year's Day so she could have time to do an in-depth story on the entry, which was popularly received.

The Bank of America again featured youth in 1971 when it presented an entry "When I Grow Up," carrying out the Tournament theme, "Through the Eyes of a Child."

36

Moon Men Land in Pasadena

MICHIGAN TUMBLES

1970

C. LEWIS EDWARDS, president of the 1970 Tournament, made the moon shot in reverse. He brought the 'moon men' to Pasadena.

Astronauts Charles Conrad, Richard Gordon, and Alan Bean, the heroes of the Apollo 12 moon landing, the United States' second successful attempt on the moon's surface, kept their date with Edwards and arrived amid the thundering applause of 3,000 football fans attending the Kickoff Luncheon the day before the big game.

"The moon will probably put Disneyland out of business if we can find a way to get the kids up there," said Commander Conrad. He told the sports fans: "The moon is good news for golfers. You can hit the ball a country mile, and with no atmosphere there is no way you can hook or slice. As for football on the moon, you'd have to make a lot of changes in the rules." Conrad added he felt a lot safer sitting in the command module on top of six million pounds of propellant than he feels on a California, Texas, or any other freeway.

The smiling astronauts, loudly cheered in every Pasadena appearance, led the parade as grand marshals in three separate automobiles. They loved the role. President Edwards made an interesting observation. "From my vantage point near them, I could tell that they were setting the pattern of our parade. Everybody was happy all along the route. This was the happiest parade I have ever seen, and it was the astronauts who set the mood of good will."

When the astronauts were leaving to go back to Houston, they graciously said good-bye to their many Tournament friends. "We had a wonderful time and everybody was great to us," they said. When they were invited back to future Tournaments of Roses, the usual custom, Conrad said: "I want to be like MacArthur. I will return."

Bean added: "I'd like to come and bring my whole family."

A tired Mrs. Gordon, who had her six children along, said: "I'd like to come back and leave my youngsters at home."

Edwards closed his momentous reign as president by saying, "The devoted and loyal volunteer workers in the Tournament make it easy for the president."

"GEORGIA: WONDERFUL LAND OF FUN,"
SWEEPSTAKES WINNER

"THE SWEET SHOP," BAKERY AND CONFEC-
TIONERY WORKERS UNION ENTRY

"IT'S A BIG, BIG WORLD," EASTMAN KODAK'S
PRINCESS AWARD FLOAT (BEST ANIMATION)

"SESAME STREET," CHRYSLER CORPORATION'S
ENTRY

"STAIRWAY TO STARDOM," THE FLOAT OF THE NATIONAL EXCHANGE CLUB

"SHOEMAKER AND THE ELVES," THE ANNIVERSARY AWARD ENTRY OF DR. PEPPER COMPANY

"BREAK THROUGH TO A BETTER WORLD," THE SALVATION ARMY'S FLOAT

"RAINDROPS KEEP FALLING ON MY HEAD," ENTRY OF HI-C DRINKS

"DOLLS FROM MANY LANDS," UNION OIL COMPANY OF CALIFORNIA

"A HELPING HAND," AL MALAIKAH SHRINE TEMPLE'S FLOAT

"DRAGONS ARE
THOUGH THIS ENTR
FESTIVAL ASSOCIAT

"HAWAII NO KA OE
LINES

"THE OLD SWIMMIN' HOLE," WINNER OF THE MAYOR'S AWARD (BEST ORIGINALITY), ENTERED BY OCCIDENTAL LIFE OF CALIFORNIA

"SEEIN' EYE TO EYE," THE FLOAT OF SOROPTIMISTS INTERNATIONAL

"TOYLAND EXPRESS," BEKINS MOVING AND STORAGE

"MOMMY PLEASE READ TO ME," THE ST. LOUIS, MISSOURI, FLOAT DRAWN BY THE FAMOUS CLYDESDALES

BO SCHEMBECHLER
LEAVES HOSPITAL

As usual, the Kickoff Luncheon was a laugh fest. This writer introduced Michigan coach Bo Schembechler with one of the shortest poems ever written: "Oh Goodie — No Woody. Gung Ho — Here's Bo." Asked about his controversial offense, Johnny McKay of U.S.C. said: "If Michigan didn't show up, we wouldn't score eighteen points."

Michigan did show up on January 1, before an all-time record Rose Bowl crowd of 103,878, enjoying the stadium's aluminum seats for the first time. U.S.C. could score only ten points. But that was enough to win 10-3 over a Wolverine team that was without its head coach. Schembechler, who had complained of stomach pains all week, went to St. Luke's Hospital with a mild heart attack and had to remain in Pasadena for three weeks to recuperate.

Following the latest $50,000 improvement program, which included new aluminum seats, new lights, new box seats, improved restroom facilities, and recessed dugouts for the players, the Rose Bowl today seats 102,016. Attendance already has exceeded that figure, as the 1970 crowd figure attests.

This is a good place, too, to note that there are 77 rows of seats in the Rose Bowl. The distance from the north to the south rim is 880 feet. The distance from the east to the west rim is 695 feet.

There were countless highlights to Edwards' gala 1970 show.

Giles L. Pellerin of San Marino, who has watched every U.S.C. game at home and away since 1926, saw the Trojans win their 300th game while he was in the stands. It was the 454th Trojan battle he had witnessed. Pellerin, an accounting supervisor for the Pacific Telephone Company, said he intends to keep watching Trojan games until he has achieved 500 of them.

E. J. Abrahamson, who helped the Great Lakes team win in the Rose Bowl in 1919, returned to the scene in 1970. Age 78, Abrahamson, owner of a resort at Clearwater Lake, Wisconsin, was amazed to see so many Caltech buildings on the Tournament Park around where he played.

CURT GOWDY
AWARDS PLAQUE
TO LATHROP LEISHMAN

Curt Gowdy, chief sports broadcaster for the National Broadcasting Company, awarded Lathrop Leishman the *Sports Magazine* award as American Sportsman of the Year. "Leishman has been the greatest good will ambassador Pasadena ever had," declared Gowdy at the Kickoff Luncheon where the presentation was made.

Miss Calla McDermid, 85, one of Pasadena's oldest native daughters, had missed only one Tournament parade during her long life in Pasadena. She and her sixty-year companion, Miss Mabel L. Forbes, age 90, viewed the parade together in a grandstand seat. When Miss McDermid was twelve years old, she rode a decorated pony cart in the parade.

The White Oak, Texas, high school band went home happy. After being on a bus for three days getting to Pasadena, the bandsmen competed in a contest sponsored by NBC. They won.

Queen Pamela Dee Tedesco was crowned at what coronation

ALEX GAAL AND C. LEWIS EDWARDS AT THE
CROWNING OF QUEEN PAMELA DEE TEDESCO

chairman Alexander Gaal called "the most impressive coronation we have ever had." More than 3,000 viewed the affair at Civic Auditorium.

When Pamela was selected as queen at the completion of competition early in December, she replied to Queen chairman Ralph Helpbringer's greeting with the following: "I can't remember what happened when the judges announced my name. I know I shook a lot because my roses were shaking. I know I must have cried — my make-up was all over my face. I kept thinking I ought to feel different — but I was numb. I said 'I'm dreaming.'" Pamela was another of the queens who early in life had wanted to be a queen. "I always pictured myself sitting on the queen's float, but now that it has happened, I can't believe it," she said.

Former Rose Queens hold an annual reunion, until recently hosted by Occidental Life Insurance Company. Horace Brower, past president and past chairman of the board of Occidental, originated the idea. The queen with the most seniority who annually attends is Mrs. Frank S. Balthis (Holly Halsted, 1930). Coming the greatest distance for the 1969 reunion was Mrs. William Kish (Nancy Kneeland, 1964), Minneapolis, Minnesota. She said, "When I got the notice of the reunion, I had a longing to see Pasadena, Tournament House, other past Rose Queens, family members, and hometown friends."

Queen Tedesco had a rose planted in her honor in the shadow of the Rose Queen fountain in the center of Wrigley Gardens at Tournament House in Pasadena. It marked the first American planting of the new hybrid tea rose, Interflora, which was developed by Universal Rose Selection, Meilland, France. Queen Pamela was assisted in the planting by A. Lewis Shingler and by Charles Hum, Interflora vice president.

The 19-year-old Pasadena City College student who reigned over the New Year's Day festivities said, "With the planting of this rose,

240

I will make it a point to visit the Wrigley Gardens, particularly during the blooming season, and enjoy the beauty. The setting will also bring back the many wonderful memories of my experiences as Rose Queen. I feel honored to be a part of this planting ceremony."

A total of 84,803 seats in grandstands constructed along the parade route were sold to the public for prices up to $8.50 each, Ben Mead, administrative assistant to the city manager, reported. Walter Reed, city licensing official, said 584 novelty peddlers, 28 food peddlers, and 78 operators of food stands along the parade route paid operating license fees of $10 for novelties and $15 for food concessions. The city charged grandstand operators 50 cents a seat for safety inspection. Although only 84,803 had grandstand seats at the parade, over a million more people watched from curbs, trees, and buildings. Many parade viewers established their "homesteads" the afternoon before and remained throughout the cold night to hold their vantage points.

The speeches of football game principals at public functions were fascinating to the sports fans who came to Pasadena for the Tournament. Craig Fertig, one of McKay's assistants, spoke at the Los Angeles Jonathan Club breakfast and said, "I was told I could have sixty minutes to review the season. I'll stand here for fifty-eight minutes and do nothing. Then I'll talk for two minutes." Of course, Fertig was referring to U.S.C.'s season of not being productive until the final two minutes of most games. The Trojans changed the pattern against Michigan, however. They played it to the hilt all the way.

Ed Essertier, then editor of the Pasadena *Star-News,* told two interesting stories in his column on the editorial page. Essertier revealed that Bob Hope was on his way to the Kickoff Luncheon the day before the game but decided to turn back. County Supervisor Warren Dorn, who was riding with Hope, told Essertier that the famed comic was determined not to come to Pasadena that noon even after getting on the freeway. Hope felt that someone might think he was trying to grab the spotlight from the three astronauts.

Essertier also told how Jess Hill, U.S.C. athletic director, almost muffed the kind of telephone call that an athletic director doesn't receive every day. Hill had been given the assignment of allotting game seats to U.S.C.'s distinguished guests in the absence of Dr. Norman Topping, U.S.C. president, who had gone on business to Seattle several days before.

FOOTBALL COMMITTEE:
LATHROP LEISHMAN,
STANLEY HAHN, RAY
DORN, WILLIAM NICHOLAS

Hill was at home shaving when his wife announced: "The president is calling you from Washington."

Believing it was President Topping calling from the state of Washington, Hill suggested to his wife to have him call back in fifteen minutes.

"No!" she said. "Not *that* president. It's President Nixon."

Hill, his face in a lather, took the call. It truly was President Nixon announcing he could not attend the Rose Bowl game and wishing the U.S.C. team luck.

Nixon called Hill again after arriving at his winter California home in San Clemente to verify that he wouldn't attend. The President of the United States also called McKay in the U.S.C. dressing room after the game to congratulate him and the team. It is believed the President did not make the fifteen-minute helicopter trip to Pasadena to see the game because he wanted the astronauts to have the full public attention without having to share it.

The city of Los Angeles won the Sweepstakes Prize in the colorful parade with a float depicting an exotic bonsai planter in the midst of an Oriental garden and pool.

Richard S. ("Rick") Chapman, twenty-eight-year-old builder, has been so successful in creating prize-winning floats for the City of Los Angeles that he was cited for his excellence by the Los Angeles City Council. He won the Theme Prize in .1968 and the Sweepstakes award in 1969 and 1970 with his designs. Chapman, who heads Festival Artists of Arcadia, captured the Anniversary Award for Knott's Berry Farm in 1970.

Again one of the parade features was the famed Anheuser-Busch Clydesdale work horses that pulled the St. Louis float called "Holidays at Busch Gardens." The float was produced by Carlota Busch Giersch, daughter of August A. Busch, Jr., president of Anheuser-Busch. Carlota is the great-granddaughter of Mr. and Mrs. Adolphus Busch, creators in 1903 of the original Busch Gardens in Pasadena.

Floral fantasy complemented authenticity on the "Holidays at Busch Gardens" float in the 1970 parade. Three Busch Gardens across the nation were selected for representation on the float, epitomizing holiday outings.

Some of the animals on two large carousels were so rare as to seem imaginary. And who says a merry-go-round prancer has to be realistic, especially when surrounded by the creamy texture of hothouse chrysanthemums — more than 500,000 being used in primary covering of the carousels and a seventeen-foot high ferris wheel between them?

Strictly real, however, was the St. Louis float's traditional use of the famed eight-horse hitch of champion Clydesdales. The horses average a ton in weight. The seemingly "bigger than life" horses drew the entry, with their drivers in circus uniforms riding a circus wagon colored red by generous application of petals from 500 dozen poinsettias used on the float.

The first or forward carousel, twenty feet in diameter and seventeen feet high, had an exterior primarily of white chrysanthemums, with accents of red. It carried six African animals to represent the African Busch Gardens at Tampa, Florida. A child rode on each animal. Holly Schmidt, National Poster Child of the Muscular Dystrophy Associations of America, Inc., rode a rare African okapi, a cousin of the giraffe with shorter neck.

The floral ferris wheel represented the Los Angeles Busch Gardens in San Fernando Valley, California, with eight bright-colored macaws riding along. They are among the trained birds who perform there.

The Houston Asian Busch Gardens was represented by another carousel of size equal to the first, but featuring Asian animals. Like the first, it revolved (but in the opposite direction), and carousel music was heard. Children also rode its animals. Its upright supports were covered by pink pruis (flowering prune) and flowering forsythia branches flown in from Holland. An orangutan (of redwood bark and orange chrysanthemums) rode a chariot seat. Other animals included a baby elephant, featuring black onion seeds, and a rhinoceros of silver dollar eucalyptus.

Designer of the float was David Miller, and the builder was Miller Brothers.

St. Louis had entered 16 previous floats.

The Farmers Insurance Company float, "Holiday in The Park," was made up of 20,000 dark red "Forever Yours" roses, but a little dog named Rosey turned out to be the sweetest rose of all. Charles Manos, a Detroit *News* reporter, bought the four-month-old pup from the Detroit Humane Society and gained a trip to Pasadena for Rosey and himself when Farmers Insurance agreed to let the pair ride on a park bench on the float in the parade.

FARMERS INSURANCE CELEBRITIES:
LINDA LANPHEAR, CHARLES MANOS,
AND PET DOG, ROSEY

Also on the float were four sets of twins in rowboats, including Dave and Doug Starkweather of Lansing, Michigan, who were on the Michigan State freshman football team. They won an all-expense trip to the Rose Bowl in a national contest sponsored by Farmers Insurance. Also chosen to ride on the float was Linda Lanphear, a Wisconsin blonde who was chosen for the honor in a Farmers Insurance contest.

Rosey came to Pasadena from Detroit via air freight but went home first class on an airliner because she had been such a big hit in the parade when she waved her tail to millions. Manos reported she stood on her hind legs when the float got near the network television cameras. "What a ham," he remarked. Before the parade started, in the early hours of the morning, Rosey received dog food and warm milk from two Tournament of Roses fans, Mr. and Mrs. Art Neff, who live near the start of the parade on Orange Grove Avenue. Rosey and Manos had stayed at the Huntington Hotel, where bellhops had brought hamburgers to the room for the prize terrier.

Mrs. J. Lambert Roberts of Pasadena especially enjoyed the 1970 Rose parade. The theme "Holidays Around the World" was an idea she had submitted. She was a second-time winner in the theme-idea contest, held annually. In 1957 she suggested "Famous Firsts in Flowers."

Although the Michigan team wore Pasadena-made uniforms (the maize and blue was "spic and Spanjian" in its garb manufactured by the Spanjian Company), the Wolverines couldn't handle McKay's "Wild Bunch," the name given to the Trojan front five-man line. The

THE WILD BUNCH: JIMMY GUNN, TODY SMITH, WILLARD SCOTT, AL COWLINGS, CHARLIE WEAVER

BOB CHANDLER STARTS TOUCHDOWN RUN FOR
U.S.C. AFTER CATCHING A JIMMY JONES PASS

reason? In this game, McKay came up with a six-man line, adding big Tony Terry, and the strategy checked Michigan's running game. The original five in the "Wild Bunch" were Jimmy Gunn and Charlie Weaver at ends, Al Cowlings and Tody Smith at tackles, and Bubba Scott in the middle.

Even the Michigan "Touchdown Pup" couldn't score a touchdown against the "Wild Bunch plus one." In its famous nose-dribble act between halves, the Michigan canine wonder ran out of bounds on the five-yard line.

It cannot be said the Trojans won only on defense, however. The Trojan offensive unit, often criticized in 1969 for attacking breakdowns until the last two minutes, "held 'em," too. U.S.C. had six scoring chances to Michigan's four and outgained the Wolverines 323 yards to 289.

U.S.C. scored first on a twenty-five-yard field goal by Ron Ayala (the boy who kicked a field goal in the last second of the game to beat Stanford earlier in the season). Michigan tied it on a twenty-yard kick by Tim Killian. Then, in the third quarter, Jimmy Jones threw a thirteen-yard pass to Bob Chandler which the fleet U.S.C. receiver took on the Michigan 20. Chandler pivoted away from Michigan's Brian Healy and then escaped a desperate reach near the goal line by Barry Pierson to score the touchdown that won the game. Ayala kicked the point.

Dwain Esper in the Pasadena *Star-News* described McKay's victory strategy: "John McKay deduced early in his Rose Bowl preparation that Michigan liked to run. Consequently he reconstructed his

245

defense to meet this team tendency — and oh, how it paid off! McKay's answer was a 'sixty-one' defense, fundamentally a six-man line with one linebacker."

McKay said, "Our strategy was to try to get Michigan to play us left-handed." He succeeded. Michigan had to resort to long passes by quarterback Don Moorhead at the finish, but he had to be content mostly with short ones to his great tight end Jim Mandich, who caught eight.

Clarence Davis and Mike Berry carried the running load for U.S.C. and churned up enough yardage to keep the attack going with Jones' well-placed spot shots to his receivers offering a change.

Punter Ayala may have made the play that saved the day for U.S.C. With three minutes to play, he stood in midfield to punt. The pass from center was high over his head. He leaped, batted it down, caught the ball, and kicked it from amidst the charge of Michigan's rushing giants, Cecil Pryor and Mike Keller. This kick, which stopped on Michigan's 8-yard line, put them too far back to go all the way with a late offensive.

Michigan players told Will Watson of the Pasadena *Star-News* that the loss of Schembechler hurt them. Moorhead said it wasn't the same without his old coach to talk to on time-outs. Michigan was under the direction of Jim Young, Bo's assistant.

"We were the most criticized ten-game winner in history," McKay told Dick Robinson of the Pasadena *Star-News*. "I don't give a damn for critics."

Player-of-the-game award winner Chandler said, "Jimmy Jones really threw me a good pass. It gave me time to see the defensive back before I made my cut."

Jones said, "We wanted to get a first down. So I called a 65-Z-snake. It sends Chandler to the short side of the field and he runs a hook pattern. I run play action fake to the right or wide side."

Loel Schrader, Long Beach *Press-Telegram,* commented: "Doubtless the Wolverines missed the presence of their dynamic young coach, who had masterminded the 24-12 victory over Ohio State in his first year at Ann Arbor. But the story of this game lay in the U.S.C. ability to stack up Michigan's running attack and force Michigan to be content with nothing more than aerial 'gimmies' of the short variety, plus the return to early season form by Trojan quarterback Jimmy Jones."

Dave Lewis, Long Beach *Press-Telegram:* "Coach Young admitted that the news of Bo being in the hospital demoralized the team at first, but in the end every player gave everything he had. The strategy had been set early in the week. We all felt it could have been a different story today if Bo had been present."

Hank Hollingworth, Long Beach *Press-Telegram:* "Jimmy Jones said 'I showed them. I've got two years to go in college and I think I'll get a lot better.' "

Don Merry, Long Beach *Press-Telegram:* "Jimmy Jones said it was very satisfying because he believed he showed 'em today that he was an all-around quarterback, something people said he wasn't prior to this game."

Bob Oates, Los Angeles *Times:* "From the first to the last, Michigan never did look like a winner except to their fans."

Mal Florence, *Times:* "The Trojans started 1970 as they lived 1969, a team that drags out every game to a tension-packed ending."

Jim Murray, *Times* "USC, unbeaten, unappreciated . . . and on the ropes at the finish."

Jeff Prugh, *Times:* "Johnny McKay said, 'I'd rather win a low scoring game like this than lose 48-42 and have somebody come to me and tell me my team sure played a fine game.' "

Dwight Chapin, *Times:* "Michigan middle guard Henry Hill said U.S.C. just punched Michigan around and kept them in bad field position."

John Steadman, sports editor of the Baltimore *News American,* covered the Rose Parade and Bowl game for the first time during his career in realization of what he described as "a life-long dream." Steadman wrote in his column: "All other games are poor imitations of this one. This has to be the all-time breath-taking spectacular. . . . Yes, Pasadena has something the rest of the world might like to copy but can't. The parade that unfolds is second to none. The color that is attendant is like a continually moving rainbow. . . . It is obvious that Pasadena takes a lot of pride in what it is. . . . There is nothing like the Rose Bowl. It comes close to being America's foremost spectacular. Thank God we lived long enough to have seen it."

When the game was over, there was nothing left for Pasadena but a gigantic clean-up. Peter Geddes, Tournament of Roses line-of-march official, had plenty of practice during the parade. Because he had missed a Tournament assignment meeting while he and his wife were in Hawaii, he drew the duty of sweeping up after the 220 equestrians passed his point. Geddes got his picture in the paper as a street cleaner the next day — in a white suit yet!

Pasadena city engineer Fritz Zapf revealed that thirty-six tons of rubbish were left behind on city streets after the festival.

Meanwhile, the citizens were tired the next day. A California Federal Savings and Loan office rented a double-decked London bus to travel down Colorado Boulevard to their new offices on Lake Avenue to advertise the firm's grand opening. The natives hardly looked up at the unusual bus. Pasadena had seen enough for one busy twenty-four hours.

A football bet was settled in downtown Pasadena in a manner to command some chuckles.

A "check" to settle a $5 bet to Don Fraser of the Pasadena Police Department was written on a plastic pigskin. Fraser took it to the Bank of America branch in Pasadena to collect.

TOURNAMENT OFFICIALS STANLEY HAHN, LATHROP LEISHMAN, BILL NICHOLAS, AND C. LEWIS EDWARDS
PRESENT ROSE BOWL PICTURE TO RICHARD NIXON DURING A VISIT TO THE WHITE HOUSE

"Will it bounce?" asked Joe Gualderon, vice president and manager of the branch.

"Where do I endorse it?" countered Fraser. "By the laces?"

"There seem to be no strings attached," replied Gualderon, who verified that the football bore the correct identification mark of the payee, bet-loser LeRoy Peterson of Merced, California, the winner's brother-in-law.

The banker squeezed the ball and concluded: "Yes, this is an inflationary period."

The Tournament Football Committee visited President Nixon at the White House during the NCAA convention held in Washington after the 1970 Rose Bowl game. The President was presented a huge color picture taken by official Tournament of Roses photographer "Mr. D" when Nixon crossed the Rose Bowl turf at halftime with Governor Ronald Reagan during the 1969 game.

A rose sticker was seen on the lapel of Conrad Hilton's painting gracing the lobby of the Statler-Hilton Hotel in Washington. Who put it there? The mystery has not been solved, although somebody chuckled: "C. Lewis Edwards was the only one of us tall enough."

The January 1970 Nielsen television ratings revealed that the Rose Bowl game ranks at the top among college bowl games in size of viewing audience. The 1970 game telecast attracted almost 37 million viewers — 36,820,000 to be exact. The Cotton Bowl had 34,460,000 viewers, the Orange Bowl 33,060,000, the National League pro championship game 30,270,000, and the American League pro championship game 30,020,000. The Super Bowl had a larger television audience, however — 44 million.

The top rated 1969 sports events on TV, according to Nielsen's average audience study, based on homes, follows:

Event	Network	AA	Homes
1. Super Bowl (Jets-Colts)	NBC	36.0	20,520,000
2. Rose Bowl (Ohio State-U.S.C.)	NBC	33.5	19,100,000
3. World Series Game #2 (N.Y. Mets at Baltimore)	NBC	29.2	17,080,000
4. World Series Game #1 (N.Y. Mets at Baltimore)	NBC	25.5	14,920,000
5. NFL Game (Various Teams)	CBS	24.4	14,270,000
6. Orange Bowl (Penn State-Kansas)	NBC	23.6	13,450,000
7. NFL Playoff Bowl (Dallas-Minnesota)	CBS	23.1	13,170,000
8. NFL Game (Various Teams)	CBS	21.3	12,460,000
9. World Series Game #5 (Orioles at New York)	NBC	21.0	12,290,000
10. World Series Game #4 (Orioles at New York)	NBC	19.5	11,410,000

NBC sold the reproduction rights to its 1971 Rose Bowl telecast to London Weekend Television.

37
Lewis the Second

BILLY GRAHAM

1971

THE 1971 TOURNAMENT OF ROSES marked the reign of Lewis the Second — A. Lewis Shingler, who succeeded C. Lewis Edwards.

Shingler is from the South — Donalsonville, Georgia, to be exact. He is an institutional fund raiser by trade, a Tournament of Roses worker by first love. For seventeen years he was a Pasadena auto salesman.

"I started selling cars here with Henry Kearns in 1936. He went pretty far, didn't he?" Shingler said of the president of the Export-Import Bank of the United States.

There was a time, because of his southern drawl, that some Tournament constituents thought Shingler was a Texan. Shingler's stock answer has been: "Fellows, I've spent only one day of my life in Texas and that was in leaving."

Shingler has some memories of all not going well in Tournament events. He is a realist. The Tournament of Roses is the greatest, but it has its problems. He tells it this way:

"Just a few years ago at 8:40 a.m., as the president of the Tournament and his charming wife awaited the starting whistle of the parade, a radiator cap blew off and steam covered the front of the president's flower-covered car. The jovial Parade Operations chairman facetiously said to the president, who was beside himself with fear and disgust, 'This may well be the only time in the history of the Tournament that a parade has gone down Colorado Boulevard without a president.' This just was not funny to the president. He may have forgiven the chairman, but for the moment there was a little tension, to say the least. Such are the events that make this the greatest show on earth.

"Then one year the Queen Committee and Tournament Entries Committee members each thought the other was securing large bouquets of red roses for the queen and princesses to carry on their float. Well, the president's wife gave her roses to the queen and the princesses waved with both hands down the line of march that year. Oh well, it was a beautiful day for a parade in Pasadena."

Shingler has served twenty-three years in the Tournament, during which time he has been chairman of five committees and served on nine. He knew how to meet all crises, just as the other Lewis did when his story of the astronauts broke over the wire services before he had official confirmation that they were coming to Pasadena. Edwards didn't get excited. He just brought the three great young Americans to Pasadena anyway and had one of the greatest of Tournaments.

President Shingler summarized his Tournament philosophy in an interview with Margaret Stovall in the Pasadena *Star-News.*

"The entire growth of the Tournament will depend on how well we are able to retain and multiply the feeling that it is more blessed to give than to receive," said Shingler. "Selfishness and personal gain should have no place in the Tournament. . . . My main interests are the church, the Tournament of Roses, and horseback riding. . . .

"The Tournament originated through unselfish motives. It was founded to strengthen community fellowship and bring New Year's Greetings to the community and the world. . . .

"The growth and success, I feel, is due to the desire to serve rather than be served. . . . I want to express appreciation for the hard work and dedication of the Tournament staff and membership. The 400 to 500 members of the 30 committees who give from 40,000 to 50,000 hours of their time each year deserve the credit for putting on the greatest show on earth. The 'men in white' should receive the praise that is given to the president each year."

Shingler enjoyed a most distinguished and successful reign as president.

His grand marshal was Billy Graham, the famed evangelist. The theme of the Tournament was "Through the Eyes of a Child."

When he spoke before 3,000 football fans at the Kiwanis Kickoff luncheon the day before the game which found Stanford (8-3) upsetting previously undefeated (9-0) Ohio State, 27-17, Dr. Graham said: "The strife in the world would end if people everywhere viewed the world through the eyes of a child."

Queen of the 1971 Tournament was Kathleen Denise Arnett, 19, of Los Angeles. She was a sophomore at Pasadena City College, a home economics major planning a career in teaching. The 5'4" brunette was the first Kathleen in fifty-two years to reign over the Rose Parade and the Rose Bowl game. Olive complexion, 125 pounds, Queen Kathleen said her hobbies were sewing, playing piano, rock-collecting, and baking.

Other members of the court were Princesses Janet Kay Hagemeier, 18, Buena Park; Cynthia Lee Coleman, 18, Arcadia; Christine Marie Hartwell, 20, Sierra Madre; Debbi Ann Gilmore, 17, San Gabriel; Patricia Hartman Burch, 17, Arcadia; and Paula Kay Hubbard, 18, Corning.

The silver anniversary of Margaret Stovall, Pasadena *Star-News* photo chief, marking her coverage of Queen activities was recognized at a past queens dinner in 1971 when Miss Stovall, who began her coverage of the royal court in 1947, was the guest of honor.

Admitting the Tournament of Roses had placed him in charge of the weather, Dr. Graham and his wife, Ruth, were happy to see that Pasadena enjoyed one of its finest sunny days for the pageant.

The Sweepstakes float winner in the parade was titled "Georgia — Wonderland of Fun." It featured attractive southern belles posed in swings beneath two majestic oak trees fashioned of flowers. Highlight of the entry was a pair of peacocks in all their magnificence perched in the trees, creating a picture of the scenic wonders and serene atmosphere of Georgia as a place of pleasure and enjoyment.

"Cinderella," drawn by six white ponies, was the winner of the Grand Prize for the Farmers Insurance Group. The two parts of this entry were synchronized so as to depict Cinderella going to the ball down an avenue of graceful trees.

"A Dream Come True in Anaheim" won the theme prize for that community. The float featured a dream come true at Disneyland. Appearing on the entry were twenty-three famous Disney characters cleverly decorated with many thousands of red and yellow roses, gladioli, chrysanthemums, irises, and a hundred different varieties of other flowers.

The President's Trophy winner was the "Birds and Bees," sponsored by the Florists' Transworld Delivery Association. The wings and arms of both species moved mechanically, and more than 50,000 roses were used to blanket the float, which depicted a giant flower garden (50 feet long, 18 feet wide, and 16 feet high). There were seventeen huge blooming flowers, each covered with a different variety of rose. This entry marked the seventeenth time the FTD entry competed in the parade, many of its entries trophy winners.

Eight major awards have been gathered by the florists, including the grand prize and six president's trophies for best use of roses. More than 40,000 individual water tubes held nearly 50,000 roses in the 1971 entry. Riding on the float were Mitch Vogel, 14, from the cast of "Bonanza"; Cindy Eilbacher, 13, from "The Bold Ones"; Johnny, Jeff, and Jan Sheffield, stars of the FTD film, *Through the Eyes of a Child,* which tells the story of the float in the Rose Parade.

Florists' Transworld Delivery Association is the world's largest and oldest intercity floral delivery association. More than 12,000 carefully selected member florists service over 5,000 U.S. and Canadian cities and communities. World-wide service embraces 35,000 members.

FTD was honored as recipient of the Tournament of Roses first Distinguished Service Award. The award was made by Tournament president Shingler to FTD president Frank Brautigam. The award read as follows:

For outstanding devotion to the aims and principles of the Tournament of Roses, for promoting and perpetuating the great American tradition this parade has become, and for its faith in our ideals as evidenced by 17 years of active, aggressive participation by reason of its float entries, including its president and key officers from all over the country each year, and in particular for its major contribution to the worldwide publicity of the Tournament through its creation of the FTD film, "Through the Eyes of a Child." Signed, A. Lewis Shingler, president, 82nd annual Tournament of Roses.

The Glendora (California) High School Tartan Band took first place in the band contest. The C. E. King High School Band from Houston, Texas, was second, and the Leavenworth High School Pioneer Marching Band of Leavenworth, Kansas, was third. Other bands competing were the Cupertino High School Pioneer Band from Sunnyvale, California, the Granada Hills (California) High School Highlander Marching Band, the Hilo (Hawaii) High School Viking Band, the Huntington Thunderers of Huntington, New York, and Plymouth Carver Regional High School Band of Plymouth, Mass.

During the days before the parade, some interesting stories developed. Kathy Howie and Kathy Parker, two nineteen-year-old coeds, claimed they would be the first women ever to pilot a float in the history of the Tournament, but evidence quickly was presented by natives to prove that Edith Wright, at the age of nineteen in 1916, piloted the

KATHY HOWIE AND KATHY PARKER, GIRL FLOAT DRIVERS

253

KICKOFF LUNCHEON INTERVIEW: JIM PLUNK-
ETT, JACK SCHULTZ, AND KYLE ROTE

Eagle Rock float. However, it was agreed by all that Miss Howie and Miss Parker were the first to pilot a float concealed in the drivers' compartment underneath the float. Miss Parker was the driver and Miss Howie operated a symbol for the State of Minnesota entry.

(That first woman driver in Tournament history, Edith Wright, today is Mrs. Edith Parr, 73, of Altadena.)

For the Grand Marshal's Ball, in the absence of Dr. Graham, who did not arrive in Pasadena in time, movie actor Robert Young returned to Pasadena where he learned his trade as a student at the Pasadena Playhouse.

Bertha Shingler, wife of the president, was confined to bed in St. Luke Hospital in Pasadena during the coronation. Hewes Bell and the telephone company rigged up an electric device so the first lady heard every word that was spoken at the official ceremonies at the Pasadena Civic Auditorium, which were under the direction of Coronation chairman Alex Gaal.

The "champion" float builders in 1971 were Wayne Herrin and Don Preston of the Portland firm that had constructed five trophy winners.

Ohio State was heavily favored to win the football game. At a Big Ten dinner at the Palladium in Hollywood, Peter Graves, of the "Mission Impossible" television thriller, said, "I assure you this Ohio State team will not self-destruct." However, Stanford turned out to be extremely destructive by rallying with two fourth-period touchdowns that overcame a 17-13 Buckeye lead and gave the Indians of Johnny Ralston a 27-17 triumph that thrilled a record 103,839 spectators viewing the game in warm sunshine.

The victory could be interpreted as a triumph for Dr. Graham. When the Ohio State team spent the night before the game at a monastery in the foothills of the San Gabriel mountains above Pasadena, Ralston countered, "Billy Graham will be on our side."

Stanford surprised Ohio State with an early end-around reverse that sprang Eric Cross for a forty-one-yard gainer to set up a touch-

254

RANDY VATAHA

down sprint of four yards by Jackie Brown. Stanford had a 7-0 lead.

Ohio State then opened up with its powerful ground attack featuring Rex Kern's pitchouts and keepers to the outside. Kern gained 129 net yards in 20 carries. John Brockington and Leo Hayden also provided solid punch, and Ohio State grabbed a 17-10 lead after the first of two field goals by Stanford's Steve Horowitz had given the Indians a 10-0 margin.

In the third quarter, Horowitz set an all-time Rose Bowl distance record for field goals by connecting on a forty-eight-yarder to cut the Buckeye lead to 17-13. However, Ohio State's ground power was asserting itself and the Buckeyes had a fourth and inches to go on Stanford's 19. If successful in this fourth down try, Ohio State appeared to be capable of moving in for a fourth-quarter score that would have clinched the game. The Buckeyes called on Brockington to punch the right side, but Ron Kadziel, Stanford linebacker, met him head-on for a yard loss. Stanford took over, and with new vigor the Indians completely took charge. Jim Plunkett, the Heisman Trophy winner who completed twenty of thirty passes for the day in an amazing demonstration of accuracy and sharp play-calling while facing one of the nation's top defenses, started to connect to little rabbit Randy Vataha and leaping Bob Moore, and it wasn't before Stanford had its

STANFORD'S STEVE HOROWITZ MAKES A
RECORD WITH HIS 48-YARD FIELD GOAL

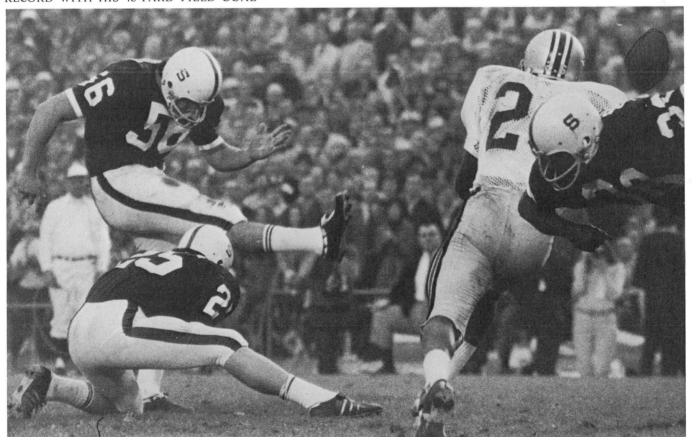

RANDY VATAHA TAKES A
PLUNKETT PASS FOR
A TOUCHDOWN

27-17 victory margin. Moore made an "impossible" catch by leaping between two defenders for a Plunkett pass on the four-yard line to set up another touchdown sprint by Brown.

South Pasadena's Jack Schultz, Stanford safety man and co-captain, who said at the Kickoff Luncheon that he always as a youngster had waited outside the Rose Bowl hoping someone would take him in, then became a Stanford defensive star. He made a big tackle and a big interception to set up a Plunkett-to-Vataha scoring strike.

"I never got inside the Bowl until today," said Schultz. "I always wondered what it was like. Now I know. It's great."

The comment in the papers after the game, as usual, was interesting.

Said Dwain Esper of the Pasadena *Star-News*: "The heroes were many on this day-of-days for the Big Red. But nobody contributed so much as the magnificent Plunkett, the peerless passer. No matter what Ohio State did on defense, Plunkett countered with shrewd audibles on the line of scrimmage. His strong arm pierced vital holes in the previously unviolated Buckeye barricade."

Dick Robinson of the *Star-News*: "Center John Sande of Stanford was one of the Indian heroes. All he did was completely shut off Ohio's great middle guard Jim Stillwagen."

Co-Captain Schultz: "Our team always won the big ones. We were no different today."

CATCH BY BOB MOORE SETS
UP STANFORD TOUCHDOWN

STANFORD CELEBRATES: POMPON DANCE
VICTORY RIDE FOR COACH JOHN RALSTON,
AND DRUM MAJOR GEORDIE LAWRY'S BICYCLE
"STRIP RIDE"
CHUCK PAINTER, S.U.N.S.

Phil Finch of the San Francisco *Examiner* reported that Ralston had planned much trickery to offset the greatness of Woody Hayes' strong team, "but we changed our plans early. Our players came back to the side lines and told the coaches to forget what we had planned, that it wasn't necessary. They could beat Ohio State with normal patterns. The receivers stuck with basics such as down and outs and curls to the inside."

Art Rosenbaum of the San Francisco *Chronicle* said, "Stanford's 'we believe' attitude remained unshaken on the field even though many in the press box wouldn't have bet a nickel after Ohio State came on to take a 14-10 lead . . . Stanford took over the game in every way . . . defense, offense, clock control, crowd noise, and of course, on the scoreboard. The coach now may get some of the national recognition he deserves."

Wells Twombley of the *Examiner* described the Woody Hayes who finally met with the press long after the game was over: "Finally, the tomb opened. There was W. Woodrow Hayes. He looked centuries older. His head was down like a man in prayer. Yes, he'd been beaten by a great team. Yes, Plunkett was a great quarterback. 'But Rex Kern was outplaying him until the third period,' said Woody. 'They beat us on two plays — that mad dog pass to Moore and when they held us on fourth down and inches . . . The only way you defend against Plunkett is to do exactly what we didn't.' In middle age, the great ogre from Columbus has discovered something he never knew he had — a sense of good sportsmanship. He was taking defeat as gracefully as he knew how. A couple of writers who had been chuckling earlier actually felt sad. An era was slipping fast away."

Yes, it was true that Woody Hayes, never beaten before in the Rose Bowl in three previous appearances and who repeatedly stated during the week before this game "You can't beat my luck," took defeat as gracefully as Woody Hayes has ever gone down.

REX KERN BREAKS INTO THE CLEAR WITH GOOD INTERFERENCE AHEAD

38
Tragedy

JOHN CABOT

JOHN J. CABOT was president of the 1972 Tournament of Roses — for less than one hour. Shortly after being inducted to succeed Lewis Shingler, Cabot succumbed to a heart attack in the Tournament House the night of January 21, 1971.

So Virgil J. White, vice president, ascended to the top position one year before he expected to. He named Lawrence Welk his grand marshal.

The Association's annual dinner meeting had just adjourned and the participants were leaving for a celebration at the president's home in Pasadena when Cabot collapsed. Doctors from the Pasadena Emergency Center, working with fire department rescue crews, worked for ten minutes to revive him before he was pronounced dead.

After being inducted as president, Cabot, just a few minutes before his death, said, "There is little doubt that this last Tournament of Roses was the greatest ever, and since it is incumbent upon the new officers to outdo the last group, that sort of puts it up to us, doesn't it? Lew Shingler's shoes will be hard to fill, but I think we can do it."

In taking over the top post of the Tournament, White declared: "John Cabot's untimely death came as a great shock to all Tournament members, and especially to me. Usually the vice president has a whole year of working with the president, learning how to conduct the office. John Cabot was a great guy, and I had looked forward to working with him, preparing for 1973. Suddenly I have to learn the job on the job, and I will need a lot of help. It is a great honor to become president, but this was not the way I wanted to achieve it. John was a very close friend."

White is a Pasadena antique dealer and importer. Cabot was associated with Cabot and Sons Mortuary of Pasadena.

White has been active in the Tournament since 1940. He is a native of Springville, Iowa, and attended elementary school in Whittier, Iowa, and high school in Barnesville, Oklahoma. During twenty years of membership in the Pasadena Kiwanis, he never missed a meeting. He has been chairman of fourteen Tournament committees and

259

OTIS BLASINGHAM

twenty-two planning units. He is a seasoned traveler, having been to Europe fifteen times and the Far East three times; he has circled the globe twice. He and his wife, Helen, have two sons, John and Robert.

"I earned my first five-dollar bill cleaning the sidewalk for the Pasadena Citizen's Bank in 1928," recalled White.

Otis Blasingham, investment broker, became the new vice president, and Edward ("Ted") Wilson, United California bank marketing director, moved from secretary to treasurer. William Lawson, contractor, became secretary.

New members of the executive committee for 1972 were Carl Wopschall and Harrison R. Baker, Jr. New members of the board of directors were Don Judson, Reid Allen, and Thornton Hamlin.

Carl Hoelscher, Pasadena clothing merchant, who is on the Executive Committee and who will be president in 1976, was informed by the American Revolution Bicentennial Commission that the 1976 Tournament of Roses will be the kickoff event for the nation's observance of its 200th Anniversary. Hoelscher said the Rose Parade will be built along the bicentennial theme, "Heritage '76." Hoelscher predicted the world-wide TV viewing of the parade will have increased to 300 million by then.

The 1925 Notre Dame-Stanford game may have been the inspiration that led to the years of Tournament contributions made by Cabot.

"I have always taken pride in Pasadena and its events, being a native son," recalled Cabot in an interview shortly before his death. "But the Fighting Irish had a hand in making me even more enthusiastic about the Rose Bowl Game and the Tournament events. I was one of the altar boys serving Mass while the Notre Dame team was in Pasadena during the two weeks prior to the 1925 game. One of the altar boys, also an eighth-grader, had a cousin on the Irish team. This increased our loyalty to the South Benders. Just before the game, Coach Knute Rockne, my boyhood idol, gave us tickets to the game."

Cabot became a member of the Tournament of Roses in 1945. He was a participant on twenty-two committees and chairman of seven.

EDWARD WILSON

Past exalted ruler George Harris of the Pasadena Elks Lodge rendered the following tribute to past exalted ruler Cabot at a memorial service: "He gave unhesitatingly and unselfishly of his time and talents toward the growth and prosperity of our order. No man I have ever known was more devoted to his family. In 1938, he married the lovely Ann Abbot. They produced six more Cabots, two girls and four boys. John's personable and sincere smile won for him a myriad of friends. His wit, his poise, his intelligence, and his compassion for his fellow men were just a few of his outstanding qualities."

President Richard Nixon sent the following message to Ann Cabot:

"Our thoughts and deepest sympathy are with you as Mrs. Nixon and I grieve at the death of your distinguished husband. The life of John Cabot will long be an example and an inspiration in the Pasadena

WILLIAM LAWSON

community and for all who knew him. His strong sense of patriotism, civic responsibility and Christian charity will never be forgotten. We hope that this thought may bring you consoling comfort now — and in the years ahead."

Archbishop Timothy Manning of the Los Angeles diocese participated in the requiem service for Cabot at St. Andrew's Catholic Church in Pasadena. Monsignor James Hourihan said the Mass.

Recalling Cabot's athletic days at Loyola, Charles Johnson, sports editor of *The Tidings,* Catholic newspaper in Los Angeles, said: "John played end on the 1932 Loyola football team, coached by Tom Leib, which astonishingly held USC's national champions to a scoreless tie until the fourth quarter when Loyola lost 6-0, thanks largely to a 15-yard penalty deep in Loyola territory."

Johnson also wrote: "Any well-versed baseball nut knows the most famous of all double-play combines — Chicago's Tinker to Evers to Chance. But in Cabot's era at Loyola, nothing was left to chance. The Lions had their own notorious combination — Karagorian to Kristovich to Cabot."

Cabot had said: "My most interesting experiences center on meeting eminent people serving as grand marshals — former President Dwight D. Eisenhower, President Richard Nixon, the Apollo 12 astronauts, Bob Hope, Chief Justice Earl M. Warren, General Omar Bradley, and Senator Everett Dirksen." He added, "It has been an equally great experience to meet and get to know such great sports writers as Wilfrid Smith, Grantland Rice, Leo Fischer, and Bert McGrane as well as the game announcers: Mel Allen, Lindsay Nelson, Curt Gowdy, Kyle Rote, and Paul Christman. I recall meeting Graham MacNamee, who dramatized the setting of the Rose Bowl 'against the backdrop of majestic mountains with the purple shadows creeping downward as dusk approaches.' "

Cabot said, "Probably the most unforgettable quote I heard during my Tournament work was in the two years when I was Queen Selection chairman. We chose Martha Sissell in 1962. At the Kickoff Luncheon, Mel Allen recognized her with 'It's fitting that a Rose Queen named Martha reigns the year Washington's in the Rose Bowl.' "

Cabot also recalled a significant quote by Ronald Reagan in 1963. "The man who is now governor of California then was the narrator of the Rose Parade for CBS, and he hosted our queen and her court for luncheon at the Brown Derby. I said, 'Mr. Reagan, meet Nancy Davis, our Rose Queen.' In complete amazement, he said, 'Why, that's my wife's name.' "

Cabot believed the Tournament's major accomplishment through the years has been its presentation of a favorable picture to the world of the American way of life.

"It is apparent the people of all lands understand the language of rosebuds," declared Cabot.

Cabot believed the Tournament has had a role in developing TV programming of special events. "In the world of video, the two-hour special telecast was unheard of prior to the first network TV coverage of our parade in 1951," said Cabot, who contended the Rose Parade telecasts have been a major stimulant to color-set sales.

Whatever the problems of the future in staging the Tournament, Cabot said they will be solved by the Tournament membership "like they always have been solved in the past." The 1972 president predicted the use of lightweight aircraft metals instead of steel in float construction, also the use of more powerful, yet smaller, engines to propel the floats, and engines that won't heat up. He suspected the high cost of float construction would lead to more large firms and fewer small communities being float sponsors. Also, the international flavor of the parade will increase, he said, with satellite TV beaming the pictures to more and more countries.

"The whole world someday may take part in our parade," said Cabot. "What a stimulant to international friendship and understanding that will be!"

The reaction of Tournament of Roses television viewers in other parts of the world is illustrated by these comments of the Roberts family of 102A Mora Road, Cricklewood, London, England, in a letter sent to the Tournament office: "It was a very cold and snowy afternoon here in London and we were having tea when the game came on. What warm sun, what a beautiful stadium, that gorgeous white horse, and the queen and her attendants. We don't have anything like that here, not even at our football cup finals. The afternoon has stayed with us for a long time. Even your cheer leaders were lovely. We felt we were there. And your football players looked like spacemen from another planet."

Paul Bryan, chairman of the 1969 Float Committee, is another of the current crop of productive Tournament workers.

"It's what you can contribute that counts in the Tournament," says Bryan. "I have received more than I've given by believing this. It's great to be part of it."

Terry Chambers, the assistant manager, annually makes an important contribution to the Tournament. Chambers liked Tournament work so well he quit a roofing and air-conditioning contracting business to get into the thick of the operation. After years of service on various committees, he joined Max Colwell's staff four years ago.

Terry's most interesting experience came when Secretary of Defense Charles Wilson was grand marshal. In his Tournament duties, Chambers was to pick up Wilson at the Huntington Hotel and drive him to a dinner party.

"What kind of a car have you got?" asked Wilson, a General Motors executive of repute.

"A Ford," replied Chambers.

TERRY CHAMBERS

"I'll ride with you," said Wilson. "They've had me in General Motors cars all day."

They got in Chambers' Ford and rode off to their destination. When they drove up to the front door with Terry's somewhat grizzly machine, the attendant at the door beckoned him to get out of the way.

"We're waiting for the grand marshal's limousine to arrive and we don't want you blocking the driveway," said the attendant.

Chambers had to move his little car and park near a phone pole several yards away. Chambers and Wilson had to walk to the door.

"It just goes to show," said Wilson, "that it doesn't matter who you are but what car you drive."

The Tournament of Roses is supported by 15 per cent of the revenue from the Rose Bowl game each January 1, and by membership dues.

"Our current budget is approximately $370,000," explained President White. "This is quite an advance from the early days when Tournament officers employed a stenographer on a per letter basis. They paid five cents for each letter written, ten cents for a formal letter to the city hall, and 15 cents for typing minutes of a meeting."

The membership dues are spent for maintenance of the Wrigley Mansion, Tournament headquarters.

White elaborated on Tournament relationship with the Pasadena city government as follows: "Currently, the Tournament pays into the city treasury one-half of whatever sum is left from income over budget. During the five years from 1966 to 1970, this amounted to $217,300. In addition, we pay from the budget one-half of the policing costs which, in 1970, amounted to $56,000. The other half of the annual surplus is placed in a trust fund that is spent from time to time on capital improvements.

"The Tournament has made many contributions to the city, including the property known as Tournament Park, which the city sold to Caltech for $600,000. This money was used by the city for the purpose of several neighborhood parks. Likewise the Tournament has purchased buildings for float construction and has given them to the city. Our investment has been approximately $500,000.

"We were instrumental in having the William Wrigley heirs contributing Wrigley Gardens to the city. Our most substantial contribution, however, has been the Rose Bowl itself."

Sam Akers and Walter Hoefflin, son of the former Tournament president, are handling public relations. Committee chairmen like Alexander Gaal, Carl H. Hoelscher, Joel Sheldon, Ramsay Lawson, Richard Davidson, Stanley E. Ward, William Leishman, Darrell Sluder, Merton E. Goddard, Frank Hardcastle, Millard Davidson, Clarence Padfield, Carl Wopschall, Harvey Christen, Peter Davis, George Harris, Donald Judson, Harrison Baker, Reid Allen, Jack Whitehead, Ralph Helpbringer, Oliver Prickett, Thornton Hamlin, E. Milton Wilson, Dan Clay, Arthur Welsh, Donald V. Miller, Jim Stivers, Fred

Soldwedel, Harland Heath, Chuck Rubsamen, and Harold E. Coombes join hundreds of others in maintaining Tournament of Roses spirit, cooperation, unselfishness, willingness to work, and common desire to do it for Pasadena and a happier world.

Perhaps the city of Pasadena has eased its Rose Bowl traffic problems at last. Despite Glendale Freeway construction and other bottlenecks due to road improvement work, traffic moved better in 1970 and 1971 than for any previous Tournament. Two helicopters added by the city to detect slowdowns and jams coordinated the best traffic direction ever. Ironically, one of the helicopters crashed five days after the 1970 event.

Perhaps in the future, if U.S.C. returns to the Rose Bowl, its student card stunts can be resumed. A computer, the latest word in modern science (so they say), conked out and made it impossible for U.S.C. to win at cards in 1970. But the Trojans did win at football.

And one final "perhaps."

Perhaps my barber, Joe Licata on Garfield near the Civic Auditorium in Pasadena, will continue to be able to say: "My customers discuss the Rose Bowl Game and the Tournament Parade more than any subject I hear in my shop."

Granddaddy's hair may turn white and his beard grow long, but he will always look young and gay.

JUST BEFORE TRAGEDY STRIKES, H. LEWIS SHINGLER PUTS PRESIDENT'S PIN ON JOHN CABOT. THIS LAST PICTURE TAKEN OF THE BELOVED PRESIDENT WHO DIED MINUTES LATER.

39
Trends and Fashions

MARY LOU WADDELL, 1931

THIS COMPLETE story of the Tournament of Roses has traced trends in many phases of history in southern California—the evolution of travel from the horse-drawn carriage to modern mechanized conveyances, the growth of football as a big-time sport, the evolution of the parade, the rise of radio and television in world-wide communications, and the penetration of a community festival into the lives of people everywhere.

Through the years from 1890 until the present, the pageantry of the Tournament of Roses also has chronicled the history of fashions in the United States. Each girl chosen to be Queen of the Tournament has reflected the charm and beauty of the era of her reign.

Phyllis Touchie-Specht, co-author with Mary Kefgen of *Individuality in Clothing Selection and Personal Appearance,* published by The Macmillan Company, briefly has summarized these changes for *The Tournament of Roses* history.

"By today's standards, the clothing, make-up, and hair styles of yesterday's queen often seem quaint," said Mrs. Specht. "It should be remembered that these were the styles of the day and a large majority of the female population of this country was affecting them.

"It is through the phenomenon of habituation that fashion moves. New styles are introduced. At first they appear strange and displeasing. After they have been viewed numerous times in the mass media and on fashion leaders, they may be accepted by the consumer and thus become fashion. The Tournament of Roses has been a part of the exposure of new styles, particularly in recent years. The wardrobes of the court have been selected as the styles are just beginning to move into popularity. The appearance of the Tournament of Roses Queen and her Princesses has been a factor in the movement of many fashions.

"The first queen of the Tournament, Hallie Woods, was selected in 1905. At this time Paris was the the center of the fashion world, with Worth, Lanvin, and Callot heading the great *couture.* It was the age of elegance, of fabulous luxury, of great skills, low wages, beautiful workmanship, rich and interesting fabrics. The portrait of Queen Hallie illustrates the exquisite detail and feminine softness of this period. In

MAY McAVOY, 1923

1907, Queen Joan Woodbury reigned. Her costume reflects a more sophisticated elegance of this same era.

"In 1913 the Tournament had both a king and queen. Harrison I. Drummond and Jean French reigned in this dual role. King Harrison was attired in a splendid military costume. Queen Jean wore the newest fashion silhouette of a straight skirt and draped bodice which was called the lingerie dress. Her huge hat of pleated embroidery or lace on a wire frame was trimmed with flowers and ribbons. This hat style was a must with the lingerie dress.

"The influence of Paul Poiret, the leading French *couturier* of the time, was reflected in the ensemble of Queen May McAvoy (1923). Poiret took women out of stiff corsets and presented them in softly contoured dresses which reflected faint touches of the East and Near East. Examples of this are found in the embroidered fabric and the drape of the bodice of this gown. Queen May was the first queen to show effective use of cosmetics. The 'cupid-bow' mouth was the rage of the time and exemplifies more of the Oriental influence of the period.

"These lovelies show how daring ladies had become by 1925. These costumes, while not accepted street wear, must have been the grandmother of the mini and micro-mini of the late 1960s. Legs were revealed and bloomers worn. Cosmetics became important to the majority of young women. The young people of the 1920s 'flappered' their parents with their modernization.

"Queen Fay Lanphier (1926) was most regal as she appeared in a crown. This was the first time a queen had worn one. Her gown was a variation of the chemise and hung loosely from the shoulder. The boyish bosom was then in vogue.

"The royal aspect of the Tournament seemed very important during the early 1930s. Queen Mary Lou Waddell (1931) posed with her elaborate crown and majestic robes of ermine and velvet encrusted richly with jewels. The coronation ceremony of Muriel Cowan (1935) was a scene reminiscent of the pageantry of an investiture in medieval times. By 1938 there seemed to be a trend away from the emphasis on royalty. Queen Cheryl Walker wore a modest crown and

THE DARING LOOK OF 1925

266

PAGEANTRY MARKS 1935
CROWNING OF MURIEL COWAN

TREND AWAY FROM EMPHASIS
ON ROYAL TRAPPINGS: QUEEN
CHERYL WALKER AND COURT

THE CHIC STYLE IS
DISPLAYED BY 1940 COURT
OF MARGARET HUNTLEY

PATRIOTIC THEME EVIDENT
IN COURT OF DOLORES
BRUBACH, 1942

robe. The dresses of the court reflected the fabrics and styles then fashionable. Hair styles were close to the head and make-up appeared more natural than in previous years.

"The court of 1940 displayed dresses that were considered very chic and beautiful. While most of them had a very covered and sleeved look, shoulders were revealed by some. If the bodice of each appeared shapeless, this was not due to lack of feminine curves, but rather to the lack of the up-lift bra, which did not appear until after World War II.

"A nation at war was reflected in the patriotic theme of 1942.

THE WAR YEARS: 1943
COURT OF MILDRED MILLER
AT WARSHIP'S CHRISTENING

While the war brought many clothing restrictions, including legislation L-85 which limited the amount of yardage used in garments, this was not evident in the gowns selected for the court of Queen Dolores Brubach. The rich satin fabric was sculptured to the torso and hipline, ending in a peplum. The 1943 court christened a warship. Their clothing for this event was typical of the war years. Suits and coats were of rather drab colors and durable fabrics. Street wear hemlines were just below the knee, shoulders were very broad. Stockings were very scarce and thus treasured; the open-toed shoes which were popular were a real hazard to this precious commodity.

"The same crown was worn by several queens during these years. It is shown in detail on Mary Louise Rutte (1945). Queens Patricia Auman (1946) and Norma Christopher (1947) wore the same crown and their gowns featured the same design details of elegant fabrics, modest necklines, wide shoulder interest, and lengthy trains.

"The man-tailored suit with short skirt and wide, wide shoulders was presented by the 1948 court of Queen Virginia Goodhue. This was the same kind of suit worn by the lady executive Katherine Hepburn in many of her movies of this period.

THE SAME CROWN HAS
BEEN WORN BY MANY
QUEENS: THIS TIME,
PATRICIA AUMAN, 1946

THE MAN-TAILORED SUIT
WORN BY THE COURT OF
VIRGINIA GOODHUE, 1948

WILLIAM HOLDEN POSES
WITH QUEEN ELEANOR
PAYNE'S COURT

PRESIDENT HARRY W. HURRY
NEARLY CRUSHED IN SWIRL OF
NYLON TULLE AS HE CROWNS
1954 QUEEN BARBARA SCHMIDT

"The Christian Dior 'new look' reached the Tournament of Roses and the silhouette changed greatly. In 1951, Queen Eleanor Payne and her court appeared with actor William Holden in ankle-hugging skirts and sweaters. This outfit was the uniform of the college girl of this era.

"Tournament President Harry W. Hurry was nearly crushed in a swirl of nylon tulle as he crowned Queen Barbara Schmidt (1954). The release of wartime restrictions on nylon brought forth a fashion bonanza. Nylon net was fashioned into an endless variety of frothy creations which graced many ladies of the Tournament parade. The strapless gowns were supported by another amazing postwar development, the strapless bra. The gown of Queen Marilyn Smuin (1955) repeats these fashion details so important then. Cosmetics of this period emphasized the mouth with dark-hued lipsticks.

"The 1956 court of Queen Joan Culver introduced the short formal, which gained a great deal of popularity because of its practicality both on the dance floor and in stormy weather.

"Pamela Prather (1959) and her court displayed the very popular dressmaker suit which was worn by several courts during this period. The design details are the natural shoulder line, boxy jacket, three-quarter length sleeves, and long straight skirts. The accessories of matching handbag and stiletto-heeled pump, breton hat, white gloves, and choker pearls were essential in the wardrobes of most fashionable women. The pageboy hair style worn by three of the court members was extremely popular.

"The 1964 court of Queen Nancy Kneeland was a fashion smash

QUEEN NANCY KNEELAND'S COURT, 1964

QUEEN PAMELA ANICICH
AND PRINCESSES, 1969

THE MINI SKIRT TAKES OVER IN QUEEN
PAMELA DEE TEDESCO'S COURT, 1970

in their brightly colored horizontal striped coats. Hemlines were on the way up and shoe heels down. Hair styles had become bouffant, make-up minimized the mouth and emphasized the eyes.

"The gowns of Queen Carole Cota (1966) and her court depicted the favored covered elegant look of the 'beautiful people.' The queen's hair seemed too full for her crown. A new fashion movement was indicated by the coats selected for Queen Pamela Anicich (1969) and her court. The natural shoulder and belted waistline revealed the curves of the figure. Hemlines were above the knee and shoe heels somewhat higher than in recent years.

"The Tournament of Roses began the new decade of the 1970s by introducing their mini-skirted Queen Pamela Dee Tedesco and her court. Fashion emphasis was on the leg. The clunky shoes attracted attention to this area along with the high hemlines. Make-up remained natural with more of a balance between eye and mouth. Extremely long hair styles were popular but most of the court had their locks shorn to shoulder length before making public appearances.

"The future Tournament of Roses queens and their courts will continue to record the fashions of women in our country. It has been said that while clothes do not make the man, they do much to explain him. The adornment of the queen and her court interprets the ideals of the Tournament of Roses in a unique form of communication which can be understood by most all. Perhaps this is another factor contributing to the enduring success of the Tournament of Roses throughout the world," concluded Mrs. Specht.

40

By Way of a Summary

JET PROPULSION LABORATORY

THE WORLD by now knows where Pasadena is located. It is a beautiful community twelve miles northeast of Los Angeles at the foothills of the San Gabriel Mountains.

Pasadena has an official population of about 120,000. Among its famed institutions are the Pasadena Art Museum, California Institute of Technology (home of many a scholar), Jet Propulsion Laboratory (home of many a moon shot), and Huntington Library. Santa Anita race track for thoroughbred horses is nearby, as is the new Ontario motor speedway where the West's famed "500" is run each Labor Day.

But no institution has done more to put Pasadena on the world map than the Tournament of Roses.

Edward Wilson, who will ascend to the Tournament presidency in 1974 to become the second in the pageant's history to round out a father-son presidential team, believes one of the prime benefits from the Tournament of Roses to society is the manner which it satisfies society's need for novelty and stimulation.

The first Tournament father-son presidential team was W. L. Leishman and Lathrop Leishman. Former president Elmer Wilson is Edward Wilson's father.

The younger Wilson cites the Random House book, *Future Shock,* by Alvin Toffler, as expressing the role a pageant like the Tournament fills.

Toffler's account states: "As leisure increases, we have the opportunity to introduce stability points and rituals into society, such as holidays, pageants and games. Such mechanisms not only provide a backdrop for continuity of everyday life, but serve to integrate societies and cushion them somewhat against the fragmenting impact of super-industrialism. . . . By regularizing such events and by greatly adding to the pageantry that surrounds them, we can weave them into the ritual framework of the new society and use them as sanity-preserving points of temporal reference. . . . We can help provide elements of continuity even in the midst of social upheaval."

272

PASADENA'S BEAUTIFUL CITY HALL, ONE OF
THE CITY'S LANDMARKS (TOP); HUNTINGTON
LIBRARY (BELOW)

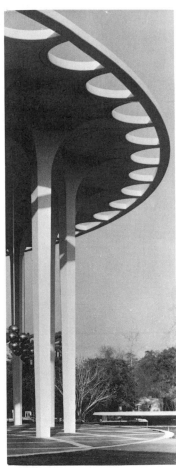

ENTRANCE TO BECKMAN
AUDITORIUM, CALIFORNIA
INSTITUTE OF TECHNOLOGY

Wilson believes the Tournament of Roses is the type of organization that carries out Toffler's recommendation for "strategies of survival." It is Toffler's contention that modern society will survive "if only we move beyond personal services for the change-harassed individual, building continuity and change-buffers into the emergent civilization of tomorrow."

So does the Tournament of Roses. It is a portrayal of ritual that aids the maintenance of equilibrium.

The ten most significant happenings in the Tournament of Roses through the years:

When the idea for a Tournament of Roses was born in the minds of Charles Frederick Holder and Dr. Francis F. Rowland in 1890; the staging of the first festival and parade.

When Tournament President F. B. Weatherby ruled in 1901 that automobiles could appear in the Rose Parade, thus beginning the era of parade mechanization that has made possible the present-day wonders.

When Tournament President James B. Wagner came up with the idea in 1902 to have a football game as the major attraction for the Tournament of Roses to attract national attention; subsequently, when Tournament officials realized in 1916 that football should become the permanent sports attraction, after chariot racing failed to command national attention.

When the first Tournament Queen (Hallie Woods) was selected in 1905.

When W. L. Leishman ascended to the presidency of the Tournament in 1920 and led the drive to build the Rose Bowl (first game in 1923), followed by the continued progressive guidance to this day provided by his son, Lathrop Leishman, as chairman of the Tournament's Football Committee.

When the first local radio broadcast of a Rose Bowl game was accomplished in 1926, followed by the first nation-wide broadcast of the game in 1927 and the first short-wave broadcast to all parts of the world in 1932.

When Isabella Coleman began decorating floats for the parade in the early 1900s and became the "queen of float construction" to lead the development of parade floats to their modern breathtaking scope.

When Max Colwell became a Tournament correspondent for the Pasadena *Post,* thus beginning a career of Colwell affiliation with Tournament activities that led to his becoming Tournament manager in 1948 and continuing to this day as the most influential man in Tournament operation and success.

When local television of the parade first took place in 1947, leading to the first national telecast of the parade in 1951 and the first national telecast of the Rose Bowl Game in 1952, de-

274

velopments that were destined to bring the Pasadena festival to all parts of the world and to create revenue from the game telecast that has assured the financial solvency of the Tournament.

When world-renowned individuals began to accept the role of Tournament grand marshal, including three men who have ascended to the presidency of the United States (Herbert Hoover, Dwight Eisenhower, and Richard Nixon), an honor to Pasadena that reached a climax in 1970 when the Apollo astronauts touched Pasadena soil after traveling to the moon.

The most significant happenings in the Rose Bowl Game through the years:

When Michigan defeated Stanford 49-0 in the first Tournament of Roses football game in 1902.

When the modern football series began in 1916 with Washington State defeating Brown 14-0 at Tournament Park.

When the first game was played in the Rose Bowl in 1923, U.S.C. defeating Penn State 14-3 in a battle that ended "by the light of the moon," because it started so late due to an argument between the opposing coaches, "Gloomy Gus" Henderson of U.S.C. and Hugo Bezdek of Penn State.

When the Fighting Irish of Notre Dame, led by Elmer Layden's great interceptions of Ernie Nevers' passes, defeated Stanford 27-10 in 1925.

When Roy Riegels of California ran the wrong way to set up an 8-7 victory by Georgia Tech in 1929.

When Alabama's great passing combination of Dixie Howell to Don Hutson put on an unforgettable aerial show in 1935, Alabama defeating Stanford 29-13.

When U.S.C.'s Doyle Nave came off the bench to complete four straight passes to "Antelope Al" Krueger in 1939 to give U.S.C. a comeback 9-3 triumph over Duke.

When Clark Shaughnessy and his Stanford team introduced the wizardry of the T-formation to a Bowl audience in a thrilling 21-13 triumph over Nebraska in 1941.

When the Rose Bowl pact between the West and the Big Ten was launched in 1947 to continue uninterrupted to today as the granddaddy collegiate game each January 1 in national television ratings.

When modern thrillers took place, such as Ohio State edging California 17-14 on Jimmy Hague's field goal; Michigan State defeating U.C.L.A. in 1956 by the same score on a forty-one-yard field goal by Dave Kaiser in the last seven seconds; Wisconsin rallying in the late afternoon fog to score twenty-three points in the last twelve minutes to cut U.S.C.'s victory to 42-37; U.C.L.A. upsetting the nation's No. 1 team, Michigan State, 14-12 in 1966 as little Bob Stiles knocked himself out preventing a late Spartan two-point try; U.S.C. gambling for two points in the final moments before losing to Purdue 14-13 in 1967 as Boilermaker George Catavolos leaped in front of Jim Lawrence of U.S.C.; and the never-to-be-forgotten fourth-quarter rally by Stanford which knocked Ohio State out of the national championship in the most exciting 27-17 game of 1971.

Appendixes

I:
Rose Bowl Scores

1902	Michigan 49	Stanford	0
1916	Wash. State 14	Brown	0
1917	Oregon 14	Pennsylvania	0
1918	Marines 19	Camp Lewis	7
1919	Great Lakes 17	Marines	0
1920	Harvard 7	Oregon	6
1921	California 28	Ohio State	0
1922	Calif. 0 (tie)	Wash. & Jeff	0
1923	U.S.C. 14	Penn State	3
1924	Washington 14 (tie)	Navy	14
1925	Notre Dame 27	Stanford	10
1926	Alabama 20	Washington	19
1927	Stanford 7 (tie)	Alabama	7
1928	Stanford 7	Pittsburgh	6
1929	Georgia Tech 8	California	7
1930	U.S.C. 47	Pittsburgh	14
1931	Alabama 24	Wash. State	0
1932	U.S.C. 21	Tulane	12
1933	U.S.C. 35	Pittsburgh	0
1934	Columbia 7	Stanford	0
1935	Alabama 29	Stanford	13
1936	Stanford 7	SMU	0
1937	Pittsburgh 21	Washington	0
1938	California 13	Alabama	0
1939	U.S.C. 7	Duke	3
1940	U.S.C. 14	Tennessee	0
1941	Stanford 21	Nebraska	13
1942	*Oregon State 20	Duke	16
1943	Georgia 9	U.C.L.A.	0

1944	U.S.C. 29	Washington	0
1945	U.S.C. 25	Tennessee	0
1946	Alabama 34	U.S.C.	14
1947	Illinois 45	U.C.L.A.	14
1948	Michigan 49	U.S.C.	0
1949	Northwestern 20	California	14
1950	Ohio State 17	California	14
1951	Michigan 14	California	6
1952	Illinois 40	Stanford	7
1953	U.S.C. 7	Wisconsin	0
1954	Michigan State 28	U.C.L.A.	20
1955	Ohio State 20	U.S.C.	7
1956	Michigan State 17	U.C.L.A.	14
1957	Iowa 35	Oregon State	19
1958	Ohio State 10	Oregon	7
1959	Iowa 38	California	12
1960	Washington 44	Wisconsin	8
1961	Washington 17	Minnesota	7
1962	Minnesota 21	U.C.L.A.	3
1963	U.S.C. 42	Wisconsin	37
1964	Illinois 17	Washington	7
1965	Michigan 34	Oregon State	7
1966	U.C.L.A. 14	Michigan State	12
1967	Purdue 14	U.S.C.	13
1968	U.S.C. 14	Indiana	3
1969	Ohio State 27	U.S.C.	16
1970	U.S.C. 10	Michigan	3
1971	Stanford 27	Ohio State	17

*Played at Durham, N.C.

II:
Individual Records

Most Points Scored, 18
    Elmer Layden
        Notre Dame vs. Stanford (1925)
    Jack Weisenberger
        Michigan vs. U.S.C. (1948)
    Mel Anthony
        Michigan vs. Oregon State (1965)
Most Net Yards Total Offense, 406
    Ron VanderKelen
        Wisconsin vs. U.S.C. (1963)
Most Net Yards Rushing, 194
    Bob Jeter
        Iowa vs. California (1959)
Most Net Yards Passing, 401
    Ron VanderKelen
        Wisconsin vs. U.S.C. (1963)
Longest Run from Scrimmage (yards), 84
    Mel Anthony
        Michigan vs. Oregon State (1965)
Most Times Carried Ball, 34
    Ernie Nevers
        Stanford vs. Notre Dame (1925)
    Carl Dietz
        W.S.U. vs. Brown (1916)
Longest Gain on Pass Play (yards), 70
    Robert Detham to Gene Gray
        Oregon State vs. Duke (1942)
Longest Pass Flight (yards), 53
    Harold Muller to Brodie Stephens
        California vs. Ohio State (1921)

Longest Run, Interception, 71
    William Daddio
        Pittsburgh vs. Washington (1937)
Longest Run, Punt Return, 86
    Aramis Dandoy
        U.S.C. vs. Ohio State (1955)
Longest Run, Kickoff Return, 103
    Al Hoisch
        U.C.L.A. vs. Illinois (1947)
Most Conversions, 7
    Jim Brieske
        Michigan vs. U.S.C. (1948)
Longest Punt, 72
    Desmond Koch
        U.S.C. vs. Wisconsin (1953)
Longest Field Goal, 48
    Steve Horowitz
        Stanford vs. Ohio State (1971)
Most Pass Attempts, 48
    Ron VanderKelen
        Wisconsin vs. U.S.C. (1963)
Most Pass Completions, 33
    Ron VanderKelen
        Wisconsin vs. U.S.C. (1963)
Most Touchdown Passes, 4
    Pete Beathard
        U.S.C. vs. Wisconsin (1963)

III:
Tournament Royalty–
Presidents, Grand Marshals, Queens

YEAR	PRESIDENT	GRAND MARSHAL	QUEEN
1890	Prof. Charles F. Holder	Dr. Francis F. Rowland	
1891	B. Marshall Wotkyns		
1892	Frank C. Bolt	Dr. Francis F. Rowland	
1893	Frank C. Bolt		
1894	Charles Daggett	Dr. Francis F. Rowland	
1895	Charles Daggett	Dr. H. H. Sherk	
1896	Edwin Stearns	Edwin Stearns	
1897	Edwin Stearns	Edwin Stearns	
1898	Martin H. Weight	Martin H. Weight	
1899	Martin H. Weight	Martin H. Weight	
1900	Herman Hertel	Charles Daggett	
1901	F. B. Weatherby	Charles Daggett	
1902	James B. Wagner	C. C. Reynolds	
1903	Charles Coleman	C. C. Reynolds	
1904	Charles Daggett	Dr. Francis F. Rowland	
1905	Charles Daggett	Dr. Francis F. Rowland	Hallie Woods
1906	Edwin D. Neff	John B. Miller	Elsie Armitage
1907	Edward T. Off	Dr. H. P. Skillen	Joan H. Woodbury
1908	George P. Cary	Dr. H. P. Skillen	May Sutton
1909	George P. Cary	Walter S. Wright	
1910	George P. Cary	Dr. Francis F. Rowland	
1911	Frank G. Hogan	Dr. Ralph Skillen	Ruth Palmer
1912	Edward T. Off	E. H. Groenendyke	
1913	Edward T. Off	Leigh Guyer	Jean P. French
1914	R. D. Davis	Charles Daggett	Mable Seibert
1915	John B. Coulston	M. S. Pashgian	
1916	Lewis H. Turner	Dr. Francis F. Rowland	
1917	D. M. Linnard	Dr. C. D. Lockwood	
1918	B. O. Kendall	Dr. Z. T. Malaby	
1919	B. O. Kendall	Frank Hunter	
1920	William L. Leishman	Frank G. Hogan	
1921	William L. Leishman	W. A. Boucher	
1922	John J. Mitchell	Harold Landreth	
1923	John J. Mitchell	H. L. Gianetti	May McAvoy
1924	W. F. Creller	Col. George S. Parker	
1925	W. F. Creller	Lewis H. Turner	Margaret Scoville
1926	Harry M. Ticknor	Col. L. J. Mygatt	Fay Lanphier
1927	Harry M. Ticknor	Dr. C. D. Lockwood	
1928	Harry M. Ticknor	John McDonald	Harriet Sterling
1929	Leslie B. Henry	Marco Hellman	
1930	C. Hal Reynolds	James Rolph	Holly Halsted

YEAR	PRESIDENT	GRAND MARSHAL	QUEEN
1931	C. Hal Reynolds	Gen. C. S. Farnsworth	Mary Lou Waddell
1932	D. E. McDaneld	William May Garland	Myrta Olmsted
1933	D. E. McDaneld	Mary Pickford	Dorothy Edwards
1934	George S. Parker	Adm. William S. Sims	Treva Scott
1935	C. Elmer Anderson	Harold Lloyd	Muriel Cowan
1936	C. Elmer Anderson	James V. Allred	Barbara Nichols
1937	Cyril Bennett	Eugene Biscailuz	Nancy Bumpus
1938	George S. Campbell	Leo Carrillo	Cheryl Walker
1939	Lathrop K. Leishman	Shirley Temple	Barbara Dougall
1940	Harlan G. Loud	Edgar Bergen & Charlie	Margaret Huntley
1941	J. W. McCall, Jr.	E. O. Nay	Sally Stanton
1942	Robert M. McCurdy	Kay Kyser	Dolores Brubach
1943	James K. Ingham	Earl Warren	Mildred Miller
1944	Frank M. Brooks	Alonzo Stagg	Naomi Riordan
1945	Max H. Turner	Herbert Hoover	Mary Rutte
1946	Charles A. Strutt	Adm. William Halsey	Patricia Auman
1947	William P. Welsh	Bob Hope	Norma Christopher
1948	Louis R. Vincenti	Gen. Omar Bradley	Virginia Goodhue
1949	Harold C. Schaffer	Perry Brown	Virginia Bower
1950	Drummond J. McCunn	Paul G. Hoffman	Marion Brown
1951	L. Clifford Kenworthy	Cpl. Robert S. Gray	Eleanor Payne
1952	Leon Kingsley	Medal of Honor Men	Nancy True Thorne
1953	William H. Nicholas	Richard M. Nixon	Leah Feland
1954	Harry W. Hurry	Gen. William F. Dean	Barbara Schmidt
1955	Elmer M. Wilson	Earl Warren	Marilyn Smuin
1956	Dr. Alfred L. Gerrie	Charles E. Wilson	Joan Culver
1957	John S. Davidson	Eddie Rickenbacker	Ann Mossberg
1958	John H. Biggar, Jr.	Robert Gordon Sproul	Gertrude Wood
1959	Stanley K. Brown	E. L. ("Bob") Bartlett	Pamela Prather
1960	Raymond A. Dorn	Richard M. Nixon	Margarethe Bertelson
1961	Arthur W. Althouse	William F. Quinn	Carole Washburn
1962	H. Burton Noble	Albert D. Rosellini	Martha Sissell
1963	Stanley L. Hahn	Dr. William H. Pickering	Nancy Davis
1964	Hilles M. Bedell	Dwight D. Eisenhower	Nancy Kneeland
1965	Walter Hoefflin	Arnold Palmer	Dawn Baker
1966	J. Randolph Richards	Walt Disney	Carole Cota
1967	Henry Kearns	Thanat Khoman	Barbara Hewitt
1968	H. W. Bragg	Everett Dirksen	Linda Strother
1969	Gleeson L. Payne	Bob Hope	Pamela Ann Anicich
1970	C. Lewis Edwards	Charles Conrad, Richard Gordon, Alan Bean	Pamela Dee Tedesco
1971	A. Lewis Shingler	Dr. Billy Graham	Kathleen Arnett

IV:
Band Participation

1950

Alhambra High School Band, Alhambra, Calif.
Bakersfield High School Band, Bakersfield, Calif.
Bonham Brothers Boys' Band, San Diego, Calif.
University of California Band, Berkeley, Calif.
Elks Symphonic Band, Los Angeles, Calif.
Glendale College Band, Glendale, Calif.
Huntington Park Band, Huntington Park, Calif.
John Muir College Band, Pasadena, Calif.
Long Beach Jordan High School Band, Long Beach, Calif.
Ohio State University Band, Columbus, Ohio
Pasadena All-City Junior High School Band, Pasadena, Calif.
Pomona High School Band, Pomona, Calif.
Riverside Polytechnic Band, Riverside, Calif.
Salvation Army Band, Los Angeles, Calif.
Selma High School Band, Selma, North Carolina
Sheriff's Boys Band, Los Angeles, Calif.
South Gate Band, South Gate, Calif.
Tournament of Roses Band, Pasadena, Calif.
United States Marine Corps Band
Ventura Band, Ventura, Calif.

1951

Bakersfield High School Band, Bakersfield, Calif.
Barstow Union High School Band, Barstow, Calif.
Bonham Brothers Band, San Diego, Calif.
University of California Band, Berkeley, Calif.
Deputy Auxiliary Police Band, Los Angeles, Calif.
Elks Symphonic Band, Los Angeles, Calif.
Glendale Police Boys Band, Glendale, Calif.
Grafton Parade Band, Grafton, North Dakota
Huntington Park Junior Band, Huntington Park, Calif.
Inglewood High School Band, Inglewood, Calif.
Long Beach City College Band, Long Beach, Calif.
Mark Keppel High School Band, Alhambra, Calif.
University of Michigan Band, Ann Arbor, Michigan
John Muir Junior College Band, Pasadena, Calif.
Pasadena All-City Junior High School Band, Pasadena, Calif.
Salvation Army Band, Los Angeles, Calif.
San Bernardino Valley College Band, San Bernardino, Calif.
Santa Monica High School Band, Santa Monica, Calif.
Tournament of Roses Band, Pasadena, Calif.
United States Combined Marine Corps Band

1952

Alhambra High School Band, Alhambra, Calif.
Antelope Valley Junior High School Band, Antelope Valley, Calif.
Bakersfield High School Band, Bakersfield, Calif.
Bonham Brothers Boys' Band, San Diego, Calif.
Elks' Symphonic Band No. 99, Los Angeles, Calif.
Glendale High School Band, Glendale, Calif.
Huntington Park City Junior Band, Huntington Park, Calif.
University of Illinois Football Band, Champaign-Urbana, Illinois
Inglewood Boys' Band, Inglewood, Calif.
John Muir Band, Pasadena, Calif.
Los Angeles Dept. of Parks and Recreation, Los Angeles, Calif.
Pomona High School Band, Pomona, Calif.
Salvation Army Brass Band, Los Angeles, Calif.
Sheriff's Boys Band, Los Angeles, Calif.
South Gate Youth Band, South Gate, Calif.
South Pasadena-San Marino School Band, South Pasadena, Calif.
Stanford University Band, Stanford, Calif.
Tournament of Roses Band, Pasadena, Calif.
United States Combined Marine Corps Band
Woodrow Wilson Bruin Band, Long Beach, Calif.

1953

Al Malaikah Shrine Band, Los Angeles, Calif.
Bonham Brothers Boys' Band, San Diego, Calif.
Deputy Auxiliary Police Band, Los Angeles, Calif.
Elks "99" Symphonic Band, Los Angeles, Calif.
Grossmont High School Band, Grossmont, Calif.
Herbert Hoover High School Band, Glendale, Calif.
Huntington Park City Junior Band, Huntington Park, Calif.
Inglewood Boys' Band, Inglewood, Calif.
Long Beach Polytechnic High School Band, Long Beach, Calif.
Mark Keppel High School Band, Alhambra, Calif.
Muir College Mustang Band, Pasadena, Calif. .
Polytechnic High School Band, Riverside, Calif.
Salvation Army Band, Los Angeles, Calif.
San Bernardino Valley College Indian Band, San Bernardino, Calif.
University of Southern California Band, Los Angeles, Calif.
Tournament of Roses Band, Pasadena, Calif.
Tulare Union High School Band, Tulare, Calif.
United States Combined Air Force Band
United States Combined Marine Corps Band
University of Wisconsin Band, Madison, Wisconsin

1954

Alhambra High School Band, Alhambra, Calif.
Bonham Brothers Boys' Band, San Diego, Calif.
Univ. of California at Los Angeles Band, Los Angeles, Calif.
Elks #99 Symphonic Band, Los Angeles, Calif.
Glendale Police Boys' Band, Glendale, Calif.
Grossmont High School Band, Grossmont, Calif.
Huntington Park City Junior Band, Huntington Park, Calif.
Jordan High School Band, Long Beach, Calif.
Michigan State College Band, East Lansing, Michigan
Mount Lebanon High School Band, Mount Lebanon, Pennsylvania
John Muir College Band, Pasadena, Calif.
Norwalk Excelsior High School Band, Norwalk, Calif.
Riverside Polytechnic High School Band, Riverside, Calif.
Salvation Army Band, Los Angeles, Calif.
Sheriff's Boys Band, Los Angeles, Calif.
South Gate City Youth Band, South Gate, Calif.
Tournament of Roses Band, Pasadena, Calif.
United States Sixth Army Band
United States Air Corps Band
United States Marine Corps Band

1955

Academy High School Band, Erie, Pennsylvania
Antelope Valley Junior High School Band, Antelope Valley, Calif.
Beaumont Cougar Band, Beaumont, Calif.
Bonham Brothers Boys' Band, San Diego, Calif.
Cardinal Whittier High School Band, Whittier, Calif.
Downey Viking Band, Downey, Calif.
Elks Toppers Band, Los Angeles, Calif.
Glendale Dynamiter Band, Glendale, Calif.
Grant High School Band, Portland, Oregon
Inglewood Boys Band, Inglewood, Calif.
Long Beach City College Band, Long Beach, Calif.
Los Angeles Deputy Police Auxiliary Band, Los Angeles, Calif.
Mark Keppel High School Aztec Band, Alhambra, Calif.
Montebello High School Band, Montebello, Calif.
Ohio State University Band, Columbus, Ohio
Saint Mary's Band, San Antonio, Texas
Salvation Army Band, Los Angeles, Calif.
University of Southern California Trojan Band, Los Angeles, Calif.
Tournament of Roses Band, Pasadena, Calif.
United States Military Academy Band

1956

Alhambra High School Band, Alhambra, Calif.
Arcadia High School Band, Arcadia, Calif.
Bonham Brothers Boys' Band, San Diego, Calif.
Burbank High School Band, Burbank, Calif.
Elks Toppers Band, Los Angeles, Calif.
Henryetta High School Band, Henryetta, Oklahoma
Hoover High School Band, Glendale, Calif.
Huntington Park Youth Band, Huntington Park, Calif.
Massillon High School Band, Massillon, Ohio
Michigan State Band, East Lansing, Michigan
Picayune High School Band, Picayune, Mississippi
Riverside Band, Riverside, Calif.
Salvation Army Band, Los Angeles, Calif.
Sheriff's Boys Band, Los Angeles, Calif.
South Gate High School Band, South Gate, Calif.
Tournament of Roses Band, Pasadena, Calif.
United States Air Force Band
United States Marine Corps Band
U. C. L. A. Bruin Band, Los Angeles, Calif.
Woodrow Wilson Bruin Band, Pasadena, Calif.

1957

Baker High Buffalo Band, Baker, Louisiana
Bellingham High School Band, Bellingham, Washington
Bonham Brothers Boys' Band, San Diego, Calif.
Edina-Morningside High School Band, Minneapolis, Minnesota
Elks Toppers Band, Los Angeles, Calif.
Glendale Police Boys Band, Glendale, Calif.
Independent Order of Foresters Youth Band, Sherman Oaks, Calif.
Inglewood Boys Band, Inglewood, Calif.
University of Iowa Band, Iowa City, Iowa
Thomas Jefferson Mustang Band, San Antonio, Texas
Mark Keppel High School Aztec Band, Alhambra, Calif.
Long Beach Junior Concert Band, Long Beach, Calif.
Los Angeles Police Junior Band, Los Angeles, Calif.
University of Oregon State Band, Corvallis, Oregon
Pacific Coast Scottish Pipe Band, Los Angeles, Calif.
Tournament of Roses Band, Pasadena, Calif.
Salvation Army Band, Los Angeles, Calif.
South Gate City Youth Band, South Gate, Calif.
United States Marine Corps Band
United States Navy Band, Washington, D. C.

1958

Alhambra High School Band, Alhambra, Calif.
Ben Ali Temple Oriental Band, Chico, Calif.
Bonham Brothers Boys' Band, San Diego, Calif.
Burbank Police Boys Band, Burbank, Calif.
Cocoa High School Band, Cocoa, Florida
Elks Toppers Band, Los Angeles, Calif.
Huntington Park Youth Band, Huntington Park, Calif.
Independent Order of Foresters, Sherman Oaks, Calif.
Long Beach Polytechnic High School Band, Long Beach, Calif.
Los Angeles County Sheriff's Boys Band, Los Angeles, Calif.
Louisville Male High School ROTC Band, Louisville, Kentucky
Occidental College Band, Los Angeles, Calif.
Ohio State Band, Columbus, Ohio
University of Oregon Band, Eugene, Oregon
Ponca City High School Band, Ponca City, Oklahoma
Riverside Polytechnic High School Band, Riverside, Calif.
Salvation Army Band, Los Angeles, Calif.
Shawnee Mission District High School Band, Merriam, Kansas
Tournament of Roses Band, Pasadena, Calif.
United States Combined Marine Corps Band, El Toro, Santa Ana, Calif.

1959

Antelope Valley High School Band, Lancaster, Calif.
Bonham Brothers Boys' Band, San Diego, Calif.
University of California Band, Berkeley, Calif.
Clifton High School "Mustang" Band, East Paterson, New Jersey
Coachella Valley Union High School "Arab" Band, Indio, Calif.
Columbus High School Band, Columbus, Nebraska
Dr. Pepper "Toppers" Band, Los Angeles, Calif.
Glendale "Dynamiter" Band, Glendale, Calif.
Jordan High School Band, Long Beach, Calif.
Los Angeles Police Junior Band, Los Angeles, Calif.
Mark Keppel High School "Aztec" Band, Alhambra, Calif.
Mt. Lebanon High School Band, Pittsburgh, Pennsylvania
Oconomowoc American Legion Band, Oconomowoc, Wisconsin
Phoenix Indian School Band, Phoenix, Arizona
Saint Mary's Chinese Girls Band, San Francisco, Calif.
Salvation Army Band, Los Angeles, Calif.
South Gate City Youth Band, South Gate, Calif.
State University of Iowa Band—and
Iowa Scottish Highlanders, Iowa City, Iowa
Tournament of Roses Band, Pasadena, Calif.
United States Marine Corps Band

1960

Alhambra High School Band, Alhambra, Calif.
John Burroughs High School Band, Burbank, Calif.
Byrd High School Band, Shreveport, Louisiana
Chicago Fire Dept. Band, Chicago, Illinois
Downey Senior High School Band, Downey, Calif.
Dr. Pepper Toppers Band, Los Angeles, Calif.
El Cajon High School Band, El Cajon, Calif.
Independent Order of Foresters, North Hollywood, Calif.
Los Angeles County Sheriff's Boys Band, Los Angeles, Calif.
Millikan High School Band, Long Beach, Calif.
Red Raider Band, Uniontown, Pennsylvania
Ruskin High Golden Eagle Band, Hickman Mills, Missouri
Salvation Army Band, Los Angeles, Calif.
Combined Santa Monica High School and College Band, Santa Monica, Calif.
Tournament of Roses Band, Pasadena, Calif.
United States Marine Corps Band
Warwick Veterans Memorial High School Band, Warwick, Rhode Island
University of Washington Band, Seattle, Washington
Weir High School Varsity Band, Weirton, West Virginia
University of Wisconsin Band, Madison, Wisconsin

1961

Adams State College Band, Alamosa, Colorado
Blackwell High School Band, Blackwell, Oklahoma
DeLaWarr High School Band, New Castle, Delaware
Dodge City High Scsool Band, Dodge City Kansas
Grossmont High School Band, El Cajon, Calif.
Hoover High School Band, Glendale, Calif.
Lakewood High School "Lancer" Band, Lakewood, Calif.
Los Angeles Police Junior Band, Los Angeles, Calif.
Manteca Union High School Band, Manteca, Calif.
University of Minnesota Band, Minneapolis, Minnesota
Montebello High School Band, Montebello, Calif.
Porterville Panther Band, Porterville, Calif.
Salvation Army Band, Los Angeles, Calif.
San Francisco Boys' Club Band, San Francisco, Calif.
S. & H. Green Stamp Topper Band, Los Angeles, Calif.
Torrance All-Star High School Band, Torrance, Calif.
Tournament of Roses Band, Pasadena, Calif.
United States Marine Corps Band
University of Washington Band, Seattle, Washington
Whittier High School Band, Whittier, Calif.

1962

Abington Township Senior High School Band, Abington, Pennsylvania

Andrew Hill Marching Band, San Jose, Calif.

Burbank High School Bulldog Band, Burbank, Calif.

El Cajon Valley High School Marching Band, El Cajon, Calif.

Fitchburg High School Band, Fitchburg, Mass.

Hillsboro Union High School Spartan Band, Hillsboro, Oregon

Independent Order of Foresters Robin Hood Band, Sherman Oaks, Calif.

Long Beach All-District High School Band, Long Beach, Calif.

Los Angeles County Sheriff's Youth Band, Los Angeles, Calif.

Mark Keppel High School "Aztec" Band, Alhambra, Calif.

Mesquite High School Band, Mesquite, Calif.

Oxnard High Coldstream Guards, Oxnard, Calif.

S. & H. Green Stamp Toppers Band, Los Angeles, Calif.

Salvation Army Band, Los Angeles, Calif.

San Francisco Boys' Club Band, San Francisco, Calif.

Santa Monica High School Marching Band, Santa Monica, Calif.

Tournament of Roses Band, Pasadena, Calif.

United States Marine Corps Band

Univ. of California at Los Angeles Band, Los Angeles, Calif.

University of Minnesota Band, Minneapolis, Minnesota

1963

Amos Alonzo Stagg Senior High School Band, Stockton, Calif.

Arcadia High School Apache Band, Arcadia, Calif.

Ben Davis High School Band, Indianapolis, Indiana

Boone Senior High School Toreador Marching Band, Boone, Iowa

Downey City Youth Band, Downey, Calif.

Glendale High School Band, Glendale, Calif.

Lakewood Lancer Band, Lakewood, Calif.

Long Beach Unified School District Band, Long Beach, Calif.

Los Angeles Police Junior Band, Los Angeles, Calif.

Mount Miguel High School Marching Band, Spring Valley, Calif.

Montebello Senior High School Band, Montebello, Calif.

Tournament of Roses Band, Pasadena, Calif.

Pocatello High School Indian Marching Band, Pocatello, Idaho

Salvation Army Band, Los Angeles, Calif.

S. & H. Toppers Band, Tarzana, Calif.

Treadwell High School Band, Memphis 12, Tenn.

United States Marine Corps Band, Santa Ana, Calif.

University of Southern California Band, Los Angeles, Calif.

University of Wisconsin Band, Madison, Wisconsin

Vinson High School Band, Huntington, W. Va.

Whittier High School Band, Whittier, Calif.

1964

A.A.W.U. Band, Seattle, Wash.

Alhambra High School Band, Alhambra, Calif.

Berkeley High School Band, Berkeley, Calif.

Big Ten Band, Champaign-Urbana, Ill.

Burbank Police Boys' Band, Burbank, Calif.

Calexico "Bulldog" Marching Band, Calexico, Calif.

Glendora High School "Tartan" Band, Glendora, Calif.

Isaac Litton High School Band, Nashville, Tenn.

Long Beach All City High School Band, Long Beach 8, Calif.

Melvindale High School Band, Melvindale, Michigan

Montana Centennial Band, Missoula, Montana

Mount Miguel High School Marching Band, San Diego, Calif.

Mutual Savings & Loan "Toppers" Band (Union Band), Anaheim, Calif.

Nyssa High School Band, Nyssa, Oregon

Prince George High School Royal Band, Prince George, Va.

Roosevelt High School "Roughrider" Band, Fresno, Calif.

Salvation Army Band, Los Angeles, Calif.

South Gate City Youth Band, South Gate, Calif.

Tournament of Roses Band, PCC Lancer Band, Pasadena, Calif.

U. S. Marine Corps Band, Hollywood, Calif.

U. S. Sixth Army Band, San Francisco, Calif.

Pasadena High School Band, Pasadena, Calif.

1965

American Legion Indian Band (Hamm's Post #501), St. Paul, Minnesota

Antelope Valley High School Band, Lancaster, Calif.

Carson High School Band, Carson City, Nevada

Colonial High School Grenadier Guard Band, Orlando, Florida

De Anza High School Marching Band, Richmond, Calif.

El Cajon Valley High School Braves Marching Band, El Cajon, Calif.

Fremont High School Band, Sunnyvale, Calif.

Glendale Schools Band, Glendale, Calif.

Inglewood High School Sentinel Band, Inglewood, Calif.

John Muir High School "Mighty Mustang" Band, Pasadena, Calif.

Lakewood High School Lancer Band, Lakewood, Calif.

Long Beach All-District High School Band, Long Beach, Calif.

Los Angeles Police Junior Band, Los Angeles, Calif.

Mark Keppel High School "Aztec" Marching Band, Alhambra, Calif.

University of Michigan Marching Band (Big Ten), Ann Arbor, Michigan

Mississippi Valley State College Marching Band, Itta Bena, Mississippi

Mutual Savings & Loan "Toppers Band", Pasadena, Calif.

Oregon State University Band (A.A.W.U.), Corvallis, Oregon

Salvation Army Band, Los Angeles, Calif.

Tournament of Roses Band (Pasadena City College), Pasadena, Calif.

United States Marine Band, Los Angeles, Calif.

Valley High School Viking Band, Albuquerque, New Mexico

1966

Arcadia High School Apache Band, Arcadia, Calif.

Bakersfield College Renegade Marching Band, Bakersfield, Calif.

British Columbia Centennial Beefeater Band, Vancouver, B. C.

Burbank All-City High School Band, Burbank, Calif.

Carbon High School "Dino" Marching Band, Price, Utah

Castleberry Lion Band, Fort Worth, Texas

Durand Area High School Marching Band, Durand, Michigan

Klamath Union High School Marching Band, Klamath Falls, Oregon

Long Beach All-District High School Band, Long Beach, Calif.

Michigan State University Marching Band, East Lansing, Michigan

Mt. Miguel High School Marching Band, Spring Valley, Calif.

James Monroe High School Viking Band, Sepulveda, Calif.

Mutual Savings & Loan of Pas. Toppers Band, Tarzana, Calif.

Sacramento City College Panther Marching Band, Sacramento, Calif.

St. Ann's Senior CYO Band of Gloucester, Mass., Gloucester, Mass.

Salvation Army Band, Los Angeles, Calif.

Sidney High School Marching Band, Sidney, Nebraska

South Gate City Young Band, South Gate, Calif.

Tenri High School Band, Tenri-city, Japan

Tournament of Roses Band, Pasadena City College, Pasadena, Calif.

UCLA Bruin Band, Los Angeles, Calif.

U. S. Marine Band (Combined), Los Angeles, Calif.

1967

Arlington High School Colt Marching Band, Arlington, Texas

Bronco Marching Band, Dos Palos, Calif.

Bucklin High School Band, Bucklin, Kansas

Capuchino High School Marching Band, Millbrae, Calif.

Columbia High School Band, Columbia, S. C.

*El Capitan High School Marching Band, El Cajon, Calif.

Glendale Schools' Band, Glendale, Calif.

**Granada Hills Highlander Marching Band, Granada Hills, Calif.

The Independent Order of Foresters Robin Hood Band, No. Hollywood, Calif.

Long Beach All-District High School Band, Long Beach, Calif.

Montclair Marching Cavaliers, Montclair, Calif.

Mutual avings & Loan of Pasadena, Toppers Band, Tarzana, Calif.

Porterville Panther Band, Porterville, Calif.

Purdue University "All-American" Marching Band, Lafayette, Indiana

Salvation Army Band, Los Angeles, Calif.

Tooele High School Marching Band, Tooele, Utah

Tournament of Roses Band, Pasadena City College, Pasadena, Calif.

Fifteenth Air Force Band, Riverside, Calif.

U. S. Marine Band, Los Angeles, Calif.

Combined U. S. Navy Bands, San Diego, Calif.

University of Southern California Trojan Marching Band, Los Angeles, Calif.

Whittier High School Cardinal Band, Whittier, Calif.

1968

*Burbank All-City Band, Burbank, Calif.

Disneyland Band, Anaheim, Calif.

Eisenhower Senior High School Band, Yakima, Wash.

(Hapeville) "The Marching 100," Hapeville, Georgia

Hilltop High School "Lancer" Band, Chula Vista, Calif.

Indiana University Marching Hundred, Bloomington, Indiana

Kalani High School Band, Honolulu, Hawaii

Long Beach All-District High School Band, Long Beach, Calif.

Los Angeles Police Junior Band & Color Guard, Los Angeles, Calif.

Mississippi Valley State College Marching Band, Itta Bena, Mississippi

Mutual Savings & Loan of Pas. Toppers Band, Tarzana, Calif.

Phoenix Indian High School Band, Phoenix, Arizona

Salvation Army Band, Los Angeles, Calif.

Strategic Air Command Band, Offutt AFB, Nebraska

**Taft High Toreador Band, Woodland Hills, Calif.

Tournament of Roses Band, Pasadena, Calif.

United States Continental Army Band, Fort Monroe, Virginia

United States Marine Corps Band, Los Angeles, Calif.

---

*Representing San Diego City & County

**Representing Los Angeles City School District

287

University of Southern California Trojan Marching Band, Los Angeles, Calif.
White Pine High School Marching Band, Ely, Nevada
Woodland High School Marching and Concert Bands, Woodland, Calif.

1969

Barnard Fire Department Band, Rochester, New York
Beaver Marching Band, Minot, No. Dakota
The Billion Dollar Band, Columbus, Ohio
  (West Senior High School)
Chatsworth High School Chancellors, Chatsworth, Calif.
Glendale District Band, Glendale, Calif.
Long Beach All-District High School Band, Long Beach, Calif.
McDonald's All-American High School Band, New York, New York
The Marching Colts (Buena High School) Sierra Vista, Arizona
Mt. Miguel High School Matador Band, Spring Valley, Calif.
Mutual Savings & Loan of Pasadena Toppers Band, Tarzana, Calif.
Ohio State University Marching Band, Columbus, Ohio
Prince George High School Royal Band, Prince George, Virginia
Riverview High School "Kiltie" Band, Sarasota, Florida
Charles M. Russell High School Band, Great Falls, Montana
Rutgers University Marching One Hundred, New Brunswick, N.J.
The Salvation Army Band, Los Angeles, Calif.
Tournament of Roses Band, Pasadena, Calif.
14th U.S. Army Band (Women's Army Corps), Fort McClellan, Ala.
U.S. Marine Band, Santa Monica, Calif.
Western States Army National Guard Band, Sacramento, Calif.
University of Southern California Trojan Marching Band, Los Angeles, Calif.

1970

Alain LeRoy Locke High School "Saints" Marching Band, Los Angeles, Calif.
Arkansas City Bulldog Marching Band Arkansas City, Kansas
Bobcat Marching Band, Marshalltown, Iowa
Burbank All-City Band, Burbank, Calif.
Burlington Teens Tour Band, Burlington, Ontario, Canada
The Garnet & Blue Marching 101 Band, Orangeburg, S.C.
Lakewood High "Lancer" Band, Lakewood, Calif.
Long Beach All-District High School Band, Long Beach, Calif.

The "Marching Chiefs," La Crosse, Wisconsin
The Marching Saints, Santa Ana, Calif.
"Marching Stag" Band, Deer Park, Washington
McDonald's All-American High School Band, New York, New York
Monarch Marching Band, San Diego, Calif.
Mutual Savings & Loan Toppers Band, Tarzana, Calif.
Port Chester Senior High School Band, Port Chester, New York
The Salvation Army Band, Los Angeles, Calif.
Tournament of Roses Band, Pasadena, Calif.
U.S. Marine Corps Band, Santa Monica, Calif.
University of Michigan Marching Band, Ann Arbor, Michigan
University of Southern California Band, Los Angeles, Calif.
White Oak High School Roughneck Marching Band, White Oak, Texas

1971

C. E. King High School, Houston, Texas
Cupertino High School Pioneers, Sunnyvale, Calif.
Englewood High School, Englewood, Colo.
Glendale Schools, Glendale, Calif.
Glendora High School Tartans, Glendora, Calif.
Granada Hills High School Highlanders, Granada Hills, Calif.
Hilo High School Vikings, Hilo, Hawaii
Huntington Thunderers, Huntington, N.Y.
Leavenworth Pioneers, Leavenworth, Kans.
Long Beach All District Band, Long Beach, Calif.
McDonald's All-American High School Band, New York, New York
Morris Brown Wolverines, Atlanta, Ga.
Mt. Miguel High School Matadors, Spring Valley, Calif.
Mutual Savings Toppers, Pasadena, Calif.
Ohio State Marching Band, Columbus, Ohio
Plymouth Carver High School, Plymouth, Mass.
Salvation Army Band, Los Angeles, Calif.
Santa Monica College Corsairs, Santa Monica, Calif.
Stanford Marching Band, Stanford, Calif.
Tournament of Roses Band, Pasadena, Calif.
U.S. Marine Corps Band, El Toro, Calif.

Index

Index

Figures in italics refer to illustrations; an italic number preceded by a *c* indicates a color illustration in the pages immediately following the reference.

Abel, Fred 52
Abrahamson, E. J. 239
Adams, Armon 86–9
Adams, Stanley T. 161; *161*
Adelman, Harry 132
Ackerman, Bill 117
Agase, Alex 139
Agase, Lou 139
Aigler, Ralph 134–5
Akers, Sam 86, 131, 263
Akins, Al 129
Alabama, University of 59, 60, 63, 73–4, 99–101, 106, 108, 131–2, 136, 141, 275; *60, 61, 105*
Alaska, 190
Albert, Frankie 122–3; *122*
Alexander, John L. 86
Alexander, William 69
Alhambra, Calif. *20*
Allen, Mel 159, 261
Allen, Reid 260, 263
Allen, Rex 82
Allen, Steve 39, 162
Allis, Harry 157
Allred, James V. 102, 106
Al Malaikah Shrine Temple 38, 232; *c238*
Altadena High School 17, 19
Altenberg, Kurt 216
Althouse, Arthur W. 196; *197*
Alustiza, Frank 97
Ambrose, Keith 28
Ameche, Alan 165–6
American Football Coaches Association 37
American Hospital Association 38
American Legion 39, 52, 143, 176
Anaheim 252
Anderson, A. B. 6
Anderson, C. Elmer 100; *99*
Anderson, Dave 108
Anderson, Mickey 113
Anderson, Ralph 151
Ane, Charlie 166
Angelus Temple 34, 53
Angus, Howard 25
Anheuser-Busch, Inc. 38, 165, 242
Anicich, Pamela 188, 231, 271; *231, 271; c110*

Anthony, Mel 210–2, 280; *212*
Apisa, Bob 216
Arbelbide, Garrett 72
Armitage, Elsie 17; *17*
Armstrong, Ike 198–9
Arnett, Jon 175, 178
Arnett, Kathleen Denise 251; *c174*
Arnold, Edward 150
Aschenbrenner, Frank 145–7
Athletic Association of Western Universities 172, 194–5, 198, 200, 217–9
Auman, Patricia (Mrs. Charles Richards) 132, 269; *132, 269*
Autry, Gene 82
Ayala, Ron 234, 245–6

Bach, Joe 54
Bachman, Charley 29
Bachorous, Pete 159
Bagshaw, Enoch 52, 59, 61
Bailey, Betty 102
Bailey, E. L. 113
Baird, Charles 12
Baker, George 56
Baker, Dawn 209; *209*
Baker, Harrison R., Jr. 260, 263
Baker, Johnny 90
Baker, Mary (Mrs. Lynn Baker) 154–5
Baker, Roy 49, 50
Baker, Royal 176
Baker, Vira 7
Bakery and Confectionery Workers Union 38, 179; *c238*
Bakken, Jim 193
Baldwin, Anita *See* McClaughry, Anita
Baldwin, Lucky 20–2
Bame, Damon 202
Bandini, Don Arturo 11
Bangs, Benton 25
Bank of America 38, 236–7; *c110*
Bank of Italy 236
Banse, George 237
Barabas, Al 98; *98*
Barker, Bob 79
Barlow, J. R. 36

Barnard, Les 29
Barnes, Ben *c174*
Barnes, Bill 198–9; *200*
Barnes, Emile 63
Barnhill, Jim 129, 131
Barr, Stanley 67, 69
Barry, Sam 113
Bartholomew, Sam 120
Bartlett, E. L. 190; *189*
Bartlett, Ken 27
Barstow, Mrs. R. C. 158
Baugh, Sammy 102
Baumhefner, C. H. 237
Beamer, Nub 183
Bean, Alan 37, 238; *c174*
Beanland, Willard and Dorothy 78
Beathard, Pete 201–3, 280; *203*
Beban, Gary 37, 216
Becker, Bill 211
Beckett, John 26–8
Bedell, Hilles 205–6; *206*
Bedell, Joan 206
Bedsole, Hal 202–3
Beecroft, Charles *c174*
Bekins Moving and Storage 38; *c46, c238*
Bell, Bert 27
Bell, Matty 102; *104*
Bellamy, Madge 62
Belotti, George 178
Bennett, Bruce 61
Bennett, Cyril 103; *106*
Bennett, Lynda 37
Bergen, Edgar 118–9; *117, 118*
Berkey, Bob 47
Berry, Howard 26–7
Berry, Mike 246
Berry, Tom 183
Bertelson, Margarethe (Mrs. Richard G. Knoblock) 193; *193, 194*
Bertonneau, A. J. 158
Berwanger, Jay 147
Bescos, Julie 113
Beverly Hills 62, 66–7, 71; *66*
Bezdek, Hugo 27–8, 48–9, 275; *50*
Bierman, Bernie 90, 91, 167; *91*
Big Bear Lake Tavern 44
Biggar, John H. 117, 148, 174, 184; *184*

Big Ten 133–6, 140, 148, 160, 172, 182, 188, 195, 200, 217–8, 275
Big Ten, The (Wilson and Brondfield) 134
Bill, Bobby 199
Biscailuz, Eugene 78, 80, 82, 103, 106, 109, 163, 184; *106*
Blackwell, Clare 125
Blasingham, Otis 260; *260*
Blythe, Ann 39
Bobo, Hubert 177–8
Bogue, George 63
Bolden, LeRoy 168
Bolinger, George 86
Bolt, Frank C. 7; *8*
"Bonanza" 82
Bond, Carrie Jacobs 62
Boni, Bill 185
Boone, Ralph 25
Booth, Allan 64
Borich, Mrs. Bessie S. 58
Bosteder, Mrs. Mildred 179
Botari, Vic 108
Bowen, Mrs. C. W. 58
Bower, Horace 240
Bower, Virginia (Mrs. Paul Nichols) 144; *144*
Bowman, Jerry 132
Boyd, Bill (Hopalong Cassidy) 82
Boyd, Willard 127
Bradley, Omar 140, 261; *140*
Bragg, H. W. 225–7; *226*
Braly, Ed 11
Breckenridge, Harold 67
Breneman, William R. 135
Brieske, Jim 141, 280
Brix, Herman (Bruce Bennett) 61
Brixuis, Frank 198
Brockington, John 255
Brodhead, Theodore J. 158
Brominski, Edward 98
Brooks, Frank M. 128–9, 132
Brooks, Phyllis *100*
Brosky, Al 160
Brothers, Paul 212
Brougham, Royal 74
Brown, Andrea 192
Brown, Gary 192
Brown, J. M. 59–61; *58*
Brown, Jackie 255–6
Brown, Marion (Senora Miguel de Guajardo) 150; *149*
Brown, Perry 143; *143*
Brown, Sam 182
Brown, Stanley K. 190–1; *189*
Brown, Tom 198
Brown, Walter ("Jap") 28
Brown, Willie 202–3
Brown University 24–6, 44, 275
Brubach, Dolores (Mrs. H. Eugene Chase) 125–6, 179, 264; *125, 268*
Bruckman, Clyde 28
Bruhn, Milt 193–5, 202–3; *203*
Bruneau, Pete 102

Brunk, Frank 147, 151
Bryan, James 52
Bryan, Paul 3, 262
Bryant, Paul 101
Buckler, Bill 60–1
Bukich, Rudy 165–6
Bumpus, Nancy (Mrs. John W. Johnson) 106; *103*
Bundy, May Sutton 18; *19*
Burbank 112, 129, 185, 197; *111*
Burbank City Schools 108
Burch, Patricia Hartman 251; *c174*
Burick, Cy 185
Burlington, Ontario, Bank 85
Burnham, F. E. 11
Burns, Doris 125
Burnside, Don *130*
Burson, Don 145, 147
Burton, R. Allen 78
Busch, Mr. and Mrs. Adolphus 242
Busch, Augustus A., Jr. 242
Busch Gardens 242, 243; *c46*
Butcher, Ron 202
Butler, Johnny 120
Butler, Steve 216
Butts, Wallace 127
Byers, Walter 117

Cabot, Ann (Mrs. John Cabot) 260
Cabot, John 259–62; *259, 264; c174*
Cafego, George 120
Cahill, Ray 224
Cain, Jimmy 73–4, 145, 147
Caldwell, Herschell 63
Calgary 214
California Institute of Technology 10, 12, 28, 70
California, University of 12, 46–9, 53, 66–7, 69, 99, 106, 108, 133, 144–7, 150–2, 155–7, 182, 188–90, 200, 275, 280; *50*
California, University of, at Los Angeles (U.C.L.A.) 102, 119, 127, 135–6, 138–9, 167–8, 177, 180–2, 199, 200, 213, 215–7, 275, 280
Callanan, Jim 130
Calland, Leo 49
Cameron, Paul 167–8
Camp Baldy 67
Campbell, George S. 103; *108*
Campbell, Gordon 49, 50
Campbell, John ("Monk") 73–4
Campbell, Tilden ("Happy") 90
Camp Lewis 27–8, 48
Cannavino, Joe 187
Capel, Bruce 208
Carey, George P. 18, 20
Carmichael, Al 165–6
Carrillo, Leo 78, 80, 82, 94, 103, 199; *102*

Carroll, Deborah *c110*
Casanova, Len 185–6; *187*
Case, Ernie 139
Casey, Eddie 44; *44*
Cassady, Howard ("Hopalong") 175, 177–8
Cassidy, Hopalong (Bill Boyd) 82
Castle, Andy 106
Catavolos, George 222–4, 276; *222*
Catavolos, Mrs. Lou 223
Celeri, Bob 147, 151–2
Central Japan Association 121
Chobe, L. H. 71–2
Chobe, Mrs. L. H. 73
Chambers, Terry 2, 262–3
Chandler, Bob 245–6; *245*
Chapin, Dwight 247
Chaplin, Charlie 45
Chapman, Richard S. 242
Chapman, Sam 108
Chappuis, Robert 140–2; *142*
Chariot racing 15–7, 19–21, 23–4, 274; *10, 18*
Charles, John 223
Chicago Bears 29
Chickerneo, John 106
Christen, Harvey 84–5, 263
Christian, A. Byrd 83
Christman, Paul 228, 261
Christopher, Norma (Mrs. Don Winton) 137–8; *137*
Chrysler Corporation 36–8, 209; *36; c238*
Church, Fred 44
Clark, Don 187; *186*
Clark, Eileen 111
Clark, Laurine 111
Clark, Steve 212
Clausen, A. W. 237
Clay, Dan 263
Clayton, Frank 165
Cleary, Paul 142
Cleman, Alan 216
Clevenger, Zora 134
Clooney, Rosemary 37
Cobb, Charles 70
Coburn, Charles 152
Coffey, Junior 208
Cole, John 60
Coleman, Charles 14
Coleman, Cynthia Lee, 251; *c174*
Coleman, Mrs. Isabella 30, 33–5, 274; *30, 40, 41*
Coleman, Mrs. Isabella and Dr. Sam, Inc. 30
Coleman, Matt 34
College All Stars 127
Colletto, Jim 216
Collingwood, Bob 6
Collins, Chuck 54–5
Colonna, Jerry 37
Columbia Hill Tennis Club 7
Columbia University 27, 96–9
Colwell, Kari (Mrs. Max Colwell) 162

Colwell, Max 1, 2, 5, 50, 86, 118, 129, 131, 158–9, 162, 171, 174, 184, 231, 262, 274; *158*
Connolly, One-eye 64; *62, 64*
Conrad, Charles L., Jr. 37, 238; *c174*
Continental Air Lines 38; *c238*
Contratto, Jim 177
Cook, Gene 61
Cook, Ron 159
Cook, T. H. 17
Coombes, Harold E. 264
Cooper, Jackie 94
"Coquette" 61
Corbus, Bill 97
Cota, Carole (Mrs. Frank A. Gelfuso) 214, 215, 271; *215*
Coulston, J. B. 23
Cowan, Muriel (Mrs. Ernest Moore) 99, 100, 266; *99, 267*
Cowlings, Al 245; *244*
Cox, Bob 166
Coy, Richard 232
Crabtree, Jack 185, 187
Cravath, Jeff 128–9, 131, 141–2
Crawford, Ernest 15
Creahan, Helen 125
Creller, W. F. 51
Crisler, Fritz 134, 140, 142, 233; *209*
Cromwell, Dean 9
Cronin, Bob 103
Cronin, Ned 120, 132, 139, 142
Crook, Bill *c46*
Cross, Eric 254
Crowley, Jim 53–7; *52, 53*
Cuddeback, Murray 53–6
Cullen, Carl 52
Cullinson, Harold 150
Cullom, Jim 147, 152
Cullum, Dick 200, 233
Culver City 110
Culver, Joan (Mrs. J. C. Warren) 179, 270; *180*
Culver, Susan 41
Cummings, Bob 39, 156
Cupertino High School Pioneer Band 253
Cureton, Hardiman 182
Custardo, Fred 208
Czechoslovakia 62

Daddio, Bill 106, 280
Daggett, Charles D. 5, 8, 15; *8*
Dailey, Ted 95
Dalrymple, Jerry 90, 91
Dana, Herb 67, 69, 91
Dandoy, Aramis 177–8, 280
Daniell, Averill 106
Daugherty, Duffy 180, 182, 216–7; *179*
Davenport, Bob 182
Davidson, John S. 183; *183*
Davidson, Millard 263
Davidson, Richard 263

Davis, Clarence 246
Davis, Con 78
Davis, George T. 46, 56, 129, 131, 160
Davis, Glenn 136
Davis, Lamarr 127
Davis, Nancy 201, 203–4, 261; *204*
Davis, Peter 263
Davis, R. D. 22
Davis, Van 127
Day, Dennis 39
Day, Ollie 113
Deagan, Bob 198
Dean, William F. 168–9; *169*
Decker, Jim 181–2
DeJong, Ray 147
Deichman, John 85
DeMolay, Order of 232
Dempsey, Ed 120
Dempsey, Jack 45
Derricotte, Gene 141
Detham, Robert 125, 280
Dickerson, Sam 234, 236
Dietrich, Jim 188
Dietz, Carl 25, 280
Dior, Christian 270
Dirksen, Everett 225–7, 261; *226*
Disney, Walt 213–4: *214*
Donahue, Terry 216
Donald Bent Parade Floats 31
Donnelly, George 208
Dorn, Raymond A. 117, 191–3; *193, 241*
Dorn, Warren M. 200, 241
Dougall, Barbara (Mrs. Clifford J. Ward, Jr.) 111–2; *110*
Dougall, Mrs. William 112
Douglas, Bill 207–8
Drain, James A. 52
Driscoll, Paddy 29; *29*
Dr. Pepper Company 38; *c238*
Drummond, Harrison 21, 266; *21*
Drury, Morley 233
Duarte 11
Duckett, Ellis 167, 168
Dufek, Donald 156–7
Duffield, Marshall 72
Duke University 63, 112–4, 124–6, 275, 280; *124*
Duncan, Randy 189–90
Dunkerley, William 71, 96, 109, 154, 158; *131*
Durdan, Don 125
Durslag, Mel 159–60, 181, 224
Dutcher, Erwin 216
Dyer, Braven 63, 72, 74, 95, 102, 112–3, 142, 155–6, 159–60, 166, 177, 183

Eagle Friend, Chief 79; *c110*
Eagle Rock 254
Early, Thomas *19*
Eastern Airlines 36
Eastern Star 42

Eastman Kodak Company 36–8; *c238*
Eckersall, Walter 25
Edelson, Harry 72
Eden, Barbara 37
Edison Company 149
Edwards, C. Lewis 173, 238–9, 248, 250–1; *240, 248*
Edwards, Dorothy (Mrs. Joseph A. Conlon) 92, 94; *93*
Edwards, Glenn 73
Eilbacher, Cindy 252
Einstein, Albert 73; *70*
Eisenhower, Dwight D. 1, 2, 152–3, 162–3, 205–6, 261, 275; *205, 208*
Eisenhower, Mrs. Dwight D. 205–6
Eliot, Ray 138, 160; *138*
Elks Lodges of California 51
Elliott, Chalmers ("Bump") 141, 211; *211*
Elliott, Pete 188–9, 207; *207*
El Monte *119*
Ely, Leroy 11
Embree, Al 86
Engle, Roy 120
Ennis, Ben 60
Ericson, Harold *50*
Erquiaga, John 216
Esper, Dwain 213, 233–4, 245, 256
Essertier, Ed 241
Etter, Les 155
Evans, Dale 179; *173*
Evashevski, Forest 182–3, 188–90; *182*
Everest, A. C. 148

Fagan, Edna 78
Fairbanks, Douglas 45
Fairbanks, Eldon 76, 78–9
Fairbanks, Patricia 41
Farmers Insurance Group 38–40, 199, 243–4, 252; *38, 39, 243; c174*
Farnsworth, C. S. 73; *73*
Farrar, Jim 147
Feder, Sid 124
Feland, Leah (Mrs. Roland King) 166; *164*
Felkins, Lee 194
Ferraro, John 130
Ferrier, William 184
Fertig, Craig 241
Fesler, Wes 150, 152; *150*
Festival Artists of Arcadia 242
Fickes, J. V. 52–3
Fidler, Janice *c110*
Finch, Frank 166
Finch, Phil 258
Finley, Bob 102
First to Fly, Chief 79
Fischer, Leo 261
Fish, Everett 31
Fisher, Bob 44
Fisher, R. S. 14

Fisk, Bill 120
Flaherty, Vincent X. 142, 160, 181
Fleming, George 193, 195, 197–8
Fleming, Willie 189–90
Florence, Mal 247
Florists Transworld Delivery
    Association 38, 252–3; c46
Folwell, Bob 52
Fonde, Henry 141
Foote, Bob 98–9
Forbes, Mabel L. 239
Forbush, Barbara 125
Force, Kenneth R. 85
Four Horsemen (Notre Dame)
    53–7; 53
Fox, Daniel F. 58
Fox, John 58
Fox, Wylie 208
Foxx, Bobby 120
Francis, Joe 183
Francis, Vike 122–3
Fraser, Don 247–8
Fraser, Malcolm 158
Freeman, Van C. 135
French, Jean 21, 266; 21
French, Thomas E. 133
Frketich, Len 212
Frost, Lew 171
Fullmer, Lianne 41
Furillo, Bud 202, 224

Gaal, Alexander 240, 254, 263; 240
Gallarneau, Hugh 122–3
Gallery, Tom 171
Galloway, Harold 50
Gardena 190
Garland, William May 90; 93
Gaspar, Phil 114, 120
Gaylord, Robert 11
Geddes, Peter 247
George, Ray 114, 203
Georgia 252; c110, c238
Georgia Tech 66–7, 69, 90, 126–7,
    275
Gerrie, Alfred L. 179; 181
Geyer, Jack 166
Giannini, A. P. 236–7
Gibson, Bob 209
Gibson, Hoot 62
Giersch, Carlota Busch 175, 242
Gillette Company 36
Gilliam, Frank 183
Gillian, Ray 236
Gillis, Grant 59, 60
Gilmer, Harry 131
Gilmore, Debbi Ann 251; c174
Girl Scouts of America 199
Glanz, Emmett, Jr. 237
Glassford, William 106
Glendale 51, 53, 65–6, 71–3, 94,
    165, 190; 51
Glendora High School Tartan
    Band 253
Glover, Harry 90–1
Goddard, Merton E. 76, 263

Goldberg, Marshall 106; 105
Gonso, Harry 228–9
Gonzales, Rebecca c110
Goodhue, Virginia (Mrs. Donald
    Hess) 140, 269; 141, 269
Gordon, Dick 200
Gordon, Richard F. 37, 238; c174
Gordon, Mrs. Richard F. 238
Goux, Marv 166, 177
Gowdy, Curt 239, 261; 239
Grabowski, Jim 208
Graham, Billy 251–2, 254; 250;
    c174
Graham, Jennie 7
Graham, Ruth (Mrs. Billy Graham)
    252
Granada Hills Highlander Marching
    Band 253; c174
Grand Army of the Republic 52
Graves, Peter 254
Gray, Bill 128
Gray, Gene 125, 280
Gray, Marv 233
Gray, Robert Stewart 152–3; 152
Grayson, Bobby 97, 101–2, 190
Green, Hotel 14–5, 71
Gregory, L. H. 160
Grider, Dallas 216
Griese, Bob 37, 218, 222, 224
Griffith, Homer 95
Griffith, John L. 133–4
Grim, Bob 212
Gualderson, Joe 248
Gunn, Jimmy 245; 244; c110
Guttormsen, George 59–61

Haas, G. A. W. 9
Hackbart, Dale 194
Hagan, Jim 64
Hagberg, Roger 198
Hagemeier, Janet Kaye 251; c174
Hagler, Collins 183
Hague, James 150–1, 275
Hahn, Stanley L. 117, 193, 201,
    204, 206; 202, 241, 248
Halas, George 29; 24
Hall, Bob 72
Hall, Frank 177
Hall, Harlan 47, 71, 158
Hall, Linda Lee 41
Hall of Fame, Rose Bowl 213
Halsey, William F. 132; 132
Halsted, Gabrielle (Mrs. Paul G.
    Bryan) 71
Halsted, Holly (Mrs. Frank S.
    Balthis) 70–1, 240; 71
Haluska, Jim 166
Hamilton, A. L. 27
Hamilton, Robert ("Bones") 97–8,
    102
Hamilton, Tom 117, 194, 219; 194
Hamlin, Thornton 260, 263
Hammack, Sterling 183
Haney, Elizabeth 41
Haney, Jacqueline 41; c174
Hanley, Dick 25

Hannah, John A. 169
Hanson, Myrna 170
Hanszen, Jerry T. 86
Harbottle, Lee 78
Hardcastle, Frank 206, 263
Hardy, Jim 128–31
Harkrader, Dick 177
Harmon, Tom 160
Harris, George 151, 260, 263
Hart, Jack 190
Hartwell, Christine Marie 251;
    c174
Hartwig, Charles 95
Harvard Club (Boston) 45
Harvard University 44–5; 45
Harvey, Raymond 161; 161
Hayden, Leo 235, 255; 235
Hayes, W. Woodrow ("Woody")
    143, 176–7, 185–7, 229, 234,
    236, 258; 176
Haynes, Vernon 91
Haywood, Ray 160
Headley, Blake 129; 130
Heath, Harland 264
Hein, Mel 73
Heller, Ron 202
Heller, Warren 95
Hellinger, Mark 108
Helms Athletic Foundation 213
Helms, Paul 213
Helpbringer Ralph 75–6, 83, 215,
    240, 263
Helpinstein, E. B. 9
Henderson, Elmer 48
Henderson, Gus 49–50, 168, 275;
    50
Henderson, John 211
Hendrickson, Joe c110
Henno, Nancy c110
Henry, Bill 39, 95
Henry, Mrs. Bill 39
Henry, Leslie B. 66, 134
Hensley, Donald 106; 105
Hepburn, Katherine 269
Herbert, Bob 128
Hermann, John 167–8
Herrin–Preston 31
Herris, Wayne 254
Herrnstein, Al 14
Hertel, Herman 10; 11
Heston, Willie 13–4
Herwig, Bob 108
Hewitt, Barbara (Mrs. David
    Laughray) 221; 221
Heydenreich, Paul 10
Hi-C Drinks 38; c238
Hightower, Patrice c110
Hilkene, Bruce 141
Hill, Fred 203
Hill, Henry 247
Hill, Jess 117, 165, 177, 219,
    241–2; 162
Hilo High School Viking Band 253
Hines, Mrs. Harold 116
Hinson, H. W. 78

Hivner, Bob 194, 197–8
Hobbs, William *194*
Hobson, C. F. 28
Hoefflin, Walter R., Jr. 162,
    209–10, 263; *210*
Hoelscher, Carl H. 260, 263

Hoffman, Bill 65
Hoffman, Bob 120
Hoffman, Fabian 106
Hoffman, Paul G. 149–50; *149*
Hogan, Frank G. 21
Hoisch, Al 138–9, 280; *139*
Holden, William 153, 270; *270*
Holder, Dr. Charles Frederick 3–5,
    15, 20, 274; *1*
Holland, Jerome 233
Holland, Lou 202–3
Hollingberry, Babe 73; *74*
Hollingworth, Hank 246
Holmes, Gordon 59, 63
Holmquist, Ray 174
Honolulu 126
Hooks, Bob 166
Hoover, Herbert 28, 96, 102, 129,
    275; *131*
Hoover, Mrs. Herbert 96
Hope, Bob 6, 36–9, 136, 138, 143,
    146, 229–31, 241; *133, 137, 230*
Hopp, Harry ("Hippity") 123
Horowitz, Steve 255, 280; *255*
Horrell, Edwin 127
Horween, Arnold 44–5
Horween, Ralph 44
Hourihan, Monsignor James 261
Houston, James 187
Howard, C. V. 5
Howell, Dixie 99–101, 275; *100*
Howie, Kathy 353–4; *253*
Hubbard, Dick 31
Hubbard, Paula Kay *c174*
Hubert, A. T. S. ("Pooley") 59–61
Hudner, Thomas J. 161; *161*
Hudson, Rock 152
Hugasian, Harry 159
Hull, Mike 222
Hull, Terri Susan 41
Hum, Charles 240
Hunter, Bill 113, 117, 134
Hunter, Bob 120, 124, 129, 131,
    142, 160

Huntington, Hollis 27–8, 44
Huntington, Shy 27–8, 44
Huntington Sheraton Hotel 38
Huntington Thunderers 253

Huntley, Margaret (Mrs. Robert
    Main) 115–6; *115, 118, 267*
Huntsinger, Ed 54–7
Hurry, Harry W. 168, 270; *169, 270*
Hurst, Bob 222
Hutchins, Colleen Kay 161
Hutson, Don 100–1, 275; *100*
Hyland, Dick 62–3, 102, 120, 141,
    159, 166, 168, 183; *63*

Illinois, University of 135–6,
    138–9, 159–60, 207–8, 227–8,
    280; *227*
Indio 183
Ingham, James K. 126, 132; *127*
Iowa Association 88
Iowa, University of 182, 188–90,
    280
Ivy League 45

Jackson, Jack 175
Jackson, Jay 175; *c110*
Jackson, Ray 194, 198
James, Jack 98, 108
Janowicz, Vic 152; *c174*
Japinga, Don 216
Jensen, Jackie 147; *145; c110*
Jeter, Bob 189, 190, 210, 280
Johns, Wilbur 117
Johnson, Charles 185, 261
Johnson, Jimmy 63
Johnson, Tom 157
Johnston, Charles 54–5
Jones, Biff 122–3; *122*
Jones, Bruce 59
Jones, Cal 183
Jones, Howard Harding 72, 90, 95,
    101, 113, 119–20, 129; *91*
Jones, Jimmy 120
Jones, Jimmy 245–7
Juday, Steve 216
Judson, Don 260, 263

Kadziel, Ron 255
Kaiser, Dave 180–2, 275
Kapp, Joe 188–90
Karras, John 159
Kearnes, Henry 220–1, 227, 250;
    220
Kefgen, Mary 265
Keller, Mike 246
Kelly, James 55
Kelly, Mark 49, 63, 100–1
Kempthorne, Dick 142
Kendall, B. O. 27–9
Kenworthy, L. Clifford 150,
    152–4; *153*
Kenworthy, Mrs. L. Clifford 150;
    153
Kerkorian, Gary 159–60
Kern, Rex 234–6, 255, 258; *258*
Kessler, Kaye 185
Kester, Katherine 116
Keys, Leroy 223
Khoman, Thanat 221, 227; *220*
Kickley, Paul 147
Killian, Tim 245
Kincaid, Howard 50
Kingsley, Leon 159
Kiwanis (Pasadena) 46
Kizer, Noble 54
Klein, Jerry 216
Kmetovic, Pete 122–3
Kneeland, Nancy (Mrs. William J.
    Kish) 208, 240, 270; *208, 270*
Knight, George 123

Knights of the Rose 22
Knott's Berry Farm 38, 40–1, 242;
    41; c174
Knott, Walter and Cordelia 40–1;
    c174
Knowlton, E. W. 20
Knox, Harvey 181
Knox, Ronnie 180–2
Koch, Desmond 165, 280
Komical Knights of the Karnival
    with King Kidder and Kween
    Karmencita 21
Kopay, Dave 208
Kopf, Herb 47, 98–9
Kornowa, Dave 228
Kouma, Ernest R. 161; *161*
Kowalczyk, Walter 182
Krall, Jerry 151–2
Krauss, Gale 79
Kremblas, Frank 186–7; *186*
Kroner, Gary 203
Krueger, Al 112–4, 120, 275; *113, 114*
Kuechle, Oliver 185
Kurek, Ralph 202
Kyser, Kay 125, 137–8; *125*
Kyser, Tommy 126

LaBrucherie, Bert 138; *139*
La Crosse, Wisconsin, State College
    Band 85–6
Lacey, Percy 126
Lach, Steve 125
Laguna Beach 112; *111*
Lakewood, Calif. 209
Lamour, Dorothy 37
Lancaster, L. H. 17
Langston, Jeff 190
Lanphear, Linda 244; *243*
Lanphier, Fay 59, 71, 266; *59*
Lansdell, Grenville 112–3, 120
Larson, Pearl 78
La Rue, Bobby 106; *104*
Las Vegas 170
Lavalle, Paul 84
Lawrence, Jim 222–4, 276
Lawrence, Mike 31
Lawry, Geordie *257*
Lawson, Jim 55
Lawson, Ramsay 263
Lawson, William 260; *261*
Layden, Elmer 53–7, 127, 275,
    280; *53*
Leahy, Frank 141
Leavenworth High School Pioneer
    Marching Band 253
Lebanon 214
Lee, Don 112
Lee, Patricia 125
Legge, Helen 153
Legget, Dave 177
Leib, Karl E. 135
Leib, Tom 261
Leiser, Bill 160

Leishman, Lathrop 42, 44, 109–11, 117–8, 148–9, 171, 184, 193, 204, 239, 272, 274; *43, 109, 126, 239, 241, 248*
Leishman, Robert 42
Leishman, W. L. 24, 42, 44, 46–8, 109, 272, 274; *42, 43*
Leishman, William 42, 263
Levingood, E. J. 21
Lewis, Dave 246
Lewis, John 182
Lewis, Mac 189–90
Lewis, Spud 65
Libke, Al 208
Licata, Joe 264
Lillywhite, Verl 132
Lindley, Lowell 50
Lindquist, G. R. 135
Lindskog, Victor 123
Lininger, Jack 152
Linnard, D. M. 16, 26
Little, Lou 27, 97, 99; *96*
Llewellyn, David 179, 184; *180*
Lloyd, Harold 99; *99*
Locke High School Band 85
Lockwood, C. D. 26
Loechler, Thomas 200
Login, Bill 126
Lom, Benny 67–9
London, Carol *c110*
Long Beach 52, 97, 132, 144, 149, 170, 176, 190, 193, 207; *97*
Long Beach Mounted Police Posse 137, 232; *c46*
Lorenz, William F. 135
Los Angeles 34, 242; *c110*
Los Angeles Chamber of Commerce 8
Los Angeles Rams Band 137
Lotter, Will 147
Loud, Harlan 111, 115–8, 134; *118*
Loud, Mrs. Harlan 116; *118*
Loudd, Rommie 168
Loughery, Mable Siebert 22
Lowe, Gayle 81
Lowe, Janice *c110*
Lowe, Thaddeus S. C. 8; *9*
Lowe, Mrs. Thaddeus S. C. *9*
Lowry, Paul 47, 59, 91
Loyal Order of Moose 232
Loyola University 56, 261
Lucas, Howard 133
Luckman, Sid 130
Lumpkin, Roy ("Father") 69
Lundborg, Louis B. 237
Lupo, Tom 202, 203
Luther, Butch 122–3
Lutheran Laymen's League 38
Lynn, Deana 152

McAvoy, May 48, 71, 266; *49, 266*
McCall, Bill 159
McCall, Don 222
McCall, J. W., Jr. 121; *122*

McCallag, Mary (Mrs. Elmer Willhoite) 166
McCarthy, Charlie 118–9; *117, 118*
McCarver, Tim 209
McClaughry, Mrs. Anita Baldwin 22
McCormick, Frank C. 134
McCormick, Walt 142
McCullough, Lou 236
McCunn, Drummond J. 149; *148*
McCurdy, Robert M. 125–6, 132; *125*
McDaneld, D. E. 90, 93–4; *93*
McDermid, Calla 239
McDonald All-American Band 84
McDonald Corporation 85
McDonald, J. Farrell 56
McDonald, Jeanette 154–5
McDougal, Doug 212
McFarland, James G. 51
McGilvray, Fisher 13
McGrane, Bert 185, 261
McGugin, Dan 14
McKay, John 28
McKay, Johnny 140, 166, 203, 218, 222–4, 229, 236, 239, 242, 244–7; *223*
McKee, Ira 52
McKeta, Don 193
McKinley, William 8
MacLachlan, Doug 130
McLemore, Henry 120
McLeod, Jack 125
MacNamee, Graham 62, 64, 261
McNeish, Bob 113
McPherson, Aimee Semple 34, 53
Mackey, Guy J. 134; *135*
Maddock, George 147
Madonna, Alex, Phyllis, and Cathie 78
Maechtle, Don 139
Main, Bob 116
Malaby, Z. T. 27
Malmgren, Frances 237
Mancuso, Joe 208
Mandich, Jim 246; *c110*
Manerud, Clifford ("Skeet") 44
Mann, Bobby 141
Manning, Archbishop Timothy 261
Manos, Charles 243–4; *243*
March Field 128
Mare Island 27, 48
Maree, Vance 67
Marine Band 84, 143
Marinos, Jim 156
Marshalltown, Iowa, High School Band 86–9
Martel, Christine 170
Martenson, Mary 1–2
Maryland, Hotel 15
Masters, Al 117, 134
Matisi, Tony 106
Mattison, F. C. E. 22
Mead, Ben 241
Meek, John 108

Medberry, C. J. 237
Medved, Ron 208
Meehan, Chick 130
Meeker, Ezra 20
Merrill, Walter *105*
Merriman, Lee 124
Merry, Don 247
Mexico, Republic of *c110*
Michel, P. B. 19, 20
Michelosen, John 106
Michigan State University 176–8, 180–2, 213, 215–7, 275
Michigan, University of 12–4, 140–2, 155–7, 210–2, 218, 239, 241, 244–7, 275, 280; *13, 238*
Mid-Pacific Carnival Assoc. of Hawaii 26
Mielke, Bob 212
Mienna, James 174
Miller, Bill 190
Miller, Bill 223
Miller, Bob 225
Miller Brothers 30–6, 243
Miller, Dan 53–4, 56–7; *53*
Miller, David 243
Miller, Donald V. 263
Miller, Edgar 54
Miller, Francesca Falk 62
Miller, Jim 216
Miller, Lee 36, 237
Miller, Lewis L. 161; *161*
Miller, Mildred (Mrs. Stevens) 126, 268; *126*
Millich, Don 194
Mills, Doug 134
Mills, Mrs. Frederick J. 71
Minnesota, University of 148, 197–200, 254
Minnesota Metro Tourist Council 38
Minute Maid 161, 201
Mitchell, Charlie 198
Mitchell, Clifford 27
Mitchell, J. J. 46–8
Mitchell, Jack 134
Mizell, Warren 69
Mohler, Orv 90
Molinsky, Ed 120
Mollenkopf, Jack 222–3
Monachino, Jim 151–2
Monrovia Town Band 6
Montana 214
Montana, Monty 78
Monterey Park 152, 174
Montgomery, Cliff 98
Montieth, Orville 26
Moore, Bob 255–6, 258
Moore, Jimmy 74
Moorehead, Don 246
Moreland, Olvin 212
Morgan, J. D. 117, 211, 217, 219
Morley, Sam 159
Morrall, Earl 168, 181–2
Morrill, J. Lewis 148
Morrill, Stella 131; *131*
Morris, Jack 187

Morrison, Fred 150
Moscrip, Monk 97, 101–3
Moss, Morton 129, 160
Moss, Perry 138–9
Mossberg, Ann (Mrs. Robert Hall, Jr.) 183; *183*
Muller, Harold ("Brick") 46–7, 280; *46*
Muller, Wes 103
Mullins, Larry 51
Mulvin, Bob 233
Munn, Clarence ("Biggie") 167–8; *167*
Munsey, Bill 198, 200
Murakowski, Art 146–7; *146*
Murphy, George 142
Murphy, Michael 65
Murray, Jim 201, 207, 224, 227–8, 247
Murray, Ken 39
Musick, Jack 132
Myerson, Bess 155

National Collegiate Athletic Association 117–8, 134, 148
National Exchange Club 38; *c238*
National Football Foundation 233
National Football League 27, 127
National Restaurant Association 232
National Safety Council 39
Native Sons and Daughters of the Golden West 38
Navajo Indians 14
Nave, Doyle 112–4, 275; *112, 114*
Nay, E. O. 121; *122*
Neale, Earle ("Greasy") 47
Neathery, Herb 160
Nebraska, University of 121–3, 275
Neff, Art 233, 249
Neff, Mrs. Art 244
Neff, Edwin D. 17
Neilson, Helen Marie 22
Nelsen, Bill 202
Nelson, Lindsay 261
Nesbet, Archie 46–7
Nettles, Jim 202–3
Nevers, Ernie 55–7, 175, 233, 275, 280; *53*
Neyland, Bob 120; *120*
Nicholas, William 117, 148–9, 159, 161, 163–4, 184, 193; *164, 241, 248*
Nichols, Barbara (Mrs. William Field) 103; *103*
Nixon, Julie 192
Nixon, Richard 2–3, 6, 86, 143, 163–4, 191–2, 194, 232–3, 242, 248, 260–1, 275; *163, 193, 248; c46*
Nixon, Mrs. Richard 163, 192, 260–1; *c46*
Nixon, Tricia 192
Noble, H. Burton 198–9; *200*
Noren, Irv 176
North Dakota, state of 152–3

Northwestern University 144–7
Notre Dame 51, 53–5, 57, 90, 135, 141, 275, 280; *52*
Nurches, Christina *c110*

Oates, Bob 247
Occidental Life Insurance Company 18, 38, 125, 179, 193, 207, 240; *c238*
Ocean Park 25
Odd Fellows and Rebekahs 38, 232
Off, Edward T. 15–7, 21, 23; *16*
Ogston, Jessie 154
Ohio State Alumni Association of Los Angeles 133
Ohio State University 46, 133, 143, 148, 150–2, 176–8, 185–7, 198, 229, 232–6, 251, 254–5, 258, 275–6, 280; *235*
Olderman, Murray 200
Olivar, Jordan 168, 197
Olmsted, Aaron G. 78–9
Olmsted, Myrta 90
O'Malley, Walter 187
Oosterbaan, Ben *156*
Oregon, University of 26, 44–5, 48, 185–7; *45*
Oregon State College 124–5, 182–3, 210–2, 280
Ortmann, Charles 155–7
Ostrich race 21
Otis, Harrison Gray 10; *11*
Otis, Jim 235
Owens, Jim 191, 193–4, 197–8, 207–8; *195*

Pacific Coast Conference 73, 119, 124, 140, 148, 182, 188, 194, 200
Pacific Eight Conference 133–6
Paddock, Charles 46, 59
Padfield, Clarence 230, 263
Palm, Mike 49
Palmer, Arnold 209; *209*
Palmer, Mrs. Arnold *209*
Palmer, Dick 123
Palmer, Ford 95
Palmer, Ruth 21; *20*
Palmer, Steve 182
Paluski, Mike 234
Pappas, Nick 113
Pandit, Korla 165
Park, Charlie 211
Parker, George S. 96
Parker, Harold A. 73
Parker, Jim 177
Parker, Kathy 253–4; *253*
Parkinson, Tom ("Pug") 72
Parr, Edith Wright 253–4
Parsons, Albert 21
Parsons, Johnny 27
Pasadena Athletic Club 1, 213
Pasadena City College 70, 84–5, 232; *c46*
Pasadena Elks Lodge 46

Pasadena High School 11, 22
Pasadena Merchants Association 19
Pasadena Pigeon Club 65
Pasadena Rotary 46
Pasero, George 185
Pashgian, M. S. 25; *23*
Pasko, Bill 208
Patrick, Frank 106
Patten, G. D. *11*
Patterson, Paul 138; *138*
Patton, Bill 190
Patton, George, Jr. 10
Patton, Harold 59, 61
Patton Field 10
Paul, E. W. 79
Paulman, Bill 102–3
Payne, Eleanor (Mrs. John Ford) 154, 270; *154, 270*
Payne, Gleeson L. 229, 231–3; *230*
Payseur, Ted 118, 134
Peaks, Clarence 182
Pearce, Clark 63
Peebles, Sylvia *c110*
"Peggy" 152
Pellerin, Giles L. 239
Pennsylvania, University of 26–7
Pennsylvania State University 48, 50, 275
Peoples, Bobby 112
Perricone, Gaspar 145
Perrin, Jay 132
Perry, Lowell 157
Peters, Doug 182
Peterson, LeRoy 248
Peterson, Rudolph 237
Phillips, Irvine 69
Pickard, Fred 64; *63*
Pickering, William A. 201; *202*
Pickford, Jack 92
Pickford, Mary (Mrs. Charles Rogers) 61, 92, 94; *92, 93*
Pickwick Cup 5
Pickwick House 5
Pierson, Barry 245
Pinckert, Ernie 72–3, 90–1; *72, 91*
Pineda, Mannie 197
Pittenger, R. M. 38–40
Pittsburgh, University of 64–5, 72–3, 94–5, 106, 280; *105*
Plankenhorn, Jim 208
Planutis, Gerald 182
Ploen, Ken 183
Plunkett, Jim 255–6, 258; *254*
Plymouth Carver Regional High School Band 253
Poiret, Paul 266
Pollard, Fritz 25; *25*
Pollard, James E. 135
Pont, Johnny 227, 229; *228*
Port Chester, New York, High School Band 85
Portland, Oregon 22
Portland Rose Festival Association 38; *c238*
Poschner, George 127

Post, C. E. 21
Post, Seraphim 65
Post Cereals 179
Postle, Wendell 135
Powers, Francis 185
Prather, Pamela (Mrs. John F.
    King) 166, 188, 190, 270; *188,
    189*
Prescott, Bob 190
Presnell, Glenn 72
Pressley, Norm 145–6
Preston, Don 254
Price, Clarence ("Nibs") 69
Prickett, Maudie 136, 226
Prickett, Oliver 263
Prothro, Tommy 168, 182–3,
    211–2, 215–7; *213*
Prudential Insurance Company 132
Prugh, Jeff 247
Pryor, Cecil 246
Pucci, Ed 166
Pund, Peter 68
Purdue Glee Club 221
Purdue University 222–4, 276
Putnam, George 80–2; *c46*
Putnam, Jil 80

Quaker Oats 154, 190, 203
Queen's Club 116
Quigley, Ernest 27
Quinn, William F. 196; *196*

Ralston, John 254, 258; *257*
Raye, Jim 216
Raymond, Clayton 6
Raymond, Gene 155
Raymond, Hotel 7, 44
Raymond, Walter 3, 20
Reagan, Ronald 154, 248, 261;
    c46
Reagan, Mrs. Ronald *c46*
Rebecca, Sam 159
Redden, Curtis 14
Redlands 19
Redondo Arrowhead Club 19
Redondo Beach 19
Reed, Bill 117, 220; *135*
Reed, Walter 241
Reno 2
Reynolds, Bob 97, 102; *104*
Reynolds, C. Hal 70–1, 117, 126,
    134; *71*
Rice, Grantland 100, 108, 261
Richards, J. Randolph 1, 213–4;
    215
Richardson, John 216
Richart, Frank E. 135
Richter, Les 156–7
Richter, Pat 202, 203
Rick Chapman's Festival Artists
    31–2
Rickenbacker, Eddie 183; *183*
Ridder, Ben 129
Riegels, Roy 66–9, 162, 275; *66,
    68, 69*
Rifenburg, Dick 141

Riley, Joe 101
Riordan, Naomi (Mrs. Martin
    Carey) 128–9; *129*
Riverside 12
Roberts, Bob 137
Roberts, Mrs. J. Lambert 244
Roberts Family 262
Robinson, Dick 256
Robinson, Sam 129
Robson, Wylie S. 37–8
Rockne, Knute 53–4, 56–7; *48*
Rogers, C. P. 21
Rogers, Charles ("Buddy") 92
Rogers, Jim 198
Rogers, Roy 82, 129; *173*
Rodriquez, Joseph 161; *161*
Rohrig, Herman 122
Rolph, James 70–1; *71*
Roman, Jim 235–6
Romney, Dick 28
Roosevelt, W. K. 14
Rosellini, Albert D. 198, 200; *198*
Rosenbaum, Art 258
Rosenberg, Aaron 90
"Roses Are in Bloom" 62
Rossovich, Tim 222
Rote, Kyle 261; *254*
Rottschafer, Henry 135
Roughneck Marching Band 86
Rowland, Al 82
Rowland, Dr. Francis F. 4–6, 20,
    23, 25, 274; *4, 5*
Royal Canadian Mounted Police
    214
Rozelle, Pete 220
Rubsamen, Charles 121, 264
Ruffa, Tony 112
Runyon, Damon 97–8
Rutte, Mary Louise (Mrs. Victor
    Wallace) 129, 269; *129*
Ryan, George 80
Ryan, John 159
Rykovich, Julius 138–9

Salt Lake Railroad 21
Salsinger, H. G. 47
Salvation Army 38, 44, 53, 84;
    c238
Sampson, Gregory *c174*
Samuelsen, Rube 128, 130, 189,
    194, 202
Sande, John 256
Sanders, Don 159
Sanders, Henry ("Red") 167,
    181; *167*
Sanderson, Lawson 28
San Diego 22, 175, 199, 232
San Francisco 140
San Gabriel 165, 190, 232
San Marino 90; *90*
San Pedro Chamber of Commerce 8
Santa Ana 84
Santa Barbara 12, 100, 103, 118;
    107
Santa Fe Railroad 21
Santa Monica 199, 203

Santa Monica City College Band 84
Santoro, Al 131, 160
Saukko, Richard 78
Saunders, Russ 72, 128; *72*
Savic, Pandell 151
Sawle, Steve 147
Schabarum, Pete 151–2, 156
Schaffer, Harold C. 143; *144*
Schembechler, Glenn ("Bo") 140,
    218, 234, 246; *239*
Schiller, Abe 79
Schindler, Ambrose 120; *120*
Schlemmer, Jim 185
Schloredt, Bob 193–4, 197–8; *194*
Schmidt, Barbara (Mrs. Terry
    Mulligan) 169–70, 270; *169,
    270*
Schmidt, Holly 243
Schmidt, Vic O. 117
Schlegel, Ben 129
Schrader, Loel 246
Schroeder, E. G. 134
Schroeder, W. R. 213
Schultz, Jack 256; *254*
Schwartz, Elmer 74
Schwartz, Perry 108
Scott, Dan 228
Scott, Treva 97; *97*
Scott, Vernon 78
Scott, Willard ("Bubba") 244, 245
Scoville, Mrs. Margaret 53
Scully, Vin 155
Sears, Jimmy 165
Sebastian, Mike 95
Sedgwick, R. Minturn 45
Shafter, William Rufus 10; *11*
Shah (of Iran) 174
Shanley, Jim 187
Shapley, Alan 52
Shaughnessy, Clark 121–3, 275;
    121
Shaver, Gaius 90
Sheffield, Jan 252
Sheffield, Jeff 252
Sheffield, Johnny 252
Sheldon, Joel 263
Shell, Joe 120
Sherman, Mrs. Caroline 58
Sherman, Les 52
Sherman, Rod 222–4; *222*
Shingler, Bertha (Mrs. A. Lewis
    Shingler) 254
Shingler, A. Lewis 2, 240, 250–1,
    253, 259; *2, 264*
Shipkey, Harold 54
Shipkey, Ted 54–6, 64
Shockley, Hillary *c174*
Shore, Dinah 162; *174*
Siler, Bill 207–8
Simpson, O. J. 37, 225, 227–8,
    232; *225, 233, 234; c110*
Simpson, Russell E. 174
Sims, Bob 65
Sims, William 96; *97*
Sinclair, Robert Harold 165
Sington, Fred 73

Sinkwich, Frankie 127; *127*
Sissell, Martha 199, 261; *199*
Sitter, Carl L. 161; *161*
Skaggs, Jim 198
Skladany, Joe 95
Slonac, Evan 168
Sluder, Darrell 263
Smith, Andy 46
Smith, Ben 74
Smith, Bobby 200
Smith, Charles ("Bubba") 37
Smith, Ernie 90, 95
Smith, Harry 120
Smith, Riley 101
Smith, T. B. 79
Smith, Tody 245; *244*
Smith, Wilfrid 139, 261
Smuin, Marilyn (Mrs. Wells F.
   Martell) 176, 270; *176*
Snow, Neil 13; *14*
Sogge, Steve 228, 232, 234, 236
Sohn, Ben 120
Solari, Ray 156–7
Soldwedel, Fred 263–4
Solomon, Fred 55–6
Sonleitner, Terry 41
Soroptomists 38; *c238*
South Carolina State College
   Band 86
Southern California Floral
   Association 161
Southern California, University of
   48–50, 64, 72, 90–1, 94–5,
   112–4, 119–20, 128–9, 131–2,
   140–3, 165–8, 176–8, 182, 186,
   200–3, 218, 222–4, 227–8,
   233–4, 236, 239, 241, 244–7,
   275, 280
Southern Methodist University
   102–3
South Pasadena 8, 103, 161, 190,
   221; *103*
Spanish Riding Academy of Vienna
   78
Spanjian Company 244
Sparling, Ray 90
Sper, Norman 47
Speth, Herb 237
"The Spirit of Notre Dame" 56
Sprenger, Jack 166
Springfield, Illinois 149
Sprott, Albert ("Pesky") 46–7
Sproul, Robert G. 184; *184*
"Stage Door Canteen" 106
Stagg, Amos Alonzo 128; *128*
Standlee, Norm 122
Stanford University 12–4, 53–5,
   57, 62–5, 96–103, 121–3, 141,
   159–60, 200, 251, 254–5, 258,
   275–6, 280; *13, 63, 123, 257*
Stanton, Sally (Mrs. Charles
   Rubsamen) 121; *122*
Stanton, W. L. 28
Starke, Tod 41; *c174*
Starkweather, Dave 244
Starkweather, Doug 244

Starr, Belle 82; *c110*
Stathakis, George 151
Steadman, John 247
Stearns, Edwin 8
Steers, Bill 44
Steger, Russ 138
Stein, Russell 47, 175; *50*
Stephens, Brodie 46–7, 280
Stephens, Sandy 197–200
Sterling, Harriet B. 65; *65*
Stevens, Don 159
Stewart, Al 221
Stewart, James 150
Stiles, Bob 213, 216, 275; *216*
Stillwagen, Jim 256
Stillwell, Don 166
Stinchcomb, Pete 46
Stiner, Lon 124; *124*
Stits, Bill 167
Stivers, Jim 263
St. John, L. W. 117, 133–4
St. Louis 165, 209, 242–3; *175;
   c46, c238*
Stockton, Vard 108
Stoecker, Howard 120
Stonesifer, Don 145
Stong, Audre 70
Storer, Moffat 125
Storum, Bill 159
Stovall, Margaret 126, 251–2
Stover, Ron 187
Strother, Linda 227; *226*
Strutt, Charles A. 132
Stuart, Charles R., Jr. 237
Stuhldreher, Harry 53–7, 134; *53*
Stupey, John 208
Suffridge, Bob 120
Sullivan, Prescott 160
Sunkist Growers 38
Suther, Flash 74
Sutherin, Don 185–7
Sutherland, John ("Jock") 65, 72,
   95, 106
Swaim, Dave 200
Swan, Fred 55
Swaner, Jack 147
Sweeley, Everett 13–4
Swor, Sammy 210
Sygar, Rick 212
Syracuse University 25

Taliaferro, Mike 208
Tannehill, Ted 132; *132*
Tappan, Francis 72
Tate, Don 159
Taylor, Chuck 123, 160
Taylor, William A. 44
Taylor and Associates 30
Tedesco, Pamela Dee 188, 239–41,
   271; *240, 271; c110*
Tegert, Lloyd 27
Temple, Shirley 109–10; *110*
Tennessee, University of 119–20,
   128–31
Tenri High School 214
Terry, Tony 245

Tesreau, Elmer 52
Tesreau, Louis 60
Texas Christian University 102
Thomas, Frank 108, 131; *106*
Thomas, Lowell 39
Thomason, Stumpy 67, 69
Thompson, Ruth 79
Thompson, William Oxley 133
Thorne, Nancy True (Mrs. John F.
   Skinner) 159, 161; *161*
Thornhill, Claude ("Tiny") 97,
   103
Thornton, Bob 178
Thorp, Ed 56
Throop Polytechnic Institute 11
Ticknor, Harry M. 58–9, 62; *59*
Timberlake, Bob 212; *211*
Timberlake, George 166
Tinkham, Harley 208
Tipton, Eric 113–4
Tobin, Jack 177
Toffler, Alvin, quoted 272–3
"Tom Brown of Harvard" 25
Top Hat Band 162
Toppers Band 84
Topping, Keith 97–8, 101–3
Topping, Norman 114, 241–2
Torrance 201
Touchie-Specht, Phyllis 265 ff
Tournament Park 10, 12, 24, 28
Tourville, Charley 187
Townsend, Eva 5
Townsend, Harry 5
Traeger, Bill 13–4
Trautwein, Bill 151–2
Treasure Tones Paint 38
Trippi, Charley 127
Trisler, Barbara 79; *c46*
Tsagalakis, Sam 165
Tsujimoto, Vicki *c110*
Tucker, Bud 224
Tulane University 90–1
Tunnicliff, Ed 145–7
Turner, Jim 152
Turner, Lewis H. 23–4; *25*
Turner, Max H. 126, 132; *131*
Twombley, Wells 258

Uansa, Toby 72
U.C.L.A. *See* California, University
   of, at Los Angeles
Union Oil of California 38, 112,
   153; *c110, c238*
Union Pacific Railroad 126
United States Military Academy
   Band 176
United States Naval Academy 51–2
Universal Studios *c174*
U.S.C. *See* Southern California,
   University of

Valley Decorating Company 31
Valley Hunt Club 4–8, 112
Vancouver Beefeater Band 214

Van de Kamp 137
Van Dellen, Elzo 101
VanderKelen, Ron 201–4, 280; *201*
Van Hueit, Carl 152
Van Schaik, H. L. 12
Varnell, George 59
Vataha, Randy 255–6; *255, 256*
Veddar, William H. 27
Verry, Norm 128–9
Vignolle, Gus 130
Vincenti, Louis R. 117, 134, 140; *141*
Vitascope Company 10
Vogel, Mitch 252
Voigts, Bob 146
"Vow" Boys (Stanford) 97, 100, 102; *104*

Wade, Wallace 25, 59, 63, 73, 124; *60*
Waddell, Mary Lou 73, 266; *73, 265*
Waddey, Frank 67
Wagner, James B. 11–2, 274; *12*
Waite, Darwin 79
Waldorf, Lynn ("Pappy") 145, 150–2, 155–6; *145*
Walker, Cheryl (Mrs. Tway Walter Andrews) 106, 108, 266; *103, 267*
Walker, Ed 56
Walker, Tommy 142–3
Wallace, Stan 159–60
Walsh, Adam 54–7
Walter, Virginia *c110*
Warburton, Cotton 94–5; *95*
Ward, Arch 160
Ward, Carl 210–2
Ward, Stanley E. 263
Warmath, Murry 197–9; *199*
Warner, Glenn S. ("Pop") 53, 55–6, 63–5, 72, 91; *54*
Warren, Earl 6, 126, 143, 261; *171, 172, 173*
Warren, Jim 208
Washburn, Carole (Mrs. Robert Lumsden) 197–8; *197*
Washington, State College of 24–5, 73–4, 180–2, 275, 280
Washington and Jefferson College 47, 99; *50*

Washington, University of 51–2, 59–61, 106, 138–9, 182, 191, 193–5, 197, 200, 207–8, 280; *61, 104*
Watkins, Bob 177
Watkins, Clifford 86, 212
Watson, Will 246
Weatherby, F. B. 11, 274; *11*
Weaver, Charlie 245; *244*
Webster, George 37
Weibel, John 54
Weight, Martin H. 8
Weill, Mrs. Edgar M. 58
Weisenburger, Jack 140–2, 280; *142*
Weissmuller, Johnny 61, 94
Welch, Ralph 128
Welk, Lawrence *c174*
Wells, Bill 168
Welsh, Arthur 263
Welsh, Lou 166
Welsh, William 136–8; *137*
West, C. C. 19–20
Whatley, Dixie *c110*
Whitaker, Johnnie 41; *c174*
White, Bob 187
White, Helen (Mrs. Virgil) 263
White, John 263
White, Robert 263
White, Virgil J. 259–60, 263; *c174*
Whitehead, Jack 263
White Oak High School Band 239
Whittier High School Band 8
Whitworth, J. B. ("Ears") 74
Wiesenbaugh, Henry 95
Wiesner, Tom 194
Wiggins, Mac 15–6
Wilce, J. W. 46
Wilcoxon, Joan Woodbury 18
"The Wild Bunch" 166, 244–5; *244*
Wilder, Newell 98
Wilensky, Joe 112–4
Wilkinson, Bud 232
Willett, Hugh 117
Willhoite, Elmer 166
Williams, Harry 27
Williams, Homer 222
Williams, Perry 222
Williamson, Stan 91
Willis, Mrs. Howard 179
Wilson, Ben 202–3

Wilson, Bobby 102
Wilson, Charles E. 179, 262; *181*
Wilson, Don 126
Wilson, Edward 260, 272, 274; *260*
Wilson, E. Milton 263
Wilson, Elmer 173, 175, 272; *172, 173, 176*
Wilson, George 52, 59–61; *61*
Wilson, Harry 49
Wilson, Kenneth L. ("Tug") 117, 133–4, 194; *134*
Wilson, Woodrow 27
Wilton, Frankie 63–5
Winslett, Hoyt 59–60, 63
Winslow, Bob 120
Winslow, Troy 222–4
Winsor, Kathleen (Mrs. Robert Herwig) 108
Wisconsin, University of 165–6, 191, 193–4, 201–3, 275, 280
Wiseman, Patricia 125
Wolf, Al 123, 128, 130, 132, 168
Women's Christian Temperance Union 44
Wood, Gertrude 184; *184*
Woodbury, Joan H. 18, 266; *18*
Woods, Hallie 15–6, 265, 274; *16*
Woolworth Company 154, 162
Wopschall, Carl 260, 263
Worden, Richard 65
Workman, Harry 46
Wotkyns, B. Marshall 6; *8*

Yale University 45
Yerges, Howard 141
Yewcic, Tom 168
Yokohama 26
Yost, Fielding H. 12
Young, Claude 138, 139
Young, Jim 246
Young, Robert 254

Ziel, Leonard 52
Zier, Harry 15
Ziff, Sid 139, 156, 165, 167–8, 176–7, 182, 186, 199, 211
Zikmund, Allen 122–3
Zimmerman, Don 91
Zimmerman, Kurt 216
Zimmerman, Paul 139, 177, 201, 207, 211, 228

About the Authors

Hendrickson

JOE HENDRICKSON has been sports editor of the Pasadena *Star-News* since 1961. He began his newspaper career in 1935 with the Minneapolis *Star* after graduating from the University of Minnesota school of journalism. After also serving as a staff writer for the Duluth *News Tribune* and the Minneapolis *Journal,* he became sports editor of *Esquire* magazine in 1944 and sports editor of the Minneapolis *Tribune* in 1945. He resigned from the latter position in 1954 to serve in a public relations capacity for General Mills, Inc., a role he held until he accepted the sports editorship of the Pasadena *Star-News.*

A native of Cokato, Minnesota, Hendrickson currently is on the board of directors of the Football Writers' Association of America. He is a past president of the Southern California Football Writers Association and served for two years as chairman of the Los Angeles-Anaheim chapter of the Baseball Writers Association of America.

In 1970 and 1971, the Pasadena *Star-News* sports section edited by Hendrickson was adjudged the best in the state for newspapers up to 300,000 by the California Publishers Association. In 1971, Hendrickson received the Exchange Club "Big M" Award for media excellence and received citations of merit from the California state senate and assembly, Los Angeles county, and the city of Pasadena.

Says Harry M. Cross, ex-president of the National Collegiate Athletic Association: "I think Joe Hendrickson's understanding of intercollegiate athletics is great. He is a warm friend of the sort of things we hope our organization is helping to assure."

Walter Byers, executive director of the NCAA, says: "Joe Hendrickson is one of the most respected craftsmen in the sports writing business."

Stiles

MAXWELL STILES was a Los Angeles sports writer for a half a century, and witnessed and reported most of the significant sport events in southern California during that time. He was a former president of the Southern California Football Writers Association.

"Virtually a half century ago, I wrote my first sports story," he said before his death in 1969. "I alternated from one person's doghouse to another, and I wouldn't trade all those years for four years in the White House."

He rated the exciting Rose Bowl games he covered among his prime thrills as a reporter.